2-

'Wilson tells a gripping tale' *Scottish Legion News*

'Kevin Wilson's excellent new book ... is a fine tribute to the men who fought and died' *Sunday Express*

'It's well worth reading ... a great deal of work's gone into this book, which is clearly a labour of love' *British Army Review*

'This gripping narrative collection is a heartfelt salute to that dwindling band of veterans and a moving memorial to the ones who didn't make it home' *Manchester Evening News*

'Kevin Wilson's compelling new study charts the fortunes of Bomber Command during its most critical year ... Wilson plots the technical developments which transformed the bomber offensive, but focuses primarily on the experiences of the men who took part' *Eastern Daily Press*

'Wilson has put together an incisive history of a phase of war ... through the testimony of former air crew and prisoners of war he relates what it was like'
Good Book Guide

' ... this exhaustively researched book ... crew members faced several grim means of meeting their death. They could be struck by flak or Luftwaffe cannon, burned alive, vaporised as the plane exploded, drowned in the North Sea or forced out without a parachute ... What amazes from this book is the amazingly youthful nature of these heroes'
Glasgow Evening Times

'The author is to be congratulated because he has been at pains to interview and research the ordinary "Joes" of Bomber Command ... a stark testimony to heroism in all its forms' *Flypast*

'This is a gripping account of everyday heroism ... a fascinating account of what it was like in the 1943 night air war. I highly recommend this book as an excellent read for all aviation historians. It shows the true nature of air warfare in a sometimes ugly light'
Cdr Doug Siegfried, USN (Ret), the US Navy aircrew journal *The Hook*,
Winter 2005

Kevin Wilson was born and educated in Yorkshire, lived for a time in North America, but now resides in Cheshire. He has spent most of his working life as a staff journalist on British national newspapers, including the *Daily Mail* and latterly the *Daily* and *Sunday Express*. He has held a pilot's licence for 20 years and has a lifelong passion for personal oral and written history. He is currently researching and writing another book about the bombing war, covering operations in 1944. He is married with three grown-up sons and a daughter.

BOMBER BOYS

The Ruhr, the Dambusters and bloody Berlin

KEVIN WILSON

CASSELL

To Mollie

Cassell Military Paperbacks

An imprint of Orion Books Ltd,
5 Upper St Martin's Lane,
London WC2H 9EA

An Hachette Livre UK company

10 9 8 7 6 5 4

First published in 2005
by Weidenfeld & Nicolson
This Cassell Military Paperbacks edition 2006

British Library Cataloguing-in-Publication Data.
A catalogue record for this book is available
from the British Library.

ISBN 978-0-3043-6724-5

Printed and bound in Great Britain by
Cox & Wyman Ltd, Reading, Berkshire

The Orion Publishing Group's policy is to use papers that
are natural, renewable and recyclable products and made
from wood grown in sustainable forests. The logging and
manufacturing processes are expected to conform to the
environmental regulations of the country of origin.

www.orionbooks.co.uk

Contents

LIST OF ILLUSTRATIONS

PHOTOGRAPHS

1 354 Air Gunner's Course, RCAF Station Mountain View, Ontario: Marcel Dowst and Reid Thomson were the only ones not killed on operations.

2 Sgt Graham Allen in his flight engineer's position.

3 Air gunner Sgt Albert Bracegirdle.

4 The remains of F/Sgt Ted Laing's Lancaster fall to earth after it exploded over Enschede, Holland.

5 P/O Dennis Bateman's aeroplane after it was shot down in Belgium on 9 March.

6 Air gunner Sgt Cliff Hill, about to take off for Berlin on 1 March 1943.

7 Peter Johnson, after he was commissioned and awarded the DFC.

8 P/O 'Bluey' Mottershead.

9 Wop/AG Sgt Walter Hedges of 102 Sqn.

10 Australian Ron Gooding, lost on the Kiel operation of 4 April.

11 Ron Gooding's fiancée, Laura Lancaster

12 The 460 Sqn crew of F/Sgt Murray just back from Duisburg in the early hours of 10 April 1943.

13 F/O Eric George Hadingham and F/O Roderick Alan Lord being rescued off the French coast after five days and nights in a rubber dinghy.

14 Air gunner P/O Albert Wallace.

15 Flight engineer John Walsh.

16 Kenneth East, pictured in 1939 at the start of his operational career.

17 Bomb aimer Sgt George Stewart, the sole survivor of his crew when their Lancaster exploded over Bochum.

18 Wing Commander Guy Gibson (standing on ladder) minutes before he took off with his crew on the Dams Raid.

19 The Eder Dam, destroyed by low flying Lancasters on the night of 16 May 1943.

20 F/Lt Les Munro and fellow New Zealander F/O Len Chambers, wireless operator in Mickey Martin's crew: a photograph taken at Scampton in the publicity blitz which followed the Dams Raid.

21 F/O Dave Rodger in an off-duty moment at 617 Sqn.

22 A reconnaissance photograph of Kassel showing flooding from the Eder, breached by the Dambusters.

23 Michaelisstrasse, Hamburg, before and after the firestorm raid of 27 July.

24 Michaelisstrasse after the firestorm.

25 Sgt Peter Swan of 44 Squadron.

26 Bomb aimer P/O Alan Bryett with his 158 Sqn pilot F/Lt Kevin Hornibrook, who gave his life to save Bryett's.

27 A reconnaissance picture of Peenemunde in June 1943, showing two V-2 rockets, the rocket storage buildings and the assembly shop.

28 W/O Dennis Slack.

29 Val Clarkson.

30 The crew of P/O John Sullivan prepare for another operation in their 467 Sqn tour at Bottesford.

MAPS

'I'm not terribly surprised to hear that Willie has won the VC. He's always been a very determined boy.'

The mother of F/Lt William Reid quoted in the *Daily Express* after the blacksmith's son won the Victoria Cross for flying his crippled Lancaster to Düsseldorf and back again despite serious wounds.

'We got to the squadron on 21 August; the first raid I went on was two days later and within eight days I had done another five and been shot down.'

Flight engineer W/O Lew Parsons of 75 Sqn, forced to bale out on the Berlin raid of 31 August 1943.

'Picked up £6 pay then rushed away as member of a funeral party for a rear gunner killed in action. Ghastly business funerals, weeping relatives all over the place. Went to pictures afterwards.'

From the diary of bomb aimer Sgt John Gilvary of 419 Sqn, killed on the Peenemünde Raid twelve days later.

'My throat became parched and I considered whether to cut myself so that I could drink some of my own blood to alleviate the terrible thirst.'

Air gunner F/Lt Eric Hadingham, DFC and bar, who spent six days in a dinghy after his 166 Sqn Wellington ditched en route to Mannheim on 16 April 1943.

'It was amazing how often a navigator would say to me, "Well cheerio, sir, I'm not coming back" and they didn't. One night I was briefed for Cologne and it was scrubbed. I was never so thankful because I knew if I went that night I wouldn't return.'

Navigator S/Ldr Alex Flett, DFC and bar, who completed a tour with 460 Sqn and a second as navigation leader with 625 Sqn.

BEGINNINGS

THE dawn of Bomber Command's year of attrition began beguilingly with a whisper. The seductive sound was carried in the tendrils of mist which both enclosed and linked billet to hangar on airfields from north to south and it held the promise of life continued. It was the soft, sibilant hiss of drizzle.

The rain crept and swept the length of eastern Britain from the flat fens of Cambridgeshire and Lincolnshire to the soft contours of Yorkshire and up into County Durham, dribbling from the wings of hooded Halifaxes, Stirlings and Lancasters poised at dispersals, glistening the grey of concrete runways lost in the fog, and carrying its damp promise into the austerity of crew huts beneath dripping trees.

Its message was that tonight there would be no war. The crack and thump of exploding flak, the urgent tearing flash of cannon fire, the shriek of plunging aircraft which would echo through the months of the great bomber offensive to come hung still. The young aircrew – from spotty-faced 18- and 19-year-olds just out of school to bloods fresh from drawing office and workbench – turned on that first morning of 1943 and slept on.

Before New Year dawned again 15,832 operational Bomber Command aircrew would be dead and 2,898 prisoners of war. Another 1,500 or so would die in training accidents on OTUs and HCUs; the rest of the doomed would be lost in the variety of horror that was the air war's speciality. Some would die instantly or agonisingly by direct contact with flak or Luftwaffe bullet or cannon; others would vanish as if they never existed in a boiling flash of oily red and orange flame as their aircraft exploded against the night sky; some would be burned alive, pinned helplessly by centrifugal force, as their stricken bombers spiralled earthwards; a number would drown in the cold waters of the North Sea as their damaged or fuel-starved aircraft failed to make the long journey home. And for a very few there would be the horror unique to their service of falling helplessly without a parachute, after being tossed from their disintegrating aircraft before they could reach for and clip on the means of survival.

In the target areas below, death would also come in a kaleidoscope of chaos never visited in such scale on non-combatants – from the blast of blockbuster bombs which could collapse the lungs without leaving a scar on the body to firebombs which threw out pats of benzol and rubber to begin conflagrations which greedily gulped oxygen from the air.

But for the moment drizzle and fog meant reprieve. The bomber boys dreamed on of the station dance the night before when they sang 'Auld Lang Syne' and held hands in a circle with the pretty WAAF they'd had their eye on for weeks or the snood-haired girl from nearby town or village, pert in her 10-shilling dance frock, seams pencilled on her coffee-stained legs to make up for stockings so hard to acquire in this fourth winter of the war. The most requested tune for the all-important last waltz had been 'White Christmas'. It was said that the new number was selling so well it could become a classic. On a few stations the more daring had tried out the burgeoning dance craze of the jitterbug, part of the cultural shock wave from the arriving American troops.

Now in the dawn as the chill drizzle with its accompanying fog seeped through blanket to the bone some aircrew would stir for an early morning raid on the coke store, waiting for the guard to disappear round the far reaches of his beat before rapidly climbing the chain-link fence and throwing shovelfuls of fuel to a comrade loitering with a kitbag on the other side.

The search for warmth from the rationed discomfort of Nissen and Maycrete billet would drive others to the sergeants' mess where at least there was a degree of constant heat from the well-supplied mess fire as men sprawled in the sagging leather of battered armchairs and leafed through the latest issue of the Air Ministry's *Tee Emm* magazine for aircrew, with its illustrations of what not to do as demonstrated by the hapless Pilot Officer Prune.

The more senior among the officers were in their flight offices working their way through log books to be signed, requisition orders to be processed, training to be organised and recommendations for promotion and gallantry awards to be forwarded. Occasionally a pilot or navigator would pop his head round the office door to ask a flight commander: 'Are we working tonight?' But the weather would keep German cities safe from major attack for a while yet.

THIS then was the scene for the ordinary aircrew of Bomber Command who would be called on to demonstrate extraordinary courage in 1943. This was the year that the resolute commander-in-chief Air Chief Marshal Sir Arthur Harris had designated for his great bomber offensive, taking war home to the enemy as never before in the history of Germany or the world. It was a year of growing success in which Harris would come close to proving his theory that the war could be won by bombing alone. In the first month of the year operations would be considered mighty indeed if the Command had managed to find 200 aircraft. By the end of 1943 air fleets of 500, 600 and 700 would be routine. Within twelve months the towns of Germany's industrial power base in the Ruhr would have been devastated one by one; a new, untried squadron would raid the region's dams, showing that the RAF could now make a precision attack at night; the Reich's second largest city, Hamburg, would virtually cease to function following the advent of a firestorm which would shake the Nazi leaders to the core; the Peenemünde V-weapon programme that could have threatened D-Day would be vitally delayed because of a remarkable night raid; and the Battle of Berlin, designed to turn the Reich capital into a Hamburg-like wilderness, would begin. It was only in the final days of 1943 that the first doubts of Bomber Command's ability to fight the Battle of Berlin to a conclusion would appear.

The year was one of innovative technical achievements by the aerial armies on each side. Remote radio signals would precisely direct Pathfinder Mosquito crews to drop their new marker bombs in the heart of Ruhr targets; a development in radar would guide Pathfinders and later Main Force crews to their aiming points; clouds of aluminium strips known as 'Window' would blind the radar sets of night-fighter pilots and their controllers. However, the advantages gained by the RAF would be swiftly met by the Luftwaffe in the game of cat and mouse above the skies of Germany and both sides would rapidly build their forces as the year progressed.

Gone were the haphazard RAF raids of 1940 and 1941 which had led to the Butt Report of August 1941 by a member of the War Cabinet Secretariat. It showed that of all the RAF bombers so far dispatched in the war recorded as hitting their target only one in three had in fact bombed within 5 miles. Now there was indeed a new dawn for Bomber Command and Harris could look forward to the coming year with confidence. He had honed his force in the ten months since he had taken office into a cohesive, united weapon from the remarkably ineffective sledgehammer it had been in the first three years of war. Since the three 1,000-bomber raids of the previous spring and early summer against Cologne, Essen and Bremen which had effectively saved Bomber Command as a separate entity the war factories were now pounding out four-engined aircraft in ever-increasing quantities and the Empire Air Training Scheme was at last producing the crews in the great numbers Harris would need in this war of attrition.

On New Year's Day 1943 Harris had received a significant gift to help him achieve the War Cabinet's aim of bringing the war to the enemy's fireside. The Canadian government had put under his control an entire heavy bomber force, 6 Group, all of which would be paid for by Canadian taxes and domestic loans, even down to the fuel and ammunition. From midnight it was his to use as he wished. His vision was for the enemy to reap the whirlwind they had sown in the 1940–41 Blitz on London and other great industrial cities of the United Kingdom. In 1943, as compared to 1942, 1944 or 1945, he would have unrestricted power to achieve that.

THIS book, however, is not about Harris or any of his senior command-ers. It's about the young aircrew who fought and died more than sixty years ago in the service of Britain and her empire and about those whose lives they touched. They joined their nation's air forces for the joy of flying and to defend their families against the terrible evil of a Nazi regime which enslaved millions and week by week directed men, women and children into gas chambers, and would undoubtedly do the same with Britons should Germany win the war. In 1943 there was no certainty of victory against such wickedness, only the hope it could be achieved.

The bomber offensive was considered by the vast majority in Britain to be, if not the way to total victory, at least the foundation for any future invasion. For a long time Britain had been losing the war, then containing it. El Alamein, the turning point, had taken place barely three months before.

The airmen who would fight this great offensive, many of whom had volunteered to be fighter pilots and now found themselves as bomber pilots, navigators, bomb aimers, flight engineers, wireless operators and gunners, rapidly realised as they began their tour of thirty operations that it was unlikely they would get more than one-third of the way through. That they, almost without exception, continued their tours until death beckoned or occasionally a capricious Lady Luck smiled shows a strength of purpose which is difficult for us, who have inherited the gift of peace, to comprehend.

How hard then that in recent years they have had to suffer the harsh criticism of themselves and their campaign expressed by those who enjoy the luxury of free debate bequeathed by the sacrifices of others. Quite simply, the war had to be won and in 1943 bombing was the way to win it. It would not be until the second half of the year that the USAAF would be able to play its full part in bombing by day with heavily armed formations and growing fighter escort. The bombing war would have to be fought by the RAF and that meant night attacks against cities because individual targets could not be guaranteed to be hit in darkness – a problem which persists today. The protection of night was considered the only way by Harris, after the harsh lessons of suicidal daylight raids by the RAF earlier in the war.

The responsibilities for taking the war to the enemy homeland would fall on the young men of Bomber Command – men from Britain and the far reaches of the empire, from Canada, Australia and New Zealand. In these pages you will meet men from all those countries. In most cases their tours were short; in a few they were long, as they appear and reappear throughout the book. All were the stuff of heroes, but some of those interviewed were officially recognised as such, waking up one morning to find themselves on the front pages of newspapers.

This book charts the bomber boys' achievements through their tours in the winter, spring, summer, autumn and winter again of 1943. It would be pedantic to follow each of the 125 major raids in the year in strict chronological order and repetitive to cover every one, but the operations that meant a new shift in the air war, large or small, are all here, remembered individually by the 137 ex-aircrew interviewed for the parts they played.

A TOTAL of 55,500 Bomber Command men would be killed in the six years of war and 8,403 wounded of its aircrew strength of 125,000. Many of those who survived the terrible strain of answering without equivocation the needs of their nation are now in failing health and squadron associations are being wound up.

They have had little thanks since the war and recently much censure. Day by day they remember with clarity the stomach-churning tension of a bomb run, the waving searchlights waiting to ensnare, the red shock of bursting flak, the sight of comrades' lives swiftly snuffed out in the night sky.

To all of them, today in their eighties, it was but yesterday. Surely there is no better time than now to say thank you to them all for bravely bearing the flame for later generations as we roll back the years to January 1943 ...

WINTER

CHAPTER ONE

TO THE HEART OF DARKNESS

THE year's campaign began as it would end: with the fury of flak and flame over Berlin. It was a desperate way to fight a war. Crews were briefed in the short winter days and in the dark would climb through cloud so cold that even the hydraulic oil to operate gun turrets was likely to freeze. Perilous ice often formed on wings and tailplanes, turning the science of aeronautics into the simple art of staying alive. When the crews finally reached the target area they had to tackle three rings of flak and searchlights one after the other, then face the same again fighting their way out. It was a nine-hour journey at 20,000 feet in temperatures of 30 degrees below zero, most of it over enemy territory where fighters could pounce at any moment, death winking its inevitability in the darkness. But at least in the beginning of the year there was hope.

Berlin was the key political target and the two biggest operations of January were mounted against it with 201 and 187 aircraft respectively. An impudent nuisance raid by Mosquitos at the end of the month would signal RAF intentions that in 1943 the Nazi leaders could expect their capital to be raided often.

Berlin was first attacked by Bomber Command at the height of the Battle of Britain on 25 August 1940. For almost a year the War Cabinet, initially reluctant to risk the loss of civilian lives, had refused to sanction operations against the capital. But after bombs were dropped randomly on London on 24 August fifty-plus bombers were dispatched to Berlin in

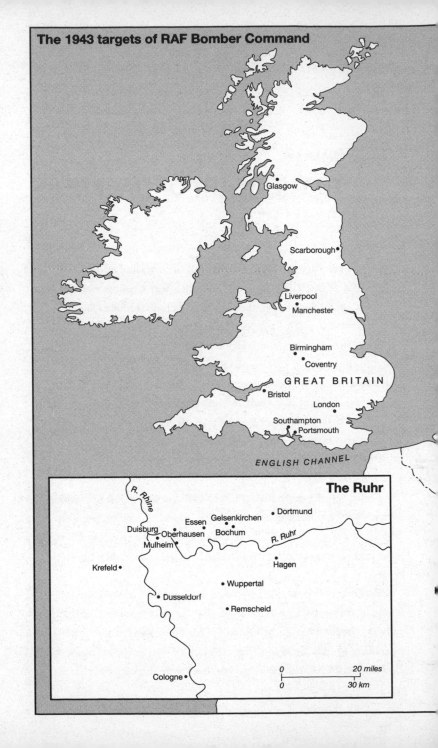

The 1943 targets of RAF Bomber Command

Glasgow

Scarborough

Liverpool
Manchester

Birmingham
Coventry

GREAT BRITAIN

Bristol

London

Southampton
Portsmouth

ENGLISH CHANNEL

The Ruhr

R. Rhine

Dortmund

Essen Gelsenkirchen

Duisburg Bochum

Oberhausen

Mulheim

R. Ruhr

Krefeld

Hagen

Wuppertal

Dusseldorf

Remscheid

0		20 miles
0		30 km

Cologne

NORWAY

SWEDEN

DENMARK

NORTH
SEA

BALTIC SEA

Kiel

Rostock

Peenemunde

Wilhelmshaven

Hamburg

Stettin

R. Elbe

OLLAND

Munster

Hanover

BERLIN

Gelsenkirchen

Bochum

refeld

Essen

Dusseldorf

Wuppertal

Kassel

G R E A T E R

R. Weser

Cologne

Ruhr Dams

Leipzig

R. Oder

POLAND

Pilsen

Frankfurt

G E R M A N Y

Mannheim

Nuremburg

MBOURG

Ludwigshafen

R. Rhine

Stuttgart

SLOVAKIA

Munich

Friedrichshafen

SWITZERLAND

AUSTRIA

HUNGARY

ITALY

0   50 miles

0   80 km

retaliation. The navigation problems that beset Bomber Command, as the Butt Report so aptly pointed out, meant the raid was a failure. The only bombs to fall within the city limits destroyed a summer house.

Bomber Command returned nine more times throughout 1940 and 1941 with negligible results and at increasing loss. Finally in November 1941, 169 Wellingtons, Whitleys, Stirlings and Halifaxes had set out, but only seventy-three aircraft had reached the general area of the Reich capital and bombed the outskirts. A total of ten Wellingtons, nine Whitleys and two Stirlings had failed to return, a horrifying 12.4 per cent. For the time being Bomber Command withdrew.

After he took over the Command in February 1942 Sir Arthur Harris had come under constant pressure from Churchill to return and indeed it was a point of some embarrassment that the Nazis could boast they had devastated London for ninety-two nights running yet the RAF could not repay. Harris was unwilling to risk aircraft of uncertain merit and decided only Lancasters could be used with any degree of safety. Furthermore, the design of this huge city of four million people, with its central Tiergarten and wide streets lined with apartment houses, meant that only a substantial force could produce significant damage.

The C-in-C had husbanded his resources until he had enough Lancasters hopefully to overwhelm the strong defences of flak and *nachtjäger*. By January the need to attack was becoming imperative. General Chuikov's final Soviet offensive on the Stalingrad front had begun on 10 January and von Paulus's Sixth Army would soon be overwhelmed. An attack on the Reich capital would demonstrate Bomber Command's growing potential to the impatient Stalin, to Hitler and to the rest of the world.

The Air Ministry publicity machine wasn't slow to take the point. News organisations were desperate to put reporters aboard bombers for eyewitness accounts. Among the reporters granted passes for the first available Berlin raid, expected to be around the middle of the month, was the BBC war correspondent Richard Dimbleby. He would experience at first hand what it was like to be shot at over the German capital and tell an expectant nation about it afterwards, safe in their armchairs in pinnies and business suits, feet firmly planted on the lounge linoleum, eager ears leaning towards the corner radio. Who better to take him to Berlin and bring him back safely than that superb exponent of operational flying, the 106 Sqn CO Guy Gibson, then with sixty-six operations behind him?

Dimbleby had arrived at 106's base of Syerston, near Nottingham, on 10 January, waiting in the officers' mess in his army major's uniform with justifiable nervousness for the Berlin op to be laid on, as all around him he heard blue-battledressed young pilots, navigators and bomb aimers, tankards in hand, discuss the relative frightfulness of the Essen, Stuttgart or Frankfurt flak, or which airman they'd known in training had just 'gone for a Burton'.

The 16th dawned fine and teleprinters at RAF stations throughout 5 Group began chattering out bomb loads, fuel capacities and time on target for Operations Whitebait, the Air Ministry code for the Reich capital. At Syerston 106 Sqn's adjutant would later record: 'Thirteen aircraft were detailed for a raid on Berlin – this being the big show for which Major Dimbleby was waiting.'[1]

Syerston was a huge, two-squadron station, with 2,500 ground staff, most of whom would be employed in getting its aircrew ready and Lancasters airborne. As the day wore on, WAAFs and airmen went through the minutiae of preparation. Escape kits with silk maps correct for the hostile area were stacked ready by the crew room and WAAFs checked CO_2 bottles on Mae Wests for signs of corrosion and leakage and parachutes for damp which would prevent the chute unfurling properly and leave its unfortunate recipient 'roman-candling' through the searchlights.

Armourers in the bomb dump, placed far away from the airfield perimeter in case of accident, fused the bombs ordered by the station armaments officer, their bare fingers blued by the cold, and loaded the weaponry onto low bomb carriers to be towed by tractor to the silent aircraft waiting at dispersals. Around the perimeter track the pregnant petrol bowsers were cruising, turning into each hoar-frosted rural dispersal to link the Merlin engines with their lifeblood. Tonight a full 2,143 gallons of high octane would be needed to take the aircraft on the testing journey to the Reich capital and back.

At the flight offices crew lists were being pored over and a battle order prepared, working back from the purpose of all this effort by so many unknown airmen and WAAFs, the time on target. The first briefing for navigators was just after noon, the main briefing an hour later, the operational meal of bacon, beans and the cherished egg at 2 p.m. and final briefing one hour before take-off. A chain and padlock had been put round the base public telephone boxes immediately the target was known, sealing the airmen in from those in that world of certainty and sanity to whom they hoped to return.

And finally, in a pathetic parody of the domestic routine, overalled WAAFs had prepared the flying rations of sandwiches, orange juice and barley sugar, a reminder to many aircrew of that short time before when they had been boys carrying their picnics on a school treat. WAAFs would hand the rations to crews with their escape kits as they went to don Irvin jackets, flying helmets, oxygen masks and parachute harnesses in the electric, ribald atmosphere of the crew room. It would also be a WAAF who would drive the men in utility trucks to their aircraft, often the last female face aircrew would ever see. As the truck halted, the WAAF would hold open the door and stand, one foot on the running board, her pretty face and bobbed hair framed by the round and pleated soft-peaked cap and gently call 'Good luck', breath holding still in the cold night air.

The Whitebait stage had been set. All that was now needed was the performers. One of them was Sgt Gordon McGregor, who was being taken on a familiarisation trip in Gibson's aircraft, with Richard Dimbleby aboard. It was a role known as 'second dickey' in which a raw pilot was introduced to the flash of flak and whiff of cordite before operating with his own crew. McGregor had arrived with his crew at Syerston just days before.

His flight engineer was Sgt Graham Allen – who within 24 hours would discover for himself the terrors of a Berlin raid – and his rear gunner was Sgt Albert Bracegirdle, a former Manchester baker and at 21 the second oldest in the crew. McGregor's tour would take his crew safely through the Battle of the Ruhr for a minimum six months' rest at an operational training unit. But before the year was over Sgt Bracegirdle would be called again for a second tour as losses mounted during November and December in the chilling campaign that would become known as the Battle of Berlin. Bracegirdle remembers:

> We had met up as a crew at 19 OTU at Kinloss at the end of July 1942. They put all the aircrew in a hangar together and we all milled around. Someone would come up to you and ask: 'Are you looking for a wireless operator or a pilot or whatever?' You had no idea what the person you were talking to had done, but it seemed to work.
>
> We joined 106 on 7 January from Swinderby where we had converted to four-engine heavies from Whitleys. McGregor met Dimbleby at the briefing on the 16th and found out then he was going with them on the Berlin raid.[2]

Another of the reporters with a ticket for Berlin was Australian Keith Hooper. He would be flying with a fellow countryman in a Lancaster of 57 Sqn from Scampton. In his subsequent report in the *Daily Express* he revealed the reaction among crews as they were called to main briefing in pre-war Scampton's purpose-built operations block:

> Our eyes instantly flicked to a huge map on the wall, across which was tacked a red woollen thread from our home station to 'Look fellows, look – BERLIN!' A tingle of more than ordinary excitement showed in everyone's face. 'Boy, oh boy,' said a sergeant pilot. 'I've always wanted to prang that dump.'[3]

It wasn't just newspaper hyperbole. There was genuine excitement that after fourteen months Bomber Command would be taking the war to where the Reich leaders lived. The adjutant's office at 9 Sqn recorded that 'the target had been received with delight' when revealed at briefing.[4]

News had been released within the past 48 hours of a Bomber Command VC, albeit a posthumous one, bang on cue to inspire crews. Australian F/Sgt Rawdon Middleton had been badly wounded by flak bombing the Fiat works at Turin at the end of November. He managed to bring his Stirling back to the Kent coast where he ordered the crew to bale out. Five did so before the plane plunged into the sea with Middleton still on board.

Gibson's aircraft was the first off from Syerston's 2,000-yard main runway at 1635 as the green of the controller's Aldis lamp flashed from the Watch Office and twelve other 106 Sqn Lancasters trundled between the blue perimeter lights, noses poised to follow. In all, 190 Lancasters and eleven Halifaxes were to take part in this important raid. Stirlings were originally to join in the operation, but had been withdrawn because it was feared their 14,000-feet service ceiling would mean them catching most of the flak. The Berlin force now represented 4 and 1 Groups and, predominantly, Sir Alec Coryton's 5 Group. Coryton had only weeks to serve as group commander. He would be sacked by Harris in February for refusing to send a small force of Lancasters on a sneak raid to Berlin in bad weather.

As the aircraft droned across the North Sea and crew members settled down at their stations for what lay ahead, skippers soon began to experience problems with the weather. Thick cloud built up and over the Low Countries and in Germany itself there were snow showers, hindering navigation.

W/Cdr Gibson was a wizard at weaving over enemy territory, rolling the aircraft slowly from side to side over its lateral arc to throw off the aim of any stalking night fighter and giving his mid-upper and rear gunners a chance to search the area below. Weaving was one of the reasons he had lived so long. But for a passenger unused to the motion in a reverberating, oily Lancaster it could be too unsettling. Says Albert Bracegirdle:

> When McGregor came back from his second-dickey raid he told me that Dimbleby had been terribly ill. He had been very sick for most of the journey. With Dimbleby there it meant they had eight on board. He was at the front with McGregor there as the flight engineer and McGregor said it was a bit of a nuisance because there wasn't that much room to move around.

After a fourteen-month absence Bomber Command caught the Berlin defences by surprise. The first sirens went off as the initial bombing by Pathfinders aiming for the Alexanderplatz railway station began and there was close to panic in the streets until block gauleiters were able to guide people to shelters. At the 10,000-seat Deutschlandhalle the crump of bombs and whump, pock and crack of exploding anti-aircraft shells interrupted the evening show of the annual circus in the hall, an event Berliners looked forward to for months.

Gauleiters evacuated the building so rapidly that twenty-one people were injured in the crush. They were led to open ground nearby and watched as the show's animal trainers calmed their charges, the frightened creatures nervously tossing their heads. Moments later sticks of incendiaries pattered across the roof of the building and because there was no one left inside to combat the fires it burned out, becoming Berlin's largest ruin so far.

The Air Ministry had high hopes of this raid. Pathfinders were using for the first time the new target indicator bomb, detonated by barometric fuse at a predetermined height and spilling unmistakable clusters of red, green or yellow candles, dripping brilliant fingers of fire against the black backdrop of the sky. German civilians were soon to christen them 'Christmas trees'. But the crews of the Lancasters droning across the city's wide expanse braving the bursting flak found it difficult to identify aiming points through the haze. The determined Gibson made three runs over the city as his bomb aimer, Sub-Lt Gerard Muttrie, on secondment from the Royal Navy, tried to pick up a TI. Finally as flak rocked the aircraft Muttrie spotted a red marker flare and released the load, an 8,000-lb bomb. As Gibson dived away the results could not be seen and at debriefing the CO reported: 'It was believed the bomb fell on Berlin, but the trip was disappointing due to the weather.'[5]

Most other skippers, including John Searby, 106 Sqn's B-Flight commander, who in August as CO of 83 Sqn would be master bomber on the important Peenemünde operation, found the raid 'rather unsatisfactory' due to the poor visibility. One 106 Sqn skipper reported that he had had to drop on an 'estimated position of Berlin coinciding with the flak concentration'.

Sgt Claremont Taylor, navigator to Sgt Bill Wendon of 460 Sqn, had come from Australia to fight the empire's war. His tour, which would end with a minimum-height moonlit operation to Stettin in April, had begun with another low-level raid in the moon period of November to Stuttgart. He remembers:

> Then we were so low coming home we were able to read the time from a church steeple just off the port wing. 16 January was my first trip to Berlin and like everybody else I was wondering what it would be like. It was ten-tenths cloud en route with the target clear for us and Bill Wendon taking evasive action all the way with an up and down movement. A Ju88 approached us from underneath, but he was seen straight away and Bill dived viciously. The bomber escaped into the night without damage.[6]

The Australian war correspondent Keith Hooper told his readers that as shells burst beneath his aircraft with poisonous red flashes he thought the trail of black puffs behind them was a balloon barrage and called to warn the pilot. 'Take it easy, pal,' he was told. 'It's only flak.'

At 9 Sqn the operational assessment was that the raid had not been a success because of cloud over the target area and the fact that 'PFF failed to conform with the technique expected of them'. The report said many decoy fires had been seen in the target area and the bombing had varied from 'bombed marker incendiaries' to 'bombed on ETA through 10/10 cloud'.[7]

F/O Les Munro was another who had travelled far to fly with Bomber Command. The New Zealander was flying his seventh operation and within months would take part in the Dams Raid with 617 Sqn, ending the war with a DSO and DFC, and becoming a national hero back home. But his first trip to Berlin was a frustrating one. 'We opened the bomb bay doors on the run-in, the bomb aimer pressed his switches and nothing happened,' he remembers. 'We were at 24,500 feet and the gear just iced up. It was a problem at that time because Bomber Command had just started flying these high-level operations.'[8]

Experienced skippers on most units had found the flak not to be heavy for Berlin and this, together with the poor weather and late identification of the target, kept the night fighters away. Only one aircraft was lost.

Stewart Sale, a Reuters correspondent on the raid in a 57 Sqn Lancaster, described in the *Daily Express* how the pilot called out 'Big City, here we come' on the intercom as the aircraft climbed on course out of Scampton. The squadron's intelligence officer had told crews that Berlin, with its industries reaching out far and wide, 'has had this coming to it for a long time. Now it is going to get it.' Over the target, Sale reported:

> The fires below spread and brightened. Incendiaries streamed across the city in glittering lanes. Looking down on this furnace I remembered nights on Fleet Street roofs when the German bombers were over. 'Pranged 'em' bawled the captain and he began to sing, not very tunefully, 'It's a Hap-Hap-Happy Day!' The navigator joined in and so did the rear gunner. I expected banks of searchlights. I saw not more than half a dozen tapered down to fine points.[9]

The flak and searchlights had indeed been lighter than normal. It had been so long since the RAF had visited the city that half of the Berlin flak personnel had been sent away on a course. Goebbels, who combined his duties as Propaganda Minister with that of Gauleiter of Berlin, was said to be furious at the poor reaction and ordered an overhaul of the system. Because so many people were on the streets, 198 were killed, including one Englishman who was among fifty-three prisoners of war who lost their lives. Prisoners of war came low on the pecking order for shelter space.

As for Richard Dimbleby, his broadcast went out to a fascinated public a few nights later. He told them of the silent, yellow, winking flashes of the flak over the enemy coast as Gibson sat straight in his seat 'as cool as a cucumber throwing the great Lancaster around like a toy'. He told them of the ring of searchlights around the city as Lancaster W for William approached Berlin and of 'a shell burst under the tail heaving us up as though a giant smacked us under the belly'.

Then he described a Lancaster underneath them releasing its load and 'a great silver carpet of fire unrolled itself. It was a retinue of brilliant lights revealing the outlines of the city. Thousands more fire bombs were released and all over the face of the German capital ran the streams of fire until the city looked like a garden filled with incandescent flower beds.' Dimbleby said he reflected as W for William droned over the Reich capital that Hitler, Goering, Goebbels and Ribbentrop a few thousand feet below might be hiding in their shelters.

The public – too well aware of what it had been like over four years to hide in a shelter and some of whom had sons and husbands in those same RAF bombers – loved it. For Dimbleby it was only the first of many experiences at the sharp end of Bomber Command. He was to make several more operational flights during the war.

Back in civilian clothes an exhausted Dimbleby had pushed his way into the crowded, cold early-morning express from Nottingham to London to record his eyewitness account. As the train slowly steamed out of the drab station with its Ministry of Information posters pleading: 'Is your journey really necessary?' Dimbleby settled into a compartment where he was the only one not in uniform apart from an elderly woman. She looked at the soldiers wearily leaning on rifle and pack in the corridor, then back at Dimbleby and said: 'I should have thought a lucky young man like you would have given up his seat.' Dimbleby was too tired to reply.[10]

THE next day the teleprinters chattered out Whitebait again as Harris put his boys back on Berlin in the hope of doing better. They didn't. Weather conditions had improved on the night before, but the raid would be carried out in a full moon and this time the Luftwaffe flak and fighter units weren't going to be caught unprepared. And Harris was using the same route out and back.

Les Munro was back over the target experiencing 'a terrific amount of searchlight activity and flak. If the flak burst no nearer than a couple of hundred metres away you just felt the thump of the explosion,' he says. 'You would feel the vibration of the explosion through the controls if it was close enough.' Munro bombed from 23,000 feet, among the highest on the raid, and on return was diverted to Harwell.

The Pathfinders had been unable to mark the centre of the city and as on the previous night the following 170 Lancasters and seventeen Halifaxes mainly bombed the southern areas of Berlin and there was no significant damage. Incendiaries fell on a BMW factory at Spandau.

It was one of several operations at this time where more RAF men were killed than those on the ground. Only eight Germans died and forty-one were injured, but nineteen Lancasters and three Halifaxes crashed, an unsupportable loss rate of 11.8 per cent. A total of 126 aircrew died and only nine became prisoners of war. Four Lancasters were lost by 9 Sqn at Waddington and another four by 12 Sqn at Wickenby, terrifying statistics for aircrew on either of those squadrons trying to calculate the chances of completing a tour of thirty operations.

Graham Allen, who had been posted to Syerston as a member of McGregor's crew only ten days before, found himself suddenly drafted onto the battle order. He recalls: 'Sgt Edward Markland's engineer went sick and I was called on for the Berlin op at a couple of hours' notice. It was some surprise.' He didn't know New Zealander Markland or any of his mainly British crew including the two gunners, 19-year-old Sgt Bob Greep and 24-year-old Sgt Ted Parry. Markland's bomb run over Berlin was uneventful, but as the Lancaster approached the Kiel area at 20,000 feet on the way back from the target a Ju88 closed in.

Allen remembers:

The first I knew we were in trouble was hearing one of the gunners shout a warning. At the same time yellow tracer shot over the top of the cockpit. Then I saw our starboard outer engine burst into flame. It was really blazing. Markland was by that time trying to corkscrew out of the way of the fighter and it was getting worse.

Markland's gunners, Greep and Parry, blasted away with their .303 Browning machine guns at the heavily armed attacker and saw the fighter spin out of control and hit the ground. But Markland still had to deal with the burning engine, spurting flames with blow-torch efficiency back over the starboard wing.

Allen recollects:

He put the aircraft into a steep dive, but it still wouldn't go out. We went down to about 5,000 feet and when he tried to pull out of the dive he had to shout to me to help him. We were both on the control column before it came level.

The fire was still blazing and Markland ordered us to bale out. The bomb aimer, who would have been first, grabbed his chute out of its clamp to put it on and pulled the ripcord by mistake. I could see it had spilled out right over the escape hatch.

Fortunately just afterwards the fire died down and I operated the extinguisher and feathered the engine, so we could get home on three. But we then ran into a lot of light flak as we were only at 5,000 feet. Markland weaved and we managed to get out of it; we could see it gradually falling away behind us and shortly afterwards we were over the sea. We had to land at an emergency airfield and were very glad to get back. I wondered if all my ops were going to be as bad as that. For a first operation it was a bit nerve-racking.[11]

The next day as fitters replaced the burned-out engine they gave the heat-twisted inlet and exhaust valves to Sgt Allen as a souvenir of his first operation.

OF the Halifaxes on the raid, seven were supplied by Leonard Cheshire's 76 Sqn at Linton-on-Ouse, taking off one by one in continuous slight rain. Two of them failed to return. Cheshire himself hadn't been on the raid, but he had been there the previous night, his seventh Berlin operation.

There had been nothing in the press the next day about the raid of the 16th as another operation on the capital was being planned for that night, but Berlin was big news in the newspapers of the 18th and the two raids were reported as if they had been one. Cheshire, who already held the DSO and DFC and was to win the VC with 617 Sqn in 1944, had a reputation for keenness with the British public and throughout the Command. On New Year's Day when most airmen were sleeping off their hangovers he had ordered all 76 Sqn aircrew to parade for a cross-country run in the rain. And to make sure no shivering gunner or flight engineer escaped he told them he would lead them. On 18 January as the Berlin media blitz broke, Cheshire was pictured on the front page of the *Daily Express* quaffing a pint.

Air Reporter Basil Cardew told readers under a story headed 'Four-ton bombs blitz Berlin' that the experiences of crews were best expressed by 'one of their aces'. Cheshire told him: 'Berlin used to be the hottest place in Germany with hundreds of guns and searchlights, but instead of a wall of anti-aircraft fire the flak was negligible compared with my previous experiences over there and I saw only one searchlight.'[12]

That may have been the experience of Cheshire and all the crews who flew on the raid of the 16th, but the next night's operation had been a far different story as the defences recovered from the debacle of the first raid. Again Berlin had cost unsustainable numbers of aircraft and crews. A percentage loss of 11.8 per cent was one which would put Bomber Command out of business in short order if allowed to continue.

There would be one more Berlin raid before the month closed, but it would be by high-flying Mosquitos, stinging Nazi pride in style. In the meantime the Main Force crews were rested when fog closed many airfields to flying. As Bomber Command's Operational Research Section at High Wycombe analysed the debit and credit of the two raids on the Reich capital, crews sought relief from the stress of operations in the pubs of Lincoln, Nottingham and York.

Among squadrons in the Yorkshire-based 4 Group, Betty's Bar in York was usually the target for the night. Tipsy aircrew fuelled up in other York pubs would weave their way past the Minster into cobbled Davygate where the feverish atmosphere of Betty's, opposite the thirteenth-century St Helen's church, guaranteed a memorable evening. The subterranean wood-panelled bar boomed with the accents of young men wearing the shoulder flashes of Canada, Australia, New Zealand and more exotic parts of the Commonwealth. Aircrew anxious to leave a mark in the world before they exited in the next few days, weeks or months scratched their names in the mirrors lining the walls.*

Reid Thomson was a 21-year-old rear gunner on 102 Sqn at Pocklington near York and a regular at Betty's. He was one of the surprisingly large number of Americans in Commonwealth air force blue, leaving his

---

* *The mirrors with the names of long-dead airmen can still be seen today in Betty's, now a fashionable cake shop and restaurant.*

Tennessee home in August 1941 to enlist in the RCAF. He joined thirteen young Canadians on Air Gunners' Course 25 at Mountain View, Ontario. They lined up for a group photograph in prickly, stiff new RCAF great-coats and, proudly displaying the white aircrew-under-training flash in their forage caps, stared hesitatingly at the camera, wondering whether they were allowed to smile. By the war's end only two of them would be alive.

A year after enlisting, Reid Thomson was flying his first operation, to Düsseldorf, from 22 OTU at Wellesbourne Mountford, near Stratford-on-Avon. Now he was rear gunner to S/Ldr John Marshall, with five trips in and a growing realisation that it was unlikely he would finish his tour. He remembers:

> When I arrived on 102 Sqn I met up with Art MacGillivray who had been commissioned at the end of our air gunners' course. I said: 'Let's go get a beer.' He told me: 'I can't, I have to fly tonight.' So I suggested the next night. He said: 'I won't be here' and sure enough he went missing that night.* [13]

Sgt Thomson remembers that sometimes the eclectic mixture of youth, alcohol, operational strain and international temperament at Betty's Bar flared into fights.

'It was dimly lit and smoky and it was mostly air force who were in there,' he says. 'I was in there and I heard a guy bragging who I knew had never completed an operation. I went over with a beer mug and told him he was a liar and a coward. I never saw him in there again.' In fact Sgt Thomson's future visits to Betty's Bar would be few. A raid on Düsseldorf described in the next chapter ended his operational career.

THE final Berlin raid of the month was staged with precision timing during daylight by six Mosquitos of Don Bennett's 8 Pathfinder Group. The date 30 January marked the tenth anniversary of the Nazis' seizure of power and festivities were planned at the ceremonial hall of the Air Ministry at which Goering was to speak in the morning, followed in the afternoon by

* F/O Aubrey MacGillivray, air gunner, of 102 Sqn was killed in air operations to Flensburg on 1 October 1942 and is buried in Kiel War Cemetery.

Goebbels. Both speeches would be broadcast live throughout Germany.

Fortunately for the British there had been ample advance propaganda by the Nazis, including timings. The first three aircraft of 105 Sqn flew out across the North Sea at low level and achieved complete surprise as they crossed the enemy coast and sped on over the Low Countries and northern Germany. The sirens went off at the exact time Goering was meant to give his broadcast message. He had planned to tell the German people of the courage of the sixth Army at Stalingrad – in fact besieged because of Hitler's intransigence – comparing them to the Spartans at Thermopylae. Berlin Radio announced that the speech had been postponed for an hour. The three aircraft all returned safely.

As they landed, three more Mosquitos of 139 Sqn were already on their way to perform the same trick again with Goebbels' speech. By this time there was ten-tenths cloud and the aircraft in the small formation were soon lost to each other. As if by the conjuror's art the cloud ran out exactly as the aircraft reached the German capital.

Goebbels, who would be reading words prepared for Hitler, had just risen to address the party faithful with rhetoric which glossed over the approaching defeat at Stalingrad in one sentence as the sirens sounded once more and the Mosquitos individually released their loads. As his audience, from hausfrau across Germany to wounded in the cellars of the Volga city, listened, they heard the crump of falling bombs over the airwaves. Tellingly the single sentence exhorted the German people to do their maximum in the struggle 'for the nation's future'. It was an admission that from now on Germany would be fighting to prevent defeat.

For the RAF the raid was not the complete coup of the earlier Mosquito attack. This time the defences were alert and shot down one of the aircraft, killing its crew. Navigator Sgt Richard Fletcher saw no activity, however, as he released his bombs.

The 31-year-old Londoner reported later:

> We all felt the Germans put up a poor show in defence. Our bombs
> went down at 4 p.m. dead, just when Goebbels was going to speak.

That night we had a pretty good do in the mess. I think I hit the hay at about 2.30 a.m. It was beer and Berlin all the way.[14]

The message to the Nazi hierarchy and to Berliners must have been clear – Bomber Command's raids on the Reich capital and on Germany as a whole were just beginning. The tide had turned for the Nazis, as was demonstrated in graphic terms the next day when Stalingrad finally fell to the Russians with the loss of 330,000 men. The aggressors were now the defenders. Harris had his finger on the pulse of Nazi fears with a signal to 8 Group headquarters after the Mosquito attacks. 'Please convey to all concerned, especially to the aircraft crews, my warmest congratulations,' it read. 'Their bombs cannot have failed to cause consternation in Germany.'

The first raid on the 16th had already stung the Nazis sufficiently for them to order revenge attacks on London and other towns in southern England the next day and night, the sound of RAF bombers returning across the Channel from the second Berlin raid being heard between Luftwaffe alerts. A few days later German air expert Major Wulff-Biel had announced in a talk on Berlin radio: 'The raid on London has again shown the decency of the methods of the Luftwaffe as opposed to the terror tactics of the RAF since the German bombers attacked military objectives only.' In fact a London school had been hit in daytime on the 17th, killing five teachers and forty-two children.

Allied attacks on Berlin would continue over the next two and a half years, with more than 340 raids by the RAF, USAAF and Soviet Air Force, thirty-five of them heavy. The *kellergemeinschaften,* as the cellar communities of Berlin became known, would endure alerts lasting a combined total of 432 hours, or eighteen full days and nights.

The next time the RAF's heavy bombers would visit the city would be on 1 March and by then it would be with newly available radar equipment, H2S, designed to take aircraft accurately to their aiming points. It and, more particularly, the Oboe blind-bombing device would devastate the cities of Germany in the next eleven months. The science of bombing was about to begin in earnest.

CHAPTER TWO

A SIGNAL SUCCESS

THE Berlin raids on which the British public had seized so enthusiastically as they braved the bitter winds, snow showers, rain and gales that lashed their heat-rationed homes in January came as a diversion from Bomber Command's main effort to experiment with Oboe and H2S on German targets. Nor would they be the only deviation the Command would experience in the first two months of the year. Harris, itching to get on with the Battle of the Ruhr, would find his command called to the aid of the Admiralty, an interruption he would find intensely irritating in a cause he considered pointless. However, for the first half of January he was allowed to carry out the bombing experiments that within six months would cause the Ruhr to be devastated.

Germany's leaders must have considered it a cruel irony that the Knickebein and X-Gerat blind-bombing equipment their scientists developed and the Luftwaffe employed to wreck Coventry and other British cities should spawn Oboe, the device with which the RAF would now locate and destroy the Ruhr's industrial cities.

The first Oboe-equipped Mosquitos in Bennett's Pathfinder force became available on 20 December 1942. On New Year's Eve itself, as the rest of Bomber Command was dancing and drinking the old year away with impressive abandon, the crews of two Mosquitos had released on an Oboe signal six high-explosive bombs on night-fighter control headquarters at Florennes in Belgium. There were rumours one bomb had gone straight through the front door of the HQ. It had been dropped from 5½ miles above, through ten-tenths cloud in complete darkness.

The Germans had developed Knickebein from the Lorenz airfield approach system. Knickebein consisted of dots and dashes broadcast to an aircraft from a powerful transmitter. If the pilot kept to the middle of the beam he heard one continuous note. A second transmitter sent a signal just ahead of where the bombs should be dropped and the point at which the two sounds intersected was where the German Pathfinder dropped his bombs for the rest to follow. Because Knickebein was easily jammed, X-Gerat was devised in which a special receiver and four beams were used. The first directed the bomber pilot along the route to his target; the second crossbeam was a check to make sure he was flying accurately. A subsequent intersecting beam cut in 20 kilometres from the target and the observer activated the timer of an automatic bomb-release mechanism. At the sound of a fourth beam crossing, the observer pressed the button again and the bombs were automatically released.

The Air Ministry ordered development of a similar blind-bombing device for the RAF. The Telecommunications Research Establishment at Worth Matravers, near Swanage, working with 109 Sqn during 1941 and 1942, came up with a radar scheme more accurate than the radio of X-Gerat. It was a precise system whereby its host aircraft could be tracked over a target by two ground stations in England emitting pulse signals, one station codenamed *Cat*, the other *Mouse*. As they were picked up by the aircraft the pulses were automatically sent back to the ground stations by transponder. The receptor Pathfinder aircraft used the signals to keep itself on the proper track – like X-Gerat – to pass over the exact target co-ordinates. Its navigator did so by setting a course to intersect an arc of a circle. The arc's centre was at Cat and its radius the distance from Cat to its aiming point. To the west of the arc the aircraft's navigator heard a series of Morse dots, to the east dashes. When on the exact arc the signal in the navigator's earphones was an unbroken tone. It was experiments with the appropriate left, right and steady tones which gave the device its name. A music-loving lab technician at Worth Matravers said they sounded like an oboe.

Under the system the Mouse operator transmitted specific Morse signals as the aircraft approached the aiming point to tell the navigator how far he had to fly. They ended in a brief series of dots followed by a dash. At the precise moment the aircraft was over the aiming point the dash would end and the TI would be released.

The drawback to Oboe was that its signal was affected by the curvature of the earth. The higher the aircraft the more accessible the signal. Originally the RAF planned to use a Mk VI Wellington with a pressurised cabin, but there were problems – one of them being that an emergency exit could only be made from the aircraft by unscrewing the floor. Then at the right time along came the 30,000-feet Mk IV Mosquito, as target indicators were developed which would fill its bomb bays. A war-winning combination was born. The Mosquito would extend Oboe's range to 300 miles – enough to cover the important Ruhr targets. Oboe had its drawbacks in that initially a pair of ground stations could only control one aircraft at a time, but it was enough for the time being as the art of target marking was developed in January 1943.

Guy Gibson had hoped his Lancasters would be used as part of the Main Force in an Oboe-marked experiment on the first day of the year. As others lounged before the mess fire reading details of the New Year's Honours List knighthood for 3 Group C-in-C John Baldwin, he had the crews of five aircraft alerted for an attack on the Krupps works at Essen. But to the disappointment of the determined Gibson showers blanketed visibility and all flying was cancelled.

It was not until the third day of the year that the weather improved enough for Gibson's squadron to operate. They put up five aircraft of the nineteen Lancasters of 5 Group which would bomb on the marker flares of three PFF Mosquitos. Others were provided by 61 Sqn – which shared the airfield at Syerston with 106 – by 207 Sqn and by 9 and 44 Sqns. Among the aircrews on 9 Sqn's battle order was that of F/Lt Douglas Lonsdale. His men included Canadian air gunner F/Sgt Robert Dickie, 23, and his friend RCAF W/O Robert Moore, a 20-year-old wireless operator.

The two Canadians had been brought up in the small Vancouver Island fishing and logging town of Duncan. One day they had each taken the train from Duncan's wooden railway station down to Victoria, caught the ferry to Vancouver and begun the long journey that now had Dickie complaining to himself of the cold as he prepared to test his guns in the pre-arranged area 25 miles out to sea while his fellow townsman protested at the flow of cabin heat, which on Lancasters came out underneath the wireless operator's table.

Waddington had proved an attractive posting for the Dominion airmen. As a pre-war station it had the comforts of hot showers and purpose-built billets, and nearby Lincoln's eleventh-century cathedral and castle at the top of cobbled Steep Hill had offered a fascinating insight into a world they had only read of at school in rural British Columbia. A couple of weeks previously there had been even more to write home about when the king visited their RAF station.

In the nose of Lonsdale's A-Apple was a Canadian born in Victoria, only 36 miles south of Dickie and Moore's home. F/O Kenneth Smith had been trained as a navigator, but was now operating as a bomb aimer in Lonsdale's crew. The other three crewmen were engineer Sgt Bert Riley, 22, from Norbury, Surrey; navigator Sgt James Morris, 22, from Kidderminster, Worcestershire; and mid-upper gunner Sgt Arthur Smitherman, 21, from Tunbridge Wells, in Kent.

As Lonsdale's aircraft slowly turned from its hard-standing and rumbled along the dimly blue-lit perimeter track following the tail light of another Lancaster, his flight engineer juggled throttles and Lonsdale peered through the rain-spotted windscreen nervously tapping brake and rudder port and starboard to keep the lumbering giant on the centre line.

This raid would take him and his crew within thirteen trips of the required thirty to be screened. He hoped there would be no repeat of the raid four weeks before when, as he released his bombs on Turin, an incendiary from an aircraft above penetrated his aircraft immediately in front of his windscreen and wrecked the autopilot. The bomb hadn't caught fire, but a second which went through the roof of the airframe just behind the rear turret had, and Dickie, Moore and their flight engineer had fought to put the fire out. Lonsdale had then flown all the way back to the emergency airstrip at Woodbridge in Suffolk staring at the 4-lb incendiary lodged in the fuselage just in front of him, hoping the slipstream whipping through wouldn't suddenly cause it to burst into flames.

As the grey runway faded beneath his turret and the mass of Lincoln Cathedral receded in the darkness, Dickie had time to reflect on those stomach-churning operations stretching over the bitter months. In Bomber Command's terms this trial raid on Essen of 3 January was an undoubted success as Oboe proved its accuracy. Bombs were reported to have hit the city centre, killing six. But the small numbers of aircraft involved made those taking part easy targets for the German night-fighter force and it was to be one of those nights for Bomber Command when more of its men were killed than those on the ground.

Three Lancasters were lost and the first was that of Robert Dickie and Robert Moore. They died on the way back from Essen at 8.14 p.m. when F/Lt Lonsdale's aircraft crashed in the Overhagense Weide on the north-east outskirts of Arnhem, after being attacked by an Me110 flown by Unteroffizier Christian Koltringer of III/NJG1 based at Twente in Holland. F/Lt Lonsdale and his crew were therefore the first of Harris's men to be killed in action in 1943, a year of escalating attrition.

At 31 Lonsdale was older than most aircrew and married. His wife, Patricia, received the news he was missing by Air Ministry telegram next day at their home in Westham, Sussex. A few days later it was followed by a letter from the squadron commander expressing sympathy for her anxiety. Then in the familiar litany of official unease there would follow the standard letter from Air Ministry ten days later telling of the 'Air Council's deep regret on learning that your husband F/Lt Douglas Herbert Scott Lonsdale is missing as a result of air operations 3/4 January. If he is a PoW he should be able to communicate with you in due course.' In two weeks the Red Cross would inform the Air Ministry from their regularly updated prisoner-of-war rolls that no one of the name F/Lt Douglas Lonsdale was in German hands and the official letter would go out to Mrs Lonsdale that her husband, previously reported as missing, must now be presumed to be dead.

Within 24 hours Bomber Command returned to Essen with four Pathfinder Mosquitos and twenty-nine Lancasters of 1 Group to continue the Oboe experiment. Crews were briefed to attack from 23,000 feet on a constant speed and course, to test the new tactics on the two-mile-square Krupps complex in the centre of the town.

The altitude was approximately twice that which aircrew had been used to bombing from in the previous year and reflected the changing tactics that would be so much a pattern of the bomber offensive of 1943. As it was, crews reported that the target was cloud covered and follow-up marking was on skymarkers, but again the attack was rated reasonably accurate with concentrated bombing north of the city centre, destroying forty-two buildings, damaging sixty-four and killing fourteen people. Two Lancasters were shot down, one of them from the Australian 460 Sqn – then at Breighton, near Selby – which was to lose more aircrew than any other Bomber Command squadron during the offensive.

In four days the Oboe experiment would be carried to Duisburg with three Mosquitos marking for thirty-eight Lancasters of 5 Group, then over the next five nights Essen would be raided four more times. The operations would find mixed success. On the night of the 12th, for instance, the Pathfinders failed utterly. The blind-marking equipment of the first PFF Mosquito became unserviceable, and the other three Pathfinder aircraft were late. Essen was not a target to hang around on and many Main Force bomb aimers released on dead reckoning. Some bombs fell on Essen, but others dropped on Remscheid, Solingen and on Wuppertal, from 12 to 20 miles south of the Krupps complex. The attack came only four days after PFF had been raised to full Group status and its commander, Don Bennett, then an air commodore, must have been an irritated man indeed.

The introduction to the next operation on Essen, the following night, was little better. Two of the Oboe aircraft had to return without dropping their marker bombs. The third did manage to release, but its skymarkers failed to ignite and plunged through the cloud. Without help the sixty-six Main Force aircraft, all Lancasters again, came through and by luck a small concentration developed. A total of fifty-two buildings were destroyed.

Among those killed were eleven French prisoners of war and six other foreign workers.

It was a bad night for Guy Gibson's 106 Sqn. Two of the missing four aircraft were from Syerston. Another of Gibson's aircraft, piloted by Sgt P. N. Reed, came back to Britain with a dead gunner. Soon after releasing his bombs and leaving the target area his aircraft was attacked by an FW190 which raked the aircraft from tail to nose, then swept round for a frontal attack, its cannon shells blasting the aircraft from fore to aft. The mid-upper gunner was killed and the rear gunner wounded. Reed managed to shake the fighter off and nurse his badly damaged aircraft to land at a USAAF base at Hardwicke, Norfolk.

Reed's squadron comrade F/Sgt Lewis Burpee also had a frustrating night. Burpee had had to abandon the raid of the 8th because of an engine failure, abort that of the 11th because of a rear turret malfunction and on this occasion had to turn back again because the bomb aimer, Sgt James Bonson, had inadvertently jettisoned the entire bomb load while testing the bomb bay doors off the English coast. The air must have been blue as 25-year-old Burpee, known as a press-on type, felt the Lancaster leap upwards when the Cookie and incendiaries fell harmlessly in the sea.

With this fourth raid on Essen in a row Harris and Bennett decided they had discovered enough and ended the Oboe trials. Bomber Command's Operational Research section had been able to estimate that Oboe was likely to be accurate over enemy territory to within 650 yards. Much else had been learned. Timing was obviously the key for Main Force to follow up on the Oboe flares, and development was needed on a ground marker. Too many of the parachute skymarkers dripping their candles of light against the blackness had drifted off the aiming point in the strong January winds before the 'heavies' could bomb.

There had also been maintenance problems with the new Lancaster, and other aircraft had shown their shortcomings as squadrons were now ordered to fly routinely at up to 20,000 feet – twice the height most had been used to – to give crews a chance of escaping the marksmanship of the increasing flak battalions.

With the two Berlin raids out of the way Harris was ready to turn to the Ruhr in earnest and rapidly ruin its armament industries. But there now occurred what he described in his memoirs as 'one of the most infuriating episodes in the whole course of the offensive'.[1]

He was diverted from his aim by Admiralty requirements to wreck the U-boat bases of Lorient and St Nazaire. Average monthly sinkings of British shipping by U-boats throughout 1942 had been 289,000 tons, a figure far higher than could be replaced by launching new vessels. Britain's ability to continue the war was approaching crisis point. Torpedoing of transatlantic supplies would peak at 385,000 tons in March 1943, then rapidly decline, largely as a result of the courageous capture of an Enigma machine from the sinking U-559 off Egypt on 13 December 1942, which meant the cryptographers at Bletchley Park were able to break the new Kriegsmarine codes. For the moment, however, the lost tonnage rate was crucial and an extremely worried Churchill provided a willing ear to Admiralty demands that Bomber Command help to stop the rot.

Lorient and St Nazaire were the two main U-boat bases being used in the Battle of the Atlantic and the Royal Navy wanted these two French towns bombed flat. Harris could understand the desire, but took the view that the Germans weren't fools and would take proper precautions to shelter any personnel who had to remain in port and disperse any vital workshops out of built-up areas. As for the U-boat shelters themselves – which Harris saw as the only worthwhile targets – they were protected by several feet of reinforced concrete, which in fact would prove bomb-proof.

The Chief of the Air Staff, Air Chief Marshal Sir Charles Portal, also took the view that the bombing would have no effect except the destruction of old French towns. The First Sea Lord had his way, however, and on 14 January Harris received his orders to bomb Lorient, St Nazaire, Brest and La Pallice in that order and to cause the 'effective devastation of the whole area in which are located the submarines, their maintenance facilities, and the services, power, water, light, communications and other resources on which their operations depend'.[2]

That night 122 aircraft attacked Lorient. Pathfinder marking was accurate, but Main Force bombing became haphazard. It was the first time the new Canadian 6 Group put up aircraft for a bombing operation and they had nine Wellingtons and six Halifaxes on the battle order. It was also the night of the group's first loss. P/O George Milne and his crew from 426 Sqn at Dishforth are thought to have gone down in the Channel.

The next night Bomber Command were back over Lorient with 6 Group increasing their effort, supplying Halifaxes from 419 Sqn at Middleton St George and Wellingtons from 427 Sqn at Croft. Almost 800 buildings were destroyed in the attack, but casualties were light as the inhabitants had fled the town after the previous raid. The American gunner Reid Thomson was in an aircraft of 102 Sqn. He remembers:

> Our main load was incendiaries for that operation. When we landed
> and taxied to dispersal the ground crew came aboard and one of them
> opened the bomb bay doors. A lot of incendiaries we thought we had
> dropped clattered onto the tarmac. Luckily none of them went off. It
> was the only time I ever saw our pilot, S/Ldr Marshall, get mad. He
> really chewed that ground-crew guy out.[3]

Bomber Command would be returning to Lorient seven more times in the next few weeks and eventually Grand Admiral Dönitz would report that it had been 'rubbed out as a submarine base. No dog nor cat is left'. Crucially, as Harris predicted, Dönitz added: 'Nothing but the submarine shelters remain.'[4]

The Lorient raids were often carried out in appalling weather in January and February and the only successes Bomber Command could see for so much expenditure of effort and courage were damage to the U-boat slipways and power supplies – temporary disadvantages. On the debit side the Luftwaffe quickly responded to the threat by moving an extra eight units of heavy flak to Lorient, plus flak ships for the run-in.

The worst weather would be experienced two days before the end of January. A total of 111 aircraft of 1, 4 and 6 Groups were dispatched to bomb Lorient's U-boat pens, but few were able to find the target. New Zealander George Barclay had just become a member of 166 Sqn at

Kirmington after it had been formed from the remnants of 142 and 150 Squadrons. He was a 19-year-old veteran Wellington pilot of both, having lied about his age to join the army at 15, then transferred to the RNZAF for aircrew training.

Of the twelve crews 166 Sqn dispatched to Lorient on the 29th only six reached the target. There was no Pathfinder marking and that and the weather resulted in scattered bombing. F/Sgt Barclay remembers:

> The night was stormy with a north-east wind of about 70 knots at 18,000 feet. I had been to Lorient and St Nazaire before and classified them as easy, so the intense flak this time was a shock. We arrived early over the target because of the strong tail wind.
>
> The return trip was far longer than usual. I went out to sea for about 100 miles and then resumed course for base. This dodged the wind, but it took one and a half hours longer to get home. My navigator, P/O Bert Marion, RCAF, got a rocket because he plotted a course off the map, onto the chart table and back onto the map – about 150 miles up the edge. The navigation leader was not amused and gave him the Pilot Officer Prune award.[5]

One unofficial 419 Sqn crewman was on the raid. F/Lt Alec Cranswick, newly posted to the squadron, took his pet Alsatian, Kluva, along. Cranswick, like all the other airmen on the operation, found the conditions to be appalling. He lifted off from Middleton St George's glistening wet runway at 1654 and climbed out to sea in lashing rain.

An electrical storm battered his Halifax, then the aircraft drifted over Guernsey where flak positions opened up. Over the target itself he found the guns 'heavy and accurate' and when he finally got back to base seven hours and fifteen minutes later his undercarriage collapsed as he rolled to a stop. Cranswick, whose dog had over twenty-five hours of air time, vowed he'd never take him flying again.*[6]

By the middle of February Bomber Command had made 2,000 sorties

*Cranswick transferred soon afterwards to 35 (Pathfinder) Sqn and was killed while operating as primary visual marker at Villeneuve St George, near Paris, on the night of 4 July 1944. By then he was a squadron leader with the DSO and DFC.

to Lorient and even the Admiralty were beginning to accept that nothing more could be achieved. In February and early March three heavy attacks, the first by 400 aircraft, would be carried out against St Nazaire. It was only after furious arguments that the Admiralty failed to gain acceptance for their demand that Brest and Bordeaux also be eradicated. Churchill, as Minister of Defence, backed Harris.

The C-in-C was by now fuming that the Germans had had time to prepare for his industrial bomber offensive. Harris wrote in his peacetime memoirs about the attacks on Lorient and St Nazaire: 'The only effect that they had on the course of the war was to delay the opening of the Battle of the Ruhr and the main bomber offensive against Germany by nearly two months.'[7]

However, he had been able to raid Germany seven more times in January, including the three Berlin operations, after the order to come to the Admiralty's aid. On 21 January he had experimented by sending seventy-nine Lancasters to Essen to see how they got on without the aid of Oboe marking. But ten-tenths cloud over the target meant bomb aimers dropped blindly on only an estimate of where their aircraft was. Four Lancasters didn't come back, two of them from 103 Sqn at Elsham Wolds. Ted Laing was the plump, fresh-faced Australian skipper of one of them, F-Freddie.

His crew of three Australians and three Englishmen had been due to go on leave that day, but it had been scrubbed because the squadron was short for the Essen raid. As fellow Australian airmen watched him and his crew prepare for the op they had a premonition he would not be returning. Laing, a former teacher, lifted off from Elsham in F-Freddie at 1743. He was caught by a night fighter shortly under two hours later, as he neared the German border from eastern Holland.

The night-fighter pilot, Feldwebel Theodor Kleinhenz,* had taken off from III/NJG1 in Twente, north of Enschede, Holland, a short time before in his Me110. In his report later he said: 'We were asked to go to Enschede where a British plane was coming from the east. We saw the plane and

---

* Kleinhenz was awarded the Iron Cross, 2nd Class the next day. He died in an air battle near Bucharest on 5 April 1944.

it suddenly started to weave. We were below it, pulled up our machine vertically and fired into the left wing between the two engines.'[8]

In Enschede an 8-year-old boy saw F/Sgt Laing's Lancaster shot down. Gerrit Zijlstra recalls:

It was about 7.30 at night when I heard the RAF going over. I stood outside our house in the garden when I saw tracer in the north-east from right to left. Suddenly the flashes turned into a fireball heading in our direction. I ran into the house to warn my parents: 'A burning plane is coming straight for us.' My family and our neighbours all came out and started running down the street heading towards some open meadows. As I looked behind, the burning plane made a sharp turn then hit the ground. Later I was told the Lancaster crashed in a field near a factory. The plane was burnt out and the crew are buried in the local cemetery.[9]

On the other side of town someone took a photograph of F/Sgt Laing's Lancaster exploding, with the four blazing fuel tanks fluttering down behind the burning fuselage, and later gave it to Gerrit Zijlstra.

HARRIS would undoubtedly have preferred to raid Essen with more aircraft than a mere seventy-nine, his experiments with Oboe skymarkers having ended, but a combination of bad weather, the two Berlin raids and continuing mechanical problems from operations now being flown at twice the average altitude of the previous year had strained his resources. For instance, 50 Sqn put up six aircraft, but four returned after jettisoning their bombs, one with W/T failure, a second because the rear turret was unserviceable, a third with intercom problems and the fourth because of gun and oxygen gremlins.

57 Sqn, which was operating off grass runways at Scampton, was having a miserable month because the airfield was waterlogged more often than not. Operations ordered on four occasions had been cancelled because of the state of the runways. For the Essen raid on the 21st six aircraft managed to take off, but three aborted – one with oxygen failure within 50 miles of the target.

While aiding the Navy by hitting the U-boat bases Harris was also called on to help the Admiralty by providing crews for regular mine-laying sorties and on the same night as the Essen raid his staff alerted Wellington and Halifax bases to put up seventy aircraft for a very large-scale mining operation off the Frisians. It met with heavy opposition from flak ships and six aircraft were lost.

F/Sgt Edwin Jury, a 20-year-old RAF mid-upper gunner on 419 Sqn, had begun his operational career over Lorient only six days before, but found laying mines much more terrifying. He recalls:

> It was the only time on ops I prayed to the Good Lord to get me out. As we flew in to drop the mines at about 800 feet five or six flak ships opened up and I could see these tennis balls of flak whizzing sideways across the water towards us.
>
> We were so low they had to depress their guns and all this stuff was going over us. I knew if we got hit we'd go straight in without a chance. We didn't fire back. We were always told not to unless you had to. There was certainly no future in pointing yourself out to a flak ship.[10]

On the 23rd, 121 aircraft were sent to Lorient but another eighty aircraft went to Düsseldorf with three Mosquitos to lead the way. Two Lancasters were lost after bombing through the ten-tenths cloud and the bad weather meant diversions for many aircraft on return. The pilot of a 207 Sqn Lancaster was the victim of oxygen failure, one of the continuing problems as engineering officers tried to adapt aircraft to the new requirements of high-level bombing. P/O E. M. Thompson was on his way to Düsseldorf at 22,000 feet when he passed out. As the aircraft went into a dive he came to, but anoxia meant he couldn't see his instruments. The flight engineer guided him down to 8,000 feet where the bomb aimer jettisoned the bomb load. The shocked pilot managed to get the aircraft home, but on landing away from base at Scampton failed to flare in time over the threshold and bent the starboard outer propeller.

For four nights Halifax and Lancaster crews were rested. Reid Thomson went to a dance and found that not everybody in blacked-out Britain was prepared to forgive the naivety of young men a long way from home. He recalls:

> I got high in the sergeants' mess with another guy I flew with and we decided to walk into Pocklington to a hop. My buddy Mitch had a flashlight in his hand and a policeman stopped him and told him to turn it off. Mitch asked: 'Why? There's nothing here the Germans would want to blow up and we would know an hour before.' The cop grabbed Mitch by his shirt and tie. I grabbed the cop and said, 'Get your cotton-picking hands off him, he came with me and will go back with me.'
>
> The cop turned him loose and we went to the dance, but another night the same policeman got my buddy about some infraction with his bike. He called at the squadron three times to serve a summons before they would let him in and Mitch eventually had to pay a fine.[11]

The hop would be Sgt Thomson's last social engagement until after the war. He was about to take part in an operation to test the effectiveness of Oboe ground markers for the first time, which would cost him his freedom and three crew members their lives.

There were two new elements to this Düsseldorf raid which would set the pattern for future raids on German cities. First – after the disappointment of seeing skymarkers drift off their aiming points – Mosquito crews would drop ground markers to burst and cascade just above the aiming point and secondly Pathfinder Lancasters would back up the TIs with flares and high explosive to keep the centre alight for Main Force rumbling and roaring along behind.

For the period the Düsseldorf operation was a major effort, calling in 124 Lancasters and thirty-three Halifaxes. The Halifax was now showing its limitations compared to the Lancaster. It couldn't reach the 20,000-feet height band required to avoid the worst of the heavy flak. Unlike the Wellington and the Stirling the aircraft would be needed as an alternative to the Lancaster for much of the rest of the bombing war and would eventually undergo more changes than any Allied heavy bomber. But as a stop gap in the first winter of 1943 the Mk II Halifax was having its front and mid-upper turrets removed at aircraft factories or on station in a temporary attempt to give extra height for what was lost in firepower.

Reid Thomson found himself drafted in as a spare gunner on one of the newly adapted Halifax Mk IIs with one turret. It was the first time the adaptation was being used by 102 Sqn and Thomson had a premonition his trip to Düsseldorf would be one-way. 'I gave a buddy all my money before we went,' he says, 'and I told him: "If we don't make it, get drunk on me." I had never worried about a particular operation before, but that time I had a strong feeling something would go wrong.'[12]

Thomson's pilot, F/Lt Bruce Lindsay, had been briefed to go in in the first wave of Main Force then orbit the target to report on results of the bombing. Lindsay hoped for an uneventful op. He'd made a date with a WAAF on the base for the following night.

As Thomson settled in for the bomb run with a crew of strangers, flak began to rock the aircraft. In the blacked-out streets below, the sirens wailed and a Wehrmacht unit prepared to disembark from a train at the main railway station. But the station was among the first buildings to be hit by high-explosive bombs blasting a path for incendiaries, and twenty-three soldiers died and nearly 170 were injured, lying trapped in the wrecked train.

Thomson's Canadian bomb aimer, F/Lt Gerald O'Hanley, released the Halifax's load, then a flak shell burst in a red ball close by, peppering the fuselage and wounding him. F/Lt Lindsay banked and dived away to observe the results of the raid, but in the confusion as smoke drifted through the fuselage the bomb aimer and navigator clipped on their chutes and jumped out. The wireless operator saw them go and thought the pilot had ordered a bale-out, so rapidly followed through the front hatch. Of the three, only two opened their parachutes successfully. F/Lt O'Hanley died as he hit the ground, his chute still intact in its chest pack.

More bombs were now tumbling down on the Ruhr town, hitting ten industrial firms and nine public buildings including the opera house, spreading blooms of red and white fire across the streets amid the crash and thud of falling masonry. The ground markers dropped over a thin cloud layer were helping to concentrate bombing in the south of Düsseldorf.

F/Lt Lindsay called the navigator for a course and discovered only he, the flight engineer, Sgt Bill Bennett, and tail gunner Thomson were still on board. Thomson remembers: 'The flak was still bursting and we flew up the Ruhr valley all the time being shot at.'

Some of the flak over the target hit the aircraft of F/Lt Henry Maudslay, of 50 Sqn, who had begun his second tour on New Year's Day and would die on the Dams Raid in May. He bombed on the last green marker after searching for a break in the cloud, but without seeing any result. Maudslay set course for Skellingthorpe with holes in both wings.[13]

Meanwhile Lindsay climbed above cloud to orientate with the stars and discovered he was flying east, the wrong direction. Says Thomson:

> He banked round and I saw the burning target again then Lindsay headed west. After a good while we dropped a flare to see where we were and I could see water, which I realised later was the Zuider Zee. We came out over an airfield on the western side, lit up like peacetime and thought we were over England so Lindsay lost altitude to prepare for a landing. The flak started floating up at us and I told the pilot to get out of there quick.

The lost Halifax droned on over the sea desperately short of fuel and the skipper turned back and ordered Thomson to jump as soon as he saw land. Waiting edgily by the rear door, Thomson saw Terschelling come up and went out at 2,000 feet, tumbling over as the Halifax's tailplane passed above him, then pulling the D-ring on his chest pack and feeling the sharp jerk on his harness as the parachute opened. 'I came down fast,' says Thomson, 'and landed smack on my back, hurting it and my shoulders. As I lay there I heard the plane droning away into the distance.'

As the silence of the night closed around him Thomson slowly got to his feet and stumbled to a nearby farmhouse. He shouted 'RAF', but the farmer refused to open up. He lurched on until he came across a canal, then walked along the towpath until he found a road. 'There I spotted two Germans on bicycles,' he remembers. 'They shouted something so I just replied:"ja, ja". Wrong answer. They unshouldered their rifles and one fired a warning shot. I put my hands up and they took me to their HQ.'

Within days Thomson would find only he, plus the navigator and wireless operator who bailed out over the target, were survivors of the Halifax crew. F/Lt Lindsay was unable to keep his date with the WAAF. He died with the flight engineer while trying to crash-land in Holland.

AS the snow, sleet and gales of January turned to what the forecasters saw as a brief period of settled cold weather Harris at last found an opportunity to test the new device of H2S against Hamburg. The crews of a predominantly Lancaster force of 148 aircraft of 1 and 5 Groups were briefed for Europe's biggest port on the afternoon of 30 January. As it turned out, the results of the operation were not immediately encouraging for the future of the new radar aid.

H2S, the second great technological step forward in the 1943 bomber offensive, had been developed by the Telecommunications Research Establishment after a happy accident while experimenting in 1941 with airborne interception radar at their headquarters near Swanage. An airborne experiment had started to produce a classic outline of the Isle of Wight when the scanner was pointing downwards.

At the heart of H2S was the top secret cavity magnetron which transmitted very powerful bursts of electromagnetic energy to be transmitted at a very short wavelength. The cavity magnetron was so far ahead of its time Harris had had to enlist the support of Churchill to use it in aircraft over Germany.

H2S worked by an aerial scanning the terrain below an aircraft and transmitting high frequency impulses. Depending on the surface the radio energy was reflected back to a greater or lesser degree and seen on a cathode ray tube. On a smooth surface such as the sea very little of the energy was reflected back, so the cathode ray tube showed that area as black. But on a built-up area the majority of energy was reflected back to the aircraft and that appeared as a bright outline in the approximate shape of the town. Its best use was over a city with large identifiable lakes or a port with a clear coastal outline. Hamburg was ideal and it was hoped to achieve a concentrated conflagration. It was not to be.

Main Force, mainly Lancasters, scattered their bombs over a wide area on the 30 January raid, starting 120 separate fires. The Operational Research Section at High Wycombe calculated that 315 tons of bombs were dropped on the Hamburg conurbation, but many are thought to have fallen in the Elbe or nearby marshland. To many of the airmen, however, weaving their way through the silver lances of the searchlight belt and the gouts of flaming flak over eight-tenths cloud, it looked as if Hamburg was being severely punished. Henry Maudslay reported: 'The dock area and the river was clearly seen and the PFF flares were on time and correctly placed. There were several really good fires in the town. The op was a complete success.'[14]

Sgt Les Knight, also a 50 Sqn skipper who would join Maudslay on 617 Sqn for the Dams Raid, thought the 'attack in the early stages showed signs of being well concentrated and accurate'.[15]

The attack had roused the people of Hamburg from their beds shortly before 3 a.m. and sent them scurrying for the shelters. Aircraft from 106 Sqn were among the first on the target. Sgt Edward Markland, who had the redoubtable gunners Sgt Greep and Sgt Parry on board – now each up for the DFM for downing the Ju88 on the 17 January Berlin raid – saw 'several fires burning below cloud' when he bombed from 21,000 feet just before 3 a.m. on the pulsating glow of a red marker.[16] His fellow 106 captain F/Lt E. L. Hayward had an alarming incident when his Lancaster entered a thunder cloud and 'very severe static temporarily blinded the whole crew and slightly burned the wireless operator, F/Sgt E. H. Mantle'.[17] As the bombers flew away they left a large railway bridge in ruins, which would prevent trains entering or leaving Hamburg for two days.

The next morning eight Lancaster dispersals remained empty as the wintry dawn light picked out the grey runways, hangars and Nissen huts of the Lincolnshire airfields, though only five aircraft were missing over enemy territory, the rest crashing in England.

The weather, which could be as formidable an enemy as Luftwaffe fighters or flak, had not been as forecast. Strong winds and freezing high-altitude temperatures had compounded problems both to and from the target. At Langar, 207 Sqn had detailed eight crews for Hamburg; one aircraft had been cancelled before take-off, but no fewer than five had returned early for a variety of reasons, only two going into the attack. At Syerston, 106 alerted seventeen crews, later reduced to fifteen, and five made early returns. At waterlogged Scampton eleven had been detailed by 57 Sqn to take off on the grass runways and four had failed to reach the target because of a plethora of problems from hydraulic failure, icing and R/T gremlins to oxygen deficiency. The frustrated adjutant on 57 Sqn had been moved to report on his Form 540 for the month: 'Crews were briefed on ten occasions for which ops were subsequently cancelled. The strain on aircraft and crews is evident in the number of early returns and cancellations.'[18]

The gales, snow, rain and fog beating, sweeping, sheeting and insidiously penetrating every crack and crevice of eastern England's airfields had made it a dreadful month to try to wage war. But during it Bomber Command had introduced not one, but two vital bombing aids which would ruin the Reich over the coming year, despite being diverted to conduct a campaign to help the Admiralty in the Battle of the Atlantic.

In sunnier conditions, for ten days in January the political, naval, military and air chiefs of Britain and America had been meeting in white-washed comfort by the side of the Atlantic deciding the future conduct of the war. They proposed and postulated in their Casablanca conference room, wrangled and reasoned, discoursed and debated and finally formulated among other matters a combined bombing policy designed to bring Germany first to her knees then to the surrender table swiftly afterwards.

It would be handed to the C-in-Cs of RAF Bomber Command and the United States Eighth Air Force in early February as the Casablanca Directive, telling Harris and Ira C. Eaker what their objectives and aims would be.

It was what Harris had been waiting for.

CHAPTER THREE

PIERCING THE GLOOM

THE plain buff file marked Top Secret which arrived on Sir Arthur Harris's desk at High Wycombe on 4 February would promote more destruction and disorder than any document in aerial warfare so far. It was tied with official white tape almost like a gift and it mirrored many of the recommendations he had made when striving in 1942 to build Bomber Command into the war-winning force he visualised.

The Casablanca Directive spelled out in clear terms to himself and Ira Eaker, head of the USAAF Eighth Air Force Bomber Command:

> Your primary object will be the progressive destruction and disloca-
> tion of the German military, industrial and economic system and the
> undermining of the morale of the German people to a point where
> their capacity for armed resistance is fatally weakened.

It went on:

> Within that general concept, your primary objectives, subject to the
> exigencies of weather and of tactical feasibility, will for the present be
> in the following order:
>
>   a. German submarine construction yards.
>
>   b. The German aircraft industry.
>
>   c. Transportation.
>
>   d. Oil plants.
>
>   e. Other targets in enemy war industry.

The document added that the order of priority could be varied to meet strategical needs and that other objectives important from a political or military point of view 'must be attacked', including Berlin, 'which should be attacked when conditions are suitable for the attainment of specially valuable results unfavourable to the morale of the enemy or favourable to that of Russia'.

IF January had been the month of Oboe, February would be the month of H2S. The five-week period taking in the first few days of March would be a time of experimentation with the new radar aid as a run-up to the Battle of the Ruhr.

Hamburg would be attacked twice more, but on neither occasion would H2S bring the results it was designed to achieve. Cologne would also be attacked three times and the U-boat provision of the Casablanca Directive complied with by the Hamburg operations, and no fewer than four raids on Wilhelmshaven and its important submarine construction yards. Crews would also make the long haul all the way across Germany to Nuremberg. It would be a sign to the Nazi leaders that no German city was now safe. And that would include their own homes in Berlin, when the city was attacked successfully on the first night of March in a raid led by H2S-equipped Pathfinders.

In Germany there was a growing awareness in February that Bomber Command was likely to make life much worse, and soon. The damage caused by the early January Essen raids, the two Berlin raids mid-month and on Düsseldorf on the 23rd had not been impressive, but – particularly in the case of a distant target such as Berlin – they were an indication of the RAF's increasing strength.

On 7 January the nominal order of battle of Bomber Command had shown thirty-one heavy bomber squadrons – of which fifteen were Lancaster equipped – and thirteen medium bomber squadrons, a front-line strength of less than 200. But by the end of February Harris would be able to send more than 400 bombers over a target and the multiplication for havoc would continue throughout the year. On 23 December, for instance, the battle order would be fifty-three and a half heavy squadrons and three and a half Mosquito squadrons. Thirty-two of those squadrons of heavies would be Lancasters. On an average night the C-in-C would have 1,072 heavy bombers at his disposal.[1]

As icy January slid into frosty February the Command was being geared up notch by notch as pilots, navigators, wireless operators and air gunners passed out of the training production line in ever-increasing numbers for the great offensive ahead. Joining them would be Merlin-trained engine fitters, armourers, radar mechanics and electrical tradesmen. To support the increasing weight of attack, bomber station WAAF sections would also grow in size. In the middle of January the king had signed a proclamation ending the voluntary status of the WAAFs and ATS, and making all single girls of 19 liable for direction into the forces or industry. At the same time ten WAAF deputy assistant provost marshals had been appointed to keep the girls in line.

There had already been a drain of women into fetching air force blue and advertisements in regional newspapers that winter begged for females to fill the gaps that were left, the unconsciously droll Jobs Vacant columns ranging from: 'Are you doing all you can to help your country in this grave crisis? Part-time workers needed at a steam laundry' to 'Good strong women needed to work in timber yard'.

The new reality across the North Sea in post-Stalingrad Germany was settling into private disquiet over the efficiency of air-raid defences. After all, Hitler Youth no more than 15 or 16 were now being drafted in to help man the flak posts. There was a contemporary joke that a soldier condemned to death was asked to choose his method of execution. He chose death by flak.

The 'happy time' of summer conquest in 1940 and 1941 was a distant memory for Germans, making way for the cold facts of winter bombardment. Department stores in the big cities were closed, Berlin no longer had its luxury restaurants and bread consisted of one-third barley meal to two-thirds wheat. Savings in gas and electricity had been ordered and a burned-out 100-watt bulb could now only be replaced by a 60-watt type. Plans were being made to erect barrack-type housing for those who might lose their homes in the bombing. The cinemas provided some relief and proved a popular outlet – though much of the content was anti-Jewish vitriol from Propaganda Minister Josef Goebbels.

The German civilian was asked to put his or her faith in the Kammhuber Line, a defensive early-warning network of radar-controlled fighter boxes protecting Germany and its occupied territories in a double string along the coast with another group of boxes around Berlin. It worked well where the RAF had only been able to put up small numbers of bombers on one raid, but it could only control one interception at a time and within months Britain would be regularly sending out 600 aircraft on a single operation, spread over an area of sky 150 miles long and 6 miles wide.

For now, however, it would suffice, claiming three victims from the first of three raids in the month on Cologne. And one of the controlled night-fighter kills would have a far-reaching outcome, causing much finger waving and head shaking at the Admiralty. They had strongly opposed taking the secret magnetron valve – which was needed in anti-submarine radar in the Battle of the Atlantic – over enemy territory in Pathfinder H2S sets, but on only the second night H2S had been used over Germany a set fell into Nazi hands when the 7 Sqn Stirling of Bill Smith, a 23-year-old squadron leader, was shot down by Oberleutnant Reinhold Knacke of I/NJG1 on the return route south-east of Amsterdam. Only the gunners got out. Ironically Knacke, an *experten* with forty-four victories, died himself later that night. His aircraft with his body inside was found near the wreckage of a Halifax he had shot down.

The H2S set, of which the Air Ministry had lately ordered 1,500 examples, was quickly dismantled from the wreckage of Smith's aircraft and taken to the Telefunken works in Berlin. Within three weeks a commission would be set up by the Luftwaffe to study means of countering the device's effectiveness. By September a detector device codenamed Naxos would be installed in a night fighter, able to home onto bomber H2S transmissions.

It was not as if much could be claimed on the credit side for such a serious loss. The mainly Lancaster attack of 2 February had been intended as a further experimentation of Pathfinder techniques in which for the first time two Mosquitoes marked the aiming point on Oboe signal, then Pathfinder 'heavies' dropped their own markers using H2S alone.

In fact it only led to confusion, some crews thinking that the Germans had dropped dummy flares. There was damage right across Cologne without any concentration of effort and the only significant loss to the enemy was six Cookies on a military aerodrome. Reid Thomson, now on his way by train to the Luftwaffe interrogation centre at Dulag Luft near Frankfurt, after baling out over Holland six days before, was an unwilling witness to his colleagues' efforts.

He recalls:

I was with five other sergeants from another crew with two guards.* The locomotive stopped outside Cologne when the raid began and the big bombs were rocking the train. We couldn't hear the planes going over, but we could see the searchlights crossing the sky and hear the loud explosions.

When the sirens wailed the all-clear the train chugged slowly into Cologne's main railway station and the prisoners were taken off and held overnight by the Luftwaffe. The next day the six prisoners were marched back to the terminus with the smell of burning buildings in their nostrils.

Thomson admits:

I was glad to have the guards with us. The civilians were quite mad at being bombed. The way I remember, briefings gave the target as a big square of a town, then the next raid another big square. I remember being told on at least one occasion: 'If you destroy the workers' houses they will not do much work having no place to eat or sleep.'[2]

Twelve days later Bomber Command went back to Cologne and achieved a much better result. This time the force was numerically stronger

* This was the crew of Sgt A. Robinson of 97 Sqn whose Lancaster crashed near Eindhoven after being hit by flak on the Düsseldorf raid. His two gunners, Sgt Ralph Muskett and Canadian F/Sgt Robert Rea, were killed.

at 243, but it was made up of Halifaxes, Stirlings and Wellingtons. Unlike the high-flying Lancaster these were poor competition for the flak and the percentage loss rate was higher, 3.7 per cent compared to 3.1 per cent. The Lancasters, 140 of them, had been sent to Milan to divert the Luftwaffe's attention and keep up the pressure on the wavering Italians.

The thirteen H2S-equipped Pathfinders met ten-tenths cloud over Cologne and had to use skymarkers, dropping their flares in clusters spread over 5 or 6 miles of the city. But Main Force – many of whom arrived before the Pathfinders – seized on them and later reconnaissance revealed wide-spread damage, including the gutting of 7½ acres of a machine tool plant. Nine aircraft were lost, seven of them claimed by night fighters in Holland and Belgium.

One of those missing was a Wellington of 466 Sqn, newly formed at Leconfield. Sgt Norman Leonard was the wireless operator in the crew of the A-Flight deputy commander, F/Lt Bill Kirk.

Sgt Leonard remembers:

We had been to Lorient the day before and had landed away from base on the return. We didn't get back to Leconfield until about lunchtime the next day and hadn't expected to be operating that night. We were scheduled to be the first off, but due to a technical problem we took off half an hour later and became a straggler in the bomber stream. I know there wasn't any weaving.

We were descending over Belgium from 20,000 feet with a view to arriving over the target to bomb at 15,000 feet when there was a tremendous explosion amidships. It blew up the oil recuperator just aft of the main spar, sparked off the incendiaries in the bomb bay and set the aircraft's fabric alight and killed the navigator, Sgt Bill Smith, outright. I have little doubt that the sheet of armour plate between me and the navigator protected me from the full force of the blast.

The bomb aimer, Sgt Ray Bentley, who was already in position, was ordered to jettison our load. Our skipper made gallant attempts to blast out the flames extending from midships to aft by putting the

plane into a sharp dive, but to no avail. At 10,000 feet or so he gave
the order to abandon. I followed Ray Bentley from the forward hatch.
I remember preparing to jump and falling into the darkness and then
nothing.

In the rear of the aircraft Sgt Bill Reynolds found he was trapped. He
couldn't turn his turret to get out because the damage to the oil recuperator had put the hydraulics out of action and the heat had distorted the doors.
He eventually used his Thermos flask to smash his way through via the
visor above the guns, snagging the triggers as he went out at about 2,000
feet. It left bullet marks on his jacket. He drifted across the burning wreck
of the plane where his captain and a second-dickey co-pilot, P/O John
Mason, lay dead in the pyre. After ordering the bale-out of his crew the
selfless F/Lt Kirk had found he was too low to escape himself and he and
Mason had tried to crash-land.

Sgt Leonard remembers:

I came to on my back, having fallen through trees at the edge of a
wooded area. I was taken prisoner by a couple of armed Belgian
gendarmes who half-carried, half-escorted me to a nearby farmhouse.
I was fussed over a bit and revived with warm drinks until Wehrmacht
guards arrived from Bourg-Léopold, where a detachment of Waffen
SS were on rest.[3]

Sgt Leonard, suffering from concussion, was put in the barracks jail at
Bourg-Léopold until a Luftwaffe major arrived and claimed to have shot
down his aircraft. He arranged his transfer to a hospital near Brussels.

A Wellington crew of 115 Sqn from East Wretham nearly became
another Luftwaffe victim. They were attacked by an Me110, but as it began
its curve of pursuit the rear gunner called out a warning to corkscrew. The
bomber tilted to starboard, sliding into the blackness, and the gunner blasted
the twin-engine fighter with his four Brownings and saw it fall away in
flames.[4]

Main Force crews who arrived over Cologne before the Pathfinders found evidence that the flak battalions guarding German cities, which at one time had blasted away at any bomber which strayed across their path, now seemed less willing to advertise their presence.

Sgt Harold McLean, in a 428 Sqn Wellington, recalls:

Everybody was flying around waiting for the target indicators to be dropped. The target was completely cloud covered and there wasn't a thing happening with the flak guns until the first bomb went down, then they opened up. It was as if they didn't want us to know they were there.[5]

Crews of 75 Sqn reported 'a red glow in the clouds as the aircraft left the target area'. They had also seen several fighters without being attacked. But the adjutant's staff complained somewhat petulantly in the post-raid report that the Newmarket base had only brought four of the seven squadron aircraft which had bombed Cologne into land when the airfield became 'completely unserviceable' because 'a stranger from 214 Sqn bellylanded on our runway'. The other three Stirlings had to divert to Lakenheath and Waterbeach, their tired crews not relishing the prospect of strange beds and an early flight back the next afternoon.[6]

There were no operations the next day, giving ground crew an opportunity to carry out repairs and catch up on the sleep they had missed in a period of intensive raids. February had opened with what were being described as the greatest gales for years with gusts of hurricane force in the Channel casting Dover barrage balloons from their moorings and depositing them in France.

In the wake of the high winds, over the next few weeks came snow and sleet. For engine fitters and mechanics living in rude huts made from discarded materials at isolated dispersals it was a bitter time working on icy engines and freezing airframes, their fingers blue with cold as they struggled to keep aircraft on line amid arctic blasts sweeping the east coast and penetrating air force serge and leather jerkin with a cruel determination.

Those same ground crew had tumbled out to wait patiently by

dispersals in the darkness of the 26th as pilots laden with parachutes and the paraphernalia of war walked stiff-legged from depositing crew trucks to accept their crouching bombers for the third Cologne raid of the month.

A maximum effort had been called and as the ground crew trudged off for their meals to await their charges' return, 424 bombers were climbing out and assembling in circuits from north to south, then droning away to the North Sea and Germany.

Several of the crews from Sgt McLean's 428 Sqn found themselves in the front line of the night-fighter defences long before they got to the target. Sgt R. A. Parkinson had just crossed the Dutch coast when his port airscrew control ran away. He jettisoned the bomb load near Noordwijk and turned for home. As he did so his rear gunner saw an enemy aircraft with a white light in its nose approaching from dead astern. Parkinson banked through 360 degrees to turn into an attack, but the fighter disappeared.

Then Sgt K. D. Fry, heading for the target at 16,000 feet, 'encountered a single-engine enemy aircraft with an orange light on each wing tip 1,000 feet below.' Fry heeled his Wellington over into a steep turn to port as the fighter closed in to 1,000 yards on the port quarter and gave the enemy the slip in the darkness. W/O A. Harrison was the next to encounter the Luftwaffe. 'At 2040 on the outward journey we saw an Me109 with a green tail light,' he reported. 'The enemy aircraft passed from the starboard quarter to the port quarter and disappeared.'

Half an hour away from the target at 15,000 feet Sgt J. A. Ferguson's Wellington was attacked by a Do217. 'The enemy aircraft made three attacks from dead astern, below,' he detailed. 'The rear gunner fired four bursts and claimed hits on the wings of the Dornier.' Deterred, the fighter pilot broke off his pursuit. But in the course of the operation Ferguson saw a total of six single- and twin-engined fighters that did not attack.[7]

For Albert Bracegirdle in the rear turret of Sgt Gordon McGregor's 106 Sqn Lancaster it was his most alarming operation so far. The air raid warning had sounded over Cologne just before 2100 and McGregor arrived over the city at 2125 to find the target clear at 16,000 feet with red and green TIs floating above a slight ground haze. His bomb aimer, Sgt Sam Birch, lined up on a blazing building in the centre of green cascades and the aircraft leapt as the 8,000-lb bomb forced its way through the bomb doors. As Birch waited for the photoflash he saw the vivid red, rippling flash of the huge bomb bursting. Then as the aircraft turned away a searchlight flicked onto the fuselage, followed by others.

Sgt Bracegirdle remembers:

We were corkscrewing to try to get out of the beams: I was really being thrown about the sky. The light was so intense I couldn't see anything. I just had to close my eyes as the aircraft went round and down and up again. The only thing to do in the end was to put the nose down and the wings started vibrating as we hit about 300 mph. There was a lot of flak coming up. As soon as we got coned we expected it and I was worried about a night fighter coming in.[8]

Eventually as the huge aircraft weaved and tossed across the sky the search-lights were lost one by one and Sgt Bracegirdle was left peering into the darkness desperately trying to restore his night vision.

Others over the target were also experiencing the full fury of the defences. F/Sgt G. H. Lancaster had just left Cologne on his way back to 57 Sqn's base at Scampton when he was bracketed by flak. 'The aircraft went into an uncontrollable dive at 18,000 feet, due to a heavy burst close under the tail,' he reported later. 'I gave the order to prepare to abandon at 4,000 feet.'

As the aircraft hurtled earthwards the three crew members in the rear, who would have had little idea how far they were from the ground, donned parachutes. Then as the aircraft plunged on, apparently out of control, the wireless operator and gunners went out. Lancaster eventually managed to pull out at only 1,500 feet and made his way home at low level with the other three crew members.[9]

The raid had been intended as a dual marking effort, with four Mosquitos dispatched to drop red TIs on Oboe signal and six H2S-equipped Pathfinders, known as Y-aircraft, loaded with greens to drop on the reds. But three of the four Oboe sorties were abortive and four of the six

H2S sets refused to work. However, all the Y-aircraft were able to aim their greens at the sole red TI and bombing was concentrated around the aiming point until what Bomber Command's Operational Research Section described as 'an inaccurately placed marker of mysterious origin caused a scatter to develop towards the south-west suburbs'.

It meant only a quarter of the Main Force bombs hit the city and most were in the south-west where the creepback headed into open country. A Cookie hit a block of flats, trapping up to fifty people in a shelter beneath. The wreckage above started to burn and most of those entombed suffocated before rescue services could reach them.

From Hemswell, 300 (Masovian) Sqn had sent its Wellingtons. The Poles, bent on revenge for Hitler's rape of their country and the aerial devastation of Warsaw, were among the keenest members of Bomber Command. In their post-raid debriefing analysis, under the heading 'Duty' – where all other squadrons put 'Bombing Target' – the Poles stipulated 'To cause maximum damage at the aiming point at the target'.

All Bomber Command crews were under strict instructions if a Cookie hung up not to bring the thin-cased bomb back where it might explode on landing, but to jettison. The Poles invariably brought back such hang-ups, so that such a powerful weapon could be loaded up again.

F/O K. Romaniszyn reported 'many large fires' when he returned from Cologne: 'There were two lines of fires running from West to East and NE to SW, approximately 2 miles long,' he said. 'A very successful trip and fires were visible for 80 miles after leaving the target.'

As the bombers flew away to take the same route back over Noordland and Southwold they had taken out they would leave more than 100 dead, 150 injured and 6,000-plus without a home. A total of twelve aircraft would not be returning to their dispersals, a small loss for numbers of bombers on target.

THERE was a stand-down for Bomber Command the next day, a chance for gunnery and signals leaders to give talks to freshmen on the latest techniques, and the opportunity for tired aircrew to lounge around the mess fire catching up on what the newspapers thought of their latest efforts.

Avidly sought was *The Aeroplane* magazine with its advertisements for vital equipment such as the GQ Parasuit ('To Which I Owe So Much' according to one satisfied NCO customer); the digest of German radio and newspapers revealing how effective Bomber Command was becoming; and the Roll of Honour, listing the dead and missing for the month.

It could make depressing reading as aircrew found so many names of friends and acquaintances they had known in training and on other squadrons. Better to turn to *Tee Emm* and chuckle over the latest debacles of the dim-witted P/O Prune and his equally clueless crew Sgt Straddle (air bomber), F/O Fixe (navigator), Sgt Backtune (wireless operator) and Sgt Winde (air gunner).

Among the lines from Prune's Shooting Gallery in the Christmas and New Year issue still hanging around the messes of bomber stations spread from Durham to Cambridgeshire were: 'I had so much metal in me after being shot up my compass followed me around' and 'I prefer the Rotol propeller to the DH – the blades are 3 inches shorter so I can fly lower.'

In the February edition *Tee Emm* had somewhat sanguine advice about staying awake on ops. Most aircrew, with the defences of Nuremberg and Cologne fresh in their memory, could attest that it was no problem, but the training magazine suggested a five-point checklist.

It ran:

Don't eat too much at the flying meal – a moderate helping of soup, meat and veg, and sweet, and only have one cup of tea.

Don't eat your aircrew rations for at least three hours.

Don't be negligent about oxygen.

Wear the recommended clothing – not too much, not too little.

Caffeine tablets will help to keep you awake and are best taken when nearing the target on an average trip of 5 or 6 hours.

Curiously it added: 'Don't take benzedrine.'

Tee Emm was an example of how forward-looking the Air Ministry could be. It educated in an amusing way and counselled instructors on how to get their message across without too much jargon.

The Ministry had also employed professional cartoonists such as Fougasse of *Punch* and David Langdon, now a serving RAF officer, to produce colourful, cartoon-style educational posters which adorned flight offices, briefing rooms and crew quarters.

Among the current crop was one by Langdon showing a comic aircraft screeching along the runway streaming smoke from its tyres as a bowler-hatted Ministry official wagged an admonitory finger. The caption read: 'With all this runway here, says Billy, to burn up brakes and tyres is silly'.

More seriously Air Diagram 2801 released in February 1943 showed airmen in a moonlit dinghy on a heaving sea with a cutting from the *Evening Standard* of 11 January detailing how three pupils on an instruction flight had survived a ditching because they followed proper procedure to the letter. It tended to bring home to crews that there was more than one way to die in the air war.

IN the two raids on Hamburg alone the death toll would add up to 155 highly trained RAF and Commonwealth aircrew. Both operations, on 3 February and 3 March, were examples of how difficult it was to successfully mark a target by H2S alone. The problems of the first raid were also compounded by bitterly cold weather.

In fact the freezing conditions over the North Sea caused many aircraft to return early, particularly the Stirlings and Halifaxes, whose pilots found that ice on the wings prevented them climbing to operational height. It proved less of a problem to the German night fighters, however, who claimed seven victories. In all, sixteen bombers were lost, half of them Stirlings, the total casualties a worrying 6.1 per cent of the force.

Rain and snow were still causing problems at grass-covered Scampton. 57 Sqn detailed four crews for Hamburg. None of them were able to take off because the runways were waterlogged. At Newmarket crews of 75 Sqn, many of whom had come all the way from New Zealand to join the Old World's fight for freedom, were instructed to return if they hit bad weather in their Stirlings, which many inevitably did. Heavy icing in cloud forced five of the nine briefed to return, but four pressed on. Half of those were picked off by night fighters.

F/Lt William Black's EQ-D of the Canadian 408 Sqn had been scheduled for the first wave of what had been planned as a major raid on Hamburg. Now the Halifax seemed to be at the very front of the attack after so many early returns in the cold air over the North Sea.

F/Sgt John Taplin, Black's English wireless operator, remembers:

We started our run-in just on the outskirts of Lüneburg and could see no Pathfinder marking ahead. We could see a lot of flak coming up and searchlights waving about, but no fires. We were hit in the fuel tanks practically straight away. We lost power to all four engines and had to jettison the bombs. There seemed to be fire all around. The pilot said, 'This is it, chaps, we'd better bale out.' The bomb aimer, the navigator and flight engineer went out through the front hatch and I sent a message to base in plain language saying we had been hit and were baling out. Flames were being whipped through the escape hatch. I just knelt forward, went out and said: 'God help me.' As the aircraft passed above I could see both wings were blazing. I counted to three then pulled the ripcord. I could see what I thought was water below so inflated my Mae West, but it was just mist on the ground.

The pilot didn't get out in time. He was found underneath the aircraft when it crashed. I landed miles away from the rest of the crew in a tree in the Lüneburg area. I couldn't find my quick release buckle for a while. My parachute harness had been out of date for inspection and I had borrowed somebody else's. It was pretty loose and the buckle was under my chin instead of across my stomach where I expected it to be.

As the last of the bombers droned away from the port the dazed Sgt Taplin got out his escape kit, checked the silk map and compass and started walking. He says:

I decided to head towards Hamburg instead of south or east because I thought it was the opposite of what the Germans expected. I didn't know what I was going to do when I got there because I was in a trauma. I was on the run for three days. I tried to catch a goods train on the first night but discovered I was on the wrong side of the lines. So I kept walking. I travelled at night for the next two nights, keeping to the woods. Eventually on the third night I was pretty exhausted, I'd only had some chocolate to eat from my escape rations, and some trainee soldiers came across me.[10]

The raid had created forty-five fires in Hamburg classed as large. The Elbe dock areas had been hit with two oil depot blazes and one in a warehouse. F/Lt Henry Maudslay, racking up the operations of his second tour, had been early on the target with Lancasters of 50 Sqn. Back in the operations block with a steaming mug of post-op tea he told intelligence officers: 'There were several really good fires in the town. This op was a great success.'[11]

But as Bomber Command's operational research section weighed the effect of the raid they came to the conclusion that half the force committed had achieved the same on the Hamburg raid of 30 January with a third of the losses. Only five of the eleven H2S-equipped Pathfinders had reached the target and the sets of two of those had failed. It was perhaps with some restraint that the section noted: 'It is apparent that unserviceability of the equipment is still a very limiting factor in the success of operating Y-type aircraft.'[12]

The second raid on Hamburg on 3 March was carried out in much better weather conditions and should have been a great success for the Pathfinders. Visibility was clear over the target area and Hamburg was an ideal city to read on H2S with its well-defined waterfront, but the receding tide may have caused PFF to misread the contours of the Elbe and they marked too far down-river, near the town of Wedel, 10 miles to the west. It proved disastrous for Wedel, but spared much of Hamburg. Hamburg's firemen first attended to the one hundred fires the bombing had started in their own city before turning to Wedel where a large naval clothing store had been left to burn out.

Harris had planned the 440-aircraft raid for days, hoping to hit the city before starting the Battle of the Ruhr. The route out to Hamburg was over Hornsea, crossing the enemy coast at Westover where PFF dropped white datum markers. The intention was to drop further route markers, in yellow, 15 miles south of the target, but as the Pathfinders were already marking the target erroneously these markers may well have been too far west.

Most crews could see it was turning into a disappointing raid as the stream's bomb aimers hunted for the green or red dripping candles of target indicators above the city. F/Lt Les Munro of 97 Sqn found the city clear of cloud, but with a smoke haze hanging over it as he began his bomb run. 'There were no target indicators to be seen and we bombed the southern edge of fires started by the previous aircraft,' he reported. 'Part of the dock area was identified visually on the run-in, but fires were rather scattered.'[13]

Some oil tanks were set ablaze in the docks and intelligence officers at 115 Sqn recorded: 'The town was observed to be well ablaze and concentrated debris was blown very high, black smoke belching up to 1,500 feet.'[14]

Sgt Harold McLean, in the rear turret of a 428 Sqn Wellington, recalls:

The smoke from burning oil tanks was several thousand feet above us. There were so many searchlights I counted them and there were sixty-six. The thin blue radar searchlight came up on our port side and flicked onto us so we switched on and off our IFF and it just went out. I also saw a Wellington brought down; a great black shape went past us.*[15]

A total of ten bombers were lost on the Hamburg operation, 2.4 per cent, in the cold tables of Bomber Command statistics a very acceptable

* This was the aircraft of Sgt J. Gauthier of 425 Sqn at Dishforth, in the same wave as the nearby Dalton-based 428 Sqn. The aircraft crashed at Schenefeld and Sgt Gauthier and all his crew are buried in Hamburg's war cemetery at Ohlsdorf.

figure on a major target. On the ground in Hamburg only twenty-seven died, far fewer again than the toll among the RAF men who were raining bombs on the streets where the civilian shelters lay. Of the seventy men in the ten aircraft lost, only one survived to become a prisoner of war.

THE Canadians of 6 Group, which had been handed to Harris on New Year's Day, were now making their mark in communities such as Middleton St George where the accents of Montreal and Toronto became more familiar than the local dialect in village pubs and dance halls. It became almost a routine to see hordes of airmen scrambling along the railway embankment near the 419 and 428 Sqn base, having pulled the communication cord of the last train between Darlington and Stockton, which inconveniently didn't plan a halt near the camp on its schedule. Further south the three Australian heavy bomber squadrons, 460, 466 and 467, were also disturbing the peace of mind of girls in rural communities.

At Breighton, 460 (RAAF) Sqn was based around the small village. The high-spirited Aussies had been changing the way of life of quiet Yorkshire farming families since they had arrived, the previous March. One night some aircrew had stolen a steamroller from the village and driven it back to their billets. Another time even the local policeman had lost his bike to an airman.

Laura Bennett was a 20-year-old typist from Winterton, near Scunthorpe, who made regular visits to her cousin Madge Waterworth at North Duffield near Breighton once the Australians had arrived. She says:

> We lived in villages where nothing very exciting happened normally, so to have all these glamorous young men in fetching dark blue uniforms from the other side of the world right on our doorstep was pretty wonderful to us. Madge helped my Aunt Harriet at a canteen and knew so many of the aircrews. She used to bring them along to my aunt's for meals. And the boys often used to pop in unexpectedly on a Friday. Friday was baking day and as fast as things came out of the oven they were snapped up. My aunt didn't mind because she realised how far

they were from home and from day to day they never knew who would still be there. In the evening we would hear the sound of the bombers as they set out on a raid.[16]

Laura Bennett would become engaged to one of the Australian aircrew and would find herself worrying in the coming weeks as she heard the bombers set out in the darkness.

On 11 February the local shops had just closed and the pubs were opening as the villagers of Breighton, North Duffield and nearby Bubwith came to their front doors and windows to hear the swelling crescendo of the Lancasters of 460 Sqn breaking through the evening mist as they taxied out of dispersals. They were bound for Wilhelmshaven on a raid that would at last prove the potential of H2S as a blind-bombing device. Navigation lights glinted and winked green and red as the Lancasters climbed out above the trees and disappeared in the cloud to the south-east of the airfield, the Merlins straining in the frosty night air as in each airframe seven men huddled to their task. Gradually aircraft of the three flights cleared the circuit and the sound of their engines slowly faded as one by one they set course. Then there was only the sound of villagers softly closing their doors on the chill of the night.

Tonight 129 Lancasters, forty Halifaxes and eight Stirlings were being employed by Harris to fulfil the primary requirement of the Casablanca Directive, to destroy German submarine construction yards. Eaker would obey the order sixteen days later, with a raid on the north German naval base by his Eighth Air Force, the first time the Flying Fortresses entered German airspace.

It had been planned for days, waiting for suitable weather. Three days beforehand nine crews of 9 Sqn had been among those briefed for the target. They were in the crew room muffled up in Irvin jackets, flying boots and yellow, buoyant Taylor suits nervously twiddling with helmets and oxygen masks as they waited for transport to their aircraft, when it was scrubbed. The next night they had actually arrived at their silent Lancasters when it was called off. The following evening seven crews had been briefed and were waiting for the Austin Tilly trucks when it was cancelled once more.[17]

Finally it was on, but the weather was far from ideal and many aircraft suffered from icing. As they struggled to overcome the cold front the Luftwaffe were out hunting. F/Sgt Graham Briggs was the wireless operator in a 103 Sqn Lancaster. He had joined the RAF before the war, was halfway through his second tour and already held the DFM, awarded in 1941 during his first tour, on Whitleys. 'It had been very misty during the afternoon and evening and the freshmen crews had been taken off the op,' he remembers, 'but the squadron commander asked our pilot, Geoff Maddern, if he would go and he agreed. There was heavy icing en route; you could hear it cracking along the fuselage.'

As the Lancaster was about to cross the enemy coastline the gunners scanned the sky in a regular search pattern and listened to the crack and thump of ice flying off the propellers. Suddenly against the dark cotton-wool clouds mid-upper gunner Frank Holmes saw a moving black shape. F/Sgt Briggs remembers:

> I heard the mid-upper call in that there was an Me109 on the port beam. We had to jettison the Cookie. Frank told the pilot to corkscrew port and the fighter went past, then he came up again and both Frank and the rear gunner, Arthur Browett, were waiting for him and they got him. The gunners saw him hit the drink.[18]

The H2S-equipped Pathfinders approached the port from the south-east to find it cloud covered, so had to employ the least reliable technique, Wanganui – skymarkers which could easily drift off the target before Main Force had a chance to bomb. This time it worked, the Pathfinders' marking accurately followed up by the crews of Main Force. As the attack developed in the moonlight the naval ammunition depot at Mariensiel was hit and exploded, devastating more than 100 acres of the naval dockyard and damaging buildings in the town.

Claremont Taylor was lying in the nose of M-Mother on the bomb run as the arsenal went up. 'What an explosion,' he recalls. 'A huge area of blue flame rose and made it so bright that for miles around aircraft could be seen coming in on the target.'[19]

One of those aircraft was that of Sgt Gordon McGregor of 106 Sqn with Albert Bracegirdle and Graham Allen on board. McGregor reported seeing 'a tremendous red glow under the cloud' as his aircraft shuddered from close bursts of flak.

At last H2S had worked successfully, and with the normally problematic skymarkers too. The operation boded well for further attacks and the cost had only been three Lancasters and the Halifax lost in England. True, six of the fourteen H2S sets had failed, but those Y-aircraft crews who found the aiming point dropped their skymarker flares according to plan. The sets which had worked had given so clear a response that many navigators picked up the echoes of a North Sea convoy on the way in. Bomber Command's Operational Research Section later reported: 'Y-aircraft were more accurate than in previous raids and this resulted in a good concentration. Most of the Main Force attacked within the first five minutes.'[20]

It looked so promising, but when Bomber Command went back to the port again a week later the Pathfinders – though convinced they had found a true picture on their H2S screens – in fact marked to the west of the target. Most of the bombs of the nearly 200 aircraft following on fell in open country and the flak took its toll. Among those who failed to return was New Zealander P/O Edward Roy Markland, whose gunners, Robert Greep and Edward Parry, had so valiantly beaten off the fighter attack on the way home from Berlin in January with Graham Allen on board.

Sgt McLean also found the defences effective. He says:

The CO of 428 Sqn was flying with us as second captain. After we landed we were standing along the port side of the plane chatting when one of the erks pointed out this large hole through the starboard tailplane about 4 feet from my turret. They thought an 8-in naval shell had gone through. We had never felt a thing over the target. A bit lower down and it would have been the end of me.[21]

Bomber Command took the risk of returning to Wilhelmshaven the following night, this time with almost twice the number of aircraft committed before, but again the Pathfinders failed to mark accurately, bombing falling to the north, and twelve aircraft were lost. The Polish crew of a 305 Sqn Wellington spent three hours being tossed around in a freezing dinghy after losing power on both engines while over the North Sea.

However, there was one positive development for the staff at Pathfinder headquarters who had found it so puzzling that H2S could be so successful over Wilhelmshaven on the 11th, yet could lead 8 Group so badly astray on the 19th. They realised the special H2S maps the Pathfinder crews had been issued with were based on out-of-date information, so the shape of the new Himmelreich suburb showing up on H2S screens bore little relation to what was on the map. A general updating of maps in Bomber Command, which would eventually install H2S in most Main Force aircraft as well, now took place.

It would make little difference for the last of the four raids on Wilhelmshaven on 24 February. Bomber Command sent 115 aircraft of 6 and 8 Groups, but again the Pathfinders failed to find the heart of the city or its docks and there was little damage. On the plus side no aircraft were lost, but the Luftwaffe ace Paul Gildner, with more than forty victories at night, died in a crash near his Gilze-Rijen base. Bomber Command would not return to Wilhelmshaven for another twenty months. There were other, more important, cities to reach.

NUREMBERG, where Hitler had gloried in his mass rallies before the war, was considered a political target and such targets were a requirement of the Casablanca Directive. Within a few weeks it would be too dangerous to risk an attack so far down in southern Germany without the benefit of darkness all the way from and to the North Sea.

It was another H2S-marked attack, but once more the Pathfinders were late after the long four-hour journey and as aircraft milled around waiting for the TIs to go down there were several near misses. Guy Gibson, leading the pack from 106 Sqn, later reported: '350 aircraft circling around waiting for the PFF was rather dangerous'. His own bomb load of one Cookie and one SBC of 30-lb incendiaries had gone down in 'excellent visibility' and he considered it had been a very concentrated attack, which caused huge fires and explosions. His verdict was 'a good but frightening trip'.[22]

At Waddington 9 Sqn had had thirteen aircraft and crews prepared, but because the weather en route was likely to be problematical two freshmen crews were taken off the battle order. The eleven that went, who had been reminded at briefing that Nuremberg was 'so popular with the Nazi party', complained that PFF had put in a poor performance, with white warning flares to mark the bomb run not going down until the first TIs had blossomed into the characteristic green blobs of fire descending over what was hoped was the aiming point.[23] In fact the first Pathfinders had marked on H2S 2 miles north-west of the AP and PFF following on had bombed very short. The result was heavy damage to two villages and none to Nuremberg itself.

At 2340 F/Sgt Taylor in a 460 Sqn Lancaster lined up a cluster of TIs around which many bombs were bursting only to find the Cookie wouldn't release. He flew off the target with the 4,000-lb bomb stuck in the shackles. Pilot Sgt Jack Murray reported: 'We had to jettison at 0020 from 12,000 feet over a searchlight and flak concentration at Karlsruhe.'

P/O J. M. Harris of 51 Sqn had one of the most hair-raising trips of all. On the outward flight to Nuremberg ice started to build up on the wings of his Halifax and further icing on the propellers sent chunks ricocheting off the side of the aircraft below where Harris was sitting. He climbed and managed to get over the front, pressing on into Germany, and dropped his incendiaries from 12,000 feet. But the effort had proved too much for the Halifax power plants.

'For a time three of the engines were not functioning properly,' says the dispassionate official report of the squadron administrative staff, 'but by skilful manipulation the captain and flight engineer, Sgt C. K. Bramfitt, were able to get the aircraft flying on three.' It gives no indication of the terror on board as the aircraft plunged 9,000 feet to 4,000 feet while Harris and Bramfitt desperately tried to restart the engines.

Maintaining 4,000 feet, Harris flew on over west Germany and northern France, out of the stream now and a target for night fighters. His luck began to improve as he flew straight through the balloon barrage at heavily defended Le Havre without damage or in fact having any guns open up on him. Then over the Channel low-level icing was encountered plus a thunderstorm. Harris had to take the risk of descending to 1,800 feet to fly under the worst of the weather. The official report goes on: 'Searchlights endeavoured to co-operate with the captain when the aircraft crossed the English coast, but this co-operation was lost in the Tunbridge Wells area. No W/T communication could be established and the pilot decided to abandon.'

Harris pulled back on the control column and trimmed the aircraft to climb to 4,000 feet to evacuate. But as he went through 3,200 feet a cone of Sandra searchlights were seen, indicating an airfield, and Harris headed straight for them. The relieved skipper came over the threshold at West Malling and breathed a sigh of relief as his wheels touched the concrete. 'He had only seven minutes of petrol left,' says the official report.[24]

THERE was one important target on which to test H2S before the Battle of the Ruhr began while it could still be reached and returned from under cover of darkness – Berlin. The Casablanca Directive had ordered it be attacked 'when conditions are suitable for the attainment of specially valuable results unfavourable to the morale of the enemy or favourable to that of Russia'.

Post-Stalingrad, a raid on Berlin would undoubtedly help the Russian counter-offensive and keep the political demands on Harris at bay. Eventually he planned a full-scale continuing onslaught against the Nazi capital, but his command would not have the strength for such a campaign against a strong, distant target for many months. In the meantime at least one heavy raid before the nights shortened would clear the field and minds to concentrate on the task in hand – destruction of the enemy armaments network in the Ruhr. The first day of March dawned bright and clear after a frost overnight. Conditions were right for Harris to order 300 aircraft to Berlin.

It would be the first trip to the Reich capital for Canadian Sgt Herbert Hoover, a 19-year-old pilot on Leonard Cheshire's 76 Sqn at Linton-on-Ouse. He and his crew had arrived on the squadron less than four weeks before and their first surprise had been their accommodation. Instead of depositing them at a bleak Nissen hut billet of the kind they had become used to in training, the dark blue RAF truck left the four Canadians and three Englishmen outside an elegant mansion in rich countryside a couple of miles from the base. They were told it was for NCO aircrew only. Officers had to make do with the purpose-built mess on the station.

Mid-upper gunner Sgt Clifford Hill, from Macclesfield, remembers: 'The bomb aimer couldn't stop smiling and the Canadian rear gunner considered it a real piece of old England.'

Beningbrough Hall, built in 1716, had been temporarily taken over from Lady Chesterfield and for the rest of the war would see aircrew from Canada, Australia, New Zealand and other parts of the Commonwealth tempted to slide down the banisters of its grand staircase. Hill, flight engineer Gordon Lloyd and wireless operator Jack Mossop selected an oak-panelled room with a panoramic view of the grounds towards the river.

'There were three other beds in our room whose occupants changed frequently as their aircraft failed to return,' says Hill. 'One trio stayed only three nights before being posted missing.' In fourteen days since Hoover's crew had become operational on 16 February they had been on five raids and a mining operation. They would now go through the Battle of the Ruhr.

They had learned to respect Leonard Cheshire and appreciate the care he showed for his crews. As they walked to the briefing room in the cold evening air of the first day of March they remembered the initial briefing they had heard there, before the big Lorient raid of 16 February in which 377 aircraft had been involved.

Cliff Hill recalls:

Cheshire spoke with quiet confidence and in a cheerful manner. After the briefing was over, he said: 'Before you go, gentlemen, I wish to say a few words to two new crews flying with us for the first time tonight.' We were sitting at the front and his confidence just flowed into us. He made it seem so easy and his gentle manner had a penetrating effect so that when he concluded with 'Good luck' we walked out almost thinking we had been to Lorient already. To be briefed by Cheshire was an unforgettable experience. He was extremely thorough.

Cheshire was on the dais again as his crews assembled on 1 March waiting to hear about that night's operation. 'When the curtain was drawn back to reveal the target and the red ribbon stretched right across the map to Berlin a gasp and a groan went up, followed by a buzz of excitement,' Sgt Hill recorded.[25]

Two of the fourteen crews listening so intently with Sgt Hill to the take-off times, courses and aiming point being painstakingly revealed by Cheshire and his section leaders would not return to their comfortable billets at Linton-on-Ouse.

Further south on 106 Sqn, gunner Albert Bracegirdle was attending the briefing by Guy Gibson as part of Sgt McGregor's crew. Graham Allen, McGregor's flight engineer, had special cause for trepidation as he saw the target revealed. His aircraft had been shot up on the last occasion he had visited the Reich capital six weeks before.

From Breighton Claremont Taylor, who had raided Berlin on 16 January, would be returning to the city in the Lancaster H-How of 460 (RAAF) Sqn. It turned out to be an event-filled night. Not long after crossing the Dutch coast at 12,000 feet the pilot, F/Sgt Jack Murray, was told about a single-engined fighter ahead. Waiting to pull into a corkscrew if necessary, Murray saw the aircraft pass 1,000 yards in front. It headed south without seeing them.

Over Berlin the H2S picture was as usual causing problems for the Pathfinder navigators. Their 10-cm H2S made it difficult to distinguish different parts of the huge city and matters would not improve until the clearer 3-cm version was used on Berlin raids later in the year.

As a result it spread bombing over the whole of the capital, but because so many aircraft were over the target with a bigger total bomb load than had been carried before, it was causing more damage than Berlin had previously seen. Among the industrial plant totally destroyed were 20 acres of railway repair workshops at Templehof.

F/Sgt Taylor, looking through the bomb sight of H-How, lined up green TIs and saw his bombs burst just south of the markers. His skipper would report at debriefing that he thought PFF had done a good job and 'these were the best concentration of fires this crew has ever seen'. The squadron's operational record book would say: 'The centre was well blitzed and many fires were left raging in the target area. It was a highly successful attack.'[26]

The long flight back had brought its problems, however. F/Sgt Taylor's aircraft went too near the Osnabrück defences and a searchlight flicked on. Others quickly followed: 'We were at 18,000 feet when we were coned,' he remembers. 'We dived at full power and passed through 6,000 feet before pulling out. The flak kept all the way with us until we hit about 400 mph. It lasted about six minutes, but seemed more like for ever.'[27]

His pilot, F/Sgt Murray, says: 'It was our thirteenth operation. We were about an hour out from Berlin and went through a wide gap between two searchlight cones. A master searchlight lit up directly on us and bursts from a few flak batteries severely damaged the aircraft.'[28]

Both Taylor and the pilot were nicked in the face by flying powdered Perspex as flak peppered the canopy. By the time Murray regained control back in the black fastness of the night H-How had suffered hits in two fuel tanks, an engine and one wheel, and a rudder trim cable had been severed. The crew struggled back to Breighton. 'The dive at 400 mph got us out of the area, but it took a month to patch up the aircraft,' F/Sgt Murray remembers. It meant taking over another Lancaster and he was offered G-George. It would see him through the rest of his tour.*

In all, seventeen aircraft had been lost, 5.6 per cent of those dispatched. At debriefing, crews of 76 Sqn were saddened to find that S/Ldr James Fletcher's was among the two crews who had failed to return. 'We all missed Fletcher,' Sgt Hill remembers. 'He was our flight commander, a big, bluff Yorkshireman, always cheerful, sporting the largest moustache I have ever seen. He used to say: "A moustache is not a moustache unless it can be seen from behind."'

Hill and most of the rest of Sgt Herbert Hoover's tired crew prepared to write the much-prized Berlin DCO (Duty Carried Out) in their log books as they left the operations room for breakfast and bed. Hill says:

* G-George in fact saw several crews through their tours. It was flown to Australia in 1944 after ninety operations and is now in the Australian War Memorial Museum in Canberra.

I remember that our second-tour wireless operator, Jack Mossop, who already had a DFM, and was the only man I met who showed no fear, remarked: 'Now that you have been to the Big City you might just survive as long as I am with you.' The following night we were stood down and headed straight for Betty's Bar.

UNKNOWN to Bomber Command there had been an ironic twist to the raid. Twenty factories had been badly damaged. Among them was the Telefunken works where the H2S set from the Stirling shot down in the Cologne raid of 2 February was being put back together and studied. It was completely wrecked by the bombing. But hours later the 35 Sqn Pathfinder Halifax of S/Ldr Peter Elliott had been shot down in Holland returning from the Berlin raid. From it the Luftwaffe picked up a replacement H2S set for the one lost in the Telefunken wreckage.

So ended an intense period of experimentation with H2S as Bomber Command gathered its strength for the onslaught ahead. There had been fewer than fourteen H2S sets available for use in any one attack. It would be September before all heavy Pathfinder squadrons were so equipped and October before the first sets trickled through to Main Force. Pathfinder crews had been enthusiastic to receive a navigation device that could see the terrain in the dark, but the results had been disappointing. They would often continue to be so until the introduction of the more precise 3-cm magnetron valve as the year drew to a close.

The problems H2S brought in its train led to a less precise, broader means of attack on targets beyond Oboe range in 1943 – in practice virtually the rest of Germany outside the Ruhr. On the first H2S-marked raid of 30 January on Hamburg, five backers-up had been used to aim not at the original markers, but at the area they encompassed. Main Force were then expected to bomb within that circle. Five backers-up hadn't been enough. From then on twenty backers-up was the norm. If the weather was good enough the backers-up were told to look for the aiming point in the light of flares the H2S marker aircraft had dropped.

It failed to produce the concentration desired, however, and in fifteen

H2S-marked operations up to the end of March, only three were considered quite successful by Bomber Command's Operational Research Section. The sets themselves proved more temperamental than the Oboe equipment, scarcely less than half working on any operation in the early months of 1943, and it was therefore impossible for the backer-up Pathfinders to arrive at a fair average and make a correct estimate of the mean point of impact.

However, this only applied to targets outside Oboe range and for the next four months two-thirds of the forty-three attacked would be within that range, in the Ruhr. Bomber Command was about to begin its first major self-contained battle, striking continuing blows at the towns and cities at the heart of Nazi industry. The aircraft were rolling out of their factories, the crews were finishing their leaves at the end of operational training and the target maps had been unfolded for the long-awaited Battle of the Ruhr.

CHAPTER FOUR

RUINING THE RUHR

THE eight Oboe Mosquitos of 109 Sqn which took off for Essen on 5 March carried more than the target indicators that would burst in a crimson pyrotechnic display to open the Battle of the Ruhr that Friday night. They also bore the aspirations of the C-in-C to prove that bombing could win the war. Harris admitted later it was the first time he had been able to pursue with real hope of success the task given to Bomber Command just before he took over a year earlier, of destroying the Ruhr towns and cities.

Essen's fate was decided when it was named the first for destruction as the biggest and most important manufacturing centre in the Ruhr. The War Cabinet had also sought the eradication of Duisburg, Düsseldorf and, on the Rhine, Cologne. It was presumed that apart from denying the enemy the use of the war material from these centres, destroying them would also undermine the morale of the sheltering workers.

The order had been issued to Sir Richard Pierse, Harris's predecessor as C-in-C. Harris, therefore, though a pragmatic advocate of area bombing, had no part in its inception. The 1,000-bomber raid in May 1942 had fulfilled in some part his obligation regarding Cologne. Now the long experiments with Oboe had shown that it was possible to find, hit and destroy Essen, Duisburg, Düsseldorf and the other great centres of the German armaments industry in the Ruhr valley.

But the Battle of the Ruhr could not just encompass Ruhr targets. To keep the enemy guessing, other operations would be launched in these first few weeks against Munich, Berlin and – as the Ruhr losses mounted – against a less well-defended target, Kiel.

The Ruhr was the largest centre of heavy industry and coal mining in Europe. Its industrial history had begun in 1838 when Friedrich Krupp had cast his first gun in an Essen forge. As the area developed into the principal producer of coal, coke, iron and steel it spawned other industries such as chemicals and gas production. By the start of the war the valley was churning out nearly three-quarters of Germany's needs for coal and coke and more than 60 per cent of its pig-iron and steel. Two-thirds of all high-grade steel alloys, needed for aircraft engines and the forging of other war material, came from the Ruhr. Coal produced the oil manufactured in ten synthetic oil plants.

The towns of the Ruhr weren't Germany's only hubs of heavy industry. But with Oboe they were in range to be successfully raided, unlike, for instance, that other great area of war production in the triangle bounded by Vienna, Prague and Breslau. They also had the advantage of being close together, in many cases one town running into another, so a scattered raid could still produce results.

The heart of it all was Krupps, and Krupps was in the centre of Essen. The attack on Essen would have to come from the north to avoid the flak belt of towns along the Ruhr valley. It would be a highly concentrated attack putting eleven bombers a minute over the target and the whole raid by 440 aircraft would last thirty-eight minutes.

Now that the RAF had two pairs of Oboe ground stations working – at Trimmingham, Norfolk and Walmer, in Kent – it would be possible to put eight Mosquitos over the target in the time available instead of the four on experimental attacks. Two Mosquitos were called upon to open the raid with their red TIs, then it was intended the other six Oboe-directed aircraft would back up with further red TIs at intervals between three and seven minutes. PFF Halifaxes of 35 Sqn and Lancasters of 83 and 156 Sqns carried green TIs to stoke the reds. Crews were ordered to aim at the reds, but if they weren't visible in the smoke and haze, to bomb the greens.

As it happened three of the Mosquitos had to turn back with technical problems, but the others dropped their reds either on the aiming point of the Krupps works or very close to it. Within minutes a circle of fire began which covered, almost without gaps, a 2-mile diameter around the pulsating TIs. Not surprisingly, ten firemen who tried to contain the blaze were among the 450 dead. It was a remarkable demonstration of what Oboe could achieve and the Nazis were well aware that all the Ruhr towns and cities were in Oboe range of the elusive, high-flying Mosquitos. More than fifty of the Krupps buildings were hit in a 160-acre area of devastation, although the main area of damage seemed to be between the armaments complex and the city centre. Krupps' proximity to the heart of the city meant more than 3,000 houses were destroyed.

The three Mosquitos weren't the only aircraft to make early returns – so did more than fifty of the Main Force, approximately 13 per cent. The mighty defences of Essen were not to be tangled with in anything less than an A1 aircraft.

The attack was made in three waves. In the first were ninety-one Halifaxes of 4 and 6 Groups; in the second, Wellingtons and Stirlings of 1, 3, 4 and 6 Groups; and in the third wave 143 Lancasters of 1 and 5 Groups.

F/Sgt Briggs was the wireless operator in one of the 1 Group Lancasters provided by 103 Sqn at Elsham Wolds. He remembers: 'The briefing was very tense. We were told it was a very important raid, there was more than usual effort being put into it. Ten were briefed from our squadron and all attacked. We could tell the operational pace was being quickened.'[1]

Cliff Hill of 76 Sqn recalls:

We were briefed in the afternoon for what was, with Berlin, the most heavily defended target in Germany. It was ringed by hundreds of searchlights and anti-aircraft guns and was usually obscured by an industrial haze, making it difficult to get a clear run-in. F/Sgt Milan, a tall, dark-haired Canadian, and his crew rode out with us in the truck taking us to dispersal and I remember we were all laughing and joking.[2]

At Leconfield the Wellington crews of 466 and 196 Sqns, both in the second wave, had been specifically ordered 'not to bomb anything but TI markers until zero hour plus 15'.

Their instructions continued: 'If no TI markers are seen before that time on arrival aircraft are to turn left and circuit to the east making another run up after zero plus 15.'

As it happened it was unnecessary; the Pathfinders, running up to the target on H2S, were bang on time. Wellington crews of 115 Sqn over the target in the second wave reported that 'large explosions were observed and fires were concentrated in one large mass, the glow of which could be seen from the Dutch coast'.[3] Sgt Gordon McGregor, piloting one of the 106 Sqn Lancasters with Albert Bracegirdle aboard, bombed at 2118 as the attack was closing and reported: 'the whole of Essen seemed to be ablaze and without doubt the attack was successful despite considerable opposition'.

The defences accounted for fourteen aircraft, four falling to night fighters. Safely back at Linton Sgt Hill was debriefed with the rest of Hoover's crew in the operations block. 'We looked at the blackboard after intelligence had finished with us,' he recalls. 'There was a blank space at the side of Milan's name where the landing time should have been. The reaper had claimed him and his crew on their fifteenth trip.'

THE onslaught on Germany as the year progressed would be felt in the pocket of the British taxpayer, and before Bomber Command returned to Essen again, Sir Archibald Sinclair presented his air estimates to the House of Commons. The Air Minister told the House 10,000 tons of bombs had been dropped by the RAF in February and 4,000 in the first ten days of March alone – creating large acreages of destruction in Wilhelmshaven, Essen, Cologne, Düsseldorf and other German towns. He said:

> The people of Britain have had their own experience of the disloca-
> tion which can be caused by bombing. When the Nazis smashed
> Coventry they introduced a new technique into bombing attacks, but the
> RAF have extended and improved on this. They sowed the seeds of
> their ultimate destruction. The seeds are now bearing fruit and it must
> be bitter to Reichsmarschall Goering, who boasted that the people of
> the Reich should be safe from the attacks of invaders.

Within 24 hours 457 aircraft would be nosing from dispersal points at airfields from Durham to Cambridge, lining up along perimeter paths, then thundering down flarepaths to make a further point to the Reichsmarschall that Germany was now a very dangerous place to be, and to Britons that their masters were spending their taxes wisely in the prosecution of the war.

This second major raid on Essen within a week caused severe damage to the Krupps complex and, according to a contemporary report from Sweden, it was the heaviest inflicted so far by the RAF on works vital to the German war effort. The town's locomotive shops and rolling stock works were burned out and in the process one-third of the total built-up area of Essen was destroyed. But the Luftwaffe flak, searchlight and fighter units were waiting. The target selectors at High Wycombe had planned to return to Essen on Saturday the 6th while the air raid emergency services were still reeling from the effects of the attack the day before, but the weather had turned foul over northern Europe. By Friday the 12th there had been time to strengthen the defences.

As Sgt Walter Hedges, wireless operator/air gunner on a 102 Sqn Halifax, prepared for the raid at Pocklington, his first, he began to realise what might be ahead. He wrote shortly afterwards:

> Our rear gunner [Sgt Ernie Hughes] told me in very plain language that it was not an easy target. I felt excited. During the afternoon I started preparing and I listened to the wireless section leader's gen. I got into my flying kit and with the other six lads went out to the aircraft. It was 1820 and the engines were being run up. The ground crew wished us 'Good luck', the aircraft taxied out to the runway and the signal was flashed to take off.[4]

The sirens sounded over Essen at 9 p.m. and the Oboe Mosquitos opened the attack fifteen minutes later, accurately marking the Krupps works. Twenty-three aircraft would not return. Sgt Hedges' Halifax, piloted by Sgt Edouard Charlebois, was among the first victims. Hedges remembers: 'We had just crossed the North Sea and over the Zuider Zee we realised we were two minutes ahead of schedule. It was rather important not to arrive before the others, so we opened the bomb doors for the target about 30 miles ahead and the pilot decided to orbit.'

His aircraft banked back on course for Dorstund where the Pathfinders were laying white TIs as a turning-point marker for the final run-in to Essen. Hedges says:

Of course, the Germans were tracking us and as we came back on course they knew exactly where we would be and the predicted flak opened up. There was an almighty bang and the aircraft lurched. A few seconds later the rear gunner reported sparks and flames shooting past him and we realised the starboard inner was on fire below the wing. Then the port inner burst into flame. The pilot said: 'Sorry, lads, you'll have to bale out. I can't hold her, it's out of control.'

The navigator, who was sitting next to me, called up the pilot and said, 'I can give you a route back', but I said, 'My God, there's no point in that, we're only going down.' The bomb aimer opened up the hatch, a blast of cold air came in and he went out followed by the navigator. I was about to go when the pilot, who was only 20 like the rest of us, called up to say he hadn't got his parachute. My heart sank, but I found his chest pack and handed it to him. I now kick myself I didn't clip it on for him. I remember saying to him, 'Come on, Charlie, there are no medals for this, get out of it.'

The rear gunner had always said he would never bale out. We always thought he wasn't serious. But I now think as he wasn't married or anything he told the skipper to go and he would stay. Charlebois was as true an Englishman as you could find and I think he couldn't leave him. I hesitated slightly by the hatch myself. It was pretty dark and cold, but then out I went.[5]

Sgt Hedges' diary records:

As I fell turning and somersaulting through the air a great glow passed my closed eyes. I knew it was the aircraft by now well ablaze. I pulled the rip-cord and the 'chute streamed out. I found myself right way up, but in complete darkness, thinking I was perhaps going up not down. I remember spitting and trying to look down, but it was difficult for my harness was tight and seemed to be choking me.

Everything was deathly quiet and I hung there feeling very helpless. After what seemed to be an age I noticed a lot of fire on the ground which appeared to be the crashed aircraft. I was right over it, so pulled on one side of my harness to try to slip away, but as this had no effect I then kept still. It began to dawn on me that I must have jumped from a great height.[6]

Sgt Hedges had in fact baled out at 17,000 feet. Finally he saw forests, fields and buildings below and pulled his feet and legs together just before he dropped into a ploughed field. Not far away his Halifax, P-Peter, had hit the ground with the bombs on board and the pilot and rear gunner still inside. He says: 'I was told later the rear turret broke off in the crash and rolled away with the gunner dead inside it. But the skipper was sitting on our bombs.'

As Sgt Hedges hit the ground Main Force was now pounding Essen. The red bursts of heavy flak, the forest of waving white searchlights and the orange glow of doomed aircraft were forming an awe-inspiring, macabre canopy above an arena of bursting red TIs, floating green candles from the Pathfinder backers-up and the winking white fires of incendiaries beginning to join into circles of orange flame. Krupps was receiving 30 per cent more damage than in the attack of a week before. As gas holders and chemical sheds were hit they sent vivid multi-coloured shock waves along the shaking ground, witnessed by bomb aimers crouched at their sights 20,000 feet above.

The final wave, all Lancasters, arrived over the target from 2130 to 2155 and by that time huge conflagrations had linked as fire watchers failed to deal with the thousands of 4-lb incendiaries and firemen lost the battle with blazing workshops. The incoming crews found the ring of searchlights extremely active. Sgt Charles 'Laurie' Lawrence was on his first operation as captain, piloting a 12 Sqn Lancaster. He and his crew had arrived at

Wickenby in early February and he had flown a second-dickey familiarisation trip to Lorient. Now they were beginning a tour together at a time
when losses would escalate. He remembers:

> Before we bombed we were coned. It only lasted thirty seconds, but
> half a minute when you are diving in an aircraft is a long time. We
> were fully coned; it lit up the whole cockpit with a bluish glow. The
> only way out was by strong evasive action, throwing the aircraft to port
> or starboard in a steep descent and then reversing the pattern in a spiral
> climb and to keep repeating it. We finally bombed at only 13,000 feet
> and the target was a mass of red and green target indicators and orange
> flames and smoke.[7]

For some the sight of blazing bombers, shell bursts from flak units
which continued to fire even when ringed by flames, and the waving fingers
of searchlights waiting to ensnare the unwary was too much to bear and
creepback developed in the later stages. Many bombs landed on towns to
the north-west of Essen, and Berbeck and Bottrop were badly hit. One 44
Sqn flight commander reported to intelligence officers: 'A very successful trip
except for some of the weaker brethren who dropped their bombs several
miles to the north of the target area.'[8]

The night fighters were now to have their moment. As the bombers
crossed the border into Holland the waiting controllers of the Kammhuber
Line fed their pilots into the stream and quickly vectored them onto targets.
A Halifax of 78 Sqn was shot down on the edge of the Reichwald Forest, a
Wellington of 115 Sqn plunged into the Zuider Zee, a Stirling of 149 Sqn
crashed east of Arnhem and a 425 Sqn Wellington near Tiel. Nine bombers
in total were brought down by night fighters. The attrition rate was 5 per
cent, compared to 3.2 per cent for a week before. In Essen 200 people are
believed to have died.

Beneath the route from Essen, gathering his thoughts after landing near
Dorstund with 'quite a jolt', Sgt Hedges had banged the quick release box on
his parachute harness and thrown the chute into a nearby stream, watching
it sink. 'In the distance was a lot of activity, searchlights, guns, fires, aircraft,

flares and explosions,' he recorded a few weeks later in his diary. 'A few of them came down in flames as I watched, then everything went quiet. Plane engines died away, searchlights went out and the guns were silent. The all-clear sounded in the distance. I was alone in Nazi Germany. I felt very, very helpless.'

As the surviving crews crossed the North Sea Sgt Hedges started walking across the flat fields of northern Germany away from the target. He recalls:

I got pretty cheesed off trying to clamber over walls. I saw the outline of a house and this farmer was standing in the doorway smoking an evening pipe after the alert. I thought I'd take a chance and strode across, opened my arms wide and said, 'British airman from London'. He took me into the farmhouse where his wife gave me 'milch' which I understood as milk and asked about 'Essen' which I didn't understand was the German word for food. I thought they were talking about the target we were going to. I wasn't brave enough to say, 'Yes, we were trying to knock the industry out of it.' I just acted that I didn't understand. They sent for the police.

Fifty years later I had the crash site pointed out to me and it was only about a quarter or half a mile away from the house. I met the farmer and his wife in the house all those years later with a local historian. He told me: 'You have this man to thank for your life' because apparently the two policemen who arrived in a car wanted to do the obvious there and then and pretend I'd never arrived. I didn't speak German so didn't know what was happening, but it seems the farmer told them: 'He is only a young man, you are not to harm him.'

I was taken by car from the house down to the little village of Wesum and there were hundreds of people waiting in the street to see me. It was getting on for midnight then and they got me out of the car and I was walked through the crowds into a building where three other survivors of the crew were sitting. We were later taken by the Luftwaffe to Reine air base and put in single cells. They weren't antagonistic. There was an informal chat with the station commander.[9]

AS Sgt Hedges was being bundled into the car outside the farmhouse the returning bombers were approaching the circuits above their English airfields, navigation lights shining in the darkness as they opened up the taps to be first home and into bed. Albert Bracegirdle remembers:

> As soon as you crossed the English coast on the way back the wireless operator would call base to get in as soon as possible. The R/T could only reach about 30 miles. You would get on the circuit of the airfield and they would give you a 5,000-feet separation with two aircraft on the circuit at the same level following each other. After they had filled all the levels they used to send you off on a cross-country run for ten minutes to clear the circuit.
>
> On this occasion after raiding Essen we were on the circuit following the Drem lights only about 2,000 feet up and on the road below I could see the dimmed headlamps of the coaches bringing non-operational people back to the base after the usual Friday night out in Nottingham. I thought: 'We've been to Essen and back and they've been to the pub or the pictures.'[10]

IN a week sixty-six of Bomber Command's heavies had been lost. To divert the defences major raids had been mounted on Nuremberg, Munich and Stuttgart as well as the two maximum effort operations on Essen. Now that the Battle of the Ruhr had begun there seemed no end to the demand for aircrew to satisfy the insatiable appetite of the Bomber Command war machine. Sgt Bracegirdle decided it was time to do something about it:

> We did four raids, had one or two days' stand-down then did another four in five nights. We'd done twelve raids in a very short time. We hadn't had any leave between moving from OTU to Syerston, well over six months. Aircrew were supposed to get a week's leave every six weeks, but they wouldn't let us go because they wanted all these maximum efforts, so I told the skipper I was going to complain. The navigator, Kenneth Davidson, said: 'I'll come with you.'
>
> We went to see the adjutant, who got us an appointment with

Gibson, the CO. We went into his office in the administration block and told him we had twelve trips in and no leave, so he pressed the intercom on his desk and asked Searby, our flight commander, to 'Step in, John.' Searby came across the corridor from his B-Flight office and Gibson said: 'I've got McGregor's crew here and they've been complaining they've not had any leave since they arrived in early January and we're well into March now. 'Searby told him: 'It's not been possible as you keep asking for all these maximum efforts', but Gibson told him: 'Get them on leave straight away, I'll phone through to the adjutant for passes.' That afternoon we were on the bus to Nottingham on our way home. There's been a lot of talk in recent years that Gibson was a bit of a tyrant, but I couldn't see anything wrong with him. He was very amenable to our complaints and I think he was a very fair man. After all, we were only sergeants yet he'd called in a flight commander to explain himself. He was thinking about our well-being.[11]

AT Linton Sgt Hill also hoped for a respite from the flak and the fighters. 'Would we obtain leave was the question foremost in our minds,' he recorded. 'W/Cdr Cheshire had given us two weeks in February, was it only last month? I remembered it was only 12 March, our leave seemed like last year. I realised I had lost track of time.'[12]

Nature was about to come to the rescue of tired aircrew. To the planners' chagrin the weather closed in over the next two weeks. For the hard-pressed administrative and engineering staff at the damp, misty bases it provided a breathing space. Many squadrons were expanding from two flights to three and aircraft with a greater range and bomb load were replacing the Wellingtons and Stirlings, which had taken such a beating. There would also be time for erks to draw new bomb symbols on fuselages marking the recent raids and by the more gifted to create colourful nose art. Sgt Herbert Hoover's Halifax, P-Peter, at Linton would be one aircraft so decorated. 'Pinnochio was painted on the fuselage just below Hoov's seat,' his rear gunner, Sgt Hill, recalls. 'The idea came from one of the ground crew who noticed Hoov had a retroussé nose.'

For most bomber boys that Saturday after the second Essen raid, it meant a late breakfast, a wash and brush-up and a dash for the liberty bus for Cambridge, Nottingham or Lincoln. In Lincoln the Lancashire comedy *Hindle Wakes* was playing at the Theatre Royal starring the actor-manager Frank Crawshaw supported by Iris Fraser-Foss. The *Daily Mail* had described it as an 'epoch-making play'.

For the less theatrical, Humphrey Bogart was on screen in *The Big Shot* at the Regal Cinema 'and Café', or for young men with other things in mind Rosalind Russell was starring in *Green-eyed Woman* at the Central. Some with recent memories to blot out would settle for a rowdy night at the Saracen's Head Hotel near the Stonebow, known to airmen throughout the Lincolnshire bases of 5 Group as the 'Snakepit'.

Albert Bracegirdle recalls:

Our crew pub was the Flying Horse in Nottingham. We didn't go often to the Trip to Jerusalem near the castle which was popular with aircrew. It was a bit too noisy for me. We used to go in on the coach on stand-downs. We would go to a matinée at the pictures, have a meal and at night we would go to a couple of pubs or go dancing at the Palais de Danse next to the bus station. We'd get back to base about 11.30 p.m.[13]

Australian crews such as those of 460 Sqn at Breighton, 466 Sqn at Leconfield and 467 Sqn at Bottesford turned the platforms of country railway stations into a sea of dark blue and headed for London. The first call was at Australia House in the Strand, straight past the commissionaire towards the main Greco-Roman-style reception room with its imposing, pear-shaped crystal chandelier and down the marble staircase to the more basic delights of the Boomerang Club to catch up on the latest happenings from Amberley to Wogga Wogga. Then it was down Fleet Street, past St Clement Danes and up into Hatton Garden where the sixteenth-century Mitre Tavern hid its charms in an alleyed courtyard from all but those in the know.

As the foggy nights continued without an operation there was a chance to get to know the pubs and villagers near the Australian bases. F/Sgt Ron

Gooding, a wireless operator on 460 Sqn, had found Laura Bennett at a local dance. They were now engaged and met in his off-duty hours at pubs such as the White Swan in Bubwith where the landlord kept a visitor's book for aircrew* or the weekend dances at the village hall in North Duffield. Laura would take a tortuous journey on problematical wartime transport by bus from her home in Winterton, Lincolnshire to Scunthorpe, another bus to Goole and then a halting country train to Selby.

On the way, in those uncertain days of late winter, she would wish for the mist to develop into an enveloping fog. 'It meant the boys wouldn't be on ops that night and we would be able to meet,' she remembers. 'I saw the boys at the dances and in the pubs. We had great times. They were a super bunch and thoroughly enjoyed themselves.'[14]

But one night while returning to camp down a darkened lane from one of those dances F/Sgt Gooding had been knocked off his bike by a car and taken to York Hospital with head injuries. He would spend much of March convalescing at Carlton Towers near York, a stately home which had been turned into a military hospital. Laura's dance dates turned into hospital visits.

IN the late evening of Saturday, 13 March as his squadron mates and the other crews who returned from Essen were weaving their way back to base after exuberantly relieving the tension with booze-ups, dances or the pictures in York, Lincoln or Nottingham, Sgt Hedges was arriving by train at Frankfurt on his way to Dulag Luft, Oberursel, the interrogation centre near Frankfurt where all downed Allied aircrew were processed to glean every snippet which could be unwittingly wheedled out of them.

'Four of us from the crew had been been taken from Reine on the Saturday and put on the train to Frankfurt, travelling through Hamm and Hagen. We got to Frankfurt very late on the Saturday night and had to sleep on the concourse,' he remembers. On the Sunday as another misty day dawned in eastern England, promising a respite from operations if not

* The book is now in the Australian War Memorial Museum at Canberra.

church parade, Sgt Hedges was put on a civilian-filled tram outside Frankfurt railway station. It stopped outside the main gate of Dulag Luft. It was not a good period of the war to arrive.

A Gestapo unit had been foisted on the Luftwaffe who ran the interrogation centre and techniques were getting tougher. Says Sgt Hedges:

> I'd never heard of the place before I got there. The RAF hadn't told us what to expect. I was put in a single cell and the heating was turned up. They pushed a plate of sauerkraut through during the afternoon. I had never heard of it and thought it was ghastly. I thought they were trying to bump me off. Pretty late on the Monday they came for me and I'd had 24 hours to think. When they do come you're pretty glad to see someone. That's when they start to ask personal questions. I was stunned by one or two comments they made. One of them was, 'How is W/Cdr Holden?' It pretty well identified us as being from the CO's squadron. It also surprised me when the interrogator told me he lived in pre-war Golders Green. But what could I tell him that he would want to know?[15]

In fact NCO aircrew weren't always subject to severe interrogation, the Luftwaffe reasoning they weren't in a sufficient position of power to know much of use to an enemy. But Sgt Norman Leonard was an exception. After his bale-out over Belgium in the middle of February he had spent two weeks in a German military hospital in Brussels recovering from concussion. While he was there he had been overheard talking German and the report had gone to Dulag Luft. The interrogators were also puzzled as to why he and the other two survivors of his crew all wore Wag brevets for wireless operator/air gunner. They thought they were onto something special. In fact Sgt Bentley had remustered as a bomb aimer without changing his brevet and Sgt Reynolds was only using his air gunner skills in the rear turret of the Wellington.

Sgt Leonard was in Dulag Luft at the same time as Sgt Hedges. He says:

They were after information about the latest navigation and bombing aids, such as Gee,* H2S and Oboe. We had Gee, but none of the others. I was put in one of their special cells for newly captured airmen, offering no means for the inmate to control the heating, lighting or ventilation. My interrogation started at 3 a.m.

The wireless operator would only give name, rank and number. Eventually a uniformed officer, after first trying to get him to complete a fake Red Cross form by offering food and cigarettes, 'went ballistic and threatened that if I was not more co-operative I would stay in solitary for the rest of the war'. He says:

> That was the start of their cat and mouse game of manipulating the heating and lighting controls of the cell to discomfort and disorientate me. Another was to interrogate me in the middle of the night under a spotlight. It was then I learned they already knew a lot about our squadron, its whereabouts and its senior officers. After about a week I was released into the main camp. The tendency was then to open up with fellow prisoners, but there was a danger of stooges and hidden microphones in the walls. Fortunately there were other prisoners of war to tell you to watch it.[16]

In the middle of 1943 many prisoners who passed through Dulag Luft complained that when they were in solitary confinement on arrival the heating was turned up so high, all metal objects such as bunk rails were too hot to touch. F/Sgt Edwin Jury, who would arrive in April, testifies: 'I was in a sweatbox for five days. It was just big enough for a 6-foot bunk. They turned on this heat every night and you sweated like a pig and had to take all your clothes off and lie on the ground to try to breathe the air coming under the door.'[17]

Eventually a complaint was made to the British government through the Red Cross and towards the end of 1943 a protest arrived from Whitehall.

---

* Gee was a cathode ray tube system whereby a bomber's course could be plotted on a chart by reception of signals from two dedicated ground stations. By the Battle of the Ruhr its effectiveness had been largely discounted by German jamming.

The extreme practice was stopped and Oberstleutnant Erich Killinger, the commandant, was said to be furious when he learned that it had been going on.

Dulag Luft was efficiently run and yielded the Luftwaffe much information. When a prisoner, still shocked at his means of arrival in enemy hands, was questioned, his interrogator would indeed already know much about his unit, gleaned from various sources. A Yellow File Room at the camp collected biographical information from newspapers, magazines and *London Gazette* award lists, a Squadron History Room gathered information on every RAF and USAAF squadron and its personalities, a Technical Room had a library on Allied equipment, and a Crash File Room plotted each downed aircraft in Germany and Occupied Europe. It was through this room that the Red Cross was able to give relatives news of whether missing airmen had survived.

The fake Red Cross form shaken airmen were handed within hours of their arrival at Dulag Luft asked the required name, rank and number. However, interspersed between innocent questions such as next of kin and home address were 'Squadron and Group' and, to rub it in that for the recipient the war was over, 'What was your payment during the war?' By far the great majority of aircrew stuck to name, rank and number, but a couple of them were turned to become agents for the Reich – one Welsh air gunner broadcasting in Welsh from Berlin and another airman infiltrating an escape line, even winning a medal for his successful evasion – and sometimes a prisoner of war's reaction to RAF information the interrogator carelessly tendered could confirm what the Luftwaffe had previously merely guessed at.

Not all airmen strictly obeyed the instructions in crew rooms to empty their pockets before being transported to their waiting aircraft. Even a theatre ticket in a pilot's pocket could be used to impress a shocked airman about how much his questioners already knew about the current social life around his station. Release from interrogation into the main huts to await transport to a permanent prisoner-of-war camp was no guarantee of sanctuary from the inquiring Luftwaffe. The huts were wallpapered and behind the paper were listening devices to pick up useful information as one airman talked to another of the men and aircraft they had known.

More Bomber Command personnel would be joining Sgt Hedges and Sgt Leonard at Dulag Luft and in the permanent prisoner-of-war camp before March was over. Some were already on their way.

TO prevent the Germans concentrating their night fighter, flak and search-light defences in the Ruhr several other heavy raids had been launched to southern Germany and two to Berlin while the nights stayed long. One of the most important and successful had been the operation to Munich between the first two Essen raids, on 10 March. Poor weather in northern Europe had forced the planners at High Wycombe to ditch any plans for the Ruhr and in fact take-off conditions for any operation would not be ideal, but the weather for the southerly targets of Germany was more promising. The die was cast for Munich.

From Grimsby 100 Sqn put up seven aircraft for the raid. 100 Sqn had been wiped out in the Far East in 1942 and had been re-formed at Grimsby as a heavy bomber unit at the end of December as part of the build-up for the planned bomber offensive. The supply chain had shown various weak links, the adjutant's office noting sarcastically at the end of January that 'the absence of a typewriter and duplicator was a very severe handicap on the formation of this unit'.[18]

Things had not gone well since. The squadron had begun operating on 4 March with eight Lancasters on a mining expedition. One aircraft had vanished over the sea in the target area and a second had crashed while trying to land at Langar, killing all on board except one gunner. Now from Munich the B-Flight commander would be missing. His aircraft would crash in France on the way home, killing all the crew, including the 18-year-old mid-upper gunner.

Night fighters operating over France also nearly claimed the crew of another 100 Sqn skipper. P/O H. Harvey was twice attacked near Amiens. The crew did not even see their pursuer. They were alerted by tracer flying by and Harvey threw the aircraft into a successful violent corkscrew away from the trajectory. Not long afterwards another enemy aircraft attacked and again he was able to shake it off. South of Stuttgart three Ju88s attacked the Lancaster of a third 100 Sqn pilot, Sgt S. Slater, but his swift evasive action and return fire from his gunners drove them away.

The losses for Munich were generally small, at 3 per cent, compared to Ruhr operations and the raid itself had hit the city hard. The important aero-engine factory at the BMW plant was plastered and was out of action for six weeks and many small subsidiary workshops were wrecked, together with a huge number of military buildings – 294, including the local flak headquarters, destroyed by incendiary bombs. The cathedral, whose twin towers would eventually dominate a landscape of rubble as the centre of Munich was blasted in subsequent attacks, was damaged.

P/O Dennis Bateman was wireless operator in a 77 Sqn Halifax skippered by S/Ldr Robert Sage, heading for Munich. He had begun operational flying in Whitleys at the end of 1941. The Munich raid was his eighteenth operation and it would be his last. He remembers:

Not far from the target a glycol leak developed in the starboard outer. We had to feather it and bombed on three engines, then on the way back we got off track and of course had lost height. Near Stuttgart the flak started coming up and we took some minor hits.[19]

Crews returning from Munich commented on the hundreds of search-lights they had seen around the city. They horrified F/Sgt Jury, tail-end Charlie in his 419 Sqn Halifax. He recalls:

We were on our way out of the target and had closed the bomb bay doors when a master searchlight picked us up and suddenly it was as bright as day. The pilot Tom Jackson immediately put it into a dive and we went down at a very fast rate to get out of the lights. I thought at one stage we wouldn't be able to pull out. We were probably coned for about thirty seconds, but it seemed much longer. Eventually we got out of the lights before the flak caught up. It was a very nasty moment.[20]

The waving wands of light over Munich also caught the 44 Sqn crew of Canadian Sgt Ken Brown, who would join Guy Gibson on the Dams Raid within two months. His rear gunner, Sgt Grant McDonald, remembers:

We were off track and were late getting to the target. The searchlights coned us before we could release our bombs, so we dropped our load and started taking violent evasive action. We lost so much height trying to lose the searchlights, we got right down into the range of the light anti-aircraft fire. Searchlight batteries each seemed to hold us then pass us on one to the other until we got to round about Augsburg. Our pilot kept trying to shake them off, but we were coned for a long time. There wasn't so much flak following us at the higher altitude, but there was once we got lower into the range of the lighter anti-aircraft fire and that was always more dangerous. Finally Ken Brown managed to corkscrew out of it and we got home.[21]

But if the searchlights were a peril over Munich, the flak was not, that night. More than 14,000 rounds were fired and only one aircraft was destroyed, exploding over the city in a savage pyrotechnic display of dripping orange fire. Of the other seven aircraft lost it is known that four were downed by fighters in France and Belgium, orbiting their beacons in the night and waiting for the *jägerleitoffizier* to vector them onto a target as the returning bombers crossed their box in the Kammhuber Line. One of the targets was KN-J, the Halifax of P/O Bateman. He recalls:

We were crossing Belgium when we were hit by the night fighter. We didn't see him; I think he came up underneath us. There had been no report from the rear gunner. There was suddenly a terrific explosion and something came up through the floor, knocking my parachute sideways. I looked out of the window and the port wing was on fire. It was all over in no time at all. The pilot was fighting to stop it going into a spin and he ordered a bale-out.

I went out through the front hatch and was the last out apart from the pilot. The aircraft was moving around all over the place and I could see the pilot's parachute rolling around, so I put it near his feet and he said: 'Off you go, Dennis', and out I went. I counted to ten and by that time the aircraft had gone by. I came down in a field rather more quickly than was normal because my chute had been damaged by the cannon fire. I couldn't see the ground coming up, so didn't know when to relax and I hurt my left leg rather badly.

Three of the crew who baled out before P/O Bateman were able to evade – flight engineer Sgt B. Walker, navigator F/Lt Bob Barker and the bomb aimer Sgt Maurice Crabtree – but S/Ldr Sage and the injured P/O Bateman were soon captured. The rear gunner, F/O Ken Adams, who P/O Bateman had flown with on many Whitley ops in 1941, was killed. P/O Bateman remembers:

I hobbled around for a while, buried the parachute and walked down a lane to a farmhouse where I shouted: 'Je suis aviateur anglais.' For reply I heard wild screaming, so I tried another house. They let me in for the night, then the next night took me to the Mons Canal where Belgium bordered France. I staggered along until I got to Condé-sur-l'Escaut, a small French town, and someone saw me and took me to the gendarmes. They sent for the Luftwaffe.

In J-Jig's fiery plunge to earth one of the engines fell away and dropped on some houses at Bousin near Mons, causing a large fire. The rest of the aircraft fell in open ground near a community and one of the Belgians living nearby was able to photograph it the next day. P/O Bateman says:

Later on the Germans showed me the rear gunner's cap and told me his chute had failed to open. I think he may have been injured in the attack and when he flipped out through the rear doors of his turret he may have lost consciousness.

Maurice Crabtree got all the way to Switzerland by escape line. I think he knocked on the right door, though the people who helped me were kind enough to give me shelter overnight. The mid-upper gunner [Sgt D. L. Morris] evaded for quite a while. He got well into France and on his way into Spain and then was betrayed by someone and picked up by the Gestapo.[22]

As P/O Bateman was nursing his injured leg in hiding in a Belgian's home the last of 76 Sqn's Halifaxes were returning to Linton-on-Ouse, on the other side of York to 77 Sqn's Elvington base. Sgt Hill recalls:

Munich was an easy trip compared to the Ruhr, but long and terribly tiring. Our eyes were red-rimmed through staring into the darkness endlessly searching for fighters. We cycled back to our billet at Beningbrough at about 5 a.m. The next night there were no ops and the seven of us went to a mess dance.[23]

For F/Sgt Briggs at Elsham Wolds a night off for his 103 Sqn crew meant a quick wash and brush-up before all the places were taken on the station bus to Scunthorpe:

We might be in the camp cinema and you would hear on the speakers 'ops scrubbed', then there would be a rush for the door and into your best blue and on the station bus for Scunny. It was the survival of the fittest to get on that bus. We'd be off to the Crosby in Scunthorpe, or the Oswald, or the Berkeley Hotel where they held dances every week. The girls were quite keen to dance with aircrew. I was married myself, but being married didn't stop some aircrew.

If it got late we used to stay the night in Scunthorpe at Irish Maggie's, a little boarding house, and catch the 6.30 bus back to camp the next day. She used to serve our breakfast and always said: 'I'm sorry I've had to charge you 6d for the egg, but I have to get those on the black market.'[24]

BOMBER Command had used the ten-day lay-off for bad weather since the second Ruhr operation of 12 March to build up the force. It meant that 450 aircraft were available for the next attack on Germany's industrial power base on 26 March, an operation on Duisburg. It turned into one of the few failures of the Battle of the Ruhr. The losses were unusually small at 1.3

per cent, but so was the result. A forecast of thick cloud meant PFF planned for the skymarking system known as Wanganui, and would set fuses for 16,000 feet. Nine Oboe Mosquitos took off, but five had to abort and the TIs of the four that did mark soon drifted off the aiming point. The Germans saw it as an ideal night to experiment with laying down dummy flares and many crews, desperately looking for the PFF reds with green stars while they suffered the Ruhr's intensive defences, were fooled. Bombs were scattered over 30 miles and in Duisburg itself the sum total of success was fifteen houses destroyed and seventy damaged. To cap it all, PFF lost the first of its Oboe Mosquitos. It ditched off the North Foreland and the crew were drowned.

From 44 Sqn one pilot officer gave an indication of the frustration felt by crews risking their lives on a wasted effort. 'Identified target by red and green preliminary flares,' he reported at debriefing. 'No release point flares followed. Searched for release point flares for twenty-six minutes, eventually seeing them ahead and and bombed. Bombing spread over many miles of Germany.'[25]

New Zealander Sgt John Martyn of 428 Sqn reported: 'Our aircraft was followed by heavy flak for fifteen minutes after bombing In the target area we sustained a hit which made eighteen holes in the fuselage and two in the port engine cowling.'[26] Three nights later Martyn and his crew radioed they were ditching on the way back from Bochum. They are presumed to have suffered the fate of so many bomber crews that year, drifting in a yellow dinghy lost and alone on the black vastness of the North Sea until the cold and exhaustion took their last reserves of strength.

THE convalescence of the 460 Sqn wireless operator F/Sgt Gooding had ended and he returned to his base at Breighton. His girlfriend, Laura Bennett, now wearing his engagement ring, looked forward to seeing him at the dances as she visited her aunt and uncle at Bubwith. But 460 Sqn now promised few nights off for its aircrew as the chop rate mounted. Only the worst of weather would prevent operations in the need to keep the enemy reeling in the Ruhr.

Bomber Command's crews were briefed for a split attack on Berlin and the Ruhr town of Bochum on 29 March despite atrocious weather, which caused severe icing en route for both the 329 aircraft bound for Berlin and the 149 bound for the Ruhr. The conditions are best summed up by one sergeant pilot on 460 Sqn with F/Sgt Gooding who had to return to Breighton because 'the windscreen and astrodome iced up inside and out and the navigator passed out through oxygen failure'.[27]

Sgt Hill, in the mid-upper turret of his 76 Sqn Halifax bound for Berlin, remembers:

> It was the coldest night I have ever experienced. I was not wearing an electrical suit but had on masses of silk and woollen clothing. We had expected a 'scrub' as the weather was atrocious. We went out to the aircraft only to be recalled to wait in the mess as driving rain lashed the windows. Back to the aircraft, more delay as the wind changed direction, enforcing a change of runway. Finally we got off, soon to be in a massive build-up of cloud ice forming on the wings and ailerons.[28]

Halfway across the North Sea they had to turn back because poor oil pressure was reducing engine power and wing ice was causing the aircraft to lose height. Those who did get through to Berlin arrived late and the marking had been too far south. Most of the bombs fell in open country, but twenty-one aircraft were lost, 6.4 per cent.

The Bochum raid fared no better and losses were much higher comparatively, a horrendous 9 per cent. Only four buildings were destroyed in Bochum. It was an all-Wellington operation and the lower-flying aircraft were even more affected by the icing conditions than those on the Berlin raid. Early returns were made by forty aircraft. Oboe Mosquitos had to skymark above the cloud and there were long gaps between TIs going down. The flak, as on any Ruhr target, was heavy and the 431 Sqn aircraft of 21-year-old Sgt Ernest Aspden exploded. The bomb aimer, Sgt D. T. Dudley-Jones, had clipped on his chute as he lay in the nose waiting for the target to come up. He was the only one who survived.

The Berlin raid had been the second in two nights. The first gave some indication of how seriously the Germans were now taking the Oboe system which was marking the cities of the Ruhr through industrial haze and cloud.

Without Oboe, Pathfinders marked two separate areas short of Berlin's centre of the city, and not one photograph was plotted within 5 miles of the aiming point. The main concentration in the scattered bombing fell on a secret Luftwaffe stores depot at Tetlow, however, more than 10 miles to the south-west of the centre. It destroyed such a large quantity of important radar and radio stores that Albert Speer, the Reich Armaments Minister, believed this had been the raid's main purpose and demonstrated a new development in marking, in which Oboe signals had been able to be extended far into Germany. The rest of the raid was thought to have been a blind.

There was a four-night respite after the split Berlin/Bochum raids as rain and low cloud washed out operations. It was a time for recuperation. The memories of Essen, Munich, Duisburg, Berlin and Bochum were etched in the hearts and minds of pilots, bomb aimers and gunners as clearly as the tally they kept pencilled by their beds on billet walls.

The whore's kiss of a target's dreadful beauty as TIs cascaded into orbs of green descending through the dark ... the winking enticement of the red markers drawing droning bombers to the core of destruction ... the urgent, crimson flash of shells ... the sly gathering of searchlights round a doomed aircraft ... the hiss of oxygen drawn sharply as blood pounded and fingers tightened on controls. The images would not be easily erased.

Aircrew were kept busy with daytime lectures by their section leaders to improve their navigation, wireless and gunnery skills. On less chilly days there were dinghy drills in the station emergency water tank or escape and evasion exercises where protesting airmen were dumped in the country-side at an unknown destination and made to navigate the 5 or so miles back to base by tiny escape compass.

Occasionally there was time for crews to explore the historic cities near their bases.

Sgt Hill recorded:

The seven of us in our crew toured York, visiting the Minster, walking by the river and the walls, going to the cinema, having tea in cafés and eventually rounding off the evening in Betty's.[29]

The young men of Bomber Command were called again to what was now ironically being called Happy Valley on 3 April as nearly 350 aircraft were bombed up for Essen.

The weather was poor in England, but it was necessary to keep up the momentum and it was hoped it would clear over the target. Just in case, PFF prepared its Mosquitos with both skymarkers and ground TIs.

Sgt Hill wrote to his parents:

> It had rained most of the day, the type of light continuous drizzle that soaks one. It cleared in the evening and there was some cloud as we went out to P-Peter. Dusk was falling as we took off. The worst part, the interminable waiting since mid-afternoon briefing was over. The faithful who stood at the beginning of the runway each trip waved and gave the thumbs up and Hoov opened up the throttles.[30]

Ten faster Mosquitos took off later from their bases in the Fens to overtake Main Force and drop both the sky and ground markers on signal from the Oboe stations in England. Backers-up with their green TIs found the target clear of cloud, but visibility was moderate. Conditions suited the hunters more than the hunted as red-eyed rear gunners peered above their Brownings into the dark.

Main Force roaring in from Holland came under attack and some aircraft started to go down. Sgt Hill saw a Lancaster lost. He recorded:

> An interchange of cannon and tracer fire and a Lancaster slightly above us to port was on fire, its starboard engines smoking then blazing furiously. Suddenly its fuselage was enveloped in flame and it began to go down, oh so slowly. I expected it to blow up, but it just fell out of the sky. A brief red flash from the ground creating a crimson glow, signalled its demise. It was doubtful that anyone got out.[31]

Two Lancasters of 83 Sqn were shot down by night fighters over Holland and another over the target. Not one of the twenty-one crew members survived. Linton, Sgt Hill's base, would lose four aircraft, three from 78 Sqn and one from 76 Sqn. 158 Sqn at Lisset would also lose three and 408 Sqn would lose another three. It would mean a rapid reappraisal of their chances of survival by surviving crews of all four squadrons and long hours awake in the night in billets as the operations lengthened and odds shortened.

W/Cdr Cosme Gomm, leading 467 Sqn on his second tour, which would take him almost up to the Peenemünde raid in August, saw four aircraft go down in flames to night fighters. Once through the fighter belt to the target, crews found the forest of searchlights and constant black and red puffs of heavy flak a barrier it seemed suicide to try to penetrate. A few flinched at the prospect and turned away. The adjutant's office of 467 Sqn would record later: 'A disturbing feature was bombs jettisoned outside the target area.'[32]

The resilient Sgt Hoover ran in towards a TI and found his aircraft coned. Sgt Hill recorded:

One searchlight caught us followed by a violet master beam which lit us up and we were dazzled. As the concentration held us heavy flak came up and burst around the aircraft in black puffs with a noise like hailstones. The bomb aimer Ken Bergey called: 'It's no use, I can't see, the lights are blinding me.' A brief OK from Hoov. Another burst rocked the aircraft, it was getting very close. I was expecting Hoov to give the order 'Jettison', but he didn't. He just swore, 'We'll have to go round again when we get out of this lot.' He took violent evasive action, throwing the aircraft all over the sky, twisting and turning in the brilliant light.

Predicted flak was bursting both port and starboard, buffeting us first one way and then the other. The whole aircraft was lit up like daylight, one could have read the small print of a newspaper. Nobody spoke as Hoov wrestled with the controls doing his utmost to shake off the searchlights. I sat there helpless, conscious that we were sil-houetted, a perfect target. I had seen others in similar positions and knew the possible outcome. Going through my mind was the thought, 'We shall blow up anytime now, have faith, have faith.'

The minutes ticked by as Sgt Hoover tried every trick he knew to break free of the tentacles of light, then the second-tour wireless operator suggested a shallow dive towards open country. It worked and the crew cheered on the intercom as the searchlights flicked off one by one.

Hoover made a wide orbit of the target and prepared to come in again. It would take bravery of the highest order to cut across the bomber stream, especially in one aged only 19. They would now be fifteen minutes late on target. By this time bombs were raining down on Essen and 65 per cent of the Goldschmidt factory making important soft metal and alloys was being reduced by fire. Widespread damage was being caused in the western part of the city, nearest to the line of attack, and the Krupps harbour foundry works, which could produce a million tons of iron and steel a year, was being wrecked from end to end.

Hoover had narrowly avoided two collisions cutting across the bomber stream and Sgt Hill recorded: 'We commenced our bombing run from 19,000 feet at 2215. Ken Bergey called: "Bomb doors open". Again predicted flak burst around us as Bergey went into his litany, "Left, left, steady, steady, right a bit … steady … steady … bombs gone".'

The starboard outer was hit by flak and had to be feathered. As Hoover continued holding the aircraft on course for the photoflash to go off, the Halifax was struck once more, then a searchlight picked it up. Sgt Hill wrote: 'We were caught again by a master beam and coned by a myriad of search-lights, lit up again like a sunny day. I swore profusely. Flak hit us again somewhere in the fuselage and I felt a draught around my legs. The acrid smell of cordite pervaded the aircraft.'

Sgt Hill found himself calculating the distance between his mid-upper turret and the parachute stowage as more shrapnel riddled the aircraft with the lights still holding the Halifax in the dive out of the target area. 'I was scared to death,' he wrote, then 'at last we were out of it into welcome darkness. Profanity converted into silent prayer. The relief was indescribable.'[33]

AN increasing number of Lancasters were now rolling out of the factories and this was the first raid in which more than 200 had been used. It was the lower-flying Halifaxes which suffered most. There were only 113 Halifaxes in the attack, but twelve of them were lost and another two crashed in England. Of the whole force a total of twenty-three aircraft were gone, 6.1 per cent.

As the surviving, battered Halifaxes rumbled into their dispersals at Linton and engines coughed and spluttered into silence the crews had time to reflect on their lucky escapes. It was one of those nights when the press were visiting the base and they listened, making notes as Sgt Hoover's bleary-eyed crew quietly related their two runs on the target and the coning by searchlights both times. Someone made a crack about a Hollywood contract for star quality and everybody laughed in the sudden stillness.

Sgt Hill remembers: 'We had breakfast and cycled back to Beninbrough, all the way laughing and joking as we tried to ride with no hands. Such was youth.'

The RAF had paid a heavy price in bomber boys' lives, 132 being killed. The losses of the Battle of the Ruhr could not be sustained, but Harris had to keep the raids rolling to maintain pressure on the enemy. An easier target was needed from the list while the women pilots of the Air Transport Auxiliary ferried replacement aircraft from factory to bomber base to fill the empty dispersals. Kiel on the Baltic, away from the main fighter bases and flak and searchlight defences, was chosen to risk 577 aircraft in a massive demonstration of power. It would be the largest raid of the war apart from the three desperate 1,000-bomber operations of 1942 when Harris was trying to keep the command alive.

AT Breighton 22-year-old F/Sgt Ron Gooding, whose promotion to warrant officer was working its way through the system, was still recuperating after his road accident. He hadn't flown on ops since he'd done six in eleven days culminating in the Nuremberg raid of 8 March. Shortly before that he'd been celebrating Laura Bennett's twenty-first birthday at her aunt's home. Suddenly he was back in the war. F/O Kay Moore, an experienced pilot with the DFC, needed a wireless operator for the Kiel raid and F/Sgt Gooding's name went on the battle order of thirteen crews.

The weather had threatened to deteriorate rapidly as the week wore on and it was thought there would just be time that Sunday to mount a major operation before forecast gales swept in. In fact thick cloud over the target necessitated skymarking and strong winds dispersed the TIs rapidly. Conditions were ideal for decoy fires and the buildings destroyed in Kiel barely ran into double figures.

A 158 Sqn flight lieutenant described the confusion to intelligence officers at Lissett:

> There was 10/10s cloud and on approaching the target at least four lots of red TI flares were observed glowing, when over the target green TI marker flares were seen to burst above and cascade into cloud. The glow of TIs and searchlights could be seen reflecting back through the clouds and lighting up the whole area above as though daylight.
>
> Conditions would have been excellent for night fighters, but there were no sightings although many of our aircraft were silhouetted above cloud. When approximately 30 miles short of the target going in, a great ball of flame burst dead ahead at 20,000 feet and then cascaded into green stars which seemed to hang in the air for some considerable time in a line north to south. At the same time a string of white flares were dropped.[34]

Some crews weren't aware the Pathfinders had marked the target at all, the conditions were so problematical. A few went below the cloud base of 5,300 feet desperately trying to find an aiming point, risking the flak. Those that were lost mainly fell to flak and the chop rate was small, twelve aircraft or 2.1 per cent. In the ebb and flow of the air war this was an acceptable figure, but behind the statistics lay the heartache. In a 51 Sqn Halifax

Cockney air gunner F/Sgt Sidney Adams died. He had lied about his age to join up and was just 17. One of the five Lancasters lost was from 460 Sqn, shot down with all on board by Kriegsmarine flak midway between Neumunster and Kiel. In the aircraft was Laura Bennett's fiancé, Ron Gooding. 'My cousin Madge used to ring me at Winterton and tell me who was missing after operations,' Laura says. 'I vainly hoped for a miracle and that he would be a prisoner of war. It was not to be.'[35]

Four days later W/O Gooding's 460 Sqn comrades were back over the Ruhr, their Lancasters among a force raiding Duisburg again. If Harris's operational research section required evidence that poor weather meant poor results they needed to look no further than this raid. Nearly 400 heavy bombers went out, twenty-one were lost and the results were negligible with only forty buildings destroyed. Thick cloud had again ruined the PFF marking – despite Oboe – leading to scattered bombing.

It was 19-year-old New Zealand pilot George Barclay's twenty-eighth operation. As he ran up the engines of his 166 Sqn Wellington at Kirmington there was a massive magneto drop on the port engine. He remembers:

> I shut down and the engineer officer came aboard and we restarted the engine. This time the mag drop was minimal and the EO more or less told me that if I did not go, 'Lack of Moral Fibre' might be considered. I was very uncomfortable about the whole thing but went anyway as it was my third go at Duisburg and it had been a milk run previously.[36]

As Sgt Barclay took off to hit Duisburg from the south-west he found he was battling with a 90-knot freezing northerly wind, upsetting the calculations of his navigator, P/O Bert Marion. Sgt Barclay arrived over Duisburg at 21,000 feet just as the TIs were going down to open the attack. The Pathfinder Wanganui technique of skymarking was producing the usual problems of drift and TIs were disappearing rapidly into cloud. It meant most crews would bomb on an estimated time of arrival over the target without many further clues as to where it might be.

Sgt Barclay released his high explosive and incendiaries, then an Me110 closed and in one pass shrapnel from its cannon hit Sgt Barclay in the right wrist and bicep and also left him with one wound near an eye and another on his shins. He dived away and managed to escape, but almost immediately the port engine died.

'I have never been certain whether the Me110 attack did it or the engine went u/s,' he says. 'I feathered the prop and jettisoned all the canisters of incendiaries, but forgot that with the port engine stopped the hydraulics would not pump the bomb doors shut.'

Sgt Barclay eventually realised why he couldn't shut the bomb doors and temporarily unfeathered the port engine to release the hydraulics, but with only a starboard engine and a 90-knot due-north wind he kept crabbing to port trying to maintain a westerly course. He remembers:

Every now and then I turned due north and retrieved lost ground, but after over two hours at about 100 knots I was somewhere over the Somme. Ice and damage had ripped off our aerials and navigation was very basic dead reckoning. The dilemma was if I tried to land in England and in fact was over the Channel it would be curtains and if we baled out and we were already over the Channel it would be curtains also. With my remaining height I turned due south and at the last moment ordered a bale-out. I got out at about 200 feet and hit a sandy field – dislocating both thumbs – and AS-H crashed and exploded nearby. P/O Marion found me, but I couldn't walk so he set off on his own.[37]

Sgt Barclay was picked up by the Germans and taken to Amiens aerodrome overnight where he was 'patched up and well treated'. Three other members of his crew were also captured, but P/O Marion made it home.

Many crews had found the cloud and icing had caused severe problems and the adjutant's office of 467 Sqn related later that the CO, W/Cdr Gomm, had said that 'the weather was entirely unsuitable for bombing'. The report went on: '10/10s cloud made it impossible to locate the target accurately. Probably because of the weather PFF were not seen and most crews bombed on a time and distance run. Flak over the target was intense and accurate.'[38]

For F/Sgt Briggs of 103 Sqn it was the last operation of his second tour. It had begun on another Ruhr target, Düsseldorf, the previous September. He recalls:

When we arrived back at Elsham Wolds the pilot, Geoff Maddern, gave the rear gunner, Arthur Browett, the privilege of calling up control to land. We were the only crew to complete a tour for several months so after debriefing there was a party in the operations block. There were crates of beer stacked up and the station commander, G/Cpt Dickens, and squadron commander took their jackets off and handed us our beer. It was a nice little do. All the crews were there and it gave everybody a lift.[39]

As tours ended, others began. Sgt Joe McCrossan made his first operational sortie, flying as a second-dickey pilot with 50 Sqn. He had arrived at Skellingthorpe, near Lincoln, a couple of weeks before. McCrossan and the rest of his crew, including bomb aimer Sgt George Stewart, had been allotted a Nissen hut on the edge of the aircraft dispersal area. The crew had stayed awake waiting for the sound of the Lancasters droning into the circuit after the Duisburg raid, so that they could ask the skipper what war was like.

'He was on the operations list to go with another crew presumably to show him the ropes which we all thought was a good idea,' Stewart recorded later. 'It was quite exciting listening to his account of the raid and I wondered how I would fare on our first op.'[40] Stewart would not have long to wait. The next night, 9 April, Duisburg was the target once more and McCrossan's crew was on the battle order. 'There was quite a hush at briefing when the CO revealed the target would be Duisburg again,' the bomb aimer wrote.

The squadron had nearly four and a half hours to wait for take-off – 'perhaps the longest period of my life,' Sgt Stewart felt. But as his aircraft joined the queue on the perimeter track for take-off, he says,

I felt excited to go on our first raid. At that time I, like lots of bomb aimers, used to lie in my bomb aimer's position in the nose for take-off for the view. They stopped it later and made you sit inside.

The plane came off then bumped back on the ground. It just wouldn't unstick and I could see the boundary hedge coming up. It lifted then bumped down again and this time the hedge was only a few feet away, but the skipper managed to get it to stagger up and we just cleared the hedge and we were airborne.

It was absolute blackness, then as we approached the target I could see the searchlights waving and the yellow and white tracks of the light flak and I thought: 'We'll never get through this'. As we flew on, the wireless operator was jamming the German night-fighter wavelength and I could hear the German voices breaking through occasionally.[41]

Over the target, he recorded afterwards:

The sky was full of black smoke and the air smelt of cordite. In front and below I could distinctly see what looked like a Stirling lit up by about a dozen searchlights and ack-ack bursting around it. Further below and to my left I could see a Wellington with an engine on fire. Light ack-ack shells were coming up towards us at a rate of knots, glowing red, green and white, but fell short as we were flying too high. The heavy ack-ack, however, was very different as shells kept bursting around us making the Lanc rock and it was very, very scary.[42]

This third raid on Duisburg within two weeks had involved only 104 Lancasters with marking by PFF Mosquitos. This time fifty houses were destroyed, but again heavy flak meant corresponding losses and eight Lancasters failed to return. The adjutant's office at 467 Sqn, which had sent seven aircraft, repeated open criticism once more. 'PFF did not do a good job and according to Gee were not on position,' they reported. 'The flares were scattered at Point A making a time and distance run difficult.'[43]

In Germany Josef Goebbels spent the next day touring the Krupps works, devastated by the attack a week earlier and the two in March. He recorded that the damage was 'colossal and indeed ghastly' and demanded more flak guns to defend the Essen factories. He wrote in his diary:

> This city must, for the most part, be written off completely. The city's building experts estimate that it will take twelve years to repair the damage ... Nobody can tell how Krupps can go on. Everyone wants to avoid transplanting Krupps from Essen. There would be no purpose in doing so, for the moment Essen is no longer an industrial centre the English will pounce upon the next city, Bochum, Dortmund or Düsseldorf.

The strength of the new Bomber Command had indeed been a mighty shock to the Nazis. Krupps' steel production would never be so high again. The record of 1.28 million tons in March would decline in all subsequent months. Albert Speer told interrogators after the war: 'To the greater part of the population the mass attacks launched in the spring of 1943 came as a complete surprise. This also goes for the local authorities as they were in no way prepared.'[44]

Before the Ruhr attacks began, however, plans for increased production laid in 1941 were already producing results and Hermann Roechling, a member of the Reichsministry for Armaments and War Production questioned at the same time, claimed that output generally from Ruhr blast furnaces and steelworks grew from January to June 1943. There was no question, however, that Krupps would ever be the same. Roechling added that he considered 'the most serious throttling of production was due to the destruction of the towns' water main, gas and electricity supplies'.[45]

This was the whole concept of area bombing – that not just the plant was hit, but there was no gas, electricity or water to maintain normal life and no transport to take the worker to and from his damaged factory.

And what of the undermining of morale, which had been a secondary aim of the War Cabinet in 1942 and a primary aim of the Casablanca Directive? The raids were having a significant effect on the morale of Germany's leaders, but in his post-war debriefing by US interrogators Speer

121

said: 'The night attacks did not succeed in breaking the will to work of the German people.'[46]

Workers walked to their bomb-damaged foundries and steelworks through the rubble of the streets. However, hanging over every German worker was the threat of being sent to an *arbeitscrzichungslager*, work education camps for 'slackers' to which the Gestapo dispatched hundreds every month. They were revealed by Walter Rohland, Deputy Chief of the Reich Iron Federation, in his own 1945 interrogation. 'They did not lack much of the terrors of the concentration camps,' he said. Forced labourers, of course, who were the basis of German industry, worked or starved.[47]

The British public were delighted to hear of the opening of the Battle of the Ruhr, particularly in the industrial North, which had seen its own factories blitzed. One Yorkshire newspaper's lurid report of the 26 March attack on Duisburg gleefully related how all the clouds above Germany's largest inland port had turned 'vivid red' with reflected fire.

There had been and would continue to be a heavy price to be paid by the RAF as the battle was pursued over the next three months. Against a total of 875 German civilians, civil defence and military personnel killed in the three Essen, three Duisburg and one Bochum raid from 5 March to 9 April an almost commensurate number of Allied airmen had died, 583.

The attrition rate had ebbed and flowed on a generally rising curve ending with more than 8 per cent on the Duisburg operation of 9 April. Before high-altitude battle commenced again perhaps it was time to try something new elsewhere – ops at low level where bombers could sneak in and out without being picked up on radar screens.

One of these operations would be a disaster.

SPRING

CHAPTER FIVE

THE BITTER TASTE OF PILSEN

IT was inevitable that, having caused such destruction to the Krupps war machine, Bomber Command's leaders would want their boys to visit that other great hive of armament industry, the Skoda works at Pilsen in Nazi-ruled Czechoslovakia. But it would necessitate a long trip with the danger of enemy fighters pecking away at the stream most of the way there and back. The Skoda complex was an impressive target. It produced thousands of tons of war material for the Reich, including tanks, shells and the 88 mm flak gun which was proving so formidable to Bomber Command. During the First World War it had been the arsenal for the Austro-Hungarian Empire and even at that time was second only to Krupps in armament production.

After the Nazi takeover of Czechoslovakia German engineering apprentices were sent there to work throughout the war and among their duties was to help man the flak guns which defended the factory itself. Seven miles to the south-west of the factory was the town of Dobrany, renamed Wiesengrund by the Germans, which contained a large mental hospital. As a result of the 1938 Munich dictate all its Czech inhabitants had been expelled and only Sudetan Germans were left. It was Dobrany and its mental hospital which would suffer from the Bomber Command raid of 16 April. Photoflash bomb plots would show the Skoda works had escaped practically unscathed.

Pilsen was, of course, way beyond the range of Oboe and picking up a solitary factory was outside the capabilities of H2S, which had manifested such mixed results in the previous few weeks. It would therefore require an attack in moonlight at low level for the H2S screens of the Pathfinders to then be married with what could be seen by eye.

But how low? If the fighters were not to gather around Pilsen ready to pounce as the bombers approached, Main Force would have to fly the whole of the route low enough so that the Würzburg radar screens of the *jäger-leitoffizier* waiting to vector his night fighters onto unsuspecting victims remained more or less blank instead of being filled with the bright dots of high-flying aircraft. As a distraction another low-level raid would be mounted following most of the same route then breaking away to bomb another target. The planners, who since the beginning of the year had been organising operations at heights of 20,000 feet-plus to deflect the worst of the flak and fighters, had started to readjust their thinking.

As the countdown began for the Pilsen raid there was no better example than the Stuttgart operation of how costly even a non-Ruhr target could be in moonlight if the Luftwaffe defenders were forewarned .

On 14 April, 462 aircraft set out for Stuttgart and 5 per cent failed to come back. Fierce flak caused creepback along the line of approach to the north-east of the target. It was the first time Bomber Command headquarters at High Wycombe were forced to officially recognise the problem of creepback by which some Pathfinder and Main Force crews facing the full fury of flak not unnaturally bombed the first available TI and dived for home. Eventually Harris would have to accept the inevitability of creepback as the year went on and plan aiming points beyond the area which was needed to be destroyed so that the bomb line ran through it.

As it happened, the creepback on the Stuttgart operation extended over the industrial suburb of Bad Canstatt and a large railway repair plant was damaged. Bombs also fell on factories in neighbouring districts. Only a few bombs hit the centre of Stuttgart, but one Cookie landed on an air raid shelter packed with French and Russian prisoners of war, killing 400 of them. Another 219 Germans had lost their lives and it became the highest toll to date from an RAF raid.

Notwithstanding the sizeable loss on Stuttgart the planners were able to call on 598 crews for the combined Mannheim/Pilsen operation, the biggest effort of the war so far, eclipsing the Kiel raid of two weeks before by more than 100 aircraft.

The spring was opening with a massive demonstration of power as a growing number of crews finished their training and a seemingly endless train of newly built heavy bombers left the factories, which hammered and riveted night and day. In the cold nights of January maximum efforts had averaged 150 aircraft. In the warmer weather of April the nights were turning heavy with the sound of hundreds of outbound bombers.

Even 467 Sqn at Bottesford, struggling with a diphtheria epidemic, would put up sixteen aircraft. The epidemic was taken as a warning in the fast-expanding command of what dangers might lie ahead as conscripts from all backgrounds were thrown together in hastily constructed wartime stations and germs were released in the warmer spring air.

Wireless operator Ken Harvey had just been posted in as a member of P/O John Sullivan's crew. Sgt Harvey remembers:

> Once the epidemic occurred there was no way you could get out again. We were put on ops and were told that if we landed away we would have to report to the sick bay there right away. It lasted about six weeks altogether. The first thing they did was put new drainage across the airfield.[1]

The adjutant had recorded the outbreak of diphtheria eight days before and 'all personnel were to be seen gargling at frequent intervals'. It hadn't prevented nine crews being sent to Duisburg that night. On the 9th the camp was sealed off and a WAAF died in Leicester Isolation Hospital. Sadly, because of the quarantine, nobody from the squadron was able to attend her funeral. The next day five squadron personnel were in the isolation wards being nursed through the virulent and deadly disease. It would be the end of May before leave was reinstituted and personnel were allowed off the camp but operations continued, and on 16 April the evening air at Bottesford popped and crackled as Lancasters nosed in line down the perimeter track laden for Pilsen.

The plan for both the 271 mainly Stirlings and Wellingtons going to Mannheim and the 327 Lancasters and Halifaxes headed for Pilsen required a climb-out to 13,000–15,000 feet before reaching Dungeness, then pilots would put the nose down to lose height and gain speed crossing the enemy coast and level out at 1,500–2,000 feet.

At this height they would fly across France through the *Himmelbett* night-fighter boxes on a line from Beauville to Mozieres and the other area of known *nachtjäger* activity between Luxembourg and Mannheim. As the stream approached Mannheim the Stirlings and Wellingtons would start to climb up to between 4,000 and 8,000 feet and turn north to bomb the centre of the inland port – where much industry was located.

The stronger force would continue on for Pilsen and itself climb to the same level to bomb. It was this second element, having to fly another 130 miles after the Luftwaffe was alerted by the rising and bombing aircraft of the Mannheim force, that would suffer most.

The force which assembled over eastern England that night brought families to their windows as it thundered south to cross the Thames Estuary. Bulbs were dimmed and blackout curtains drawn back to see the red and green navigation lights of the mightiest bomber fleet yet to leave Britain droning on to Dungeness and beginning to let down over the Channel.

For members of a Wellington crew from 166 Sqn a horrendous ordeal in the sea was about to begin. F/O Jack Lupton was mid-Channel almost at the 1,500–2,000 feet height required to cross the enemy coast at Cap Gris Nez when the starboard engine cut. It picked up, then both engines stopped and with little warning the Wellington dived into the ocean.

F/O Eric Hadingham, a 22-year-old Rhodesian, was in the rear turret. He remembers:

The impact was quite gentle. The turret had been facing the port beam and I was able to open the doors behind my back and tumble into the sea. The aircraft sank like a stone and there was a moment of utter panic until I realised I hadn't disconnected my oxygen supply. I tore off my helmet and floated to the surface.[2]

The rest of the crew were still in the aircraft. F/O Alan Lord, the navigator, recorded in a letter from hospital to a friend:

> I was in a cabin in total darkness, being cut and bashed about by nearly every hard object available. I remember cursing inwardly because I hadn't been killed outright. I started struggling in a futile sort of way and was suddenly amazed to find myself moving upwards without any obstruction.

The aircraft had broken its back and Lord came up to find Hadingham was aboard the self-inflating dinghy. Hadingham guided the shocked Lord to it and helped him in. 'We soon heard the bombardier [Sgt John Paul Merton*] shouting for help in the darkness, so I presume he came up through the same hole as myself,' Lord wrote.

'We found him hanging onto the pilot, who I think was already dead.' Merton was paralysed below the waist and had severe head injuries so while Lord held Lupton, Hadingham, with great difficulty, got Merton aboard. The dead pilot drifted away. There was no sign of the wireless operator, Sgt William Whitfield. The last of the bombers droned overhead on their way to Mannheim and Pilsen and Lord, Merton and Hadingham were left in their loneliness on the rolling expanse of the moonlit sea.

There was little or no cloud to hinder the navigators and bomb aimers plotting the routes of the aircraft waking towns and villages the width of France as they roared on towards Germany and the first of the two targets. Nor was there much evidence of the feared night fighters; only one aircraft – a 214 Sqn Stirling – is known to have been shot down en route, crashing near Beauvais.

But deadly light flak took its toll from the French coast to Nuremberg. One of the aircraft hit was skippered by Sgt Charles Lawrence of 12 Sqn, who had been coned over Essen on 12 March on his first operation with his own crew. He recalls:

---

* Sgt Merton was an American in the RCAF and the younger brother of the Trappist monk Thomas Merton, who post-war wrote the bestseller *The Seven Storey Mountain*.

I was some 20 miles short of Nuremberg when I was shot up by ack-ack and a shell went through the starboard outer. The engine caught fire and my flight engineer pressed the extinguisher button and I dived immediately to port away from the flames. There wasn't much room to go down because I was at about 800 feet at the time. We then got well behind on three engines and about half an hour before we were due to arrive at Pilsen I asked the navigator to give me a course to cut across the course of the returning bombers to join up with the main stream because we were at low level on a moonlit night. A forest came up so we got rid of the bomb load there.[3]

Many navigators got off track as their pilots obeyed instructions to fly low and bomb aimers struggled to pick up pinpoints. There were losses to heavy flak over gun-defended areas off the main route at Laon, Saarbrücken, Stuttgart and Nuremberg.

Some squadron commanders seem to have briefed their crews not to fly at 1,500–2,000 feet because of the danger of navigation problems taking them out of the stream. The subsequent report by Bomber Command's Operational Research Section into the combined raid recorded: 'There was considerable variation in the planned flying heights. A survey of the heights at which crews were flying when they made observations suggests that aircraft were distributed fairly evenly between 1,000 feet and 17,000 feet en route with a few even below and above these heights.'[4]

The night fighters arrived after the Stirlings and Wellingtons of the Mannheim force – now down to 205 after early returns and losses to flak – split from the stream and turned north to bomb the inland port. PFF laid their red ground markers accurately in good visibility and early arrivals bombed close to the aiming point. Later the attack drifted away, but there was moderate concentration and 130 buildings were totally destroyed, stopping or reducing production at forty-one industrial plants. The considerable scattered damage included the works of I. G. Farbenindustrie and the tank and vehicle works of Joseph Vogele, where 5.5 acres of factory space was devastated.

As the Mannheim force turned for home more night fighters arrived and were still in the area as the returning Pilsen force came back through more than an hour later. Crews would report eleven combats in the Mannheim zone.

The force tasked with destroying the Skoda factory arrived in the Pilsen area shortly after 0140 as the weather began to deteriorate into a slight drizzle, hindering problems of target identification. The Lancasters and Halifaxes thundered in from the south-west, the sound of their Merlins and Hercules filling the sky only a few thousand feet over Dobrany and the nearby village of Chlumcany.

The Skoda works lay 7 miles further on track on the western edge of Pilsen near a bend in the Radbusa river just before it joined the Mze river. But there was another bend near Dobrany, a town which now contained 10,000 Sudetan Germans. It was this the Pathfinder bomb aimers came across first on their H2S screens. The first three dropped white flares to try to visually identify the Skoda works. At 0141 one of them dropped a green TI in the mistaken belief he had pinpointed the factory complex. More Pathfinders then arrived.

Just to the east could be seen big buildings and a railway line. It couldn't be anything but Pilsen. In fact it was Dobrany, 7 miles to the south-west on the flight plan before the force should have reached the Skoda works. The big buildings were a vast mental hospital in Dobrany with factory-like tall chimneys.

From 0146 more green TIs went down and the Main Force crews now milling over the area came in, bomb doors gaping, and released their loads of high explosives and incendiaries. The complete bomb load of 249 aircraft which had reached Pilsen was going down in the wrong area. The night raid report by Bomber Command's Operational Research Section written immediately after the failed attack puts it succinctly:

> It appears that the first green TIs were dropped at Dobrany about 0146
> and that those PFF aircraft which arrived later were only able to identify
> the 'target' by means of green TIs due to drizzle and smoke and the

fact they were forced to fly above a thin layer of cloud in order to drop their markers.

They therefore all marked Dobrany and it is not surprising that the concentration of flares which lay athwart the main line of approach to the target should have attracted most of the main force so that practically all the subsequent bombing was concentrated in this area.[5]

Pathfinders would never get it so wrong again, but seldom would a town so close to an actual target copy an aiming point so faithfully in both geographical and structural terms. PFF were also having to face heavy and light flak guns in the area sending up an effective barrage to aircraft flying at an average of 4,000–8,000 feet, not the usual 20,000 feet.

Sgt Len Bradfield, a 49 Sqn bomb aimer, remembers:

Pathfinders were miles out. It was patently obvious when we got there that nobody knew what anyone else was bombing. We picked what we thought was the brewery next to the works and bombed that. Everybody was doing what they could to pick out the target. I had map-read fairly well and I confirmed with the navigator that Pathfinders hadn't found the target.[6]

Scattered conflagrations after bombing by other aircraft in two areas nearer to the Skoda works convinced some brave crews battling the flak that the Germans had lit false fires. Sgt George Stewart of 50 Sqn, who had begun his tour with the 9 April raid on Duisburg, recalls: 'It was a long haul in moonlight. The Pathfinders failed to mark the target properly and the Germans lit a lot of decoy fires. I couldn't see any sign of this mile-long factory. It was a real cock-up, with lots of aircraft shot down.'[7]

The flak guns manned by the Skoda apprentices brought a Pathfinder down over Dobrany itself. The 83 Sqn crew of P/O F. C. Milton were all killed. One of Skoda's young German workers, a Herr Schmied, of Wranova, near Mies, saw the bomber crash. He said: 'The aircraft turned to the left, caught fire and started to drop in spirals. I could see it hit something, maybe the bell tower (of St Nikolaus church in the Ringplatz).' In fact

P/O Milton's aircraft missed it, but crashed near Dobrany railway station.[8]

The heavy bombers jockeyed for position on the bomb run trying to identify the works as smoke from the wrongly placed TIs drifted across the forests south-west of Pilsen. A 44 Sqn sergeant pilot reported: 'The concentration of Lancasters and Halifaxes was more than the flak itself.' He had felt the shock waves of the bursting Cookies as he ran up at low level.[9]

The sixteen Lancasters of quarantined 467 Sqn at Bottesford all made it to the target area with their CO, W/Cdr Gomm. The adjutant's office detailed later: 'Our crews were able to bomb factory buildings, railway sidings and installations which they could see through the clouds of smoke from fierce fires.' The buildings, railway lines and 'installations' were in fact all in Dobrany.

The report went on: 'There was a small amount of fairly effective flak. The residential area was practically untouched, the whole area was covered by fires with bombs bursting among them. W/Cdr Gomm said the PFF flares ignited too low so burned on the ground and formed a fairly efficient smoke screen.'[10] In fact the smoke was from the burning woods north of Dobrany which had been set alight.

The mental hospital at Dobrany was laid out in blocks and had a boilerhouse, a tall chimney and a water tower, giving it the look of an industrial complex. South of it was a former cavalry barracks of the Austro-Hungarian Empire now being used as a military hospital for the wounded of Stalingrad. Both the mental hospital and the military hospital were hit by many bombs and eyewitnesses said 300 people, including many women patients, had died in the insane asylum and the military hospital. The Nazi propaganda machine claimed 1,000 wounded soldiers had died.

Eyewitnesses said later that the buildings of Dobrany, mainly bungalows, 'burnt like hell', fires from one side of a road connecting to another to form 'a flame roof'. The baroque tower of one of Dobrany's two historic churches collapsed after the raid. It was temporarily repaired and later when it was replaced a time-capsule letter was found from the then burgomeister, Herr Schwanig, reading: 'The bulb-shaped baroque tower was destroyed by fire in the dreadful night of British bombing. All five bells, the clocktower and the steps to the tower were destroyed, 261 buildings and sheds were destroyed by fire or destruction bombs and 224 [sic] people died.'[11]

A squadron leader of 77 Sqn was typical of the courageous captains who thought they had struck a major blow at the enemy armaments industry. He bombed at 0144 from 8,500 feet and reported at debriefing: 'Viz fairly clear. Bombs dropped on buildings illuminated by incendiaries. These buildings had tall chimneys. HEs were seen to be throwing up debris in the target area, while a few incendiaries were seen burning.'[12] His photoflash would in fact show his bombs had gone down on the southern edge of the bombing arca, ncar Chlumcany, miles from the Skoda plant.

Another 77 Sqn senior captain reported: 'Bombs dropped from 7,000 feet. A big factory seen in bomb sight on release of bombs.' His load would show on the bomb plot later prepared by High Wycombe's Operational Research Section as having gone down on the western edge of Dobrany. A third 77 Sqn skipper, F/Sgt J. S. Lea, reported dropping his bombs at 10,000 feet 'when the railway line was in the bomb sight and the target appeared to be one mass of fires'. As he turned away, a Ju88 was seen on the port quarter. 'It closed in and opened fire from 600 yards,' he reported. 'I dived to port and the rear gunner replied with a three-second burst from about 400 yards, but no results were observed and the aircraft was lost to sight.'[13]

It may have been the same Ju88 that then attacked T-Tommy of the squadron flown by P/O Richard Fitzgerald. He told debriefing officers it closed in from above and astern at 14,000 feet and opened fire at the same distance as the attack on F/Sgt Lea. As P/O Fitzgerald took violent

RIGHT The photo-flash bomb plot prepared by Bomber Command's Operational Research Section after the Pilsen raid of 16 April 1943. It clearly shows only one bomb load on the Skoda works; most of the rest have fallen on Dobrany and Chlumcany, demonstrating the difficulties of accurate target marking beyond Oboe range.

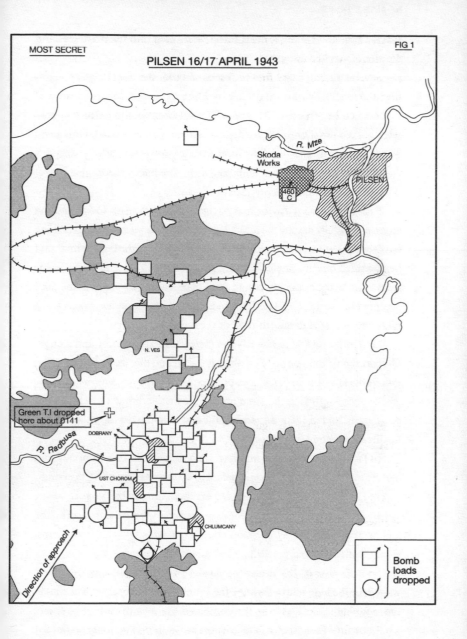

FIG 1

PILSEN 16/17 APRIL 1943

R. Mze

Skoda Works

PILSEN

460 C

N. VES

Green T.I dropped here about 0141

DOBRANY

R. Radbusa

UST CHOROM

CHLUMCANY

Direction of approach

Bomb loads dropped

135

evasive action his rear gunner's tracers streamed into the blackness and the aircraft banked away.[14]

Several aircraft made two or three runs over the target area trying to find a green TI. A warrant officer of 9 Sqn expressed the frustration of many when he reported: 'No green TI until after bombing. Illuminators seen, but did not illuminate factory on first run nor on second. Only river, wood and built-up area.' Making more than one run over a heavily defended target at low level was not attempted lightly. The pilot's report also stated: 'Flak hole in port wing, aerial shot away'.[15]

F/Sgt Claremont Taylor had navigated G-George of 460 Sqn to the target successfully despite the difficulties of the low-level route. 'On reaching the Danube I estimated another ten minutes to go, but the bomb aimer said he identified our nominated turning point,' F/Sgt Taylor recorded in his log book. 'As the bomb aimer had been map reading throughout the pilot accepted his position. A later plot indicated my position was correct. On ETA we were 28 miles north-west of the target.'

G-George, unable to identify the target, turned for home and a target of opportunity. But one 460 Sqn aircraft would find the Skoda works. F/Sgt P/O Eddie Hudson, in C-Charlie, bombed the south-western corner of the vast complex at 0141 at the same time as the first Pathfinder green TI went down over Dobrany. 'He was among the first to bomb the target,' 460 Sqn's intelligence section would record.[16]

In fact Hudson was the only one to do so, the sole aircraft of 327 that had set out more than four hours before to achieve its object. All the bombs except Hudson's that had been loaded earlier in the day had gone to waste, as had all the fuel brought at great expense across the Atlantic and all the labour of airmen and WAAFs on countless RAF stations, arming guns, checking electrics and preparing food, maps and paperwork.

Soon the lives of 181 airmen would also be going to waste as the fighters waited for the long return flight of the Pilsen force against the wind and in the moonlight. The loss from the combined Mannheim and Pilsen forces would be fifty-four aircraft, the greatest attrition on any night so far. Sgt Stewart remembers:

About half an hour after leaving the target we had the moon behind us and a night fighter came up behind and from about 1,000 yards away started pumping cannon shells at us. I could see the tracer coming slowly in then whipping past us. We were taking evasive action, but the rear gunner said he couldn't engage him as he was out of range, so I jumped onto the front guns thinking I would get him going by. But he seemed able just to hold off. We were corkscrewing and knew it was only a matter of time before we were hit, but we were lucky, dived into a cloud and escaped. I couldn't understand how he could slow down so much.[17]

F/Sgt D. B. Moodie of 460 Sqn related that he'd had to jettison his bombs south-east of Nuremberg at 0225 hours when he was attacked by a night fighter at 8,000 feet. He had been seeking a secondary target after being unable to locate the primary 'through lack of detail'.[18] The Cookie and three 1,000-lb bombs were released in such a hurry as Moodie corkscrewed away from the fighter that the bomb doors were buckled by the weapons passing through. His rear gunner scored hits on the fighter's fuselage and it broke off the attack.

Moodie was one of the lucky ones. Under the full moon the Luftwaffe would begin pecking at the bomber stream all the way from burning Mannheim to Trier and continue across France and Belgium. Some aircraft were still over France as dawn was breaking.

F/Sgt Jack Murray in G-George of 460 Sqn decided to have the bomb aimer drop the Cookie and three 1,000-lb bombs on Koblenz as they followed the Rhine. They expected a barrage of flak as they were alone over the city at 6,000 feet. But the only thing that came up was the escape hatch over the pilot's head, lifted by the explosion of the Cookie just over a mile below, which gave the aircraft 'a hell of a belt' and caused some surprise to a second-dickey pilot, Sgt Walter Pridgeon.

Fickle fate would select some squadrons for attrition more than others. The Commonwealth squadrons were particularly unfortunate. The Canadian 408 Sqn, one of the founding squadrons of 6 Group on 1 January, lost four of the twelve Halifaxes it sent to Pilsen; 460 (RAAF) Sqn lost three, as did W/Cdr Gomm's 467 (RAAF) Sqn.

At Snaith RAF 51 Sqn had five aircraft missing, but it was Linton-on-Ouse which suffered the biggest blow. The base's 76 Sqn lost three and another three were lost by 78 Sqn, which shared the airfield. The mid-upper gunner of one of the 76 Sqn aircraft was 17, a Canadian who had fooled the authorities. It was a sad scene in the operations room at Linton as waiting WAAFs slowly realised so few were coming back.

Sgt Cliff Hill, mid-upper gunner in Sgt Herb Hoover's 76 Sqn crew on the Pilsen operation, remembers the shocked atmosphere the next day as the empty dispersals signposted so clearly that six crews had not returned to Linton. He says:

> Three of us in Sgt Hoover's crew shared a large oak-panelled room at Beningbrough Hall with three other aircrew who were on this operation and were among the missing. They had only been with us for about a week. In fact all of the ones who were lost hadn't been with the squadron more than a month. The following morning we saw our roommates' beds were empty. It wasn't a very nice feeling. After almost ten hours in the air we had slept late, going to lunch after 1 p.m. When we arrived back all their possessions had gone.
>
> There was a sense of shock on the airfield, more with the ground crew. They would have waved them off and later seen the empty dispersals until replacement aircraft were flown in. The aircrew tended not to discuss it; you kept your feelings to yourself. Having previously lost two flight commanders in consecutive months, S/Ldr James Fletcher over Berlin and F/Lt Tony Hull on the way back from Frankfurt, and numerous other aircrew, our attitude tended to harden.[19]

In all, thirty-six aircraft were lost from the Pilsen operation, a huge 11 per cent, and to no avail. From the successful Mannheim raid eighteen were missing, 6.6 per cent. Another fifty-four aircraft in the Pilsen force were damaged by flak and fighter attack and an additional forty-one of the Mannheim element returned with damage. Several of these aircraft would never fly again. If a grain of comfort was to be found it was that a surprisingly large number of aircrew evaded capture, twenty-eight in total, and would rejoin the fight.

Within hours the German apprentices at Skoda would be drafted in for clearing-up operations at Dobrany. Among them was Herr Schmied, who had seen P/O Milton's aircraft crash. He reported: 'The morning after the attack I took a look at the wreck. The left wing was missing, the trunk was broken, but not too much burned.'[20]

That night some of the residents of Pilsen would break the law and risk tuning in to the BBC. They heard that their armament works had been heavily damaged, as RAF intelligence officers at first thought it had. 'The people of Pilsen were astonished when they listened,' a resident, V. Kratky, wrote. 'When they went to work in the Skoda factory the next day everything was in place and the production of weapons could continue without distraction.'[21]

In England there was the usual inquest by Bomber Command's Operational Research Section who had to explain the huge losses to Harris and his senior officers. The ORS report, which had earlier noted that bombers had been observed flying anywhere between 1,000 feet and 17,000 feet, concluded:

> In conditions favourable to both fighters and light flak part of our bomber force flew at heights offering no difficulty to fighters and the remainder at heights offering good opportunities to light flak. This resulted in heavy losses to both of those forms of defence.
>
> The cause of the heavier loss sustained by the Pilsen force is not clear. There is no evidence that more than three aircraft were destroyed in the target area or that many losses occurred on that part of the route not common to both the bomber forces. It is possible that the increasing effectiveness of the defences, as shown by the greater night-fighter effort made against the returning bombers, continued throughout the operation and therefore fell with greater severity against the Pilsen force, which returned later.[22]

One other person conducted his own inquest into the Pilsen debacle, Air Vice Marshal Don Bennett, the Pathfinders chief. Clifford Hill remembers: 'AVM Bennett went round the groups raising hell. It was the Pathfinders who had committed the initial error, marking the wrong buildings as the target.'[23]

A crew still remained to be accounted for in the Pilsen/Mannheim losses: that of F/O Lupton, which had gone down in the Channel as the 598 aircraft had set out. The ordeal of the survivors was just beginning.

As the last of the returning bombers passed over the Channel in the dawn, F/O Hadingham was coming to in the dinghy after twice passing out in the night. The first time he awoke he discovered that the deeply religious Sgt Merton, who had been fingering his rosary beads and praying after being helped into the dinghy, had died. 'It was light, the sea was absolutely dead still and there was a heavy sea fog with visibility about 10 feet at the most,' he recorded later. 'There was no sound, wreckage from the aircraft had disappeared and we felt very strange and lonely. A really eerie situation. I was scared.'[24]

When the fog lifted at about 11 a.m. Hadingham and Lord discovered they were near the French coast and could see buildings on it. 'We didn't want to be picked up by the Germans or the French so made no attempt to attract the attention of the few small vessels that passed close to us,' Hadingham wrote.

The day wore on, the sea remained calm but the two – without water, as the dinghy pack had been lost – began to get very thirsty in the hot sun. A few aircraft flew overhead, too high to wave to. They drifted away from the French coast and the sun went down. They had taken stock of their supplies and found they only had one escape pack between them. It amounted to thirty Horlicks tablets, a bar of chocolate and a tube of condensed milk. Hadingham and Lord slept fitfully that night, waking occasionally to pump air into the dinghy.

The next day dawned with another fog over the calm sea. As the fog lifted, the two discovered they had drifted back towards the French coast and were even closer in than on the previous day. The sun beat down and in the afternoon they drifted further out into the Channel. 'That evening we each had a Horlicks tablet and a small portion of condensed milk,' Hadingham wrote.

As Hadingham and Lord ate their meagre supper 170 Lancasters left their bases to fly south to bomb the dockyard at La Spezia. The bombing spread to the north-west and the main railway station and central buildings were hit, but in comparison to two nights before only one Lancaster was lost.

The dawn came up again with a breeze that started to pitch the dinghy, but it was moving in the direction of the English coast. Hadingham remembered:

> We had picked up some pieces of driftwood and using them as paddles we tried to reach various buoys and markers that we could see. Despite the breeze it was still very hot and Alan was getting very burned about the face and hands. We rationed ourselves to two more Horlicks tablets and a taste of condensed milk.

Lord wrote:

> I had received a bad cut over the right eye when we crashed and although I did not know it at the time there was a large hole in my left arm just above the elbow from which I lost a lot of blood. Consequently I was very weak and had to be assisted into a sitting position by Hadingham every time we used the paddles.[25]

AT Linton Sgt Clifford Hill and the rest of Sgt Hoover's crew took advantage of the spring sunshine. The Pilsen raid had been their nineteenth operation. After such a beating it was time to enjoy life while they could. Sgt Hill remembers:

> There came our initial introduction to the Alice Hawthorn country pub at Nun Monkton, ferried across the river behind Beningbrough by the good Captain Nick, a silent character who would appear from nowhere across the stretch of water as he saw us standing on the opposite bank. He was always able to convey without words that it was he who was doing us a favour in letting us share his boat, charging

two pennies per person across and sixpence for the journey back.

An evening at the Alice Hawthorn was something to savour. Its atmosphere would allow one to forget the war for a few hours. There was a lounge with a small wind-up gramophone with, I recall, a number of Inkspot records, 'Whispering Grass' and 'Java Jive' etc. Outside was a stretch of grass on which we used to sit in warmer temperatures.[26]

IN the Channel the night of the 19th passed fitfully for Lord and Hadingham. They woke to find they could just see the cliffs of Dover. Hadingham wrote:

> This heartened us tremendously. But as the day progressed they receded and once more we neared the French coast. Our hopes of rescue were beginning to diminish and after much anguished discussion we finally decided to commit John Paul's body to the sea. This we did in as Christian a manner as possible. His body remained afloat and in the vicinity of the dinghy for the remainder of the day. We hadn't thought of this happening and were most distressed.

That night as 339 aircraft set out for Stettin on another experiment in low-level, long-distance raiding, Hadingham and Lord continued to drift in the Channel. They awoke the next day in deteriorating weather to face a cold wind and rough sea. During the previous afternoon the Typhoon patrol guarding against nuisance raids on south coast ports had flown over. F/O Hadingham had summoned his strength and stood up in the dinghy, waving in a bid to attract its attention. The only result had been that he had fallen in the sea, then brought salt water flooding across the floor of the rubber boat as he clambered back in. Both he and Alan Lord had been too weary to bale it out.

Two evenings previously they had eaten two Horlicks tablets each and finished off the tube of condensed milk from the dinghy rations. The only sustenance they then had left was four of the tablets. They were now so parched Hadingham had considered cutting himself to drink some of his own blood. As the bombers had flown out to Stettin he had finally given up hope. The dinghy was losing air and, weak as he was, Hadingham had to desperately keep pumping with the bellows.

The first rays of light through cloud revealed a heaving dark sea with waves occasionally breaking. Hadingham recorded:

A number of small coastal vessels passed quite close to us and aircraft were flying to and fro overhead. They all went about their business and we eventually stopped even trying to attract their attention. Although we were not consciously aware of the fact, this was our sixth day afloat and the outlook was grim. I began to think more and more about my family; by now they would know I had gone missing and while there was always the chance I might have survived as a PoW, it was a pretty slim one. The chance that I might have survived in a dinghy was a great deal slimmer.

Suddenly a strong easterly wind sprang up and at about 10 a.m. Lord and Hadingham began holding the shelter tarpaulin as a makeshift sail. Lord later wrote:

We sat on either side of the dinghy holding up the tarpaulin until our arms almost dropped off. We bowled merrily westward from 10 a.m. until about 4.30 p.m. and sure enough we soon saw white cliffs ahead and about 3 a.m. we were only three miles or so from Dover, the nearest we had ever been to land. But the wind suddenly dropped and our progress stopped. We tried paddling for half an hour, but made hardly any headway and reduced ourselves to complete exhaustion.

In the late afternoon Lord and Hadingham lay listlessly in their drifting dinghy in the Channel slowly dying from dehydration. They watched the Typhoon patrol come out and fly near and over their 4 ft 6 in boat several times over the next two hours without seeing them, its pilots looking for Luftwaffe fighters. 'When one of these planes flew right over us at a height of about 50 feet without seeing our frantic evolutions with the tarpaulin, our language was scarcely civilised,' Lord recorded.

Then dramatically the downed airmen's luck changed. 'The second Typhoon suddenly broke formation and came swooping down towards us, continuing to circle our dinghy,' Lord wrote. 'For a long time I couldn't believe we had been spotted at last until the first machine also came swooping over us and waggled his wings.'

Hadingham remembers: 'I was delirious with joy and waved frantically as the two planes circled us. Eventually they flew off, but we knew that they would have radioed our position and that help would soon be on its way.'

An RAF photographic team had been stationed at the Dover Air Sea Rescue Station for some time, waiting to record an actual rescue for an ASR instruction manual. So far each call-out had been for German airmen, which, while it might have been an encouraging sign of the direction the war was taking, did nothing towards fulfilling their brief.

The team leaped aboard one of the two ASR launches heading out for Lord and Hadingham's dinghy and clicked away as the downed airmen were spotted and brought aboard to be transported to Dover Hospital. Hadingham recalls:

> Within a few hours of our rescue a violent storm broke over the Channel and we were told there was no way our tiny little dinghy would have survived the maelstrom. We were spoilt by the staff at the hospital in Dover and had an endless number of visitors including the Mayor of Dover.

Lord and Hadingham were soon transferred to the RAF hospital at Halton, Buckinghamshire. 'While we were there the Sunday papers published the story of the rescue together with some of the photographs,' Hadingham remembers. 'We were treated like heroes.'

The tragic Pilsen/Mannheim records could at last register a note of triumph. But this was not the end of the Pilsen story. On 13 May, 120 Lancasters of Harris's favoured 5 Group went to Pilsen to see whether with the help of thirty-six Pathfinders they could find and hit the important Skoda works where so many had failed in the disastrous raid of almost a month before. They couldn't and nine aircraft were lost. But this time the bombing fell in open country to the north. Dobrany to the south was spared and the route to and from the target had been at a much greater height band. Skoda armaments production would continue uninterrupted for almost three more years, until an attack by the USAAF destroyed major sections of the factory.

By then low-level operations were a matter of history for Bomber Command. But before the second Pilsen raid and only four days after the first a second low-level long distance operation had been laid on by Bomber Command headquarters.

Again the losses would be high, but ironically it proved to be the most successful raid out of Oboe range during the period of the Battle of the Ruhr.

CHAPTER SIX

THE TOSS OF A COIN

THE low-level flight plan to raid Stettin in the moon period had already been formulated before the Pilsen operation that had resulted in such huge losses and rapid recalculation by aircrew of their chances of surviving a tour. There was little question of abandoning the plan and it was considered the northern route over Denmark and the Baltic would result in fewer casualties. As it turned out, the planners were right, though the losses would still be a worryingly high 6.2 per cent. Such losses could not be sustained. Even a constant 5 per cent meant that after twenty such operations all the crews on a squadron would have gone, ten trips short of the magic number that completed a tour.

The operation was designed to aid the Russians by eliminating supplies being stored for shipping to the Eastern Front, so came under the 'political' umbrella of the Casablanca Directive, but many airmen were told at briefing it was the RAF's present to Hitler on his birthday. The prospect of another low-level operation, after the Pilsen raid only four nights before had proved how dangerous this could be, did not go down well with aircrew. Groans echoed round briefing rooms throughout Britain's bomber counties as the flight plan was revealed.

Crews were told that, as with the Pilsen operation, there would be a heavy diversionary raid to distract the defences, with eighty-six Stirlings on the battle order to attack the Heinkel factory near Rostock. A few Mosquitos would also drop bombs on Berlin to further confuse the fighter controllers.

By the night's end the combined operations would have delivered another thirty-five aircrew into the Reich's prisoner-of-war camps – now showing visible signs of the increasing RAF offensive as their populations grew – one of them arriving after a terrifying ordeal at the hands of German civilians. Before the year was over nearly 3,000 young bomber crew would be looking at life from behind the wire. A whole network was being built up in England and Switzerland to cater for their needs, and in Germany to keep them out of the war.

The route to Stettin would take aircraft over the North Sea at 3,000 to 5,000 feet, then, before crossing the Danish coast, 1 Group's Lancasters would descend to 1,000 feet, 6 Group's Halifaxes would go down to a breathtaking 500 feet or less, and 4 and 5 Group's Halifaxes and Lancasters would cross Denmark on loose orders of 'as low as possible'. All groups would climb in the final stages across the Baltic and none of them were to bomb at above 12,000 feet, then they would all descend to minimum height until well on the way home. The eighty-six Stirling crews who would accompany this force would also be required to fly as low as safety allowed, then at Drasser Point north-east of Rostock they would break away to attack the Heinkel works as the rest flew on to bomb Stettin.

The attack on Stettin would be opened at 0100 with red TIs by three Pathfinders using their H2S equipment, the Rostock raid shortly before, again with the aid of H2S. It was hoped the coastal outlines would help Bennett's Pathfinders to mark the target accurately. They did and the Stettin raid proved a tremendous coup for PFF, smarting somewhat after leading Main Force astray in so spectacular a fashion at Pilsen.

In the cool afternoon at Middleton St George, near Darlington, as the battle order went up for 419 Sqn, F/Sgt Edwin Jury looked to see which spare crewman would be flying with him as the second gunner on D-Dog. He was pleased to see it was F/Sgt Dennis Watkins, who had completed two tours and was acting as a gunnery instructor on the squadron.

D-Dog had had its mid-upper turret removed to give the Mk II Halifax more height and speed. Instead it now carried a ventral gun position, not popular with gunners called to man this position on the fuselage floor, because of the lack of visibility and mobility.

Both F/Sgt Watkins and F/Sgt Jury normally occupied a rear turret with its four Brownings and neither fancied the ventral position. As they waited to go out to the aircraft the two gunners ruled there was only one way to decide it. Watkins spun a coin with Jury and won the toss. Watkins would go in the rear turret, but to ease Jury's disappointment he offered to swap over for the return trip.

To the south G-George of 460 Sqn was being prepared at Breighton for F/Sgt Murray and his crew on the last trip of their tour. Sgt Pridgeon, who had accompanied them as second dickey to Pilsen, was taking his own crew on their first operation in J-Jig. It was 9.30 p.m. as the Merlin engines of the first of the squadron's Lancasters bellowed across the grass and it rumbled with growing speed along the runway and up into the night sky. Its pilot and those of the other 444 aircraft for both targets swept on over the North Sea, watching waves glinting in the moonlight, then descended as they approached the Danish coast, nervously gripping juddering control columns as they flew under the beams of German radar.

For many crews there was the welcome sight of Danes greeting the bombers as they roared overhead. Air gunner Cliff Hill in the 76 Sqn crew of the newly commissioned Herbert Hoover remembers: 'It was full moonlight that night as we flew low over Denmark just above roof-top height. I remember the Danish people sitting at open bedroom windows and waving to us. Hoover had to lift the aircraft over windmills, we were so low.'[1]

As the aircraft flew on across Denmark, however, light gun batteries began opening up and alerted flak ships in the Baltic. F/Sgt Jury in D-Dog saw aircraft falling one after the other. 'They were going down like ninepins and nobody had a chance to get out,' he remembers. 'They were going straight into the deck; it was most frightening to see.'[2]

Sgt Herbert Fuhrmann of 460 Sqn had to abort his attack after fire from a flak ship south-east of Mon Island damaged his Lancaster's port outer, the starboard fin and the bomb doors. It also put between twenty and thirty holes through the fuselage between the mid-upper and the rear turret and wounded the navigator in the thigh.[3]

The Lancasters, Halifaxes and the few Stirlings climbed over the north German coast for their bomb runs on Stettin and found the Pathfinders' red and green TIs already glowing ahead. But the heavy flak from dug-in positions now began to take its toll. The port outer of Sgt Fuhrmann's aircraft packed up and the crew were warned to prepare for a bale-out as he headed for Sweden. The bomb load was jettisoned.

The aircraft of a 20-year-old 9 Sqn skipper was hit by flak over Stettin before his aircraft could bomb. 'The port outer engine caught fire and a fire started in the cockpit under the pilot's seat,' he reported later. 'The port wing tip was hit and the port side of the fuselage was hit. The fires were extinguished.' But he added that at low level 'the explosion of bombs caused severe damage to the aircraft'.[4]

A pall of smoke which would rise to 10,000 feet was building over the port and began to spiral above the aircraft unloading their Cookies and incendiaries in red and white flashes below. In total nearly 600 people would die as residential areas along with industrial premises caught fire from the rain of incendiaries.

To the west Rostock had been covered by a smokescreen alerted by the Stettin force and the bombing had been scattered, but night fighters and flak claimed eight Stirlings, 6.6 per cent of the force. The captain of a 214 Sqn Stirling was on its bomb run east of the Heinkel works when a flak burst damaged the port inner engine and sent shrapnel through the fuselage, hitting him in the leg. The bomb aimer had to take over the controls for an hour until the wounded pilot could regain his seat.

Another of the squadron's captains reported later that he was 'repeatedly shot at by flak en route'. Evasive action made it too late for him to reach the primary target and he had to jettison his bombs near Naksov. Then a fighter swept in, blasting the rear turret and tailplane and fatally wounding the rear gunner. No fewer than four 214 Sqn aircraft would return with wounded on board.[5]

The night fighters were now moving in over Stettin. One of the first to be hit was D-Dog of 419 Sqn. F/Sgt Jury remembers:

Two Me110s came in directly from behind and hit us with their .5 mm cannons. We were full of incendiaries that night. As the fighters attacked, the rear turret was knocked out, the aircraft immediately caught fire in the bomb bay and the intercom went. The fire was so intense with the incendiaries going up, I knew it was the end for us. I reached for my chest pack, clipped it on, then turned the lever on the escape hatch near the ventral position. It fell out and out I went. I counted to ten and pulled the ripcord. Unfortunately I hadn't tightened the leg straps on my harness and as the chute opened there was the most appalling pain in my testicles. It was so painful I thought about twisting the quick release box and letting myself go. It was terrible.

I could see the burning aircraft diving away below me and the two Me110s flying around and I thought they were coming to finish me off. As I got near the ground I saw I was heading for a forest so I pulled on the risers to swing away. I landed about 20 feet away from the woods near a place called Eberswalde to the north of Berlin.[6]

Over the Baltic, E-Easy of 460 Sqn was now maintaining height after jettisoning its bombs, so Sgt Fuhrmann abandoned the plan to bale out over Sweden and set a course for home. The squadron's G-George was also over the Baltic at this time. On the way out from Stettin following a railway line the bomb aimer, W/O Tom Osborn, had taken advantage of flying low level to climb into the front turret and shoot up a train. It had stopped, blowing steam. The crew's navigator, Claremont Taylor, remembers:

The Baltic was very active with light flak and we saw quite a number shot down. As it was the last trip of our tour the pilot said, 'Let's get out of here', so we diverted well to the north, climbed up to 7,000–8,000 feet and after crossing Denmark continued out to the west to avoid the Frisian Islands before turning for home.[7]

It was as the returning bombers crossed the Baltic from Stettin to Denmark that the night fighters gathered en masse to pick off the bombers trying to avoid the flak ships. One crew reported seeing nine aircraft go down. The unlucky 100 Sqn, which had lost two crews on the Pilsen operation, was about to lose its CO. W/Cdr J. Swain cleared the dangerous Baltic and Denmark but was shot down as he left the west coast. None of the crew survived. A Stirling Pathfinder of 7 Sqn was flying on three engines after being hit by flak. As it neared the island of Sjaelland off the east coast of Denmark an Me110 opened fire, hitting the fuselage with cannon and machine gun. The second pass set the wing tanks on fire and the captain, F/Lt Charles Parish, ordered the crew to abandon as the aircraft went into a steep dive.

Sgt David Smith,* the Canadian flight engineer, was the only one to escape, climbing up to the rear hatch by using cannon-shell holes in the floor as a ladder. As he reached the hatch the slipstream pulled him out, his chute pack dangling above his head. With difficulty he reached up for the D-ring and pulled the ripcord at less than 1,000 feet.

The 460 Sqn aircraft of F/Sgt Kenneth James was also shot down over Denmark. Residents of Vestbirk in eastern Jutland woke up at 3.30 a.m. to hear a low-flying aircraft under attack by a night fighter. They saw the Lancaster catch fire then dive into the ground. The entire crew was killed. In all, three Lancasters were lost by the Australian squadron on the Stettin raid. The second was that of Sgt Walter Pridgeon, second dickey to F/Sgt Murray on the Pilsen raid. The third was the Lancaster of F/Sgt Reg Hogben, the 20-year-old Australian whose crew had been the first to bomb on the Pilsen raid four nights before. He and his crew vanished without trace.

A total of twenty-one aircraft failed to return from Stettin to add to the eight from Rostock. Of the ones which taxied into their dispersals from Stettin, fifty-two had flak damage; from Rostock fourteen would need drastic repair. Many crews showed their resentment at debriefing about the low-level planning, the adjutant of 100 Sqn recording for instance: 'The view was expressed that many aircraft were lost owing to flying low.'[8] A senior pilot on 460 Sqn reported that 'he saw no virtue in the low-flying

---

* Sgt Smith evaded and was taken by small boat to neutral Sweden, the first Bomber Command airman to evade from Denmark. He got back to Britain in July and was awarded the DFM.

tactics'. Another 460 Sqn crew also recorded bitterly: 'Several aircraft were seen shot down entirely due to low flying.'[9]

Some had found the experience of facing flak at low level where there was no chance to escape too nerve-racking to bear. Sgt George Stewart of 50 Sqn remembers:

> In Lincoln after the raid I met a fellow bomb aimer I knew on another squadron and he was white with shock. He told me he was up for being stamped Lack of Moral Fibre. His aircraft was being hit by flak ships over the Baltic, which were pretty good. He panicked and as they went over the land he jettisoned the bombs at 500 feet. The aircraft turned half on its back and it was only for a hillside deflecting the blast it was saved.[10]

F/Sgt Charles Lawrence of 12 Sqn was flying his fourth operation in a week including being shot up on the Pilsen raid and found the low flying required tough duty. 'We were on Gee initially for the raid, but it cut out early because of jamming and you were left with dead reckoning,' he says. 'Unless you plotted your course pretty well and knew where the high ground was, you were in trouble. I think some of the casualties were from aircraft flying into the ground.'[11] F/Sgt Lawrence had landed back at Wickenby after a seven and a half-hour trip with a holed petrol tank from a flak burst over Stettin.

Among the last of the Stettin aircraft to cross the North Sea was that of Sgt Fuhrmann. He finally brought his badly damaged aircraft into Breighton at 7.10 a.m. after a harrowing nine hour and thirty-three minute flight. The shocked Fuhrmann was immediately ordered to bed by the medical officer. His bomb aimer, F/O C. B. Anderson, gave the raid details at debriefing. Fuhrmann would soon receive a DFM for his efforts that night and his bomb aimer the DFC. Both were killed on a Remscheid operation at the end of July.

THE next morning as reconnaissance pilots were being alerted to establish what a success in terms of damage the Stettin raid had been, F/Sgt Jury woke in the woods near Eberswalde and weighed his chances of evading capture in the Reich. As with many downed airmen his flying boots had fallen off as the chute snapped open and he had put his leather gauntlets on his feet and started shuffling by the forest he had landed alongside.* 'I heard some people coming who sounded as if they had been to a party, so I hid in the bushes all night,' he recalls.[12]

In the early dawn his freedom was about to come to an end:

I saw some Volksturm troops with an Alsatian dog looking for my crew and heading my way. They fired at me, so I put my hands up and shouted 'Engländer' and they still fired at me. Fortunately they weren't very good shots. The dog came up and sniffed me and wandered away. Then I was taken into Eberswalde and as I shuffled through the village women came out in their nightgowns and started spitting at me and hitting me. A Wehrmacht officer came along on a bicycle, got his revolver out and put me up against a wall. I thought, 'This is the end', but he turned it round on the people. If it wasn't for him they would have torn me to pieces.

The crowd demanded that something be done to me, so he bashed the daylights out of me. He knocked me to the ground, kicked me, picked me up, then bashed me around repeatedly. I was taken to the police station bleeding profusely. I was told the Gestapo was coming to question me.

The Gestapo turned up on the second night. F/Sgt Jury says:

They kept pointing at maps and asking, 'Where did you come from?' I just gave them my name, rank and number, then they found a dagger I flew with. They said, 'You got this to kill German troops.' I said 'No', and pointed to a can of orange juice I'd had with me and thrust the dagger into it to open it to show why I'd had the knife. They laughed their heads off, but I didn't find it very funny.

---

* The RAF went to many lengths to provide aircrew with escape kits, but their efforts were negated by the 1941-pattern suede flying boot which invariably came off in a parachute descent, leaving the airmen with little chance of walking home. Eventually the design was modified with an adjustable strap round the ankle. Later in 1943 the escape boot was issued which came with a knife to cut off the calves and leave a pair of normal walking shoes. The calves themselves could be tied into a warm waistcoat.

Then I was put on show in the village hall full of women. The jailer took me and said, 'You must not escape or we shoot' and I was paraded around. There were about forty or fifty people there; nearly all were curious rather than aggressive. They asked me questions such as 'Do you have ration books in England?' 'Do you eat well?' 'Have you a lady friend or wife?'

Later the Gestapo took F/Sgt Jury to see the wreckage of his aircraft. They kicked aside a piece of engine cowling to reveal the body of F/Sgt Watkins. F/Sgt Jury reflected that if he had won the toss for who would occupy the rear turret, he not Watkins would be lying there.

More torment was to follow for F/Sgt Jury when he was put in the sweat box at Dulag Luft. He says that after he had refused to talk for five days the interrogator 'pulled out an RAF book with "Secret" on the cover. I was amazed at what they said was in it. They knew the name of my flight commander. The interrogator promised me cigarettes and that they would take me out of the sweat box if I talked, but I wouldn't. Finally the Red Cross arrived in the camp and they had to put me in a holding cell.' He was later transferred to Stalag Luft I at Barth and learned that all but Watkins had survived the shooting down. Watkins's DFM came through a few weeks later.

Barth was one of three camps for RAF prisoners now beginning to feel the first intimations of overcrowding. Within two months the 1,700 NCO population of Stalag Luft III at Sagan would be moved to a new camp at Heydrekrug and Sagan expanded for officers only, as RAF prisoners of war Goering had never expected to see began arriving in the Reich on a weekly basis. At Stalag IVB at Mühlberg a whole compound would have to be constructed within an existing Russian prisoner-of-war camp just to house Allied aircrew and others such as paratroopers who might be likely to escape. Two more huge prisoner-of-war camps would be designated RAF only and aircrew would be distributed in large numbers to army prisoner-of-war camps within the greater Reich.

A supportive network in England was growing by the day to cater for the needs of British and Commonwealth troops behind the wire and those of their worried relatives at home. A magazine, *The Prisoner of War*, was produced each month by the Red Cross and was available free to relatives of prisoners of war. It included knitting patterns for gloves, for thick three-ply socks and for warm waistcoats to go in next-of-kin parcels. It also answered the anxious questions of relatives, which ranged from 'Can I send a coloured photograph of myself to my fiancé?', to which the answer was 'Yes', to 'Can I send my husband his civilian sports jacket?', to which the answer was, not surprisingly, 'No'.

In a spring issue the honorary secretary of the Old Etonians Association asked the next-of-kin of OEs for the addresses of their camps so that communications from the association could be dispatched to them. In the previous edition Penguin listed the ten most popular books they had been asked to send to prison camp libraries. They included Jane Austin's *Northanger Abbey*, Vita Sackville West's *Passenger to Teheran* and *The Dark Flower* by John Galsworthy. Relatives were advised that works by J. B. Priestley, who was making popular BBC radio broadcasts at the time, were banned, as were any books by Jews.

Many prisoners were using the enforced incarceration to improve their technical skills, a pursuit encouraged by the Germans, who wanted prisoners of war to visualise time behind the wire as long-term rather than temporary, and one early 1943 issue read:

> An RAF sergeant from Clacton writes from VIIIB of the excellent study facilities at the camp. In the main school there are classes in agricultural knowledge, advertising, veterinary work and hotel management. The sergeant has just been asked to take over a class of 60 to 80 in Elementary Automobile Engineering. 'Preparing lectures and attending them keeps me busy and seems to make time fly', he says.

But a truer picture of the boredom and strangeness of prison camp life was perhaps to be found in the May magazine. Under the heading 'Adventures in Kriegieland' a newly arrived flying officer set down his first impressions of Stalag Luft III. It read:

An ardent individual clothed in a pair of pyjama trousers and an old scout's hat perched on a tree stump in the midday heat, a little way away from the wire, diligently executing the chromatic scale on a saxophone. I was amazed at the indifference of the sentry in the box a few yards off and of the Kriegies marching round the perimeter track, busily, quickly in little knots of two or three, as if they had somewhere to go, a train to catch perhaps – or an important meeting to attend.

Then there were the dozen or so yachtsmen, skilfully navigating home-made sailing boats round the fire squad's 12 ft square reservoir. Some wore old socks on their heads; cut down RAF trousers served as shorts; pyjama jackets, shawls and other quaint swathings abounded. I'm sure that only the season prevented the March Hare turning up at teatime. Kriegieland – a land much stranger than fiction.

Airmen were fed by their guards the Reich rations of a non-productive human and needed Red Cross parcels to stay alive. The June issue of the *Prisoner of War* magazine described to relations what foods an average parcel contained to provide a well-balanced diet, many with vitamins added, and how much they cost. The list read: Biscuits, cheese, chocolate, fish, fruit or pudding, syrup or jam, Margarine, hot meat, cold meat, bacon, milk, sugar, tea, vegetables, oatmeal and eggs – plus cigarettes for an after-meal smoke. With overheads the cost came to 10s (50p). Freight to the neutrality of Switzerland from where the parcel was shipped into Germany cost an extra 1s 2d (about 6p).

THE RAF did its utmost to ensure downed personnel never actually got to a prison camp. Evasion lectures by those lucky and determined enough to have done it were a regular feature of the routine at bomber bases on days when the weather prevented flying. There were also constant reminders that an airman who fell into enemy hands could unconsciously yield much useful information if he wasn't careful.

Cartoon posters hung in crew rooms showing an airman with a blonde on his knee above a pile of mail and advising: 'You Can't Take It With

You'. *Tee Emm* magazine had made its own contribution in the campaign to make sure downed airmen told their captors nothing but name, rank and number. In an article entitled 'Just All He Knew', it related:

> William Henry Buster Prout
> Stopped some flak and baling out
> Landed safe, but somewhat shaken
> North of Schnitzel-unter-Laken

It went on that after he had fallen into the hands of his fellow flyers in the Luftwaffe:

> They didn't seem to ask him much
> Just 'How are all at home'? And such
> Gin followed brandy, then came port
> Our Buster talked – without a thought

Outside the world of cartoon characters most of those who did find themselves prisoners considered it their duty to continue denying the enemy and fighting the war. In fact a total of thirty-four RAF prisoners of war were able to escape back to Britain during the war.

At Stalag Luft I RAF prisoners of war were sending military information to MI9 in London via a five-letter word code known as Bob, which had been introduced into letters home to pre-alerted relatives. When some of these prisoners of war were transferred as part of a batch into Sagan's East Compound they introduced it there, and when 850 prisoners of war were then switched to Sagan's North Compound in April, 1943 RAF letter-writing spies went with them. Eventually, when bursting Sagan's Belaria Compound was opened shortly after Christmas, the spy network set up a fourth station there. Code Intelligence Officers were set up in each compound to sift the information.[13]

RAF prisoners also set up an organisation known as Plug to undermine the morale of German guards. When German propaganda sheets circulated in the camps telling of heroic military actions a parallel was sought which had been similarly advertised and had then had disastrous results, such as Stalingrad. Cuttings from both were then displayed without comment on camp notice boards.[14]

Both actions were symptomatic of the RAF prisoner of war's refusal to accept that he was now a pawn of the Reich. It was an attitude that puzzled and infuriated the Nazis. A 1943 SS report on Internal Security complained that the attitude of British prisoners was 'extraordinarily self-possessed, one could almost say arrogant and over-bearing. The British are always decently dressed, their uniforms are always in faultless condition, they are shaved, clean and well-fed. When they march in formation they frequently look better than our own German replacement units.'[15]

The SS were concerned that such an image tended to demoralise a nation who were constantly being assured they were the master race. As an example of the 'challenging' attitude of the prisoner of war it described forty such prisoners who were being transferred. 'They arrived at the station near their camp with masses of heavy luggage and ostentatiously carrying large packets of food, corned beef and other things which were very short in Germany,' the SS report said. Worse was to come: the British then cheekily requisitioned handcarts and paid some German boys in chocolate to push the carts to the camp.

The SS were horrified that prisoners made fun of Hitler, an offence punishable by the executioner's axe for Germans. 'The manner in which the British behave to the population leaves no doubt of their confidence in victory,' the report concluded. There lay the key. The Germans were being told they would succeed, but the rubble of their cities which grew week by week provided a mountain of doubt it was impossible to climb. The average RAF flyer might complain about operational planning which cut a swathe through Bomber Command messes, but night after night he was prepared to go on because not only was it necessary that Britain and the Common-wealth triumphed, but it was also unthinkable that they wouldn't.

The only hope was that low-level operations would be rare if not a thing of the past. The losses from Pilsen had been catastrophic without benefit; those from Stettin and Rostock, severe but at great benefit. Bomber Command's Operational Research Section had reported: 'An extremely accurate ground-marking attack was delivered causing immense damage to industrial and military installations. In the Pommersdorf district 100 acres of closely-grouped industrial installations were devastated including the whole of the Bommerensdorf-Milch chemical factory.'[16] Even at Rostock, where the rapid smokescreen had prevented any hope of hitting the Heinkel works, there had been 'a fair amount of damage to the docks'. The ORS went on: 'Four and a half acres of the Neptun Werft Submarine Yards were laid waste.'[17] No small prize.

But it was clear the loss of eighty-three aircraft from two split operations in four days could not be continued. Obviously Bomber Command would have to return to high-level flying. However, there would be one more operation at tree-top height in less than a month.

The Dams Raid would be a spectacular success but, as the crews on Pilsen, Mannheim and Rostock had found, the light flak would prove deadly.

CHAPTER SEVEN

THE POWER OF WATER

'AS I always thought – the weapon is balmy. I will not have aircraft flying about with spotlights on in a defended area. Get some of these lunatics controlled and if possible locked up!' So wrote Harris in a reply to a minute about the answer to keeping 617 Sqn's aircraft at the correct height for their coming attack on the Ruhr dams by fitting converging guide lights under the fuselage.

His memo, to which he angrily added the note: 'Beams of light will not work on water at glassy conditions. Any fool knows that', was penned on 18 April. Less than a month later he was able rightly to hail the operation as a great success and a 'major disaster' for the enemy. It was almost entirely due to the relentless tenacity of the weapon's inventor, Dr Barnes Wallis, and the steadfast courage of W/Cdr Guy Gibson and his Dambuster crews that such a miracle of metamorphosis was so obviously to occur in the C-in-C's opinions.[1]

There was nothing new about the idea of ruining Ruhr industrial output by denying the factories the electricity and water they needed. In anticipation of a European war a list of thirteen strategies known as the Western Air Plans had been drawn up by the Air Staff in October 1937 and a special Industrial Intelligence in Foreign Countries Committee set up.

WA5 concentrated on taking out nineteen power plants and twenty-six coking plants in the Ruhr, Rhineland and Saar. But the body's Target Sub-Committee realised this was an impossible dream and instead devised a plan to destroy the Möhne and Sorpe dams to partly realise these aims by flooding large areas of the Ruhr, and disrupt its industry by cutting off the electricity and water supply.

The problem was that the RAF, at that time coping with 500-lb HE bombs, had nothing like the weight of weapon to realise such an objective, but the IIFCC chairman, Sir Maurice Hankey, swept aside such piffling Air Ministry objections and said consideration should also be given to locks, aqueducts and canals. It meant that the Eder dam, which controlled the level of important waterways in the Fulda and Weser valleys, would eventually be brought into the equation.

The question was how was all this appetising denial of enemy resources to be achieved? Both Special Operations Executive and Combined Operations staff considered ways of breaching the Möhne. Wilder thoughts involved flying boats and pilotless aircraft.

However, the research department at Woolwich Arsenal had pinpointed the nub of the problem in 1938 when they advised in a minute that 'the development of a *propelled* piercing bomb of high capacity would be essential to ensure the requisite velocity and flight approximating to the horizontal to attack gravity dams'. Bomber Command's operational plans section at Uxbridge decided themselves that April that 'Bomb penetration at right angles to the face of the dam would have to be obtained. This penetration is not possible under present conditions of release.' The underlining is theirs.[2]

Meanwhile the Woolwich researchers decided to conduct their own investigations into solving the issue and almost three years to the day before the dams were eventually breached the department instructed W/Cdr C. A. Finch-Noyes to go over all previous papers concerned with attacking such objectives. Four months later he reported that if 20,000 lbs of explosive was detonated 40 feet below the crest 'there seems a probability the dam would go'. To resolve how to get the explosive against the dam wall and over net defences or booms he accepted the principle of a 'hydroplane skimmer'. The various ideas were coming together.

As for Wallis, at the outbreak of war he had begun independently to examine the means of destroying natural sources of energy such as coal mines – and dams. He fastened on the Möhne and Eder in Germany and the Tirso in Italy as suitable for attack. He drew plans for a 10-ton bomb shaped like the R100 airship he had designed for Vickers-Armstrong and became involved in experiments at the Road Research Laboratory, Harmondsworth, where he explained that 10-ton bombs could be dropped in a lake above a dam to create a shock wave. The lab began using the Möhne as a model.

As there were no bombers at that stage of the war able to carry such a bomb, Wallis, being Wallis, designed one. Vickers knew it as the Victory. But by early 1942 Wallis realised he was getting nowhere with service chiefs and felt himself that his techniques might be impractical. He hit on the idea of ricocheting a missile up to a dam wall where it would sink. Only later did he find out naval gunners in Nelson's time had used the technique to increase range. It was probably this information that led him to extend the uses of the weapon to hit capital ships, and through the early part of 1942 he seemed to become convinced that it was a more suitable weapon for the Fleet Air Arm.

The Admiralty were by now certainly interested and through scientific contacts told the RAF of their hopes for the weapon. By January 1943 three versions of Wallis's weapon were being considered: Upkeep, which the four-engine Lancaster could deliver against enemy dams; the smaller Highball, to be dropped by Mosquitos for bouncing up to ship hulls; and Baseball, a leaping mortar shell to be used by MTBs against enemy surface vessels.

For the second time in the war Wallis produced a major paper on the bombing of enemy industrial targets, entitled 'Air Attack on Dams'. (His first, in the autumn of 1940, 'A Note on a Method of Attacking the Axis Powers', in which he correctly told the air chiefs how wasteful of resources their bombing policy had been so far, had – not surprisingly – been treated with some disdain.) The turning point for Wallis from abstract into actuality came at the end of January when Vickers-Armstrong agreed to manufacture 250 Highball bombs.

Wallis knew that if Ruhr industry was to be denied the water it needed, the Sorpe dam, too, would have to be attacked, and senior Air Ministry figures themselves realised this in promulgating the Western Air Plans before the war. Wallis admitted in his paper that the important Sorpe did appear 'at first sight' not to be susceptible to a bomb which bounced. But he went on to say that earth dams with concrete cores practically destroyed themselves if a sizeable leak 'can be established within the water-tight core'.

He said it was such a leak that had occurred at the Bradfield Dam, near Sheffield, in 1864. It had started with a small crack on the crest which eventually resulted in 3½ million tons of water pouring from the reservoir in forty-five minutes, causing 'great loss of life'. However, apart from the fact neither of them were concrete alone like the Möhne, the Sorpe and the Bradfield Dam bore little comparison. The Bradfield Dam became susceptible because it had a solid clay core – not 30 feet of concrete, supported by earth banks covered with stone slabs, as the Sorpe was constructed.

Wallis believed the Sorpe could be destroyed by a bomb sinking to 'a suitable distance' on the upstream side of the dam. The bomb would have to be released at extreme range, so that its momentum was virtually spent when it reached the dam's sloping wall and it wouldn't fly over the crest. He claimed a shock wave through earth would crack thick concrete and once the concrete core had been cracked, seeping water would damage the earth bank on the opposite, downstream side of the dam. The concrete core would then collapse through lack of support. However, all the experiments at the Road Research Laboratory and at Nant-y-Gro in Wales had been against concrete, gravity dams, not earth dams like the Sorpe. In fact, earth dams had tended to be favourite for areas subject to earthquakes for the very reason that they were not vulnerable to shock waves.

As it would turn out, the Sorpe element was the flaw in the operational plan for the Dams Raid.

HARRIS was opposed to the project from the start, considering it a waste of his precious resources and an unnecessary risk for his crews. But Portal, the Chief of the Air Staff, Air Vice Marshal Saundby, Harris's deputy, and Air Vice Marshal Cochrane, C-in-C of 5 Group, had seen the experimental films and were interested. And on 22 February when Harris himself was shown the films by Wallis at Cochrane's instigation he let slip that Portal had already authorised the conversion of three Lancasters for Upkeep trials.

Harris, who had less than sixteen squadrons of precious Lancasters at that time, reacted to Portal's pressure like the disciplined subordinate he was. Despite his personal misgivings he told Cochrane on 20 March to form a special squadron for the task ahead, 617 Sqn. It came in the nick of time for Wallis. Vickers had just told him they were cancelling the dams project and he indicated he would resign, then three days later he was called to Whitehall and told to develop a working bomb. The last possible date to attack the dams while they were full and could provide the maximum water pressure was 26 May, barely eight weeks away.

The order came just as the ideal man for the task had finished his third tour. Guy Gibson returned in the dawn of 12 March after the Stuttgart raid with his port outer feathered and a keen desire for a week's leave in Cornwall before his new posting. Instead he got a call to 5 Group headquarters in Grantham where he was told he would be writing a book. Days later, however, he was called in to see Cochrane, who had lately taken over from the sacked and popular AVM Coryton, and asked to do one more bombing operation. It would be his seventy-second. The following day Cochrane sent for him again, told him low flying would be required, he would be based at Scampton – still a grass aerodrome – and crews who had completed or nearly finished two tours would be needed. He would also be expected to start flying within four days.

As it turned out only six of the crews had the optimum operational experience and only a few of their pilots were personally known to Gibson. Joe McCarthy, however, was. His bomb aimer, George Johnson, remembers:

We were at the end of our first tour and supposed to be going on end-of-tour leave, then Guy Gibson personally asked Joe if he would join and Joe said he would and asked us what we thought. We said we would go with him. We thought it was for one special trip, then that would be it. I don't know what the connection was, but Gibson was very fond of Joe, perhaps because he respected his ability as a pilot.[3]

Les Munro, who would fly AJ-W on the Dams Raid as an acting flight lieutenant, recalls a less personal approach:

We hadn't finished our tour at 97 Squadron, we had twenty-two trips in, but 5 Group squadrons were circulated asking for volunteers for a special squadron of pilots nearing the end of their first tour or engaged on a second. I talked to my crew about it and we agreed we would volunteer.

The crew were reasonably happy about it. Nobody expressed any particular concern or opposition to volunteering for a special duties squadron. I wouldn't have taken the crew with me if they hadn't been happy. But it was a natural assumption it was going to be a difficult job. Looking back I think it was just a question of, 'OK, they're looking for volunteers for something, here we are nearly at the end of our first tour, let's have a go.' But it was a matter for conjecture what we were volunteering for.[4]

Grant McDonald, an RCAF rear gunner whose aircraft would be one of only two to attack the Sorpe, has a different memory of how he came to join the Dambusters. 'Ken Brown was our pilot on 44 Sqn and we transferred as a crew to 617. I think it was a matter of you, you, you and you. I don't remember volunteering.'[5]

The personal approach certainly helped at Syerston. From Gibson's old squadron came F/Lt John Hopgood, Lewis Burpee – soon to be commissioned – and indirectly F/Lt David Shannon. Shannon, still only 20, had finished his tour on 106 Sqn, been posted to Pathfinders, then, hearing Gibson was forming a new squadron, volunteered to join him. From his crew only his Canadian navigator, F/O D. R. Walker, agreed to go to 617 Sqn.

Seven crews were posted to Scampton by 24 March, seven more the next day and a third seven by 25 March. Like Bomber Command itself it would be a cosmopolitan outfit. Three of the skippers were in the RAAF, one in the RNZAF, five in the RCAF – albeit one of them, McCarthy, was American – and twelve in the RAF, one being an Australian, Mickey

Martin. The spanning of the Commonwealth would be an Air Ministry press officer's dream in the wealth of publicity demanded following the successful operation.

P/O Vernon Byers, RCAF, F/Lt H. S. Wilson and F/Sgt G. Lanchester were early pilot arrivals on 617 Sqn. Then from 50 Sqn came Old Etonian Henry Maudslay and P/O Les Knight; from 97 Sqn F/Lt David Maltby and Joe McCarthy; from 49 Sqn – who in fact had just vacated Scampton – Sgt Bill Townsend and Sgt Cyril Anderson; and from 61 Sqn F/O Robert Barlow. Maltby was beginning his second tour when he transferred and his navigator, Sgt Vivian Nicholson, had not flown operationally. The dams would be his first target.

Four crews of 57 Sqn's C Flight, skippered by S/Ldr Melvyn Young, P/O Geoff Rice, F/Lt Bill Astell and Sgt Lovell, were posted straight across the airfield on 26 March and eleven days later P/O Warner Ottley and his crew arrived from 207 Sqn.[6]

Training began on 27 March, though at first with Lancasters borrowed from other squadrons. Gibson was told his squadron would have to navigate its way in moonlight at low level and make a final approach to the target at 100 feet at a speed to be determined, but around 240 mph. He was not told what the target or targets were, but was advised to practise over water.

McCarthy used the excuse of there being no aircraft to ask for leave for his crew. Just in case the CO showed any reluctance he was prepared to point out that his bomb aimer, Sgt Johnson, had a long-standing arrangement to get married in Torquay within a few days. Johnson remembers:

> I was getting married on my post-tour leave, then I phoned my fiancée saying we were just going to do this one trip. She told me: 'If you don't turn up on 3 April don't bother again.' Needless to say I was there on 3 April. We were married in the Torquay church on the Saturday and I was back on the Monday.

As the crews began their training Portal was circulating to members of the Chiefs of Staffs Committee a note with the self-explanatory if long-winded title 'The Economic and Moral Effects of the Destruction of the

Mohne Dam and the Added Effects which will result from Destruction at the same time of the Sorpe and Eder Dams'. The paper, credited to scientific advisers to the War Cabinet, said: 'The capacity of this reservoir [the Möhne] is therefore great enough to cause a disaster of the first magnitude which would spread to densely populated areas between the Ruhr and the Dortmund–Ems Canal.' It reminded its readers of one of the primary aims of the Casablanca Directive, by saying morale in the Ruhr had been weakened by the recent months of 'devastating' bombing and 'breaching of the Mohne would undoubtedly have further and serious repercussions on morale'. Destruction of the Sorpe, which with the Möhne produced 75 per cent of the Ruhr's water, would 'produce a paralysing effect on the industrial activity in the Ruhr and would result in a still further lowering of morale'.

In early April the Ministry of Economic Warfare made the necessary aims of the operation clearer, warning that it was essential to destroy the Möhne and the Sorpe at the same time – breaching the Möhne alone would not necessarily cause economic devastation in the Ruhr. A note by Mr O. L. Lawrence of the Ministry said: 'It is not possible to state that a critical shortage of water supplies in the Ruhr would be a certain and inevitable result of the destruction of the Mohne dam', though if the Sorpe was wrecked at the same time 'it would be worth much more than twice the destruction of one'. Hopes were building and to fully achieve the dreams of the pre-war Western Air Plans it was clear a significant number of aircraft would have to be assigned to the Sorpe.

Gibson launched into serious training himself on 28 March by flying a Lancaster with Hopgood and Young on board to the Derwent Reservoir near Sheffield. He found the required low flying in daylight no problem, but as dusk descended on the surrounding hills he misjudged his height and nearly crashed into the dam. Clearly his crews would need to swoop and sweep over the dark lakes and valleys of the Midlands and Wales until it became second nature to make an attack over water for whatever they were meant to hit. In fact 617 Sqn would put in more than 1,000 hours of airtime training for the raid.[7]

The next day Gibson was called to 5 Group headquarters and shown models of his major targets, the Möhne and Sorpe. At last he knew what he was practising for. Gibson admitted he had thought it was the *Tirpitz*. It had been an inspired guess, because 618 Sqn had been formed eleven days after 617 Sqn with the express aim of attacking the German battleship with bouncing Highball bombs.

Daily intensive flying training took place throughout April and Cochrane's headquarters suggested crews practise over the following reservoirs in three groups: Group One over Lake Vyrnwy, Bala Lake and a reservoir 10 miles south-west of Denbigh; Group Two at Fewston, 11 miles north of Bradford, Goatwater Reservoir, 10 miles north-north-west of Fewston, and Barnard Castle Reservoir; Group Three to cover Cropston Reservoir near Leicester, Thornton Reservoir near Leicester, and Blackbrook Reservoir near Loughborough. It may well have been these water features best approximated the Möhne, the Eder and the Sorpe in that order.

In fact, Gibson found the Eyebrook Reservoir, near Corby (known as Uppingham Lake in Operation Chastise documents), the Abberton Reservoir, near Colchester, and the Derwent Dam, together with the bombing range at Wainfleet, most suitable for training. In particular the Eyebrook contours had been seen as most like those of the Möhne, the Abberton a reasonable facsimile of the Eder and the Derwent Dam area most like that surrounding the Sorpe, though in fact the Derwent has towers like the Möhne and its construction would not help an operational crisis at the eleventh hour. The Wainfleet coastal bombing range was widely used after reconnaissance showed that the two sluice towers of the Möhne were 700 feet apart and sight screens were erected on the beach to exactly represent these in dimension. Similar representations were put up at Eyebrook (Uppingham). It was on this basis that a plywood triangular sight, with a peephole at the apex and two nails at the opposite end to represent the towers, was designed by W/Cdr C. L. Dann at Boscombe Down.

Most of the young crews found it thrilling to thunder over hills, valleys and lakes at low level as they practised day after day, night after night. George Johnson remembers watching ground features whip by only feet away as he lay in the nose of his Lancaster looking through the bomb aimer's window. 'I found the low flying exhilarating,' he says. 'We'd been so used to the high-level stuff and it was great. The Lancaster at low level gave us no problems.'

F/O Dave Rodger, rear gunner on the same crew, F/Lt McCarthy's, also found it intoxicating. 'Low flying was a new experience after doing operations at 20,000 feet and above,' he says. 'You didn't know what was coming up as you dipped up and down until it went by.'[8]

But tail gunner F/Sgt McDonald wasn't so keen:

We had no idea, of course, what we training for on 617. Low level flying was a bit worrying and quite a bit different from what we were used to. At that time Bomber Command had been attacking targets from higher and higher. We had all been stacked up at 20,000 feet and above. Suddenly it was low level and quite alarming in the rear turret watching the ground go by so quickly. You heard a lot about people flying under high tension wires and so on. Some aircraft suffered some damage through going through the tops of trees.

In fact, Henry Maudslay came back with branches stuck in his tail wheel after too steep a descent to the Abberton Reservoir.

Les Munro was among the majority who enjoyed being let off the leash. He says:

Once we started the low flying in training it was exhilarating, it was an enjoyable change from the high-level trips we had been used to. It would depend on the ability of the particular pilot, but I enjoyed low flying. Most of the crews did because normally it was a court-martial offence if you did it unauthorised.

However, F/Lt Munro himself nearly came to grief as he dropped a practice Upkeep off the north Kent coast on 12 May at too low a height and the plume, as the mine bounced off the water, hit the rear turret and damaged the tailplane. He says:

The airspeed would affect the rate of projectory of the weapon, and it could have been a combination of that and being a bit lower than the 60 feet required. My rear gunner [F/Sgt H.A. Weeks, RCAF] was jammed in his turret because of damage caused by the splash. I felt the thump, but there was no danger of going in the drink even though I didn't climb away as we had to stay at low level for the training.

Training accidents weren't the only problems the new bombing concept was causing. The order had been for spherical steel bombs to have the correct properties to bounce across the water 'like footballs', but as the cylindrical mock mines with their round wooden casings hit the sea, the casings shattered and sometimes so did the metal itself. However, when dropped at the correct height, in nearly every case the cylinders themselves bounced onwards in a straight line as the weapon had been designed to do.

The result was that Upkeep became a cylinder, not a sphere and in fact, as 618 Sqn crews practised on a Scottish loch for their own war against the *Tirpitz* with the smaller Highball, they found the sphere shape gave the weapon a tendency to run wildly off course in a swell. After all the sweat and worry Upkeep was now little more than a huge depth charge. The difference was that it was a depth charge which would be back-spun to make it bounce. To protect it 617 Sqn's crews would also now be going into the attack at a mere 60 feet where a mere hiccup, as some of them observed, would land them in the water.

The problem of maintaining that height beyond the accuracy of normal altimeters also had to be addressed, which was where Harris was moved to scrawl his astringent memorandum. The idea of two spotlights converging into a figure eight when the bombed-up Lancaster was at exactly 60 feet was that of Benjamin Lockspeiser, Director of Scientific Research at the Ministry of Aircraft Production. He believed it was more likely to work on a calm lake, rather than a choppy sea – entirely the opposite of Harris's cryptic script.

Eventually an Aldis lamp was mounted in 617 Sqn's aircraft on the port side aft of the bomb aimer's window and the second to the rear of the bomb bay. This would normally have been impossible because of the bomb bay doors, but the special Type 464 Provisioning Lancasters for the raid had had their bomb doors removed for the Upkeep mine to obtrude below the aircraft.

Harris's objections were overruled. He was pleased, however, to discover that the four-cylinder engine being mounted in the Lancaster bomb bays to provide back spin at exactly 500 rpm was a standard model for submarines. It allowed the C-in-C, who never had an easy relationship with the Senior Service, to boast later that the RAF had 'pinched' a small engine from the Navy. The special Lancasters would find extra speed from reduced drag occasioned by the removal of mid-upper turrets at the suggestion of Roy Chadwick, the aircraft's designer.

As the date for the operation approached, Gibson, who was suffering from operational fatigue with a painful carbuncle on his face that the rubbing of rubber oxygen mask clipped to flying helmet did nothing to help, exerted a tight grip on his squadron. Sgt Lovell and his crew were returned to 57 Sqn, their places taken by P/O Divall's, and Lanchester's crew were posted at the skipper's request because Gibson wanted to replace his navigator. And days before the raid itself Gibson would have an air gunner posted for 'a course' at the aircrew discipline unit at Brighton. The man would be missing on the aircrew strength for the attack.[9]

Bomb aimers who fell short of Gibson's standards in practice were likely to be hauled before him to explain themselves and F/Sgt Ken Brown expressed personal fears he wouldn't be seen to measure up. The CO, for some reason, seemed not to be keen to have so many Canadian pilots on the squadron, though their figures were representative. Canadian homes supplied 60 per cent of the Commonwealth pilots in Bomber Command, which themselves amounted to 37 per cent of the total skippers.

But Brown had found a different side to Gibson off duty. The Canadian liked to go swimming at the pool in Lincoln to relax from the constant strains of buzzing hill and dale and one day, standing by its side in a bath robe he was rather proud of, he found himself pushed in the water. He came up spluttering to discover it was the CO who had pushed him in.

Les Munro also remembers: 'While we were training for the raid Gibson was a very keen disciplinarian, but off duty he was prepared to socialise with the crews in the mess. In my opinion he was a fine leader.' But Brown apart, NCOs found they had little contact with the CO. Grant McDonald recalls: 'As a flight sergeant I didn't have any association with Gibson except to see him in the briefing room. That was the only time.'

As training continued the gremlins were beginning to show themselves. On 4 May, in the countdown to the attack, a final communications trial had proved air to air communications on the TR1196 R/T set 'completely unsatisfactory'. F/Lt G. Bone from Bomber Command headquarters was drafted in and had VHF radios of the type used in fighters installed in all 617 Sqn aircraft within five days. They would later be fitted in all Bomber Command aircraft, just one of the successful by-products of the Dams Raid.[10]

For the first time a Group AOC would be able to have a direct involvement in an attack over a target. Special frequencies of 4,090 kc/s and 3,680 kc/s were arranged for two-way Morse-code signals from the target area to be sent directly to 5 Group headquarters at Grantham where Cochrane would help to direct which targets an airborne reserve force of five aircraft would attack.

Wallis, however, was having some misgivings. He might very well by now have discovered that the Bradfield Dam core was clay, not concrete like the Sorpe, and nervously scribbled in a memo to Bomber Command operations that the air side of the dam was made of 'pretty heavy material' that might not collapse even if the core cracked. He suggested, therefore, that the air side be cratered before an attack on the water side. As it turned out, the two crews who attacked the dam would be briefed only to do so on the water side.

There was also another significant development which would reduce the ability to destroy the important Sorpe. On 13 May the intrepid 21-year-old Maudslay, who had already proved his determination to fly low by picking up foliage and branches in his aircraft as he roared by, lost the starboard flap from his aircraft to the water plume when he dropped a dummy Upkeep off Reculver. ED933/G would not be repaired in time for the operation and it would mean nineteen aircraft would fly to the dams, not the twenty originally planned. The end result would be fewer for the Sorpe.

Then 48 hours before the operation was due to take place it was very nearly called off. It had been planned 618 Sqn would attack the *Tirpitz* within days of the Dams Raid with their smaller, bouncing Highballs. But they were still having problems releasing the spheres and getting them to keep on track. The Navy wanted to delay the RAF's operation because they felt once Upkeep was used, its secrets would be revealed and the Highball plans would be jeopardised.

The vice chiefs of staff could not agree on Upkeep being used independently and asked the chiefs, who had accompanied Churchill to Washington where he was meeting President Roosevelt, to give a decision. On 14 May, the day after a live Upkeep was dropped for the first time, 5 miles off Broadstairs, Portal personally signalled the go-ahead. It is not known whether Churchill had intervened – however, Operation Chastise was on.

A decision had been made, however, that would limit its success. On 11 May Wallis told G/Cpt Sidney Bufton at the Air Ministry's directorate of bomber operations that the previously proposed method of attack on the Sorpe dam might not breach it. It had also been realised that the Sorpe, unlike the Möhne and the Eder, had no towers for the bomb aimers to lay their Dann sights on as they had practised to do. Cochrane decided to embark on a different tactic. He ordered that the Upkeep aircraft attack along the 1,965-foot wall of the dam and that the bomb not be spun – which had after all been inherent to its design for the Möhne attack – and it be dropped near the crest into the water. The Sorpe was out of the bouncing bomb programme.

AS the crews were called to briefing during the afternoon of 16 May they were surprised to see a civilian take centre stage with Gibson and that alongside him was the 5 Group AOC, Cochrane. Wallis wanted to explain specifically what it was they were being asked to do and why it would work. The weeks of wondering were over as the handsome 24-year-old CO, the very image of a war hero, now sporting the ribbon rosette of a bar to his DSO, referred to 5 Group Operation Order B976 detailing an attack on the great dams of the Ruhr.[11]

F/Sgt McDonald remembers:

When we went into the briefing room to hear what the target was there was a very tense atmosphere. It really didn't hit home when it was revealed. In those days you knew there was nothing you could do about it, you were going to go anyway. I was pretty confident I would come back.

Sgt George Johnson says:

I don't know of any particular concerns about the possible danger at the briefing. I don't think any of our crew had any particular thoughts about anyone getting the chop. Nobody on our crew mentioned it. We just thought of it as a job to be done and if it wasn't going to be successful we wouldn't be being asked to do it.

F/Lt Munro had little idea what they had been practising for until Gibson, arms folded in characteristic pose, stood up to speak:

Even after the bulk of the training had been completed there was no indication of the exact nature of the target. We didn't find out we were going to the dams until the briefing. It may sound silly, but as a crew we never discussed what the target might be. We were aware, particularly because of the nature of the training over the Derwent Reservoir and the Uppingham Reservoir, that it was something to do with water. I think we had discounted early on that it might be the *Tirpitz*.

Sgt Johnson also had a surprise when he heard what his particular bomb was meant for. He learned as well that it would involve a method of attack for which he and his crew had no training, as had nobody else on 617 Sqn because it had only been realised at the last minute that the Sorpe had no towers to line up a bouncing-bomb attack on. He says:

We had no practice of our type of attack on the Sorpe at all. We didn't know in fact what kind of attack it was going to be until the briefing. That gave us the style of attack, but the actual geography of it we didn't know until we got to the Sorpe. All our practising had been with the bouncing-bomb method at right angles to the objective. None of it had been running along the line of a dam wall. There were a few specific bombing practices. We used the range at Wainfleet where we had two posts set up on the beach. These were obviously meant to simulate the towers on a dam. If a cross-country route ended up in that area then you did bombing practice as well. We also practised on Uppingham Lake but that again was on route for cross-country exercises. We had no indication until the briefing, of course, what the targets were going to be. There was conjecture, but dams were never considered. We thought it would be shipping of some sort.

It was warm in the briefing room and the airmen could empathise as they were told that 'the inhabitants and industry of the Ruhr rely to a very large extent on the enormously costly water barrage dams. Destruction of Target X [the Möhne] would bring about a serious shortage of water for drinking purposes and industrial supplies' taking effect over several months. 'The additional destruction of one or more of the five major dams in the Ruhr area would greatly increase the effect and hasten the resulting shortage. Target Z [the Sorpe] is next in importance.'

The operation order also said that flooding 'might well cause havoc' in the Ruhr valley and there 'would be a large loss of water for the large thermal plants'. In the Weser district the destruction of Target Y (the Eder) 'would seriously hamper transport in the Mittelland Canal and in the Weser and would probably lead to a complete cessation of the great volume of traffic now using these waterways'.

The nineteen Lancasters would take off in three waves. The first wave of nine aircraft with Target X, the Möhne, as its primary aim, would take off in three sections with ten minutes between each. Gibson, Hopgood and

Martin would leave first, followed by Young, Astell and Maltby, then Maudslay, Knight and Shannon.

The second would have McCarthy, Barlow, Munro, Byers and Rice lifting off one after the other to attack the Sorpe. The third wave, Townsend, Brown, Anderson, Ottley and Burpee, would be an airborne reserve, taking off hours behind the others. This force would not know their exact targets until well on their way. Under the direct control of Cochrane from Grantham they got their radioed instructions from 5 Group's headquarters long after they had crossed the enemy coast.

The first and third waves would use a southern route into the target, crossing the coastline near the Scheldt estuary; the second would cross at the Dutch island of Vlieland then fly south-east over the Ijsselmeer to join the route of the first wave. It was the second wave on the northern route, timed to hit occupied territory at the same time as the first further to the south, which would suffer the initial casualties.

The crews listened carefully, bending forward on the benches like attentive sixth-formers with matriculation to worry about, as the route and fighter and flak defences were painstakingly outlined. They were told Bomber Command had laid on light bomber diversionary strikes against Luftwaffe bases, but any failure to keep on track could be fatal. It would prove prophetic for many of those listening so quietly, their hearts beating rapidly as the fundamentals of the attack were outlined.

In fact a total of eighty-eight Bomber Command aircraft would operate that night, including thirty-six dropping mines off the Dutch coast, which would help to disguise Operation Chastise, and another eighteen towards the Bay of Biscay. There would also be light raids by three Mosquitos on Berlin, two on Cologne, two on Düsseldorf and two on Munster.

As the briefing finished and the armed guard unlocked the door, models of the Möhne and Sorpe were available for crews to inspect. Sgt George Johnson had paid particular attention to what Barnes Wallis had to say. 'I'm certain I heard Barnes Wallis say at briefing it would take at least six of the special bombs to crack the Sorpe and the weight of the water would do the rest. In fact six crews were briefed for that particular dam,' he says.

SECURITY throughout 617 Sqn's training had been tight and few of the station's permanent staff realised that the new unit was about to take off on an operation that would make history. There were none of the usual small party of WAAFs and ground personnel waiting by the control caravan to wave good luck when the first Lancaster turned onto the active runway as the sun set on a perfect late spring day.

It was the second wave on the longer northern route that took off first, with Barlow getting the signal from the caravan at 2128, followed by Munro, Byers and Rice. Then eleven minutes later Gibson, with Hopgood on his right and Martin on his left, took off in formation. Young, Astell and Maltby, then Maudslay, Knight and Shannon followed in their own vics of three rumbling across the grass and barely clearing the boundary fence with the Upkeep weapons spoiling the classic lines of the aircraft.

F/Sgt McDonald, Brown's rear gunner, had a view of the runway with other aircrew in the reserve force. 'I recall watching the second wave take off independently followed by three flights of three aircraft each take off in formation,' he says. 'I had never seen Lancasters take off in formation. That was quite a sight. We still had two hours to wait being in the reserve wave and didn't leave until shortly after midnight.'

Meanwhile, F/Lt McCarthy was in crisis. The ex-Coney Island lifeguard had found his own aircraft, Q-Queenie, unserviceable with an engine coolant leak. He rushed his crew over to the spare aircraft for the operation, T-Tommy, before anyone else could grab it. The aircraft had been flown in from Boscombe Down as a fortunate spare only a few hours before because the aircraft Maudslay had lost the flap on would not be available. It was bombed up with the Upkeep weapon, but there had not been time to fit the VHF radio or the spotlights.

McCarthy's rear gunner, Dave Rodger, remembers: 'Joe nearly went without a parachute. In transferring equipment from one aircraft to the other he caught his foot in his chute and it blew open so he had to send someone running for another.'

McCarthy also discovered there was no compass deviation card for T-Tommy. Without it there was no way his navigator, Don MacLean, and bomb aimer, George Johnson, could keep to the precise route needed to survive. The WAAF utility truck sped away to the flight offices where a card and replacement chute were thrust into quivering hands. The inability to carefully calibrate the compass card once the magnetic field of the enormous bomb had been discounted would cause navigation problems for the return.

By now the last of Gibson's first wave was bucking and bouncing over the grass as McCarthy, meant to depart first, anxiously turned his aircraft through the wild flowers growing at the runway check point and lined up. 'We were very late taking off and that probably saved our lives,' says Rodger. 'We did about 200 mph over the sea trying to catch up.'

McCarthy was airborne at 2201, thirty-four minutes late. It was the ill-fated second wave which had been briefed for the Sorpe. What happened to that wave in the next two hours would remove any possibility that the important dam, which supplied much of the water needs of the Ruhr industry, would be destroyed or even damaged sufficiently that it would have to be drained. The Dams Raid would still be a great success, but not the cataclysmic blow Wallis had envisaged it might be.

IN the north tower of the Möhne, Unteroffizier Karl Schutte traversed his 20 mm light flak gun and looked forward to another boring night duty. The monotony of life at the Möhne had been broken that day, a Sunday, as families from nearby Guenne had come to picnic near the water and celebrate Mother's Day. Now Schutte had only hours of staring at the still lake to look forward to.

THE first and second wave of Lancasters entered enemy territory at the same time, miles apart, at the two pre-arranged points to confuse the Luftwaffe. The first to go down was Byers on the northern route. Without pinpoints and only flame floats to check drift over the wide expanse of the North Sea his navigator, F/O J. H. Warner, got off track and flew over the heavily defended island of Texel instead of Vlieland. Geoff Rice's crew saw the yellow light flak curling up at 2257 then K-King hit the sea about

20 miles off Harlingen into the Waddenzee. The body of Byers's rear gunner, F/Sgt J. McDowell, was later recovered. It would mean one less for the Sorpe.

Less than an hour later Barlow was lost. His aircraft is believed to have been hit by light flak as he flew past Rees, near Harlen, at 2348. Then, possibly because the Australian was wounded, he climbed and is thought to have struck high tension wires running parallel to the Rhine and railway. At 2350 AJ-E plunged into the ground on fire and rapidly burned out, killing all its crew.[12] The Upkeep mine was, of course, still aboard and because its fail-safe destructive timer had not been activated by release, German scientists would know within days the secrets of Upkeep the Navy had fought so hard to preserve for their own purposes.

Six minutes later Munro, who had got to know Barlow over many a pint in the mess, was heading over the waves in the moonlight with Vlieland just ahead of him where the North Sea joined the IJsselmeer (Zuider Zee). He remembers: 'Going in over the North Sea I saw the dunes of the coast ahead of us and gained height to make sure I cleared the dunes then subsequently put the nose down to get back down to 60 feet approaching the water of the Zuider Zee on the other side.'

A marine light-flak unit, alerted by Barlow's aircraft passing nearby minutes before, was waiting. Munro recalls:

We were flying at 240 mph and I would have been at 70 or 60 feet when we were hit over Vlieland on the port side of the aircraft. The intercom immediately went dead. I felt the thump of the shell. The damage from that shell exploding blew a hole in the side of the aircraft where the squadron code letters were, but didn't cause much damage on the other side and no damage to the rear gunner and his turret because it was probably only a 20 mm. We could see a line of tracer coming up towards us, but it was only a single shell which hit the aircraft.

That lucky shot from a Kriegsmarine gunner with a single 20 mm shell would help considerably to save German industry from a cataclysm that loss of the Sorpe's water supplies would have caused. Munro was now unable to communicate with his crew, essential if he was to carry out such a precise attack at low level. The New Zealander flew out of range then orbited at 150 feet while his Canadian wireless operator, W/O P. E. Pigeon, faced the task of trying to re-establish the intercom. Munro says:

> I asked my wireless operator to go back and see if there was any possibility of connecting up the wiring or anything like that so that we were able to converse with each other. I did a few circuits round the Zuider Zee while he was looking at that and when he came back and said it was impossible to make any repairs I made the decision to return to base. It was just one of those things.

Three of the intended six mines Wallis had contended would be necessary to crack the Sorpe's concrete core would not now be delivered. Only an immediate success with few Upkeeps at the Möhne or a full effort by the airborne reserve now leaving their dispersals at moonlit Scampton and clumsily taxiing for take-off would save the ultimate ambition of the planners.

THE experience of P/O Rice, fourth in the second wave, was about to make success at the Sorpe more unlikely than ever. One minute behind Munro and slightly further to the south he passed between Vlieland and Texel at such a low level he had to pull up over the sand dune then put his nose down again. It had been rammed home to 617 Sqn's crews that, in an exact turnaround of what they had been trained to do in Main Force, height meant death and keeping at 150 feet or below on the way to the target would save their lives.

Rice had not used his spotlights to check height and he misjudged. The mine touched the water, jolting H-How. The skilful Rice immediately pulled up and applied full boost, but a second violent movement proved his worst suspicions. The mine had been torn away. It was fused, but the shallow depth of the Afsluitdijk polder meant it would not explode. Like Munro, Rice reluctantly turned for home and went back through the narrow gap between Vlieland and Texel.

Of those briefed for the Sorpe in those hours of hope and sunshine in the warm operations block at Scampton, only McCarthy remained.

AS Rice cleared the enemy coast Gibson's wireless operator, the 25-year-old Liverpudlian Bob Hutchison, was radioing Group headquarters to tell them of an uncharted flak position east of Dülmen which had punched 20-mm shells through the port wing of Hopgood's aircraft as twelve searchlights sprang up. Group alerted all 617 Sqn aircraft, codenamed Cooler, four minutes later.[13]

Gibson's Canadian navigator, Torger Taerum, and Australian bomb aimer, Fred Spafford, had had difficulty charting their course across the North Sea and found the wind pushed them south of track, so instead of crossing into enemy territory in the Scheldt estuary they flew over heavily defended Walcheren. To allow his navigator and air bomber to pick up a pinpoint Gibson had led Martin and Hopgood to an intersection of three railway lines to the west of Breda. Then, as Spafford uncurled the specially constructed map roller before him, they had followed canals to the Rhine where there was an exchange of fire with flak guns mounted on barges.

Flying beneath high tension cables, Gibson went to the north of Hamm, south between Werl and Soest, at some point becoming separated from Martin, then finally roared over a forest on a range of hills and saw the Möhne lake glinting in the moonlight below him. Martin was already there, but Hopgood was behind Gibson and joined the other two in a left-hand circuit of the lake. Gibson got his first view of the dam and thought it looked 'squat, heavy and uncomfortable', a grey and solid 'part of the countryside and just as immovable'.

As the three aircraft navigated their final leg to the dam, McCarthy, who had made up considerable time, was flying across Holland on the northern route, having crossed into enemy territory via Vlieland. Rear gunner F/O Dave Rodger remembers: 'Going over Holland I was looking for flak guns. Well inland I took a whack at a battery that started shooting at us.'

The biggest trouble was to come, however, when Rodger and Sgt Batson in the front turret spotted a train. Right below Batson in the nose Sgt Johnson heard the gunners ask McCarthy if they could open fire. 'He said, "Sure" but it was an armoured train and fired back,' says Johnson. 'If we'd known it was armoured we perhaps wouldn't have been quite so keen. The train's response to our .303s was a little heavier. We knew we'd been hit, but it didn't impair the aircraft so we could still press on.' But the damage from the train would cause problems later.

It was at about this time that Astell in B-Beer crashed, apparently caught by the flak Hutchison had radioed base to alert other aircraft to. He had flown in formation with Maudslay and Knight, twelve minutes behind the vic of Young, Maltby and Shannon and twenty minutes behind Gibson's flight. Astell became uncertain of his position, and turned south down a canal instead of crossing it. He fell behind the other aircraft whose crewmen saw two lines of yellow flak lazily float into the sky behind them and Astell flew into it. His gunners returned fire, but Astell crashed in a ball of flame.[14]

Ten minutes later Gibson opened up the attack on the Möhne. The engine to spin the mine was turned on and Gibson tilted G-George's 100-foot wingspan, looking over his shoulder towards the water as he swept wide over the hills to position with the moon to port. Then as he cleared the pine trees at the eastern edge of the lake his Yorkshire flight engineer, Sgt John Pulford, pushed the throttle levers fully forward. The huge dam with its twin towers stood stark against the industrial haze of the Ruhr valley dead ahead. All those weeks of training, all those frightening flights over dark British moors and lakes, all that studying of maps and models now crystallised into one momentous moment in history.

Gibson's crew found their hands acting before they had time to wonder as the mechanics of the attack took over. There was a shock as Taerum turned the spotlights on and, head thrust into the starboard cockpit blister, started calling off the height: 'Down, Down'. Spafford in the nose lined up his Dann sight and realised with relief that he could see the towers.

In the north tower on the dam wall Schutte reacted with horror as he heard the four Merlins, saw the lights hit the water and realised at the same time that the fast-approaching shape was a Lancaster. His 20 mm light flak gun sounded out an urgent 'pok, pok, pok', hurling shells into the blackness. Other 20 mm guns followed.

Gibson, staring at the new altimeter in front of his windscreen, was now at exactly 60 feet, the spinning Upkeep noisily shaking every rivet in G-George through to the control column gripped in the wing commander's sweating hands as the white balls of flak began arcing lazily towards the dark shape of the bomber, then shooting past the cockpit.

F/Sgt Joe Deering in the front turret had opened up now, the 100 per cent tracer all 617 Sqn aircraft had been armed with doing its job in frightening Schutte and other gunners guarding the huge grey mass. Deering had been told he could expect three anti-aircraft positions on the dam with another in the fields below. It seemed like more. Gibson could hear the pounding roar of Deering's twin Brownings and see his white tracer bouncing off the south tower as the dam wall swept closer.

At that moment, Gibson admitted later, he almost lost his nerve. He believed that in less than a minute he and his crew would be dead and 'didn't want to go'. Instead he screwed down his fear and perspiring in his shirt sleeves told the crouching Pulford beside him to leave the throttles open now and stand by to pull him out of the seat if he got hit. Then the mine, spinning at exactly 500 rpm, dropped away. It bounced once, twice across the water and Hutchison fired the agreed red Very signal as Gibson swept over the wall and climbed rapidly up the valley, balls of flak chasing the dark shape of the aircraft.

A minute later the first of the hydrostatic pistols on Upkeep clicked at exactly 30 foot below the surface. The explosive power of 6,600 lbs of Torpex tamped by millions of tons of rainfall collected over generations shot a column of concentrated water up the concrete face of the dam and into the air. More water rushed in to fill the prospect of vacuum below and the glistening, foaming, writhing, bubbling tower kept rising until it was 1,000 feet high, a solid, living, swirling memorial to ingenuity and courage in the moonlight.

Gibson, orbiting to port and looking back over his shoulder, expected to see a violent surge of water sweep all before it into the valley as the dam wall collapsed. Instead, as Maudslay and Knight arrived ten minutes later, he had to call in Hopgood to begin his attack. This time as M-Mother floated lower and lower over the dark surface Unteroffizier Schutte got the range and pumped 20-mm shells into the starboard petrol tank. Hopgood left a streak of flame reflected in the water as his mine fell and he cleared the wall. But the mine had been dropped too late and it followed him over the wall and plunged on the transformer station at the base, blowing it apart.

Hopgood struggled to climb his burning aircraft to 500 feet and ordered his crew to bale out. Both the Canadian bomb aimer, P/O John Fraser, and the Australian rear gunner, P/O A. F. Burcher, realised they were too low for a proper exit and pulled their ripcords in the aircraft, Fraser going out through the front hatch, clutching his chute, Burcher through the rear door – after first pulling open the chute of the wounded wireless operator Sgt J. Minchin and bundling him out – then the red tongues of flame ate through the wing root and the starboard wing fell away, the blazing wreck plummeting to the ground near the village of Ostönnen, a few kilometres to the north of the Möhne. Only Burcher and front-exiting Fraser, who had married a Doncaster girl only seventeen days before, survived the low-level bale-out.

Gibson told relatives later that when he saw his friend shot down something snapped. Hopgood had been with him when 5 Group had launched the low-level daylight attack on the Le Creusot armament works the previous October. Now the fear had gone and he only had revenge on his mind. He called in Martin to attack.

Swirling black smoke, from coke and oil ablaze in the remains of the power station wrecked by Hopgood's mine, was shrouding the south tower as Martin swept in and from one and a quarter miles away he could only see the north tower. Then the Upkeep weapon fell away and bounced across the surface and he saw a spout of water reaching above the smoke as the mine plunged under the water, his Australian gunners Toby Foxlee and Tammy Simpson doing 'wizard work' against the defences. But again there was disappointment for the circling aircraft above the valley as they saw the Möhne was still intact.[15]

Gibson could afford to lose no more mines or aircraft and decided to try something new. He called in S/Ldr Young in A-Apple and as Young hurtled across the water Gibson flew a parallel course to the starboard side, hoping to draw fire and allow Young's mine to be accurately placed. It bounced three times and seemed to be on target, sending a huge wave of water over the wall as it exploded. But again the message to base was 'Goner' for a mine exploded, not the code for the Möhne destroyed.

THE time was 0043. The five aircraft of the third wave were over the sea on track for the mouth of the Scheldt, and 70 miles to the south of the Möhne Joe McCarthy was over the Sorpe. After being shot up by the train over Holland T-Tommy had come under attack again. F/O Rodger remembers: 'As we were reaching the Sorpe we flew past a battery of five 20 mm flak guns on the side of a hill. They had a crack at us, but didn't hit us.'

Air bomber George Johnson and navigator Don MacLean had also had several headaches trying to cope with navigation at low level. Johnson recalls:

Don and I had an arrangement whereby we both had maps with the track marked on. I would pick out various pinpoints not necessarily on track and report back to him and he would use the information to keep our course. We didn't use the roller map method. Don was of the opinion that should the situation arise where you got badly off track you would have no map to refer to because the roller kept you to a certain width of track. The ordinary maps took up that much more space, but they were so much better, we felt, for us.

As they approached the valley where the Sorpe lay they had difficulty picking up the dam because of thick mist as air over the water cooled and condensed after the heat of the day. 'The dam itself wasn't misty, but it was misty in the area around,' Johnson remembers. 'We had difficulty finding it in the first place then, having found it, it was difficult to get down to the height and the correct line.'

They expected to see Barlow, Munro, Byers and Rice already over the dam carrying out their attacks or circling in the hills around. Johnson says: 'As we were late off we couldn't understand why nobody was there when we got there and none came after we got there. It wasn't until we got back that we learned what had happened.'

The crew had been told at briefing to line up the inner port engine nacelle with the dam wall on their bomb run, but attacking a dam by a method they had never tried before was causing Johnson severe problems and McCarthy had his own worries making a steep descent from the south-west over Langscheid church on top of a 1,000-foot hill, then throwing the Lancaster hard over in a rapid climbing turn to port up the other side of the valley.

Flying the spare aircraft with no spotlights made it difficult to get down low enough to drop the Upkeep weapon close enough alongside the Sorpe wall on the water side. Fortunately there were no flak positions actually over the dam. Johnson says:

> We made ten runs on the Sorpe and dropped the weapon on the final run. I found out that night how easy it was to become the most unpopular member of the crew very quickly. Nine times I called dummy run. It didn't do the morale of the crew much good, but I knew that if we had to do it we had to do it properly.

Josef Kesting, a machinist at the Sorpe power station below the dam, saw the Upkeep fall away. 'It dropped an instrument like a huge septic tank over the crest of the dam on the water side,' he says. 'A column of water rose 100 metres high.'

F/Lt McCarthy reported at debriefing later:

> I saw a half-circular swelling of water with the wall of the dam as its diameter, followed by a spout of water about 1,000 feet high. The crown or causeway of the dam crumbled for a distance of about 15–20 feet.[16]

Johnson says:

When the mine exploded it was a terrific sight. We were nose up at that stage and turning. The explosion was between our aircraft and the moon and Dave Rodger in the rear turret had a clear view. He said: 'God almighty', then as we turned I saw it. By then it was starting to fall back, but it was still a fair amount of water.

Rodger remembers:

I saw a big blast of water as the bomb went off, then we flew past a clock tower with a flak gun on it which made life interesting. We could see the tracer coming down to us, but they missed.

Johnson recalls:

We didn't have the spotlights, of course. But I think we dropped from 30 feet. It had to be a bit of a by guess and by God attack. The idea was that the lower you got, the forward travel of the bomb was reduced that much more. We lined up the port engine with the dam wall, so that when we dropped the bomb it went down the water side of the dam and rolled down to the prescribed depth before it exploded allowing us time to get away, pretty essential. As we orbited we saw it had crumbled about two-thirds of the way along the dam wall. We were hopeful, but that was as far as it got.

Johnson couldn't help feeling sorry for Rodger in the rear turret:

He got the worst of the dummy runs because coming down very steeply, then flying a short distance straight and level, then climbing like hell to get out he was getting a lot of G-force. He was wondering what the hell was going on. Even when the bomb splashed into the water the spout went into his turret. He said afterwards, 'I thought I was drowning.'

BACK at the Möhne, David Maltby was making his attack. This time Martin joined Gibson in trying to confuse the gunners on the dam. Gibson came in to starboard of Maltby and Martin flew along the port side, both of them breaking away as the mine fell from J-Jig. In that moment Maltby had seen that the Möhne was already damaged. The top of the dam was crumbling and there was a hole right in the centre of the concrete.

Young's A-Apple had been the only one of the aircraft so far to put its mine in the right position as Gibson drew fire and it had done just as Wallis said it would: it had breached the dam.

Maltby broke away to port following Martin in a flurry of flak streaking white against the blackness and his mine bounced across the now choppy water once, twice, thrice, four times before smacking into the dam wall then exploding, sending a spout of mud and water 1,000 feet into the air, a visible shock wave powering away from the base of the jet as it put another hole in the dam.[17] But Maltby's wireless operator, 22-year-old Sgt Tony Stone, quickly sent the signal 'Goner' to Grantham for the release of the mine, not for a breach, and it's possible that he did not know at that instant the dam had been destroyed.

Gibson, circling in the hills, called in Shannon to make his attack. Then looking down and to his right he saw the dam had gone. Days, weeks, months and years of trickling, babbling and pouring down the hills had been held by the hand of man to create a mighty weight of water. Now a maelstrom of fury was shooting out from the shattered concrete and tumbling, tripping and twisting with awesome power as all the years of pent-up energy were released in an instant. In the few minutes it took the seven surviving Lancasters to lazily unwind circuits over this theatre of destruction their crews could already see the changing form of catastrophe as the wallowing, pitching and tossing turned into one solid wave, a thing of terrible, symmetrical beauty, powered at its base and hissing in a seamless, glistening wall of destruction sweeping before it all the pathetic attempts of man to control nature.

IN the underground operations bunker at 5 Group headquarters at Grantham Wallis, somewhat dejected after four bombs without apparent result, was sitting on the steps of a raised platform staring at the ops board on the opposite side of the room when the telephone rang again and the group chief signals officer heard the code word signifying the Möhne had been breached. Wallis jumped to his feet and excitedly waved his arms in the air. Cochrane sought a Morse transmission asking for Gibson to confirm and a minute later it came through. This time Cochrane joined officers shaking Wallis's hand and Harris came over to apologise for his disbelief and to tell him that in future the scientist could 'sell him a pink elephant'.

AT Wickede (Ruhr) a few miles beyond the dam in the valley Clement Mols, who ran the village post office, had been looking from a first floor window towards the Möhne lake when Gibson opened the attack. 'The humming of planes came from a distance,' he says in an official report after the attack. 'Suddenly an unusually loud detonation was heard and I saw in the direction of the Möhne lake a high column of water.' He said that he also heard further explosions, but he understood from the air raid warning broadcast to his post office that the immediate danger had passed. Instead a few minutes later the post office at Arnsberg, 3 miles nearer the Möhne, called him to warn of the tidal wave approaching.[18]

He told his wife to prepare to flee and without success tried to phone villagers to rouse them from their beds. Then as the couple left the post office for higher ground in the village, 'we had only gone fifteen or twenty paces when I felt the air becoming damp'. In the 'cold and damp' fog they ran back into their home and 'the water caught us in the hall'.

Frau and Herr Mols slammed the entrance door behind them and hurried upstairs. 'We saw the water penetrating the house with a terrific speed,' Herr Mols says. 'A sulphurous vapour cloud mounted from the cellar, short-circuiting the battery. The water continued to rise in the ground floor. I counted ten steps to the first floor under water.'

From the window he saw the avalanche of water submerge a goods train, saw furniture and farm wagons sinking and rising in the rushing tide and heard the clamour of 'the cries for help of floating people, the roaring of drowning cattle'.

In the few minutes it took the remorseless, unstoppable tidal race to reach the village of Neheim, 8 miles from the dam and at the point the

Möhne river reached the Ruhr, it had already wrecked the village of Himmelpforten-Niederensee where the village priest had died trying to ring a warning on his church bells, swept away several bridges, and isolated Guenne, from where villagers had walked to the dam to celebrate Mother's Day just a few hours before.

Now at the foot of the Wiesenberg by the Möhne river it was to drown hundreds as the flood bore down on a Ukrainian women's forced labour camp and swiftly plucked from their bases the wooden sleeping huts. It bobbed and tossed the huts downstream hurling the women round inside, then smashed the buildings to matchwood against a concrete bridge.

At Neheim a Dutch forced labourer working in a factory had stood fascinated on a ferro-concrete bridge watching the strange sight of planes low-flying with lights on amid the rattle and pok-pok of machine gun and flak. Suddenly he heard the dam go, got an impression of a dark greyness rushing towards him and ran for the hills, calling to others to follow. Only he and one other worker escaped. Not even the concrete piles of the bridge he had been standing on would be left by the flood.

The torrent rushed on, wrecking twelve Neheim factories, washing away railway lines, wrecking power stations and gas plants and drowning farm animals by the hundred. Many villagers died in their cellars. They had taken shelter as the air raid warning sounded on the approach of the Lancasters and were still there when the deluge struck Neheim.

AFTER one last look at the gaping holes in the wall of the Möhne and the tumbling torrent hitting the valley below, Gibson had ordered Martin home and Young, Shannon, Maudslay and Knight in A, L, Z and N to the Eder. As they flew away, the wreck of Hopgood's plane in the spring meadows beyond the Möhne was still burning.

Now the mist was gathering and Gibson wandered off too far to the west before finding the squat dam at the head of the tree-lined reservoir. Young was also there, but Shannon was well and truly lost until Gibson contacted him on the VHF set, which had so proved its worth, and fired red Very lights over the undefended Eder to guide him in.

Shannon went into the attack first. But the Eder, which necessitated a rapid descent from 1,000 feet, an acute bank to the left to clear a spit of land, then quickly getting down to 60 feet to release the mine, needed the same kind of attention as Sgt Johnson had found at the Sorpe an hour before. Shannon made four approaches without success, so Gibson called in Maudslay. He also could not get the right line on his two dummy attacks, however.

Eventually Shannon, with the moon directly behind him, dropped down to 60 feet and released his spinning Upkeep at the dam wall. It bounced twice, then as he climbed away at full boost his rear gunner, F/O J. Buckley, saw 'an enormous spout of water' rise 1,000 feet above the grim, grey wall.[19]

But the dam still held and now Maudslay made his third run. Desperate to get it right this time, Maudslay's bomb aimer, 23-year-old P/O Michael Fuller, held on to the last possible minute for release as the spotlights raced over the water, but it was too late. As Maudslay flew on so did the mine and exploded on the crest 'with a slow, yellow, vivid flame which lit up the whole valley like daylight for a few seconds' as Maudslay climbed away ahead. To Gibson's urgent R/T message, Maudslay faintly answered he thought he was OK. The damaged aircraft vanished into the night and headed for home.

The wing commander called up Astell in the faint, desperate hope that B-Beer had not been shot down, but it was too late. Now only one bomb, that of Australian Les Knight, remained. Knight made one dummy run to get the line of the curving attack, then came in 15 degrees to the left of Shannon's approach. The moon was shining brightly to his right as he released the mine at 0152 heading straight for the centre of the dam wall. He soared away at maximum rate of climb, his rear gunner looking straight down onto the concrete line. Sgt H. O'Brien saw it shatter with the force of the explosion. A huge jet of glittering, foaming water was roaring from the dam while the crest held.[20]

Knight, somewhat humbly, described his attack at debriefing as 'straight-forward and as predicted', but as he banked to port after clearing the hills he saw the crest of the dam had now collapsed and a 30-foot tidal wave was cleaving a glistening path. The orbiting Shannon and his crew saw car lights disappearing under the treacly water as the hissing deluge of destruction heralded dreadful death down the valley.[21]

Three-quarters of the 202 million cubic metres of water in the dam were on their way down the cleft in the hills. The alert was raised by the postmaster at Bad Wildungen, who had a call cut off in mid-sentence that the wall had broken. He rang other villages in the Eder valley and people began to leave their homes for higher ground. The sheet of solid, unbroken water swept on, swiftly levelling the church, school and houses at Affoldern, buckling and dismembering the iron suspension bridge at Hemfurth, inundating the farmland at Fritzlar. Areas over 250 miles from the dam would feel the force of the three Upkeep bombs.

THE wireless operator on G-George tapped out the codeword 'Dinghy' and there was further elation at Grantham, but not before the cautious Cochrane had again asked for and received confirmation. He also asked how many aircraft in waves one and two were left to attack the all-important Sorpe, which with the last-minute change of tactics Wallis thought would need six accurate bombs. The wing commander told him none. Gibson then ordered Young, Shannon and Knight to set a course for home and headed back over the Möhne to witness the scale of the Germans' catastrophe.

McCarthy had made his own detour there an hour before. His bomb aimer Johnson recalls:

> We went back over the Möhne more from curiosity than anything. It was tremendous to see – an amazing sight I'll always remember. It was just like an inland sea. There was water everywhere in the moonlight, where before it had been a pretty reasonable valley.
>
> We could see the hole in the dam and the water shooting out. The level was well down. There was a great sense of satisfaction to see the job had been done.
>
> It hadn't happened as far as the Sorpe was concerned, but we had the satisfaction of doing the job we were sent to do. We reckoned we had done it properly, but there was a disappointment there was no end result.

Rear gunner Rodger remembers: 'McCarthy said we'd go back from the Sorpe the same way we came in and the same 20 mm guns on the side of the hill had a crack at us again, but again didn't hit us.'

As the exhausted Gibson flew away from the Eder towards the scene of his triumph at the Möhne he knew that only the third wave under the direct orders of Cochrane could achieve the ultimate aim of Operation Chastise by cracking the Sorpe.

At that moment the last hopes of such a success were fading as an aircraft of that wave came under attack. The flight had been led into the air by P/O Ottley, airborne at 0009, followed by Burpee, Brown, Townsend and finally Anderson.[22] Burpee's crew were the first to die. They committed the fatal error of getting off track at the most crucial part of the route, flying between the *nachtjäger* airfields at Eindhoven and Gilze-Rijen. Burpee flew over the edge of Gilze-Rijen and was immediately hit by ground fire.

F/Sgt Brown's crew in F-Freddie, 10 miles behind at 150 feet, saw what happened. 'We saw the flak coming up towards him, then the explosion as he hit the ground and his bomb went off,' recalls rear gunner McDonald. The time was 0153 and at debriefing Brown said he had seen a blast in the air before Burpee's S-Sugar, the fire spreading a fierce red light, hit the ground, demolishing some airfield huts. Burpee had shaken Brown's hand before take-off and told him only he, Brown, would be returning to Canada. Hopgood also had confessed a premonition to Shannon that he would die.

Half an hour later Ottley had just received airborne orders to attack the Lister dam – changed one minute later to the Sorpe as Cochrane realised how few Upkeeps he now had left – when he also was downed to the east of Hamm on the Boselagerschen Wald. McDonald says: 'We also saw Ottley shot down. We were further away this time, but saw the white anti-aircraft fire curling up, then the explosion.'

Amazingly, one member of Ottley's crew survived the low-level crash. Sgt F. Tees in the rear turret saw his aircraft lit up by searchlights, then flames streaking past the tail as Ottley reported they were falling. As C-Charlie hit the ground from 150 feet the turret broke away and Tees was later picked up, badly burned.

Three miles away to the east, over Hamm itself, the crew of T-Tommy heading homewards in the opposite direction were experiencing their own problems. Because F/Lt McCarthy had had to switch aircraft at the last minute Sgt Johnson and navigator Don MacLean had had trouble keeping on track. Johnson says:

The problem occurred because we had to take the reserve aircraft. While there was a compass card in for the deviation with the bomb on there wasn't one for a swing having been taken before the bomb was loaded, so the deviations were very much different coming back than going out. When Don noticed that and realised we were using the wrong deviations Joe said: 'Right, we'll go out the same way as we went in.'

How we did it I don't know, but we got home. But there were navigational problems and we wandered over the marshalling yards at Hamm. Fortunately we were so low the flak gunners couldn't depress their guns enough to get at us. As Dave Rodger put it, it wasn't so much flying the aircraft as changing the points, we were so low.

As F/Lt McCarthy diced with the defences at Hamm and P/O Ottley was dying, S/Ldr Maudslay was also losing his battle to reach home. His aircraft was caught by light flak just east of Emmerich, fifty minutes after his ill-fated attack on the Eder. His aircraft plunged to earth near the village of Netterden, killing him and all his crew at 0236, one minute after Ottley went down.

The floodwaters from the Möhne raged on through the Ruhr valley. An unnamed eyewitness in post-raid German records describes how at 2.40 a.m. his watch on a piece of furniture in his house was stopped by the swollen Ruhr smashing into his home. His wife had woken him to ask: 'Is it hailing outside?' Then he looked out to see waves slapping his house near the river meadows and fog hanging above the water 'like steam'.[23]

Living miles away from the dam burst, he unwittingly thought drainage pipes had broken in his rural community. Then 'the waters came with a terrific speed, all the doors were blocked up by the pressure, the furniture in the kitchen was afloat, so I jumped through a window'. Wearing only his shirt he clung to a large elder tree. 'Everywhere one could hear cries for help, the crash of beams,' he says. 'Men, animals, houses, furniture and all sorts of things floated past me. Trees and beams bounced against my tree yet it kept firm.'

Eighteen minutes after the slapping of floodwater against his home woke the hapless civilian, S/Ldr Young was lost. He was shot down by flak within sight of the last leg to safety at IJmuiden and crashed just off the coast with the total loss of his crew.

F/SGT Brown now received his airborne orders to attack the Sorpe and flew south-east, whipping over power lines as he saw them rising up his windscreen, glinting under the moon. As Burpee went down Brown had pushed the nose of F-Freddie further forward and hummed down a road, below tree-top height, then later narrowly avoiding crashing into a castle. His crew saw Townsend's O-Orange ringed by flak near Dülmen, where Astell had been caught, but Townsend, after throwing his aircraft about the sky, flew on with orders to attack the Ennepe dam.

Cochrane did not know at this stage that he had lost two aircraft tasked with the Sorpe, otherwise he might well have switched Townsend to join Brown as he later did Anderson, but there was now no chance of Wallis getting his six bombs to what was rated the second most important target of the night.

Also at that time the AOC did not know the Sorpe had been attacked at all as the hills had prevented McCarthy's message getting through and two Sorpe-bound aircraft, Munro's and Rice's, had by now returned to Scampton. McCarthy re-broadcast by routine thirty minutes later and twenty minutes from home at 0303.[24] It had been an equally hair-raising ride beyond Hamm for McCarthy. F/O Roger recalls: 'Near the IJsselmeer we were at 150 feet when a flak gun opened up. Fortunately it was shooting below us.'

Brown arrived over the Sorpe to find problems with visibility similar to those McCarthy had encountered. His approach to the dam would be at right angles along the water as on training exercises because, as a member of the airborne reserve, Brown had not been told of the last-minute change in method of attack. Nobody seems to have thought of it. We will never know whether two, not one attack along the dam wall would have made a difference. Sgt McDonald recalls: 'We made six runs along the dam before we dropped the bomb because of mist on the reservoir side.'

On the third attempt Brown nearly crashed as he dived into the mist. He rapidly climbed and decided to mark out a circuit with flares to establish his bearings. The flares set fire to woods on either side of the lake and helped to clear the mist. On the sixth run across the Sorpetalsperre Sgt Steve Oancia dropped the still Upkeep at 60 feet. It hit the water just in front of the dam wall.

Brown reported:

> We could see everything on the run-up with the moon on the starboard beam. I could see the target from 900 yards away. The missile was dropped about 10 feet away from the dam, about two-thirds of the way across. A semi-circular swelling of water against the dam was followed by a spout of water about 1,000 feet high.

He also reported: 'There was a crumbling of the dam for about 30 feet.'[25]

In fact the mine may have exploded early, soon after entering the water. Eyewitnesses on the ground reported a much louder explosion than that caused by McCarthy's Upkeep and that there were deep fissures on the ground near the water as if the mine had first struck there. The explosion also blew all the tiles off the roofs of houses 500 yards beyond the dam.

AT the exact time of 0323 that Brown's bomb was exploding at the Sorpe its previous attacker, McCarthy, was coming in to land at Scampton. Luftwaffe flak personnel on the train who had so surprisingly fired back when the American's exuberant gunners raked it were now to have their skill discovered. F/O Rodger says:

> The starboard tyre had been flattened, unknown to us. As we came in to land, though, Joe did a wonderful job. He managed to hold that

wheel up by applying aileron until we were just about stopped. We just spun round once. Then when we got out we had a welcome cup of tea. We were relieved to be home.

Like McCarthy, Brown went to see what had happened at the Möhne on his way back. Herr Mols, watching the flood's remorseless devastation from the loft of his post office in hours of anguish during which his wife 'complained, wept and prayed', heard Brown 'flying up and down the river'. He says: 'The aircraft kept very low and we thought, "Is it going to drop bombs?"'

After landing at Scampton F/Sgt Brown told the intelligence officer at debriefing:

The flight engineer [Sgt Baz Feneron] saw two large breaches close together between the two targets [sic]. Each breach was about a quarter width of space between the two towers. Water was pouring through both gaps, shooting well out before falling in two powerful jets. The valley seemed to be well covered with water. The front gunner [Sgt Daniel Allatson] reported a third breach beyond the tower on the North-East end of the dam with water pouring through.

In fact what Allatson saw was a large section of banking on the north side of the dam which had been collapsed by Martin's bomb veering to the left and sending a wave of water over the wall, staining it. The two breaches in the dam had become one 250-foot gap by the time reconnaissance photographs were taken the next day, but it is possible that at the time Brown – or McCarthy – flew over this had not happened.

Brown was in the Möhne area when the last attack of the operation was launched a few miles away to the south-west, by F/Sgt Townsend headed for the Ennepe. The dam had proved difficult to find and mist over the water was making up for the lack of defences. The shape wasn't exactly as described. What had been shown as an island was in fact a peninsula.

Townsend came in for an initial approach with the spinning Upkeep shaking his aircraft and his navigator desperately trying to get the two lights to join into an eight over the water. But the bomb aimer called a dummy run at the last minute. Twice more Townsend tried without success, then at exactly 0337 and flying at 220 mph he dropped the weapon. It bounced twice before sinking, but it was short and the circle of water as the mine went off only reached out to the dam wall. It wasn't against it and the dam held. Wartime German reports seem to indicate that Townsend had mistaken the Bever dam nearby for the Ennepe and attacked that instead. There is no indication that he would have found greater success at the Ennepe in the conditions.

ONE more 617 Sqn aircraft was ordered to the Sorpe, that of F/Sgt Anderson, the last to leave Scampton at 0015. This would be Cochrane's final chance to destroy the second most important target of the night. But severe navigational difficulties developed for Anderson when he was forced off his course north of the Ruhr by heavy flak. Mist was now covering much of his route and it was difficult to find pinpoints. Searchlights in the strong-point near Dülmen which had claimed Astell threw him off track again.

Then his rear gunner reported he couldn't turn his turret fully. Anderson pressed on, but with dawn approaching and miles to go before he reached the area of the Sorpe he realised he could be caught over a large section of enemy territory in daylight. Now all other 617 Sqn aircraft had gone he would be alone with the Luftwaffe without the proper means of defending himself.

Bombers were making early returns night after night instead of completing operations because of faults with their aircraft, and a faulty rear turret was a common cause. He took a skipper's decision and decided to turn for home by the quickest exit route, via the Scheldt estuary.

F/SGT Brown and his crew nearly died in their last few minutes over enemy territory at a terrifying 50 feet as the dawn streaked the North Sea ahead. Sgt McDonald recalls:

> We had crossed the Zuider Zee and were coming onto the Den Helder peninsula when a searchlight hit us. At first they didn't have the range

right and it went past the rear turret, but then they picked it up so that we had to fly through it and that's when we got hit. You couldn't do anything, you couldn't go any place, you couldn't go up, you couldn't go down, you just had to go through it and that's all there was to it. We were hit on the starboard side at the back of the cockpit. There was quite a large hole and many other perforations, but nobody was injured.

IN the debriefing room at Scampton Harris and Cochrane mingled with some of the eleven tired crews who had returned as they nursed rum-laced mugs of tea, smoked welcome cigarettes and told the stories people would be listening to into the next century. Their accounts would help to frame the official report to Winston Churchill in Washington, where he was able to defeat some American scepticism of what Bomber Command could achieve.

Within days American newspapers would take their cue from the mass of publicity pumped out by the Air Ministry to the avid, waiting presses of Fleet Street, hungry, after news of the Axis capitulation in North Africa four days before, to publish another British and Commonwealth success. The *New York Times* raved about the RAF's 'unexampled daring, skill and ingenuity'. Coming the day before Churchill's fifty-minute speech to the US Congress, it was heaven sent. He told the congressmen of the 'unparalleled devastation' Bomber Command was wreaking in the 'great centres of German war industry' and then went on to remind them of 'the gallant operation' they had just read about, which would play 'a very far-reaching part in reducing the German munition output'. Any waverers to the idea that a war in Europe had to be funded and won ahead of finishing the Pacific campaign were won over. This alone would have made Chastise a success, as indeed it was.

There were other benefits in the dreadful profit and loss account of war. As the crews shuffled away from the debriefing tables ready for their post-operation breakfast and nerve-restoring sleep, the waves of destruction they had unleashed were sweeping on through western Germany. The Wabern and Felsberg districts were now under water, 16 miles from the dam. The floodwaters were heading for Kassel, parts of which would remain submerged for days. Road and rail communications had been broken, telephone and power lines destroyed, and where industrial premises weren't swept away they were silted up by mud. In a wide area 70 per cent of the harvest and all the root crops were destroyed.[26]

The primary aim of the attack had been to deny the Germans a large proportion of their water supply and this it did. The water held back by the Möhne dam supplied the needs of four and a half million people. Its release halved the amount available to them in this highly industrialised area.

As the surviving 617 Sqn crews tucked into their bacon and eggs the German Armaments Minister, Albert Speer, was making plans to fly to the area of devastation, having been woken in the early hours to be told the Möhne had been breached and emptied and three other dams attacked. He flew in by Feiseler Storch soon after dawn and toured the area for two days, reporting that 'industry was brought to a standstill and the water supply of the population imperilled' because electrical installations at pumping stations had been soaked.[27]

That morning another British aircraft was flying high above the devastated dams as Speer's Storch landed. S/Ldr Jerry Fray had been sent out in a PRU Spitfire to photograph the devastation. He had no trouble finding his way. The sun was glinting on the enormous inland sea which had been created. The picture he took of water still shooting from the shattered Möhne would be printed in newspapers throughout the free world.

The BBC had by now announced how the raid had been pressed home with great valour and the survivors were waking to find themselves heroes. Sgt Johnson recalls: 'It was just another job and I don't think I realised the significance of what we were being asked to do until it was done. Then I found out very quickly with all the publicity.'

F/O Rodger recollects: 'The next day we were pretty numb. It took a while longer than that to realise someone you knew was gone. Some we didn't know well at all because we hadn't been together that long before we went on the trip.'

F/Lt Munro says:

THE POWER OF WATER

We had only been together for six weeks before the raid. It wasn't as if we had been together on a squadron for several months, getting to know people in the mess before and after operations. In this case some of them were quite well known to me, like Henry Maudslay. He was my instructor at 1654 Heavy Conversion Unit at Wigsley. It was sad to know a lot of those blokes, like John Hopgood for instance, a first-class chap, and Bill Barlow the Australian, weren't coming back.

Sgt Grant McDonald also remembers a sense of subdued loss:

At Scampton we were billeted in what had been station married quarters in the pre-war period. The day after the raid we were pretty stunned when we saw the lorries coming along the houses to pick up the effects of the ones who were gone. Until then we didn't realise it had been so many.

There was a sense of shock that so many had been lost, but we hadn't been together that long because the training period hadn't been that prolonged. You knew people casually in the mess.

Les Munro gradually became aware of how lucky he had been:

On reflection afterwards I felt a sense of relief that because I was hit and had to return to base it probably saved my life. Even to this day I think if I had gone on there was a strong possibility I wouldn't have come back. If you look at the percentage of the ones who got there and didn't come back the possibility is that if I hadn't been hit by flak I would have been among those who didn't come back.

In the days that followed, the Air Ministry publicity machine besieged Scampton, taking colour pictures of Gibson then his crews one by one on the same recognisable stretch of grass. The fact that the Commonwealth had been so well represented was a bonus to be exploited. New Zealander Munro remembers: 'After the Dams Raid they took pictures of the various nationalities involved and they took a picture of the New Zealander Len Chambers and myself.' He still has it.

THE cost was still being counted in Germany. Two days after the raid Hitler had approved 7,000 workers being drafted in to clear up, ready for rebuilding, the destruction in the Möhne valley, Eder valley, Dortmund and Kassel. Soon workers from the Todt Organisation working on the Atlantic Wall would be diverted to join another 20,000 labourers at the scene. But Speer told Goebbels that he hoped to have the armaments industry in half production by the beginning of the following week and in full working order again by the end. Hitler was deeply concerned about the effects on armament production and was furious that the Luftwaffe had let the raid happen. Goebbels himself recorded that 'the attacks of British bombers on the dams ... were very successful'.[28]

In human terms, the Germans now knew that 499 of their countrymen and 718 forced labourers from countries they had occupied had died. Teams would work throughout the summer to restore the damage. It wouldn't be until September that the 19,000 cubic metres of concrete blasted or washed away at the Möhne would all be replaced.

The RAF detailed analysis of reconnaissance photographs reported flood damage at Grunne, Dellwig, Fröndenberg, Neheim, Langscheid, Wickede and between Schwerte and Hattingen. The railway viaduct near Herdecke carrying the main line between Dortmund and Hagen had gone. But the assessment by 617 Sqn's intelligence staff was that:

> The most important consequence of this operation is that the Ruhr industries will be deprived of a great deal of their industrial water for the coming summer. The immediate effect of the floods from the two dams breached was to cause devastation and disruption through the valley of the Ruhr as far as Duisburg and serious flooding below the Eder at Kassel and other places down the Weser valley.[29]

It had undoubtedly been a severe blow to the Nazis, far beyond the effects of a routine bombing raid involving hundreds of aircraft, not just nineteen. In Bomber Command terms the losses of fifty-three men had not even been severe. Experienced squadron leaders and flight lieutenants were being killed on a regular basis in the Battle of the Ruhr. If the Sorpe, with its greater supply of water for industrial needs, had been breached as well it would have been a calamity for German industrial production.

The change of tactical plan at the eleventh hour gave little chance of success and the Air Staff went ahead despite Harris's misgivings. The War Cabinet was told the aim was not to breach, but to cause leakage which would enforce the Germans to drain the dam to make repairs. One of the aircrew who attacked it was told later this was what had happened. But in fact the Sorpe was little damaged, never drained and the crest was soon repaired. Three days after the raid Immediate Interpretative Report No. K1564 from RAF High Wycombe revealed to the Air Ministry: 'No vital change can be seen except for violent activity on some sort of repair work and clearance of the road over the crest of the dam.'[30]

Would the cumulative effect of six of Wallis's bombs have caused the Sorpe core to crack? Sgt Johnson, bomb aimer of McCarthy's successful crew, says:

I think if all the crews had got through there would have been a very good chance of cracking the dam. If people had got there and got their attacks in it would have made a serious impact and, of course, if that dam had gone it would have made a much more serious impact on the German war industry.

Joe McCarthy's son told me that when his father went to the Sorpe after the war he said that if he had seen it before he wouldn't have thought it was possible to breach it. Coming from Joe that was quite something because he would try anything. It obviously was possible because we hit it.

SGT McDonald, rear gunner in the other crew to hit the Sorpe, F/Sgt Brown's, says categorically, however: 'You could never have breached the Sorpe with that bomb.'

It is certain that once the second wave – on course for the Sorpe – was decimated, there was practically no chance of success. Perhaps more trained crews and aircraft would have been the answer for such an important operation.

There were other accretions to the Bomber Offensive from the Dams Raid. The technique of a formation leader directing his aircraft in the target area was to blossom into the master bomber method of controlling attacks – a dangerous but valuable position which was eventually to claim the life of Guy Gibson himself. Harris was now so convinced of Wallis's genius that he encouraged development of the 10-ton bomb Wallis originally thought was needed to breach the dams and it was used to great effect by two RAF squadrons in the final months of the war. 617 Sqn, under the leadership of a later commander, Leonard Cheshire, was to develop low-level marking techniques which turned it into a 5 Group rival to the Pathfinders and may have enhanced the performance of each of them.

Perhaps most importantly of all, it showed the Nazis, who were feeling the full effects of the Battle of the Ruhr, that Bomber Command could now hit a pinpoint target at night and get away with it. The days of the Butt Report to Churchill's Cabinet, which showed that by the middle of 1941 only one in five of British bombers dispatched to attack all targets had got within 5 miles of them, were over.

THIRTEEN days after the Dams Raid the awarding of thirty-four gallantry medals was announced, from a VC for Guy Gibson to a DFM for Sgt Johnson and also for Sgt Vivian Nicholson, a medal winner on his first foray against the enemy. One other person had already received an award as a result of Operation Chastise. Unteroffizier Karl Schutte was wearing the Iron Cross, Second Class, for shooting down F/Lt John Hopgood's M-Mother over the Möhne dam.

CHAPTER EIGHT

POINTBLANK AND RETURN TO THE RUHR

IF the leaders of the Reich needed a further example of what Bomber Command could now achieve to end their regime they would find it nine days later with the sound and fury of 826 aircraft unloading their high explosives and incendiaries on Dortmund. There were now many three-flight squadrons in Bomber Command and the Battle of the Ruhr was about to enter a key phase of destruction as the region's industrial cities were regularly hammered by bomber fleets of 700-plus.

The better weather and improved servicing would mean fewer early returns and – in theory – more aircraft at one time through the boxes of the Kammhuber Line would mean smaller percentage losses with return to bombing heights of between 14,000 and 20,000 feet. The theory would seem flawed in reality.

In this period, less than a month after the Dams Raid and six weeks before the cataclysm of Hamburg, Harris and Ira Eaker of the US Eighth Air Force received a revision of their directions on how to prosecute the bombing of Germany. The combined chiefs of staff were aware of how much it was costing in aircraft and airmen's lives and the concern was that Bomber Command and the USAAF, whose day attacks were at last making an impact, would eventually be ground to a halt by sheer lack of material and men for the round-the-clock bombing of the Reich. The new directive, known as Pointblank, admitted that Harris's and Eaker's incursions have 'forced the enemy to deploy day and night fighters in increasing numbers on the Western Front. Unless this increase in fighter strength is checked we may find our bomber forces unable to fulfil the tasks allotted to them by the Combined Chiefs of Staff.'

Pointblank continued that the combined chiefs had decided that 'the first priority in the operation of British and American bombers based in the United Kingdom shall be accorded to the attack of the German fighter forces and the industry upon which they depend'.

Dams Raid apart, Harris's force could not attack precision targets at night. He interpreted his part of the directive as bombing those industrial towns and cities in which there lay large numbers of aircraft component factories. But these were to the east and south of the Ruhr and until the longer nights of the autumn and winter arrived it would be suicide for his crews to attempt such distant targets.

The original requirements of the Casablanca Directive remained and Harris continued in his task of wrecking the industry of the Ruhr and pressed for improvements in H2S radar equipment to allow him to attack more precisely outside Oboe range. The Americans would concentrate on destroying the German airframe, engine and component factories and the ball-bearing industry without which German fighter manufacture could not continue.

As the spring nights shortened towards summer, Duisburg, Düsseldorf, Essen, Münster, Bochum, Oberhausen, Krefeld, Mülheim and Gelsen-kirchen would resound to the whine and crump of bombs. Five operations would be mounted in six nights in the last week of June – Bomber Command's own *Big Week* – and two heavy raids would be mounted on Wuppertal, the first of which would create a 'firestorm' effect, soon to be seen in its full terrible fury in Hamburg to shock the Nazis to the core. But the losses in aircrew would rise proportionately, a single squadron losing six of its aircraft in one night.

Dortmund on 23 May was a case in point. It was the largest raid of the Battle of the Ruhr and the biggest of the war so far apart from the three

1,000-bomber raids of 1942. The Pathfinders were able to mark the target accurately in clear skies marred by the lurid flashes of bursting shells as they faced the flak's red rage. The centre, the north and the east of Dortmund were devastated, one large steelworks being wrecked completely. Night fighters claimed twelve bombers and twenty-six more fell to flak or disappeared without trace into the North Sea.

Bomb aimer Sgt George Stewart was in the nose of his 50 Sqn Lancaster watching the destruction unfold below. He recalls:

I could feel the slipstream of the aircraft in front on the way towards the target, but as on any op the only time I saw other aircraft was over the target itself. We looked down from 20,000 feet in the Lancs on the Wellingtons and Stirlings and I saw one or two coned and attacked.

The light flak coming up was red, green and yellow. It came up towards us then died away because it was only effective to 15,000 feet, but the heavy flak you didn't see at all – just the flashes of it exploding – and there was the smell of the cordite and the white searchlights crossing the sky.[1]

Members of 467 Sqn had found the barrage flak nerve-racking to fly through, but – unlike later crews on target – saw so few searchlights it caused speculation that the enemy were trying new tactics. The adjutant's office reported: 'Numerous aircraft were seen shot down, apparently by enemy fighters.' One of them was that of F/O Giddey and his crew, who had barely had time to unpack before going missing. Giddey was shot down over Holland and both his gunners were killed.[2]

The squadron lost one other aircraft that night, but others were hit far more heavily. 51 Sqn lost four and another crashed with hydraulic failure shortly after take-off; 78 Sqn lost three, as did 166 and 214 Sqns.

Josef Goebbels, the Reich Propaganda Minister, considered the raid had been 'probably the worst ever directed against a German city'. He recorded in his assiduously kept diary: 'Reports from Dortmund are pretty horrible. The critical thing about it is that industrial and munitions plants have been hit very hard. We are in an almost helpless inferiority and must

grin and bear it as we take the blows from the English and Americans.'
Dortmund's gauleiter, Hoffman, had told him that hardly a house in the
city was habitable and 'other big cities on the Rhine and the Ruhr can just
about figure out for themselves what fate is soon in store for them'.

Bomber Command was indeed making its might tell and Harris's private
prediction as he watched the London Blitz, that having sown the wind the
Nazis would reap the whirlwind, was ending in the reality of blasted streets
and the smell of death in the smoky morning air.

But while cities such as Dortmund smouldered and the Nazis specu-
lated about what was to come, the attrition rate in Bomber Command's
ranks mounted throughout the Battle of the Ruhr. Canadian P/O Albert
Wallace was one of those it touched. He had arrived at Middleton St George
in February, posted as a mid-upper gunner to 419 Sqn, and his operational
career ended during a May raid on Duisburg. P/O Wallace had arrived at his
Halifax to find it had undergone the conversion overnight which removed
the mid-upper turret to gain more height and speed. Nobody had told him
about the change at briefing, which strictly obviated the need for him to
go. He remembers:

When I got out of the crew bus at dispersal I discovered there was a
large hole in the floor of the aircraft covered by plastic. Apparently
my job was just to lie down over this hole and look for fighters. There
was very little between me and what might come up from below and I
felt very vulnerable.

It was my second trip to Duisburg and this time looking down at
the view over the target was spectacular. I could see the bombs going
down and the incendiaries fluttering in the air. I could see the shock
waves as the Cookies hit with a red glow and then the incendiaries
going off like sparklers.

We had bombed and closed the bomb doors when the bomb aimer
discovered we had a hang-up so the bomb doors were opened again
and we kept flying straight and level. It was a fatal error. The flak had
us zeroed in and they got us. We lost the starboard outer from the burst

and feathered it. There was a hole in the wing and I could see a blue flame coming up through it. Then we lost the starboard inner and the engineer told the pilot the fire was going to go through the main spar of the wing. With that the pilot, W/O Glenn McMillan, said: 'Bale out' and then he countermanded it and said: 'Hold on for a roll call'. Everybody chimed in except the rear gunner, Hank Bees, so the pilot asked me to check on him. When I got to the rear turret I saw it was turned around and the two doors were flapping in the breeze. Hank had heard the bale out order and gone.

I went to the port hatch and sat down and I couldn't get the nerve up to jump. I think I was having hallucinations through lack of oxygen and thought if I jumped I would hit the ground. I plugged my intercom back in and asked the pilot, 'Mac, how high are we?' He replied, '12,000 feet, Wally, get out, get out.' With that I unplugged and moved forward and the slipstream pulled me out. I had my hand on the D-ring as I went and pulled the ripcord immediately. There was a great crack and a jerk as the chute opened up and I seemed to be hanging up there for ever. It was pitch-black without a horizon, then I saw the earth coming up. I'd gone to one lecture about what to do if you had to bale out and the instructor's words all came back to me. I closed my legs, bent my knees, hit the ground and rolled over. It was just like getting out of bed. There was a barn about 10 feet away and I hadn't even seen it. I started to gather up my chute and two farmers came up and grabbed me. They weren't unfriendly and I thought we might have made it to Holland so I asked, 'Dutch?' and they said, 'Ja, Deutsch.'[3]

Gauleiter Hoffman's prediction after the Dortmund raid of town after town destruction was realised two nights later at Düsseldorf as 759 aircraft dropped 2,000 tons of bombs. Five Cookies were released every minute, spilling their pink shock waves over the target. But skymarkers had had to be used and there were two layers of cloud across Düsseldorf, causing scattered bombing. It was a grave disappointment compared to the headlines in the British press the previous day, which had trumpeted the same tonnage on

Dortmund and told a pilot's story of 'single searchlights waving aimlessly about the sky as if the defences couldn't stand up to the weight of bombs'.

It was an example of how the same planning, professionalism and weight of weaponry could be committed to two similar operations yet the caprice of weather was the final deciding factor. From Grimsby 100 Sqn had sent twenty-five aircraft, 'the squadron's best effort so far', the adjutant's office proudly reported, but they lost two crews among the twenty-seven aircraft missing and one was led by another experienced squadron figure, the young C-Flight commander S/Ldr Philip Turgel. Holding senior rank on 100 Sqn was proving a short experience.[4]

The attrition rate from the Battle of the Ruhr was causing a manpower crisis on many squadrons and the gentle introduction to operations favoured by many COs at the beginning of the year, even by firebrands such as Guy Gibson, was giving way to the harsh realities of maximum effort demanded by Harris.

Sgt Peter Johnson was over Düsseldorf, beginning operations in a 101 Sqn Lancaster. The 21-year-old Londoner's rapid tour would take him through the height of the Battle of the Ruhr into the Battle of Hamburg and would encompass two tough Berlin raids. Sgt Johnson, newly graduated from OTU, had reported with his crew to Holme on Spalding Moor only 48 hours before the Düsseldorf operation. He quickly discovered the squadron had more aircraft than crews:

> I signed in at Holme on the Monday morning and they put me on ops on the Tuesday night, no second-dickey trip, just straight in. I was assigned to B Flight and the commander was away. The deputy was a real press-on type. He gave me an air test and then I was on the op. I was excited about it at the time. All my training had been for that. Things deteriorated.[5]

As Sgt Johnson's tour began, that of Albert Bracegirdle and Graham Allen ended on 106 Sqn as their pilot, the newly commissioned Gordon McGregor, was screened. They had had to return early from the Düsseldorf operation because the air speed indicator failed in the thick cloud.

The same weather problems which had prejudiced the attack on Düsseldorf were present at Essen two nights later. However, the RAF had just got a third pair of Oboe ground stations working and it meant the target could be marked almost continuously throughout the fifty minutes of the attack. Essen was covered by eight-tenths cloud and skymarkers had to be used leading to scattered bombing, but the central and northern districts were hit by many of the 500-plus aircraft dispatched and nearly 500 buildings were destroyed. Bomb aimers later on target reported seeing the glow of fires turning the clouds red. Krupps, placed so centrally, was inevitably damaged again.

Wireless operator Sgt James Arnold was on his fourth operation with 49 Sqn when he found himself coned over Essen. He recalls:

One moment we were flying along in complete darkness, then it was just like day. I felt naked when the searchlights fastened on us. I used to have the blind across the window by my position and it was just as if someone had switched a light on in a darkened room. There was a sensation you were being looked at from below. The pilot, Sgt George Cole, dived and corkscrewed us out of it. It seemed ages, but it was a matter of minutes. We could feel the explosions from the flak and could see the flaming onions of the flak bursting. We had seen other aircraft explode when they were hit. There would be a great big blow in the sky, then nothing.[6]

F/Sgt Robert Gill, an air gunner on 158 Sqn, was making his first operational flight and had the same experience:

In the Ruhr you went along from one lot of flak to another. We were suddenly coned and everything went quiet. Then the flak started coming up, but the pilot, Archie Hardy, put us into a very steep dive. I thought: 'I wonder where we're going from here', but we got out of it. Later the pilot admitted he didn't know how much the wings of the aircraft would stand.[7]

A total of twenty-three aircraft were lost in the raid, a just acceptable

4.4 per cent for a Ruhr target, but in personal terms 51 Sqn, so badly mauled on the Dortmund operation, lost another two crews.

THE clocks had gone forward two hours – 'double summer time' as it was known – and the warmth of spring meant few evenings spent in the mess for aircrew not on the battle order for the Ruhr. Canadians, Australians and New Zealanders roamed the historic lanes of York, Lincoln and Cambridge in the sunshine, rowing down the Ouse or punting on the Cam as they contemplated how good life could be away from the war.

Herb Hoover and his crew spent most free evenings in the Alice Hawthorn pub at Nun Monkton, rowed across the Ouse from their billet in Beningbrough Hall by the ferry boatman, 'Captain Nick'. The problem was that the ferry service stopped before closing time. Sgt Hill remembers:

> We would then call at Captain Nick's house. His wife would admit us into a small hall from where we could see him eating his supper. Gradually we would enter into his dining room. His wife would say: 'If he has taken his boots off he won't take you back.' Captain Nick would completely ignore us as we craned our necks to catch a glimpse of his feet to see if his boots were on or off. Invariably they were off.

There then followed a game, which only had one outcome for the anxious young airmen. Sgt Hill recalls:

> After dining he would light his pipe and sit in contemplation puffing serenely. Still not giving us the merest glance he would say: 'You know the rules, you can walk back,' signifying the bridge miles away.
>
> After much cajoling by the pilot he would reach for his boots and an audible sigh would go round the room. His wife would then say: 'You naughty boys, Mr Nichols is not pleased.' On arrival on the other side Herb Hoover, who being a Canadian was wealthy by our RAF standards, would tip him with a 10-shilling note and we would stump up the regular fare plus a bit extra. He knew and we knew he would take us across.[8]

Hoover and his crew were now the most seasoned on 76 Sqn in the last third of their operational tour and the Canadian had been commissioned. They found themselves on the battle order for the Wuppertal operation of 29 May, their twenty-fourth target. The raid in terms of damage by fire was the most successful of the Battle of the Ruhr; up to 80 per cent of the Barmen half of the straggling town was burned out, including five of its six largest factories and more than 200 other industrial premises. It was also an operation from which thirty-three aircraft would be lost, 35 and 75 Sqns losing four aircraft each and 466 Sqn three.

F/Sgt William Garfield was the bomb aimer in one of the 466 Sqn Wellingtons, skippered by Sgt Lindsay Upjohn. He remembers:

As we flew over Holland and were about to cross the border into Germany it was realised someone had left the armour plate doors open in the centre of the fuselage so I went back to close them. As I did so the bullets from a fighter banged against them. I heard the 'tonk, tonk, tonk' sound of the machine-gun bullets hitting.

The pilot went into a corkscrew to port, but the rear gunner, F/Sgt Jock Hay, had already been killed. There was a clang as the fighter fired again, hitting the top of the fuselage, and he set the starboard engine on fire. He then disappeared and I think he was out of ammunition because he hadn't used his cannon. We were descending because we couldn't fly on one engine and the pilot asked me to go back to see if the rear gunner was all right. I shouted to Jock, but didn't get any answer, then I felt along the back of the turret and it was full of bullet holes and there was blood there, so I knew he was dead.

I hadn't plugged in my intercom and didn't hear the pilot order the crew to bale out. When I went back to the front I saw they had all gone through the front hatch. I was afraid the Ju88 might still be around, so I kicked open the diamond hatch on the right-hand side and went out. There was a lot of smoke from the burning engine and I just missed the tail. The Wellington was still flying, but going down. I landed in a newly ploughed field into two feet of soft earth near the village of Hasselt, not far from Venlo. The rest of my crew landed miles away and I never saw them again. I hid the parachute and went to a farmhouse nearby. I heard the family talking in Dutch in the basement. I shouted, 'Anybody home?' The farmer came up and said: 'You're English.' I said: 'Welsh actually' and he said: 'I'll take you to see the priest.'

Father Gerard, parish priest of St Lambertus in Hasselt, ran the local underground, helping Allied airmen to evade on the Comet escape line. Within days F/Sgt Garfield was in Brussels after being helped by a 14-year-old Resistance member:

A few of us stayed with a couple of old ladies in a house next to the German Embassy. If you went into the garden you could see Germans through the windows. The two old ladies were picked up later and the Germans did for them.

As we got further down we were picking up people all the time and we got down as far as Paris. There were about twenty of us on the Paris Nord tube station when the gendarmes came in at both ends. On the way to Fresnes Prison one of them apologised very deeply to me. He said: 'I've got to do this, I've got a wife and child', so I told him he'd have his deserts after the war.[9]

WHILE aircrew were being shot out of the skies en route and over Wuppertal others on the ground would die in much greater numbers. Three of the eleven Oboe Mosquitos had to return early, but the rest dropped their red TIs accurately to guide more than 650 aircraft to the old, narrow streets of Barmen. Raging fires quickly began to link up. There were indications of a firestorm, where cooler air was sucked towards the conflagration, shooting sparks and burning material into areas untouched by flame. That particular fire spread for more than 3 miles. In the chaos following the raid, which effectively brought Wuppertal to a halt, few proper records were made, but it is thought approximately 3,500 people lost their lives, by many times the highest death toll of any air raid so far.

F/Sgt Robert Gill of 158 Sqn, who had been coned over Essen two nights before, remembers:

> At briefing we were told Wuppertal was one of the centres of the textile industry. From the rear turret at 18,000 feet the fires were absolutely spectacular. It was a clear night and everything was blazing from end to end. As far as I could see the whole city was on fire. There was the yellow fire and the red and green markers going down and the white searchlights outside, an amazing spectacle.[10]

For bomb aimer George Stewart it was a struggle to survive the moment the target came in view of his 50 Sqn Lancaster:

> As we approached we could see two rows of searchlights standing straight up without moving and it looked like a trap, so we started to turn to starboard. The TIs were visible and then accurate flak started to come up. One shell came straight in and out through the roof. There was a hole the size of a bucket by my side. Then flak hit a port engine; the engineer used the extinguisher and feathered it.
>
> But two or three minutes later we were hit again with a blow like a sledgehammer and then flak hit an engine on the other side and that caught fire. The engineer put it out and it too had to be feathered. We seemed to be in predicted flak and the bomb doors fell open and the wheels dropped down as all the hydraulics were shot away. We had a full bomb load and I was always worried about being hit in the bomb bay.
>
> We were down to 8,000 feet and bombed from there. We turned away from the target and because of the lack of power and the wheels and bomb bay doors causing drag we kept losing height until we were down to about 2,000–3,000 feet. The skipper told us: 'If we can't maintain height we'll have to abandon.'
>
> He got everyone to throw out their ammo and the flight engineer undid the armour behind the pilot and threw it out and we steadied the aircraft at about 800 feet. The navigator had to route us through

Holland to avoid the high ground in Germany and we were lucky enough to get back all the way to the drome. Everybody except the pilot had to sit with their backs to the main spar for the landing and as we came in, the wheels collapsed. As the aircraft slithered to a stop we got out as fast as we could and the ambulance crew was waiting. They seemed disappointed nobody had been hurt. We counted forty-seven holes in the aircraft but nobody had been hit. The kite was a write-off.[11]

Pilot Joe McCrossan woke the next morning to find himself officially recognised as a hero. He and his flight engineer, Sgt 'Yorkie' Wilkinson, were up for immediate DFMs and his horrendous journey home had been written up by a news agency reporter, the story appearing the following day in several regional papers.

Sgt Cliff Hill returned safely to 76 Sqn's base after 'a very busy raid with plenty of fighters and a lot of flak and searchlights' and as the weather deteriorated waited to find an unwelcome improvement and his name on the crew roster again. It was not to be. He says:

The following week the flight commander told the pilot our tour was finished. We went out to the pub later and it was a marvellous do. It was a day I never expected to see. We'd been screened early as a morale-booster; crews were going missing on the squadron on their twenty-seventh and twenty-eighth op. We came off at twenty-five. I phoned my parents. I didn't appreciate at the time how worried my mother had been – all you wanted to do was get home on leave and go out and have a good time.[12]

Four of the crew would return for a second tour with Pathfinders in 1944. All aircrew knew that the end of one tour would probably only be a temporary reprieve. At the end of a minimum six months away from operational flying they could be recalled for a second tour of twenty operations, which they could not refuse. In the unlikely event they survived those they were free of ops unless they volunteered for a third tour. Some did. Few survived.

IT had been a gruelling month for the command, with 180 heavy bombers lost in ten major operations. The medical officer of 214 Sqn, which operated Stirlings from Chedburgh – considered by many to be flak and fighter bait – was moved to report: 'Some of the new crews are shaky and they present some difficulty suggesting rather that training is finished too hurriedly.'[13] The squadron had lost nine aircraft in the month, three alone on the Dortmund operation of 23 May. Little wonder new crews showed signs of nerves as they realised how slight their chances of surviving a tour were.

In the Canadian 6 Group, where squadron commanders thought their crews got the worst of the targets or were placed in the most hazardous of waves, losses amounted to 8 per cent. The Commonwealth prime ministers had been promised that the cream of their country's manhood would be well cared for under British leadership. It was time to improve morale and one of the ways to achieve that aim was by providing better quarters.

The result was that many RAF squadrons in Yorkshire and Lincolnshire were moved out of their comfortable, permanent pre-war stations and Commonwealth squadrons moved in. Two RAF squadrons, 9 and 44, left the purpose-built order of Waddington so that concrete runways could be laid. It would be Australian squadrons, 463 and 467, which would be posted in when they were ready. The aircrew of 9 Sqn would shiver in Nissen huts at Bardney and 44 Sqn at the equally inhospitable Dunholme Lodge.

The Australian 460 Sqn was moved from spartan Breighton to well-constructed Binbrook, and 78 and 76 Sqns moved out of the red-brick grandeur of Linton-on-Ouse. 78 Sqn went to Breighton and 76 Sqn, which now had a new CO since Leonard Cheshire had been promoted to group captain a few weeks before, to bleak Holme on Spalding Moor, from which 101 Sqn now moved to the new airfield of Ludford Magna near Louth in Lincolnshire – hardly an improvement for 101 Sqn. Ludford became universally known throughout the command as Mudford Magna.

It was at Linton, where the NCO aircrew had been billeted in a stately home, that the switch was felt most keenly. At one time they had been used to civilised evenings lounging by the grand piano in their own bar at Beningbrough Hall where a dark-haired navigator used to wander in wearing gloves and play Chopin's 'Polonaise in A Flat'. Sgt Hill remembers: 'It caused a lot of resentment swapping Beningbrough for Nissen huts.'[14]

THE Command had been idle for almost two weeks as rain and cold winds swept the British Isles, but Harris could wait no longer. He had now lost 2 Group, with its medium bombers transferred to the Second Tactical Air Force, but extra flights and even whole new squadrons of 'heavies' were being formed as his force expanded. In the two weeks of bad weather considerable numbers of new Lancasters and Halifaxes had rolled out of the factories.

By 3 June Bomber Command's nominal front-line strength stood at 784 heavy bombers with another 148 on standby, up from 608 on 4 March.[15] Slowly the Stirlings were being phased out and replaced with Lancasters, but Halifaxes constituted an important part of the command. On 11 June there were enough Halifaxes to send more than 200 to Düsseldorf, the first time so many had been used on a raid, and part of a total powerful force of 783 aircraft.

Harris now had so many aircraft he could employ part of his force on a diversionary raid and on the same night seventy-two aircraft from Pathfinder squadrons were sent on an important experimental operation against Münster in a mass trial of H2S. Just under half the aircraft carried flares, the rest were the bomber force. In less than ten minutes severe damage was achieved against railway installations, but the small force suffered expensive losses, five aircraft failing to return, two of them from 35 Sqn.

Of the 783 aircraft in the Düsseldorf force many turned back in ten-tenths cloud and icing conditions over the North Sea, but 655 bombed over skymarkers. It would have been a perfect Wanganui attack if one of the Oboe-directed Pathfinder aircraft hadn't inadvertently released its TIs 14 miles to the north. Some Main Force aircraft followed and bombed in open country.

As it was, more than sixty factories were damaged in what Harris later described as 'a vast conflagration' sweeping the town, and the fire brigades lost control. There was the heavy loss of life that had now become the pattern on Ruhr raids and 140,000 residents were bombed out. The embers were still smouldering a week later.

The Lancaster squadron 619 had lately been formed at Woodhall Spa and the Düsseldorf raid was its first operation. F/O Stewart Harris, navigator in B-Beer being flown by F/Lt Colin Taylor, was working on the route halfway across the North Sea to the Frisian Islands when the air speed indicator failed, which meant they could no longer keep an accurate course. F/Lt Taylor took the views of all the crew and decided to press on.

Over Belgium a night fighter attacked from the port quarter and raked the aircraft with cannon fire, setting fire to three engines and destroying the pitch control to all four. The fighter came in astern to finish them off, but the gunners blasted him with the combined power of six .303 machine guns and the German aircraft exploded.

The crew put out the fires in two of the engines, jettisoned the bomb load and managed to turn the aircraft on a homeward course despite heavy damage to the ailerons and tail fins. But the fire in the starboard outer raged on and it seemed likely the Lancaster would blow up. The pilot ordered the crew to abandon. Says F/O Harris:

> I put on my chest pack, threw all the contents of my pockets on the navigation table and followed the bomb aimer and flight engineer out. I squatted momentarily on the edge of the roaring black hole which was the escape hatch and rolled out. I don't remember pulling the ripcord and was knocked senseless. When I came round, the aircraft could still be heard, but in a few moments it was gone and it was eerily quiet.
>
> I had been hit in the face by the chute harness and my face was well bloodied. There seemed to be a light shining in my face. I eventually worked out that a torch which I had stuffed into my battledress had switched itself on. I landed in the middle of a wheat field.*[16]

* The pilot, F/Lt Taylor, landed on the back of a cow and successfully evaded through Belgium, France and Spain to Gibraltar. The rest of the crew became prisoners of war, but F/O Harris evaded capture for five weeks until being arrested by the Gestapo. He spent nine weeks in solitary confinement, receiving little food. He was finally sent to Stalag Luft III and repatriated because of his poor physical state in February 1945. As a result of his treatment by the Gestapo he is now blind.

A Halifax of 77 Sqn was also shot down over Belgium at about this time as it wandered off track over the German night-fighter base of St Trond. Hauptmann Eckart-Wilhelm von Bonin was already in the air in his Me110, having shot down the 35 Sqn aircraft of F/Lt Stan Howe over Holland, and was vectored onto the aircraft.

Sgt John Walsh, the Halifax's flight engineer, recalled in notes he made after the war:

> We were to the east of Brussels when a burst of machine-gun fire raked the underside of the starboard wing, knocking out the starboard inner engine and setting the fuel tanks alight. The rear gunner Sgt Stan Hammond called, 'Christ, I've been hit.' I thought at that time he baled out.

Two more Me110s now came in on either side of the crippled Halifax and the one on the port side opened up, but the mid-upper gunner, Sgt Dennis Burrows, drove him off with accurate fire and he had to make an emergency landing at St Trond airfield. The starboard fighter then came into the attack and the gunner shot it down in flames.

The Halifax's starboard wing was now burning furiously. The pilot called: 'Bale out', and the crew went out except Sgt Walsh and the mid-upper gunner. Hauptmann von Bonin was still behind, loosing off cannon and machine-gun fire.

Sgt Walsh wrote: 'I trimmed the aircraft level and by turning the elevator trim handwheel fully up and down tried to get the aircraft to wallow for Dennis to get a shot at him. This was not successful, so I told him we were the only ones left and to get out.'

They then discovered the armour plate door between the mid-upper turret and the front of the aircraft was jammed. Sgt Walsh wrote:

> With him pulling and me pushing at the buckled door and with the aid of the fire axe I got the door open. I will never forget the white face that greeted me.
>
> With Dennis out I dived head first down the steps and out of the

escape hatch behind the navigator's position. The aircraft was at 14,000 feet and the slipstream hit me and tumbled me over with the rubbish and cinders from the burning aircraft getting in my eyes. I straightened up and was falling vertically and reached for my D-ring. It was not there! The fact that I had not held the pack to my chest when I jumped meant it was blowing about above my head. Reaching up I found the release handle first time and pulled. The canopy deployed in textbook fashion to much relief.[17]

Sgt Walsh saw his burning aircraft fly on, slowly make a diving turn to port and crash in a quarry with its bombs on board, killing three civilians, the blast sending him skidding across the sky. Of the crew all but the rear gunner had survived. Sgt Walsh was captured the next day.

The Düsseldorf and Münster raids were acclaimed by the British public, one regional newspaper noting that the two-week stand-down since the apocalyptic attack on Wuppertal had been 'the longest after-dark bombing lull on Germany this year'. Any frustration had now been blown away with what were being described as devastating attacks.

Both newspapers and the public were still coming to grips with how serious for the Germans had been the March and April raids on the Krupps plant at Essen. Essen was now being described in the press, in these days before Hamburg, Dresden and the Atomic Age, as the most bombed city in the world.

A four-column photograph appeared in the *Daily Express* on 13 May under the headline 'What we did to Krupps'. It showed many of the one hundred industrial buildings and offices destroyed, with an accompanying key. The Air Ministry picture was considered such good propaganda it was made into a leaflet dropped on the Ruhr in June and July, one of a total of 265 million leaflets produced by the Political Warfare Executive and distributed over Germany throughout the war. Harris considered them a complete waste of time, taking up incendiary bomb space and only providing the Germans with unlimited toilet requirements.

Meanwhile the British public stuck war savings stamps on bombs for

Germany as 'Wings For Victory' weeks were held by towns throughout the land in the warm spring weather. There was satisfaction to be had for those who had endured the Blitz on Britain in ads such as the one for Weston's Biscuits which appeared in the *Daily Express* of 14 June, showing a sketch of a laughing pilot. It read: 'Jim's back from Essen. "Krupps," he says, "are all that they are cracked up to be." He fairly takes the biscuit!'

It was obvious now to all that German industry was being hit hard and even the Nazis were recognising the series of raids under the title of the Battle of the Ruhr. The German radio network beamed to neutral countries had admitted in June: 'It is true that the people of the Ruhr spend their nights in the cellars ... but the work goes on. We must not forget that the hour of retaliation will come and then the battle will bear the name of one of the English counties.'

In fact the Luftwaffe reply at this time consisted of the odd nuisance raid against a south coast town, the sound of sirens no match for the church bells which had pealed throughout the land to celebrate the successful end of the campaign in North Africa.

But as the RAF raids grew the *nachtjäger* were getting better and more numerous and stories were beginning to appear in the press to answer worries over longer RAF casualty lists. In April the *Daily Express* had run, under the headline 'RAF send more bombers: Losses not disturbing', a story explaining that more aircraft were failing to return because more were being sent, not because the Germans had developed new skills. It read: 'Losses in RAF raids on Germany, which have sometimes reached 20 a night recently, will have no restraining effect on our attack. Bomber Command continues to expand every week.'

By June and July losses of twenty in raids were common and thirty or forty were not unusual. Of the 503 aircraft sent to raid Bochum on 12 June, for instance, twenty-four failed to return. And this was considered an almost acceptable figure, a percentage rate of 4.8 compared to the 6.3 on Krefeld or Gelsenkirchen.

Among the crews lost on Bochum was that of Sgt John Cornish. The Canadian air gunner had arrived on 460 Sqn only 24 hours before finding himself on the battle order for Wuppertal and was now making his third operational flight. As his Lancaster neared IJsselmuiden east of Amsterdam there was a large explosion in the aircraft. He says:

We had been hit by cannon shell from underneath and everything was on fire. The only one to speak was the pilot, Sgt Ron Vaughan, who said: 'Abandon aircraft.' I climbed down from the mid-upper turret and opened the doors to the rear gunner so he could come in and bale out, but he was not there – he must have been blown off.

Sgt Cornish opened the rear door and baled out, the tailplane catching him a glancing blow. That and lack of oxygen caused him to pass out:

I came to at about 10,000 feet. My intercom cord had partly split across my chute, but I got out a knife and cut it, allowing the chute to fully open. I saw my aircraft burning in the distance. All of a sudden tree tops came up and I landed on my butt in a cow pat. Cattle were mooing all around. I had a bullet in my left leg, a toe missing on my right foot and a badly burned face.

The body of the RAF rear gunner, Sgt Andrew Gordon, was lying about 200 yards away. 'My face was very sore, so I took out my escape kit and spread the condensed milk over my burns to soothe them,' Sgt Cornish says. 'I took off my parachute and got up to walk but fell, so I had to crawl. I headed towards what looked like buildings.'[18]

Sgt Cornish hammered on the door of a farmhouse and was helped inside by a farmer and two of his sons. In the morning he would be unable to see and his ordeal would continue as night by night the raids continued.

The Main Force was harried into the Ruhr valley by night fighters as it thundered on to Bochum. A 77 Sqn sergeant pilot reported: 'Six miles west of Munster tracer was observed, then an aircraft in flames, which exploded and was followed down by a fighter which was still firing.' It wasn't the only combat he observed that night. He went on: 'Ten miles north of Almelo red and green tracer was seen, also return fire, and the aircraft was seen to fall and hit the ground.'[19]

For a skymarking attack the raid was extremely accurate and 130 acres of the centre was destroyed. Over the target flak bursting alongside killed a 12 Sqn bomb aimer as he looked through his bomb sight. The pilot had to use his own jettison control to release the bombs.[20]

The newly decorated Sgt Joe McCrossan, on his eleventh operation, found himself at the tail end of the stream. The op had gone wrong from the moment he left 50 Sqn's base at Skellingthorpe. His bomb aimer, Sgt Stewart, remembers:

> The gremlins were with us that night. When we got in the aircraft to start up, the navigator found someone had switched the gyro compass off, then when we climbed up to 10,000 feet and were ordered to go on oxygen we found all five bottles had been switched off. We had to go and switch them all back on. Then the engines started overheating. Because the engines were acting up it made us late on the target.

By that time the flak units of Bochum were demonstrating their full awesome power. 'As we went into the target there was a lot of AA and we started weaving and I could hear crashes at the back as we were getting hit,' he says. 'So I put my chute on and I lay over the escape hatch to set up the bomb sight ready to drop the bombs in three or four minutes' time.'

At that moment the aircraft took a direct hit by a flak shell and blew up. Those members of the crew whose bodies survived the blast were tossed out to fall through the sky at terminal velocity with pieces of the wrecked aircraft around them. Only Sgt Stewart and the dead pilot, whose survival equipment was part of his seat, were wearing chutes. Sgt Stewart says:

> I had no sensation of it happening. When I regained consciousness I was in my chute, I could feel blood running down the side of my face, my feet were freezing and my left shoulder was aching. I didn't pull my ripcord, so the explosion must have ripped my pack open. I must have drifted over the target, through all that flak, unconscious for about fifteen or twenty minutes because I hit the deck in two or three minutes and we had been flying at 20,000 feet.

POINTBLANK AND RETURN TO THE RUHR

I had awoken hearing the terrific 'rip, rip' noise of the bombs coming down. There was a big glow at the back, but darkness in front. Then I crashed down into a cemetery in a village between Bochum and Dortmund. Bombs were falling all around me. I lay there for about an hour and could hear a flak battery firing not far away. I tried to get on my back but couldn't and lost consciousness again.

I awoke once more to hear the flak men moving around me and they carried me in a stretcher to a maternity hospital 50 yards away. Dawn was breaking at this time and women were coming out of their houses and spitting at me and trying to get at me, and the flak crew were warding them off.

At the hospital there were a lot of Frenchmen from a forced labour camp we had bombed and they had a French padre with them. The doctor was in the SS and he wanted to finish me off with an injection as a *terrorflieger*, but the padre told him not to. I had a big wound in the front of my head which left an indentation.*[21]

THE cloudy Continental weather continued and two nights later Oboe-directed Mosquitos dropped skymarkers right over the centre of the old town of Oberhausen.

They were followed by an all-Lancaster force of 197 aircraft, which destroyed or damaged 850 buildings. It was also the first time Serrate, a device by which British night fighters could home into the search radar of German *nachtjäger* transmissions, was used. The RAF fighter pilots, however, had no success as they patrolled the German bases.

Lancaster pilot Sgt George Cole of 49 Sqn was asked to take an extra navigator on the raid – Sgt Biggin – to show him the ropes prior to Biggin operating with his own crew. Sgt James Arnold, wireless operator in the Cole crew, remembers: 'The loss rate was so high at that time we were one of the most experienced crews on the squadron even though we had only done five operations.'[22]

* *Sgt Stewart's wounds were such that he was repatriated from a prison camp the following year.*

On the way to the target the flight engineer of a 103 Sqn Lancaster would carry out a running repair which would win him an immediate DFM for cool ingenuity.

Sgt Sandy Rowe, whose dramatic tour would end over Mannheim in September, recalls of the Oberhausen raid:

> We were over Germany when the rear gunner called up to say he was being covered in hot oil. I picked up my tools and went back with a 10-minute oxygen bottle. I found a feed pipe was broken to one of the guns. I bent the pipe to stop the oil flow, but the turret still wouldn't work because too much oil had been lost.
>
> As it happened, this particular aircraft was fitted with a complete hydraulic system for a turret underneath, although it had never had under-guns. So I thought I'd use that oil. I took an axe and cut the feed pipe and tapped some oil into a thermos flask and transferred it to the rear guns. We managed to get two guns working with it.[23]

The gun turret now operational, the Lancaster of Sgt Rowe headed into the bomb run, as did that of Sgt Arnold. Sgt Arnold remembers:

> We bombed and were coming away from the target when we got a direct hit by flak. The two starboard engines were knocked out and Biggin, who was sitting on the step next to me, was killed instantly and our own navigator was wounded.
>
> We were then jumped by fighters and the pilot went down to the deck to avoid them. We didn't have much power and to maintain height I was throwing extinguishers and everything I could out of the escape hatch. I even tried to get the rear door off. I think the rear gunner, Dusty Rhodes, had baled out and we were too low for his chute to open. Suddenly I heard this swishing sound and it was us going over the top of some woods at Oosterbeek near Arnhem. I came to outside the aircraft, which was going up in flames with a terrible noise. In my confused state I tried to get back in for safety, but it was too high. I was also worried about the carrier pigeons. I knew the crew wouldn't have

survived. I'd hurt my back and could hardly walk. I went to a castle to get help and met some Dutch people who sat me on their bike and took me to a barn and gave me an apple, then a saloon car drew up and out came a German officer, who said: 'For you the war is over.'

I was surprised to see the mid-upper gunner, Johnny Bryan, in the car. Apparently he also had got out of the crash. I was taken to the main hospital in Arnhem and then to a Wehrmacht barracks where I was put in a cell.[24]

The toll on the Oberhausen raid was heavy for the bomber boys. Flak and fighters accounted for seventeen Lancasters, a percentage rate of 8.4. Within 48 hours squadrons would have to find new crews for an experimental raid on Cologne. The city had not been raided since the 1,000-bomber operation the previous May. Much of the damage from the previous year had now been repaired and to take it out of the target list it would be subjected to a series of four raids in all.

Cologne was within Oboe range, but it was decided to use sixteen heavy bombers fitted with H2S to mark the AP. It was not a success. The sets were still proving unreliable and heavy cloud meant skymarkers had to be used, leading to scattered bombing in which only sixteen industrial premises were hit. Fourteen of the 202 aircraft on the raid were lost. One was from 83 Sqn carrying signaller F/O Kenneth East. East's war had been long. He had made his first operational flight on 3 September 1939 as an AC2 wireless operator on a Whitley from Linton-on-Ouse dropping leaflets on Cologne and the Ruhr. Almost a year later he finished his tour with a bombing raid on Berlin and was awarded the DFM.

He had returned for a second tour in May 1943 and now found himself listed to return to Cologne in the crew of Canadian P/O Charles Murray. He remembers:

I was filling in for the regular wireless operator who had been commissioned and gone to get uniform. They were a young, inexperienced
crew. I had only met them at the air test earlier in the day. We were
across Cologne and had bombed, then got hit by two Me110s. All we

heard was the sound of the cannon fire. One shell exploded under my radio set and put a row of holes across my log book in front of me and left a bit of shrapnel in my thumb. I had been jamming the German fighter transmissions with a 'wobulator' which broadcast our engine noise over their frequency. There was no further sound of the fighters and I could see the mid-upper gunner getting down to tackle a small fire in the fuselage so I closed the armour plated doors and carried on.

Then the aircraft started doing funny things; one minute I was off my seat and the next thing I was pinned to it. I was off intercom because I had been working the radio, so I looked forward to see what was happening and there was no one there. I clipped on my chute and walked forward. I tried the pilot's controls but they were just flopping around and whatever I did didn't affect the aeroplane, so I went to the front hatch and baled out.

We were at about 18,000 feet when I went out. I found out later there were bodies laid out alongside the site of where the aircraft went in. The pilot didn't survive, but he wasn't in the aircraft when I left so he must have died on the way down or on the ground. The rear gunner was also killed, I think in the fighter attack. I landed in a cornfield several miles west of Cologne near Jülich. I hid the parachute in the corn and waited, wondering what to do.[25]

THERE was no doubt the losses in aircraft and crews were worrying, but against them Harris could balance the catastrophes which were now overcoming the Ruhr towns and their industry. He was pressing for even more resources and priorities to successfully attack cities outside Oboe range and to this end began his Blue Book in which after each attack the ruined area was marked with blue paint over a mosaic of aerial photographs of the target city.

This book was shown to every important visitor to High Wycombe and to Harris's nearby home, Springfield. To create a three-dimensional effect of what the RAF was achieving Harris borrowed a Victorian stereoptican viewer from a relative. There were few guests at Springfield who would not be steered into the 'conversion' room after dinner to view the photographs and study the charts. Eventually the Blue Book would extend to two or three enormous volumes.

In Germany, Goebbels had his own carefully kept book, his diary, and he was complaining in it about the 'sensational publicity' the English were giving to their successful bombing raids. 'They exaggerate a lot, but unfortunately much of what they claim is true,' he admitted. 'The industrial and munitions plants have been hit very hard,' he wrote. 'One can only repeat about air warfare, we are in an almost helpless inferiority.'

For all Goebbels's private concerns the official propaganda line that the Reich was successfully striking back at Britain's cities continued. A song sheet entitled 'Bomben auf England' was going the rounds from a film about the Luftwaffe entitled *Feuertauffe*. Just in case anyone didn't feel inclined to sit through the lies, a law had been passed making it an offence for anyone to enter or leave a cinema during the showing of a wartime documentary. Taking shelter during an air raid was a justifiable exception.

The Nazis tried to divert the public gaze from the growing gaps, like teeth painfully removed, in urban streets, and luxuries such as permanent wave hair-dos continued despite objections from realists. Members of the Girls' League were still being sent away for youth hostel weekends where they competed to run 60 metres in 12 seconds. *Kraft durch Freude* (Strength through Joy) was still an evident slogan. But a more often seen message now was *Wir Leben* – chalked on the ruins of bombed houses to show that the one-time occupants were still alive.

HARRIS, impatient to return to ruining the industrial might of the Ruhr, was about to begin the most intensive week of the battle. From 23 to 29 May he had sent his force on four major raids against the Reich's industries. Now from Monday, 21 June to Sunday, 28 June his Lancasters, Halifaxes, Stirlings and Wellingtons would be lining up at their grass and concrete runways in a seemingly never-ending stream to be dispatched on four major operations to the Ruhr and a second heavy raid on Cologne. The operations would cost another 166 bombers and their crews.

Harris did not wait until the moon period was over to begin the attacks, with a maximum-effort raid on Krefeld, the largest producer of high-grade steel in Germany. The town, with a population of 170,000, was an important railway junction for traffic travelling north to Holland and south to central Germany.

As the bomb train of 705 Lancasters, Halifaxes, Stirlings and Wellingtons rumbled and roared on their path to the Ruhr across the moonlit skies of Holland, starting air raid warnings from Amsterdam to Osnabrück, Sgt Cornish was lying blinded in a hospital bed below.

He had woken in the farmhouse of the Dutch family who were sheltering him after he was shot down in the Bochum raid of 12 June to discover his eyes were swollen shut from his burns. He recalls:

> I could not do much to help the family to help me and the Germans were already searching for me. They had found the bodies of the other boys in my crew and were looking for the seventh. I was in no shape to escape and the Germans came for me and sent me to the Queen Wilhelmina Hospital in Amsterdam.[26]

It would be almost three weeks before, with his sight recovered, he could be transferred to a hospital in Germany and prisoner-of-war camp.

F/O East, shot down on the Cologne raid, also heard his RAF comrades going over. He had lain up for two days in the cornfield near Jülich. He recalls:

> I got the escape map out but it wasn't much use because the scale was too small. I started walking westwards on the third night. I hid up during the day, often scared out of my wits in case anyone saw me. On one occasion I was hiding in a field when some children came along who had been haymaking at the end of the field. I hadn't very good cover and thought I might be spotted.
>
> After a few nights of travelling, trying to live on raw potatoes and onions, there was the air raid. I had to hide in a field while they went over because everyone was on the alert. I could hear the bombers and

the ack-ack guns going off and see the explosions in the sky and bits of shrapnel were coming down. I remember wishing I had a steel helmet.[27]

F/O East eventually made it to a village near Maastricht where he got in touch with the resistance and was taken to Brussels, but he was betrayed by a double agent known as the Captain and eventually ended up in a prisoner-of-war camp.

The bombers flew on to Krefeld to demonstrate what could be achieved if the target was marked in clear skies. More than three-quarters of the heavies dropped their bombs within acceptable limits of the aiming point as the Pathfinders' red TIs glowed hotly against the winking surface of the town. Large fires quickly linked and joined up for a conflagration that raged out of control for hours, destroying nearly 50 per cent of the built-up area. One by one the Ruhr's industrial towns were being turned into a wasteland.

The moonlight which made the Krefeld raid so successful also created conditions for the hunters. A total of forty-two aircraft were shot down and the great majority fell to night fighters vectored into the vicinity of glowing exhaust stubs, which stood out for up to 10 miles against the black sky. It was a disastrous night for 35 Sqn. They lost six aircraft out of nineteen dispatched, the worst loss by any RAF bomber squadron throughout the whole of 1943 apart from the specialist 617 Sqn on the Dams Raid. Six crews of 35 Sqn had already been lost in the past three weeks.

F/Sgt Roy Macdonald was in the last of 35 Sqn's aircraft to go down on the Krefeld raid, piloted by Canadian F/Lt Tom Lane. Macdonald was officially the mid-upper gunner on Lane's crew, but as the turret had been removed to improve the performance of the Halifaxes he had no guns to use. He says:

There wasn't a question of mid-upper gunners being reallocated, so I flew as a sort of second pilot. We had dropped our markers and bombs on Krefeld with absolutely no opposition, no flak, no searchlights – nothing.

We flew west into a brilliant and huge moon and were attacked from the rear by a Ju88 night fighter. He hit the rear turret, putting two guns out of action and the other two jammed. He was only seen by the rear gunner when he fired and by the engineer from the astrodome when he broke off an attack. He made three very close attacks. I was standing next to the pilot and I could see sparks as shells ricocheted off the starboard wing then exploded up ahead. He was very close and we were silhouetted against the moon. We couldn't give directions to the pilot for evasive action as we didn't know where the fighter was. Eventually he hit the port petrol tanks. There was a great, big 'woof!' and the whole wing was on fire. There wasn't much we could do then and the pilot gave the order to abandon the aircraft.

The rear gunner went out through the back door, I got my chute on and plugged back into the intercom and was standing on the step looking down into the nose where they were opening the hatch. The escape hatch was under the navigator's seat and this had to be put away. The navigator, the bomb aimer and the wireless op were all having a bit of bother doing this. The engineer was standing behind me and kept giving me a nudge as if to say 'Get a move on'. I kept turning round and telling him they weren't ready yet. I saw the three in front go out and turned round to tell the engineer we could go and found he wasn't there; he'd run down the back and gone out through the rear door.

I was just leaving and heard the skipper say he couldn't find his Sutton harness release clip, so I went back and pulled his clip out and he followed me. I think I got out at about 18,000 feet and came down in a field between the Maas and Vaal in Holland, not far from Tiel.[28]

As dawn broke, F/Sgt Macdonald found himself in the hands of the police, who called the Germans. That day the sergeants' and officers' messes at Graveley were sad places indeed and remained so until the gaps of six missing crews could be filled.

Air gunner F/Sgt Robert Gill had arrived as a new posting to the Pathfinder squadron as its aircraft were being prepared for Krefeld. He remembers:

They wanted to put us on the op straight away. The skipper, Archie Hardy, was able to persuade them not to because he said we didn't have any flying kit, it was all coming on by road. We were shocked the next day when we found out six of eighteen had been lost by 35 Sqn. We thought, 'We won't be here many weeks.'[29]

For a few the strain of Krefeld's defences had been more than could be borne. Sgt 'Bluey' Mottershead of 158 Sqn returned from making his first trip with his own crew, to hear the rear gunner categorically say: 'I'm not bloody going again.' Mottershead remembers:

I asked him: 'What did you say?' and he repeated it. He was stripped of his rank, given as Lack of Moral Fibre and was off the station in quick time. I never saw him again. I think he was sent to the glasshouse in Sheffield.* I had spare gunners from then on, fifteen in all. It was the only case of LMF I ever came across, yet our squadron lost 851 young men in action.[30]

TWENTY-FOUR hours later, on the Tuesday, the squadrons of Bomber Command were briefed for a Ruhr target important for its foundries, furnaces and rolling mills, which had never been attacked before. Eight Oboe Mosquitos opened the raid on Mülheim at 0120 through thin cloud. The fire and rescue services quickly broke down as 550 aircraft dropped their loads and fires spread into neighbouring Oberhausen. More than 60 per cent of Mülheim was destroyed.

Two nights later it was Wuppertal's turn again. A total of 630 aircraft were on the battle order, eighty-nine fewer than for the operation of three weeks before, demonstrating the losses which were now being felt on the squadrons.

On 101 Sqn at Ludford Magna, Sgt Peter Johnson was by now one of the more experienced skippers with seven operations completed in less than a month. He was on the crew list for Wuppertal in K-King. 'I was exhausted,' he remembers. 'It was my third operation in the aircraft in four

* *The Aircrew Discipline Unit at RAF Norton.*

days.' The attack was aimed at the Elberfeld half of the town, the Barmen half having been badly hit in the raid at the end of May. More than 90 per cent of Elberfeld was wrecked in a highly successful raid which destroyed or wrecked more than 220 industrial premises and the loss of life was severe, 1,800 people being killed.

Sgt Johnson found himself coned on the run-in:

One or two searchlights picked us up, then they all joined in from all over the sky. I couldn't see a thing, it was so bright. I just let my seat down and dived and weaved in and out. It wasn't a question of diving towards the lights because I didn't know where they were coming from. The only thing I could do was to check my instruments to make sure I wasn't upside down or whatever.

I could smell the bursting flak. We were terrified. We bombed at 14,500 feet instead of near 20,000 feet and we had to climb to get there because we'd dived to get out of the lights. Afterwards the navigator's log book showed we had been coned for eight minutes. We'd been peppered, the Heywood compressor was damaged and a piece of the canopy disappeared from flak. All the maps were blown off the navigator's chart table by the draught and ended up at the back of the Elsan. We had to find our way home by the Pole Star, leaving it always on my right so that we knew we were heading west. When we got back we had no brakes because of the compressor damage. Fortunately Ludford had a very long runway and we just ran on to the end. The aircraft had to have a complete overhaul.[31]

Gelsenkirchen was selected for the last of the four Ruhr raids in this most taxing week for exhausted aircrew. Many had begun the week hopeful of gradually getting through a tour. The empty bed spaces in billet after billet had turned confidence to despair.

Situated in the middle of the Ruhr, Gelsenkirchen could not be approached in any direction without running the gauntlet of searchlight and flak for several minutes. It had not been on the target list since 1941, but had taken much of the creepback and jettisoning from other Ruhr raids.

Losses and damage to aircraft which returned from Wuppertal, Mülheim and Krefeld meant the maximum-effort order from High Wycombe could only yield 473 bombers. The raid was not a success. Cloud cover necessitated skymarking by the Oboe Mosquitos. The problems this would create were compounded by the poor serviceability of aircraft which had been called upon too many times in the previous four days. No fewer than five of the twelve Oboe Mosquito crews briefed would return without dropping their TIs because of unserviceability. Bombing was scattered, spreading to other Ruhr towns, and the toll on the ground was minor, fewer than forty deaths being recorded. It was one of those nights when more died in the air than on the ground. A total of thirty-two aircraft failed to return and 188 British and Commonwealth airmen lost their lives.

THE last raid of *Big Week* came on the Sunday against Cologne. It did not begin well. Only half of the twelve Oboe Mosquitos were able to drop their TIs, heavy cloud meant a less reliable skymarking attack and the marking began seven minutes late and carried on intermittently, but it resulted in the most severe damage in Cologne of the war. More than 80 per cent of the centre was destroyed. Forty-three industrial, six military and 6,368 buildings were wrecked and more than 4,000 people lost their lives.

One resident, Josef Fischer, described in a diary how he sheltered in a cellar feeling the 'pressure–suction–pressure–suction' effect of the rain of bombs which began shortly after 1 a.m. By now the people of the Ruhr, like the residents of London, Coventry and Sheffield before them, had learned to distinguish the different sounds of bombs tumbling through the air. A rustle like a flock of startled birds was the noise of approaching 4-lb incendiaries, a short, sharp crack the 30-lb incendiary, which could throw out fire for more than 75 yards. Then there was the shocking air-sucking thump of the Cookie, blasting out doors and windows over a wide area to open up factory, office and house to the oxygen-consuming flames.

Fischer described how, as the house next door burst into flames, the residents leaped through from their cellar to his own. When the bombs stopped and the shelterers crept up the stairs they found that every house in the neighbourhood was burning. Every corner, every tree was outlined against the flames. The blazes in Cologne reached their zenith at dawn, joining up and demonstrating many of the facets of a firestorm. It would be noon before Fischer could finally leave his cellar.

Sgt John Walsh, shot down over Belgium on the Düsseldorf raid of 11 June, changed trains under heavy guard in Cologne that night on his way with other aircrew from Brussels' harsh St Giles Prison to Dulag Luft. 'The guards were more necessary to protect the aircrew than to prevent them escaping,' he wrote in his recollections. 'The civilians were quite menacing and vocal and not above lynching.'[32]

Industrial town after town in the Battle of the Ruhr had been laid waste, but the attrition in the air was reducing the ranks of squadrons in massive proportions.

The Reich Armaments Minister, Albert Speer, had remarked to a conference of gauleiters in June on the serious losses in production of coal, iron, steel and other vital war requirements caused by Harris's night raids. It had, therefore, been decided to draft in 100,000 men to shift the growing rubble and carry out repairs. More importantly for the crews who were already facing such daunting defences over the Ruhr, a decision had also been made to double its anti-aircraft defences.

In the nineteen weeks of the Battle of the Ruhr Bomber Command made a total of 18,506 sorties and 872 aircraft failed to return (4.7 per cent). Another 2,126 were damaged, some so seriously that they never flew again. There was a less than one-in-three chance that any crew beginning a tour with the Essen raid of 5 March, recognised as the start of the battle, was still alive by the time the last operation in the campaign was mounted.

There had been forty major raids in the period, twenty on the Ruhr itself with its canyons of sentry-like searchlights and crazily coloured corridors of bursting red and white flak against the dreadful, quick orange flare of exploding aircraft. But at the end of the battle Bomber Command was stronger, not weaker. The Command's effectiveness was undoubted by the German leaders in mid-1943 as they looked at brick piles that were once industrial centres or smoking ruins that were once factories.

Goebbels, who as a propagandist had his finger on the pulse of Germany more than most, wrote as the battle was at its height: 'The English wrested air supremacy from us not only as the result of tremendous energy on the part of the RAF and the British aircraft industry but also thanks to unfortunate circumstances and our own negligence.' He went on: 'It seems to me that the air situation should be considered one of the most critical phases of the war.'

The young crews of Bomber Command who went out night after night to fight that phase thought little of the bigger picture, or even beyond the next raid as the prospects of a future shortened. But they had achieved victory at great cost to themselves. That battle's final toll was arrived at on the night of 30 July against a previously unbombed industrial town, Remscheid. It was a remarkably successful operation in which 83 per cent of Remscheid was devastated, but the losses were above average: 15 crews out of 273, or 5.5 per cent, did not return to their familiar billets and the comfort of mess and pub.

Press and public who had cheered the airmen on day by day found little to interest them in the Remscheid raid. Three days earlier an operation had been launched in a new battle which had staggered the crews of Bomber Command and shocked the Nazis to their black hearts. It was the firestorm raid in the Battle of Hamburg and nothing like it had happened before in the history of warfare.

SUMMER

ABOVE 354 Air Gunner's Course, RCAF Station Mountain View, Ontario. Marcel Dowst, third from left, front row, and Reid Thomson, second from right, front row, were the only ones not killed on operations. (*Private collection*)

ABOVE Air gunner Sgt Albert Bracegirdle began operations on Guy Gibson's squadron. (*Private*)

RIGHT Sgt Graham Allen in his flight engineer's position. He was attacked by a night fighter on his first operation, the Berlin raid of Jan 17th, 1943. (*Private*)

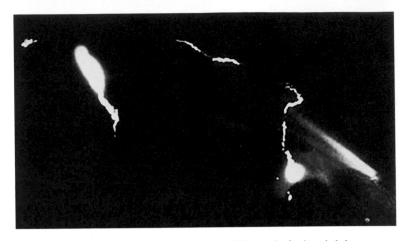

ABOVE The remains of F/Sgt Ted Laing's Lancaster fall to earth after it exploded over Enschede, Holland. Top left is the blazing fuselage. The other four fires in the sky are the fuel tanks. (*Private*)

BELOW P/O Dennis Bateman's KN-J of 77 Sqn after it was shot down in Belgium bound for Munich on March 9th. The Halifax fell near a housing estate in the Mons area and a resident took this photograph the next day. (*Private*)

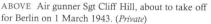

ABOVE Air gunner Sgt Cliff Hill, about to take off for Berlin on 1 March 1943. (*Private*)

ABOVE RIGHT Peter Johnson, after he was commissioned and awarded the DFC. (*Private*)

RIGHT P/O 'Bluey' Mottershead: his 158 Sqn Halifax was hit by a 30lb incendiary bomb over Mannheim on 23 September. (*Private*)

BELOW Wop/AG Sgt Walter Hedges of 102 Sqn, who was shot down on his first operation, the Essen raid of March 12th. His was one of 23 aircraft which failed to return. (*Private*)

ABOVE Australian Ron Gooding, lost on the Kiel operation of April 4th, the largest raid of the war so far. (*Private*)
RIGHT His fiancée, Laura Lancaster, in wartime. (*Private*)

TOP The 460 Sqn crew of F/Sgt Murray just back from Duisburg in the early hours of 10 April 1943. W/O Taylor is second from left, and F/Sgt Murray second from the right. It was their second trip to the Ruhr port in two nights and they had four ops to go to finish their tour. (*Australian War Memorial*)

ABOVE F/O. Eric Hadingham and F/O Alan Lord pictured at the moment of rescue off the French coast after five days and nights in a rubber dinghy. Only Hadingham has the energy to greet the crew of the ASR launch. Lord is lying exhausted out of view in the dinghy. (*IWM*)

ABOVE Air gunner P/O Albert Wallace. A hang up over Duisburg caused his Halifax to be shot down. (*Private*)

ABOVE RIGHT Flight engineer John Walsh. His 77 Sqn Halifax strayed over a night fighter base en route to Dusseldorf on June 11th. (*Private*)

BELOW Kenneth East, pictured in 1939 at the start of his operational career. He was shot down on the Cologne raid of June 16th 1943. (*Private*)

ABOVE Bomb aimer Sgt George Stewart. He was the sole survivor of his crew when their Lancaster exploded over Bochum. (*Private*)

TOP Wing Commander Guy Gibson (standing on ladder) minutes before he took off with his crew on the Dams Raid. (*IWM*)

ABOVE The Eder Dam, destroyed by low flying Lancasters on the night of 16 May 1943. (*Ullstein*)

ABOVE F/Lt Les Munro, right, and fellow New Zealander F/O Len Chambers, wireless operator in Mickey Martin's crew. The photograph was taken at a Scampton dispersal in the publicity blitz which followed the raid. (*IWM*)

ABOVE RIGHT F/O Dave Rodger in an off-duty moment at 617 Sqn. (*Private*)

BELOW A reconnaissance photograph of Kassel showing flooding from the Eder, breached by the Dambusters. Kassel's ordeal by fire would come later in 1943. (*IWM*)

LEFT AND ABOVE Michaelisstrasse, Hamburg, before and after the firestorm raid of July 27th, which so shocked the Nazi hierarchy Hitler's armaments minister told him six more similar raids could end the war. (*RAF Museum*)

ABOVE Bomb aimer P/O Alan Bryett, left, pictured at Lissett with his 158 Sqn pilot F/Lt Kevin Hornibrook, RAAF. The Australian gave his life saving Bryett's over Berlin on 23 August. (*Private*)

TOP Sgt Peter Swan. The 44 Sqn bomb aimer was shot down off Holland returning from the Hamburg raid of 2 August. (*Private*)

ABOVE A reconnaissance picture of Peenemunde in June 1943, showing two V-2 rockets (A), the rocket storage buildings (B) and the assembly shop (C). (*Corbis*)

ABOVE W/O Dennis Slack, one of the 158 Sqn bomb aimers shot down on the Berlin raid of 23 August, a night when 158 Sqn lost five of its Halifaxes. (*Private*)

ABOVE RIGHT Val Clarkson, who met her friends among 158 Sqn aircrew at their adopted Bridlington pub, the Brunswick. A young air gunner wept as he told her of his fears. (*Private*)

LEFT The crew of P/O John Sullivan prepare for another op in their 467 Sqn tour at Bottesford. They were shot down the same night as their CO on a "piece of cake" op to Milan. From the left: Sgt Buddy Spurr (mid upper gunner); F/O Terry Entract (bomb aimer); Sgt Jimmy Power (rear gunner); Sgt Ken Harvey (Wop) at top left of doorway; W/O Alec Grange (navigator); Sgt Johnnie Newland (flight engineer); P/O Sullivan. Only Entract and Harvey baled out in time. (*Private*)

Dulag-Luft. Kriegsgefangenenkartei.

	Erkennungsmarke (Gefangenen-Nummer)	Dulag-Luft Eingeliefert
	Nr. *222626 IV B*	am: 2.9.43

NAME: P A R S O N S

Dienstgrad: Sgt   Funktion: Eng.

Vornamen: Lewis Patrick

Command	Group	Squadron	Flight	Station:

Matrikel-No.: 1 455 528   Religion: C of E

Geburtstag: 7.5.33 Ort: Pitsea, Essex

Verheiratet mit: nein

Staatsangehörigkeit: G.B.

Anzahl der Kinder: -

Zivilberuf: Schlächter

Heimatanschrift: *MR. PARSONS*

Vornamen des Vaters: *ARTHUR*

19 HIGH Rd.
VANGE-PITSEA-ESSEX

Familienname der Mutter: *PARSONS*

Abschuß am 1.9.43   bei: Aarbruck

Flugzeugtyp: Stirling

Gefangennahme am: wie oben   bei:

Nähere Personalbeschreibung

Lichtbilder	Figur	Größe	Schädelform	Haare	Gewicht	
	schlank	D. 5.10 E.	eckig	blond	am	Ko
						67
	Form	Gesichts- Farbe	Augen	Nase		
	eckig	gesund	blau	gerade		
	Fingerabdruck des rechten Zeigefingers		Bart	Gebiß		
			--	2 Vorderzähne fehle		
			Besondere Kennzeichen:			

unt   Profil

OKW.Befehl. v. 1o-1-4o. b...   -8. SEP. 1943

	PARSONS	*Lewis*				*2.9.43*	

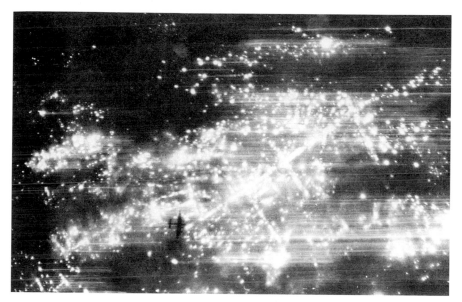

LEFT The POW identity document of flight engineer Lew Parsons. His Stirling was one of five lost by 75 Sqn on the Berlin operation of 31 August. (*Private*)

ABOVE A Lancaster flies over Hanover during the attack of October 8th, the city's burning streets clearly outlined below it. (*National Archives*)

BELOW A photo reconnaissance picture of Hanover the next day, showing the same streets, their buildings roofless, gutted ruins. (*National Archives*)

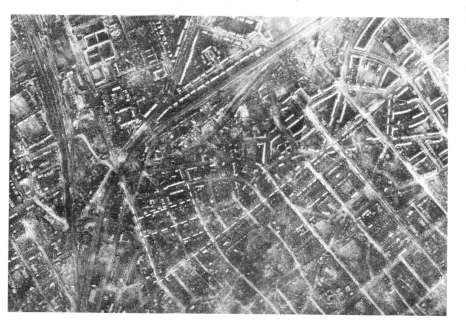

ABOVE Burning Kassel on the night of 22 October, the most destructive attack since the Hamburg raid of 27 July. The tracks are caused by the time delay in the photoflash. (*National Archives*)

RIGHT Post-raid reconnaissance shows how fires raged unchecked through Kassel's old town, marked A, between the Law Courts (B) and the main station (C). (*National Archives*)

ABOVE A surprised F/Sgt Bernard Downs, centre, arrives back at Breighton with his crew from the Berlin raid of 22 November to meet a barrage of press photographers. The picture appeared in a national newspaper the next day. (*Private*)

BELOW The Finlay crew at Elsham Wolds. From left, bottom, standing on the ladder: Sgt Steel, a fitter; signaller Harry Wheeler, who was killed; Australian mid-upper gunner Jim Vivers; F/O Douglas Finlay at top; engineer Sgt Sandy Rowe; Canadian Sgt Bill Gillespie, rear gunner. From left, bottom five, unknown fitter; Scottish bomb aimer Sgt Ian Fletcher; the crew's M/T driver Peggie Forster (now Lyons); navigator Sgt John McFarlane; unknown fitter. They are sitting on a 4,000lb bomb. (*Private*)

CHAPTER NINE

THE POWER OF FIRE

THE disaster that was about to engulf the citizens of Hamburg as they enjoyed the hot sunshine of late July happened more by accident than design. If the city's shape, only 60 miles from a clear coastline, had not shown up so well on H2S screens, it might not have been so attractive a target.

If those same citizens had not been hammering and riveting a profusion of U-boats with such efficiency, their city would not have fallen so neatly within the first proviso of the Casablanca Directive; if it hadn't had a role to play in the aircraft industry, it wouldn't have come conveniently within the demands of the more recent Pointblank Directive; and if it hadn't been the second largest city in Germany, it would not have beckoned so invitingly as a means of demonstrating to the Nazis that Bomber Command could indeed undermine the morale of the German people to a point where their capacity for armed resistance was fatally weakened. If none of those advantages had applied, Harris would not at last have been given permission to use 'Window', the foil strips showered from aircraft which would so effectively put out the eyes of radar-dependent fighter and flak. And if it hadn't been such a glorious July, touching 86°F degrees Fahrenheit in low humidity only hours before the RAF's second, cataclysmic raid while colder air outside the city created a funnel effect, the firestorm which snuffed out 40,000 lives in one night would never have happened.

The plan to hit Europe's largest port with four maximum-effort raids had been smouldering since May. Harris had told his group commanders on the 27th to start preparing for such attacks. He said:

> The Battle of Hamburg cannot be won in a single night. It is estimated that at least 10,000 tons of bombs will have to be dropped to complete the process of elimination. To achieve the maximum effect of air bombardment, this city should be subjected to sustained attack. On the first attack a large number of incendiaries are to be carried in order to saturate the fire services.

The campaign would have the codename Gomorrah and the USAAF would be part of the plan.[1]

Window had been ready since April 1942, but permission for its use had been denied because it was feared the Germans would copy it and use it in raids on Britain. A strange decision – Britain's air defence was nothing like as well developed as Germany's had had to become and Luftwaffe bomber operations in the West compared little with the might of Harris's command. Finally, as late as 15 July, nine days before the first of the four raids on Hamburg, the War Cabinet had relented.

As the citizens wandered by the Elbe river or the Alster lakes in the sunshine or prepared for a Hitler Youth canoe-race rally on the coming Sunday with suitable flexing of master-race muscle, it would have seemed impossible that a piece of black paper, 30 cm long and 1.5 cm wide with a piece of aluminium foil stuck to one side, could so drastically change their lives for ever.

Bomber Command's last raid had been an unsuccessful Halifax operation against the Peugeot motor factory at Sochaux in France on the night of 15 July. Hamburg had been on the target list since then.

SGT John Kevin Gilvary was one of the thousands of men from the Irish Republic who had forgone their country's neutrality to take up arms for Britain. He had qualified as a bomb aimer and been posted to 419 Sqn now at Croft, near Darlington. As he waited to take part in his first op he began jotting down his experiences in a pocket-sized red Air Force Diary he had

THE POWER OF FIRE

purchased from the NAAFI. It gives a unique insight into the vagaries of life for bomber aircrew in the summer of 1943.

On the Tuesday before the first Hamburg raid he noted: 'Allotted an aircraft in E-Easy. We live or die in him in all probability.' Then two days later, on 22 July, came the entry: 'Quite shocked this morning at suddenly being told I was on ops tonight. Got over it, however, and spent morning and afternoon rushing madly about. Briefing for Hamburg after tea.'[2]

At Ludford Magna Peter Johnson had also found himself on the battle order. He'd already worked out before the briefing what area of Germany it might be:

> In the morning I used to go to the Met office and get an idea about where the clear paths of Europe were. Then I'd get the petrol load from the ground crew, so I could work out how far we were going. Mine used to say, if the load was 1,500 gallons for instance, 'We've given you a bit more,' thinking they were doing me a favour. But I used to think: 'Oh no, that's a bit more to lift off.'[3]

Sgt Gilvary made a further entry in his diary, perhaps seeking to inscribe prosaic immortality in the event of not returning. He wrote: 'Went for operational meal after marshalling and then got dressed.' But the final entry for 22 July read: 'Just turning onto runway for take-off when aircraft was scrubbed.'

Weather-gauging reconnaissance sorties by the four-month-old 1409 Meteorological Flight at Oakington had shown less than ideal conditions over the Continent. If Window was to be used for the first time it was important that the advantage wasn't negated by poor Pathfinder marking against wind or cloud.

In these final few days aircraft were still being delivered from the factories to the aerodromes of Lincolnshire and Yorkshire, making good the losses from the Battle of the Ruhr, and eventually 792 would take off. Many of the nearly 6,000 aircrew who would be aboard those bombers had still not got used to the sight of blond locks being shaken loose as the woman pilots who delivered the powerful machines switched off and removed their flying helmets before climbing down from fuselages.

Two months before, the Air Transport Auxiliary had been expanded to cope with the growing needs by Bomber Command for more deliveries. Stories in the national press in May had explained that girls could now be paid to learn to fly with the ATA. Previously the ferry organisation would only take those women who already held a civilian flying licence.

It was obvious to many in Britain's aircraft factories in the closing days of July that something big was coming. On the 10th, the Minister of Aircraft Production, Stafford Cripps, had forecast in a broadcast to aviation industry workers 'an intensification of our air war at almost any moment'. At the end of June, in a speech at the Guildhall, Churchill himself had promised: 'There is no industrial or military target in Germany that will not receive, as we deem necessary, the utmost application of exterminating force.'

On Friday, 23 July crews were briefed for Hamburg again, though the reports of Pampas flights, indicating the likely weather, still needed to come in. Sgt Gilvary wrote in his diary: 'Exactly the same procedure as yesterday only with less panic. Did an air test in E-Easy. Briefing again after tea. Ops scrubbed halfway through briefing.' The weather reconnaissance had shown cumulonimbus clouds gathering.

Sgt Johnson recalls: 'I had had the very welcome pre-op bacon and egg. Once I'd had the briefing I felt ready to go. It was disappointing when they called it off because I knew I would have to face it again. Hamburg was unusual because I was briefed for it three times before I actually went.'[4]

Peter Johnson's third Hamburg briefing was the next day, Saturday. Crews were told Bomber Command would take off from 2145 onwards, beginning with the slow and low Stirlings, and the attack would open just before 0100. Sgt Gilvary, who had spent an hour in a local pub, the Wheatsheaf, after ops were called off the previous night, was reprieved. Only his Australian skipper, F/Sgt Stan Pekin, would be going to Hamburg, to gain experience as a second-dickey pilot.

Crews were told they would start dropping Window 35 miles from the islands of Heligoland and Sylt where it was thought the range of the Würzburg radar installations on the mainland became crucial. The bundles of 2,200 strips held by elastic had been delivered to each aircraft and the airmen were now trying to work out just how such strange packages could possibly be effective in holding off flak or fighter.

F/Sgt Harold McLean, who had been on the Hamburg raid of 3 March as a rear gunner with 428 Sqn, was now flying with 427 (Lion) Sqn from Topcliffe. He remembers: 'The new device was delivered in packets to the aircraft and one of our crew conveniently dropped a packet to open it. We couldn't make head nor tail of it. One chap peed on it to see if it reacted. It didn't.'[5]

Bomb aimer Sgt Len Bradfield at 49 Sqn was also bewildered by the packages. He remembers:

All these large brown paper packets had been dumped on the dispersal and we didn't know what they were. At the briefing we were told they were to be thrown out of the starboard cockpit window by the flight engineer.'[6]

The silver strips would cause his crew a big problem over the target.

As his pilot went to Hamburg Sgt Gilvary went to visit an uncle in Redcar. They heard the aircraft of 6 Group assembling after 10 p.m. then the thunder of the engines gradually fading away as the fleet flew south to Hornsea and followed the rest of the Main Force across the North Sea. Among them were seven Wellingtons of 432 Sqn. Eight crews had been detailed originally, but the adjutant's office reported: 'One aircraft was cancelled by orders of the medical officer owing to insufficient rest of the crew.' Only six of the Wellingtons would make it back to base; the seventh would ditch within a mile of the English shore.[7]

In Hamburg people were coming out of the cinemas in their shirtsleeves after watching the diet of propaganda newsreels and escapist comedies and musicals from the UFA film studio. *Die Grosse Liebe* (The Great Love), made in 1942, was still being shown at some cinemas, its sentimental story of a classical singer entertaining wounded troops a hit throughout the war. There was little to be found on the newsreels about the fighting in Sicily. Palermo had fallen two days before, following the invasion of Sicily on 10 July, and Mussolini would be overthrown the next day.

HARRIS could reflect that Saturday night on how far his command had come in six months. In January there had been the first tentative Oboe-directed raids on Essen by fifty or so aircraft, then the largely wasted effort of smashing the French U-boat ports, followed by the tentative forays to Berlin and at the end of the month Hamburg. In March the Battle of the Ruhr had begun as his force grew into a mighty fleet of 700 aircraft wrecking the Reich's industrial towns one by one, albiet at great cost to the crews.

In Hamburg, from 25 July until 3 August, Harris's vowed intention made during the London Blitz that the Nazis would reap the whirlwind they had sown would be realised, and with a vengeance even the commander-in-chief must have found astounding. It would bring him closer than at any other time to date, and for many months to come, to fulfilling his ambition of winning the war by bombing alone and making the German people accept defeat.

There would be an added factor to keep the stream together and aid concentrated bombing. For the first time, aircraft of the Pathfinder force would break radio silence to send back to PFF headquarters the wind direction and strength navigators had found. The mean of these would then be worked out by Bomber Command experts and re-broadcast to every navigator in the stream, so that each crew was operating with the same wind.

Among the Pathfinders leading the 750 bombers of Main Force, now filling the sky and radar screens with fluttering clouds of Window, was 35 Sqn. Twenty-three aircraft had been sent, but New Zealander F/Sgt Nicholas Matich hadn't got very far. One engine cut as he sped along the Graveley runway. He managed to brake in time and turn onto the perimeter track, where the engine picked up again.

Demonstrating a press-on spirit so appreciated by group commanders, Matich decided to try again. But this time his wheels had just left the ground when petrol shortage struck once more. 'When taking off both outer engines failed at a height of 2 feet and the aircraft crashlanded in a field beyond the aerodrome,' the adjutant later reported. Matich and his crew escaped without injury.[8] Three more aircraft had had to make early returns, but now nineteen of the squadron's aircraft were heading for the final turning point that would take them through Hamburg.

In the Heide national park 10 miles to the south of the city Hans Erich Nossack was enjoying a break with his wife in a holiday cottage. He had been complaining about how much his wife had wanted to bring from their home near the university. As the Nossacks prepared sleepily for bed in the dark of the warm summer night, in the distance came the faint sound of the *Kleinalarm*, signifying raiders approaching. It was shortly followed by the strident and urgent *Alarm* to take cover. Then there came a buzzing noise which grew into a droning cacophony. 'We had experienced already about 200 attacks, some were really heavy, but this was something completely new,' Nossack wrote at the time. 'However, one was sure immediately, it was what everyone had waited for. It had lain like a mantle over us for months.'[9]

Within minutes there was the sound of rustling as thousands of tinfoil strips began falling through the trees of the Heide. Crews of 35 Sqn at the head of the stream were unable to benefit from the glittering showers. Later crews on target would report seeing searchlights flicking aimlessly across the sky and flak bursting where there were no aircraft, but the aluminium clouds descending at 300 to 400 feet a minute as the Window bundles broke apart had not the volume at the spearhead of the assault. It meant one 35 Sqn Pathfinder crew found their aircraft was picked out by a flak unit about 12 miles from the target, which followed it in and well to the south of the city despite evasive action and change of height. Because he could not then identify the aiming point on time the pilot had to bring his target indicators home.

The crews of 35 Sqn had been selected to act as blind markers, some helping to open the attack with white flares and an ancillary bomb load to be followed by red TIs, and the less experienced crews as backers-up, remarking with green TIs. Yellow TIs were to be used as route markers on the way in and out. As the Pathfinders of 35 Sqn approached they found conditions excellent with only a slight wind, and the docks and river approaches of Hamburg clearly showing up on H2S screens. Some of this group, who would be joining Pathfinders from 7 and 405 Sqns, were late but their accuracy was good, several TIs going down near the aiming point of the Church of St Nicholas, near a distinctive bend of the Binnen Alster lake.

S/Ldr E. K. Cresswell was a blind marker. He told intelligence officers later:

> The weather was clear and the visibility excellent. The first yellow TI was seen at 0059 and was north east of the aiming point. The first red TI seen later was to the east of the aiming point and several green TIs were seen. TIs appeared to be falling close together and near the aiming point between 0100 and 0104 hours. Between 0104 and 0106 there was a very large, vivid explosion to the south-east of the aiming point in the dock area, also a number of other explosions scattered in the town area.[10]

Window was now having a dramatic effect. Sgt Len Bradfield, lining up the bomb sight of his 49 Sqn Lancaster, remembers:

> It was absolutely fantastic. We came up the Elbe and could see the river quite clearly. The radar-controlled blue master searchlights were standing absolutely upright and the white ones were weaving round, just searching. There were no night fighters because they were all in their boxes waiting to be given the vectors. The flak was just in a block over the target. We were quite early in on the second wave and the fires were just beginning. The target had been very well marked with red and green TIs. It was the only time on any bomb run I was able to have twenty seconds completely unimpeded, without being stalked by the flak.[11]

However, the unfamiliar device was also causing problems for the bomber crews. Sgt Bradfield recalls:

> When the flight engineer undid the packages and threw the strips out of the cockpit window they hit the mid-upper turret and stuck there.

Because of the black on the underside of each strip they nearly blacked out the turret. The mid-upper gunner, Terry Wood, was most aggrieved about it when we got back. Later they put a little chute in the aircraft to drop the Window through.

Most of the target indicators fell close enough to the aiming point for a concentrated raid to quickly develop and 2,253 high-explosive bombs and 349,000 incendiaries went down in fifty minutes. The plan had allowed for creepback from the AP and bombs were falling in a 6-mile line across the city. German radar screens were indicating their airspace had been invaded by thousands of aircraft as crew members in the bombers shovelled out the bundles of Window. At the same time the airborne sets on the orbiting night fighters were showing a mass of aircraft which split up and multiplied, then seemed to flash past the hunters. It was frustrating chaos for the defenders.

F/O Alex Flett, a navigator in 460 Sqn halfway through a tour that would take him to Peenemünde and a savage Berlin raid in August, remembers the relief of seeing the effect of Window:

We looked out and the searchlights were all over the sky like probing fingers. The flak also was completely disorganised. Normally you would see at least one chap get caught by a couple of searchlights then the whole lot would sweep onto him. If it was you it was just like daylight. But this time there was nothing. We dropped our bomb and saw the bloody great flash, then we got hit in a petrol tank. We got back OK and it did us a favour because although we weren't due for leave, the flight commander said it would take a week to fix our aircraft so we went on leave early.[12]

Some crews of 156 Pathfinder Sqn were acting as backers-up in the third and fourth waves of the six-wave attack and they reported a carpet of fire below dense smoke with approximately 150 ineffective searchlights in the target area.[13] Curiously, two 156 crews reported a new type of flak. One described it as an 'explosive rocket form' and another, who bombed at the same time of 0130, said it was 'bursting and shooting out in all directions, yellow in colour'. In fact this report of a 'scarecrow' was probably an exploding Stirling. Two Stirlings were shot down by night fighters over the city, the only aircraft to be so, and the Stirling element was in the third wave.[14]

Hamburg had 41,000 firemen at that time and the first of them were on the scene within ten minutes of the attack opening. Bombing was at first fairly concentrated, but the creepback started fires all the way across Altona, St Pauli, Neustadt, Hoheluft, Eimsbüttel and parts of the docks. Finally there was a major breakdown in the city's fire-control system when the telephone exchange caught fire and the lines were cut. Fires raged unchecked and after the raid it was estimated that in the city's western districts there were burning buildings with a frontage of 65 miles. Fire engines could not negotiate the rubble-strewn streets and water had to be pumped from storage tanks or waterways.

Gas, water and electricity lines were damaged, one of the key benefits to the attackers of area bombing. As the all-clear signal sounded just after 3 a.m., 1,500 people lay dead. Among the blitzed landmarks of the city was the Church of St Nicholas. The choir and nave were destroyed and the steeple was burned out, but did not collapse. It now stands as a memorial to the bombing.

The defences, so overwhelmed by Window, had little to show to counterbalance the success of the raid. Only twelve RAF aircraft were missing all told, most of them shot down by night fighters on the return, some over the North Sea, as the effects of the radar-screen snowstorms dissipated. Remarkably, crews who returned reported forty-nine interceptions, but only seven had ended in combat with the Germans.

Hamburg's flak units, firing blind across the sky, had brought down only one British bomber. It was that of the W/O George Ashplant, who had been awarded the RAF's first Conspicuous Gallantry Medal in February for giving his own chute to his bomb aimer to bale out after a collision, then managing to crash-land his Wellington. Ashplant, only 21, died with all his crew. It is particularly ironic that someone lucky enough to pull off a crashlanding in the dark should die by the one shell, fired randomly in the Hamburg night sky, to effectively hit a target.

From Elsham Wolds 103 Sqn had put up twenty-seven aircraft for the raid, the maximum number of any squadron. It meant they also suffered the maximum losses. Three of the missing twelve aircraft were theirs. Not one of the twenty-one men on board survived to become a prisoner of war.

The final aircraft to be lost on the operation was that of S/Ldr C. B. Sinton of 432 Sqn. He had to ditch his Wellington a mile off the Norfolk coast, but he and his crew were soon rescued, the squadron adjutant recording: 'Special thanks to the Life Saving Station at Cromer and the landlord and staff of the Red Lion Hotel. Also the station at Coltishall did all they could to see that the crew were outfitted to return to the station.' Sinton and his crew were back at Skipton-on-Swale 24 hours later.[15]

At Leeming, near Harrogate, the adjutant's office of 427 Sqn declaimed in the Operational Record Book after so many hard-fought raids over the Ruhr: 'Today saw the first stage of the Battle of Hamburg. Twelve crews were detailed. This was one of the best ops the squadron has ever done. There were no boomerangs and no losses.' He ended, somewhat prematurely, 'According to the crews Hamburg "had it".'[16]

In Germany Goebbels would soon receive a report of the operation, noting in his diary: 'During the night an exceptionally heavy raid on Hamburg took place with most serious consequences for the civilian population and for armaments production. This attack definitely shatters the illusions that many have had about the continuation of air operations by the enemy.'

The propaganda minister, who knew nothing then about the aluminium strips which had defeated the Luftwaffe, was furious that only twelve aircraft had been shot down, a 'wholly inadequate number'. He went on:

Unfortunately only two days previously Colonel General Weise took the heavy anti-aircraft guns away from Hamburg to send them to Italy. That was the last straw! One can imagine what a field day the enemy planes must have had over Hamburg. The eastern section of Altona is particularly hard hit. It is a real catastrophe.

It wasn't, but a real catastrophe unimaginable to the leaders of the Reich, who had instituted area bombing, was on its way.

The raid had been a spectacular advent for Window. It had sown fires in western Hamburg which would still be burning three nights later and would keep the firemen in that part of the city when they were needed to tackle the opening conflagrations of the next raid. And those conflagrations would end in the phenomenon the world had not yet truly seen, known as a firestorm.

GENERAL Ira Eaker's Flying Fortresses were already engaged on a series of sustained attacks which became known as Blitz Week throughout the USAAF when his role in the removal of Hamburg's part in the war locked into place. The plan had been for 300 bombers to hit Hamburg and Hanover on 25 July, but assembly techniques over cloud were then in their infancy with the Eighth Air Force, and delayed groups were recalled. It meant that only two combat wings, comprising a total of ninety Flying Fortresses, would reach the North Sea port.

The fires from the previous night's raid were still burning furiously when the B-17s arrived to strike at the Klockner aero-engine factory and the Blohm and Voss shipyard. Supplies of coal and coke stored in cellars for the winter months had caught fire in the previous night's raids and were proving difficult to extinguish, sending smoke billowing thousands of feet into the air.

The city's formidable flak battalions did not now need radar to see their targets. They put up a barrage which damaged seventy-eight of the American bombers. The Blohm and Voss yard, producing five U-boats a month, was not badly damaged, most of the bombs falling in the water, and the Klockner target had been abandoned because of the smoke cloud, the B-17s hitting a generating station instead. Throughout the day delayed-action bombs from the RAF attack had been exploding and six Mosquitos raided the city to keep the sirens wailing. Firemen, some of them now brought in from as far away as Hanover, Lübeck, Kiel and Berlin, were battling with the smouldering coal in cellars, and buildings were still falling.

That day another two combat wings of the VIII Bomber Command had raided Hanover, but most of the Hanover Fire Department was in Hamburg tackling its problems. The result was that many fires in Hanover raged unchecked, a classic example of what the two-pronged effort of the RAF and USAAF could achieve. The cracks from bombing were spreading to bring the Thousand Year Reich tumbling down.

Despite the fires the infrastructure of Hamburg was beginning to recover. Local newspapers had combined to produce a free Sunday edition and special three-day food rations were made available together with 50 grams of non-ersatz coffee, 10 extra cigarettes, 125 grams of sweets and a half-bottle of spirits for the nerves. Some, perhaps prescient, residents had packed up what few possessions they had left and started to leave the city, despite threats by the Reich authorities who needed their labour for war industries. Those whose houses and flats were still standing were told they were not entitled to accommodation elsewhere.

As the sun went down, the tired crews of Bomber Command were preparing for another maximum-effort raid, this time back in the Ruhr valley. Harris had planned his second major raid on Hamburg that night, but reconnaissance had shown that thick smoke was blotting out the city, so instead the 705 available aircraft were dispatched to Essen. Another six Mosquitos were over Hamburg once more.

Because of Window the loss rate was much lower than could have previously been expected on the second most heavily defended target in Germany, thirty aircraft, or 4.3 per cent. The death toll in aircrew was 141 and there were the usual tales to tell of courage and remarkable escapes. One member of 158 Sqn lost his parachute as he baled out, but managed to grab it and put it on as he plummeted through the air.

At Croft in Co Durham Sgt Gilvary would wake to begin a five-day battle course with the RAF Regiment. His pilot, Stan Pekin, who had gone on the first Hamburg raid as a second dickey, would also be going on the battle course with the result that he and his crew would miss the operation on Hamburg in two days' time, the night of the firestorm.

In Hamburg the machines of the Hanover Fire Department were leaving the city, personally ordered back by a furious Goebbels. It meant they would not be where they were most needed when the thunderclap of Gomorrah descended.

The USAAF kept up the momentum by sending four combat groups the next day to attack the Blohm and Voss shipyard again, but this time the Germans lit scores of smoke pots which created the same smokescreen the fires had the previous day. Lead bombardiers chose alternative targets, the two leading groups hitting the Howaldtswerke U-boat construction yard and the 91st and 303rd Bomb Group the Neuhof Power Station. It supplied half of Hamburg's electricity and would be out of commission for a month. A little over thirty-six hours later Hamburg would effectively cease to exist as 787 bombers arrived over the city. There was little difference between this attack and the one of the 24th; the bomb loads were the same mixture of HE and incendiary and a total of 4,417 tons would be dropped that night.

The Germans were, however, changing technique to catch up with the effects of Window. The system of vectoring night fighters onto their targets as they passed through the deep boxes of the Kammhuber Line had now largely broken down because of the snowstorm of blips on radar screens. Major Hajo Herrmann was forming a full-strength *geschwader* of Wilde Sau fighters in Bonn. It was an idea he had tried out on 3 July over Cologne. Herrmann, a former bomber pilot himself, had long promulgated the theory that single-engined fighters should be allowed free range over a target city while the Zahme Sau controlled by the Himmelbett fighter boxes attacked the bombers heading to and from the target. He had been allowed to put forward his theories to Reichsmarschall Hermann Goering amid the summer splendour of the Obersalzberg and Goering had agreed that he could test his beliefs under combat conditions during the next heavy raid in the West.

It came during the Cologne raid of 3 July. Major Herrmann and nine other pilots in Me109s and FW190s circled the Ruhr towns and followed the bombers to Cologne, claiming twelve victories. Wilde Sau was clearly a success and the next day Herrmann was ordered to form his Jagdgeschwader

300. On 27 July he got a personal call from Goering telling him his hour had come.

The Wilde Sau were allowed free range over the bomber-route turning points where marker flares went down and over Hamburg itself. The flak were ordered to limit their fuses to 18,000 feet and the searchlight batteries co-operated with the single-engined fighters by light signals, calling them in when they had an aircraft in their beams. A running commentary was also given of any scrap of information the fighters might find useful about the enemy's route, strength or intentions.

It set the pattern of operations over Germany from then on and spelt future doom for many aircrew now still tussling with lectures and training at OTU. So the advantage Bomber Command had gained with Window was now to be quickly sapped by the growing countermeasure of Wilde Sau. That night the loss rate was seventeen aircraft, only 2.2 per cent, as the anti-aircraft defences were swamped by the bombs. Twelve of those aircraft, however, are known to have fallen to night fighters, the majority from Wilde Sau.

THE *Kleinalarm* warning that the bombers were fifteen minutes away from Hamburg sounded at 11.40 p.m., but because the stream was flying further to the east before hooking back to the city it was forty-five minutes later before *Der Alarm*, signalling an imminent raid, bellowed its fifteen-wails-to-the-minute warning and the drone of the first of the heavies leading six waves was heard. It came as no surprise. After the heavy night attack three days before and the two USAAF and two Mosquito raids that again had sounded the alert, many residents, like the citizens of London in their Blitz, were now sleeping in their cellar shelters or on the grass outside in the hot night air, waiting for another attack after what had been another swelter-ingly hot day with remarkably low humidity of 30 per cent.

There were eight different types of shelter in Germany's second city. Air raid precautions in Germany, as in Britain during the Blitz, depended on how efficient city authorities were and the administration of Hamburg had been very efficient indeed.

That night the city's citizens could choose from 1,442 underground public shelters, 773 splinter-proof shelters, 60,000 reinforced cellars and 139 massive bomb-proof, above-ground *hochbunkers*, each capable of accommodating 1,000 people.

In the narrow streets of the Borgfelde, Hamm and Hammerbrook areas most of the accommodation consisted of large old apartment buildings with their interconnecting cellar shelters fitted with blast-proof steel doors. Hamburg's pre-war census showed one-quarter of the city's population living there. Those shelters were now full as the first of the bombs began to fall, around 1 a.m. In many cases the shelterers would never leave. It became the heart of the firestorm area and as the blockbusters blasted the old buildings and opened them up to the rain of incendiaries, flames leaped from one side of streets to the other, joining in a roaring, twisting sea of fire which demanded oxygen to breathe. The air in the cellars now became superheated and was sucked away to feed the voracious fires. Those who obeyed standard ARP instructions to remain under cover while bombs were falling died of suffocation.

SEVERAL squadron and station commanders had been anxious to take part in the operation, among them W/Cdr D. A. Reddick, CO of 101 Sqn. He had found the PFF route markers perfectly placed just at the time they were expected and his bombs went down on the Hamburg TIs at 0102. 'We were the first to bomb, but numerous HE explosions and TI markers were seen to fall in close concentration,' he reported. 'A large orange explosion was seen in the target area at 0108.'[17]

American Sgt Alexander Reid of 106 Sqn was in the same wave and bombed four minutes later. He had seen a large explosion on his run-up and reported: 'Bombs were aimed at a cluster of yellow and green TIs from 20,000 feet. Fires were well concentrated. Searchlights and flak were quite accurate and fighters appeared to be operating in large numbers.'[18]

Charles Lawrence, now a pilot officer, was flying his twentieth operation with 12 Sqn. He had been on the previous Hamburg raid of 24 July and as an experienced bomber pilot he was in the first wave over the city. By this period of 1943 the first wave was entirely made up of experienced crews from various groups who could be relied on to attack the TIs accurately and promptly start fires for the less knowledgeable to follow.

'It was thought the defences were harder for the first waves,' P/O Lawrence recalls. 'Because we were early in the raid we didn't see the firestorm beginning, but as we flew away towards home, the rear gunner called up to say: "By God, you should see what's happening there now, fires springing up all over."'[19]

F/O F. A. Randall bombed towards the end of the first wave. His 460 Sqn Lancaster had been late on target because of engine trouble, but he bombed the centre of green TIs. 'There was concentrated fire, smoke up to 20,000 feet and several large orange flashes,' he reported. The defences would rapidly be overwhelmed, but as Randall turned for home they were still active. 'I had great difficulty trying to evade the searchlights for a considerable time after leaving the target,' he related back at Binbrook.[20]

Wireless operator Sgt Ken Harvey, who had arrived on 467 Sqn at the height of its diphtheria outbreak, was in a Lancaster over the city. He would be over Hamburg again two nights later and shot down within three weeks. He recalls:

> I left my position to look down on the target and it was unbelievable. It was dreadful. There was one mass of flame and smoke. I'm surprised anyone survived in it. It was a case of the more the fires the greater the fire because of the firestorm.
>
> It really hit the German leaders. We weren't very popular as prisoners of war because of it. As we were moved through towns our guards told us, 'We're here to keep the population from you, not in case you try to escape.' There would be shouts and screams from the people of *luftgangster* and *terrorflieger*.[21]

The horror in the streets of Hamburg was being replicated by dread above. Sgt Douglas Boards was acting as second pilot in the 15 Sqn Stirling of F/O R. Waugh in the third wave, due to bomb from 0120. Thirty miles from the target the starboard inner caught fire and F/O Waugh ordered the crew to stand by to abandon the aircraft.

Boards had been by the rear spar, but went forward and stood by the second pilot's seat while putting on his chute. The engine had now been stopped, but the fire was still blazing and the propeller would not feather. Then the revs dropped on the port inner and the port outer also looked as if it might quit. Waugh ordered a bale-out, but Boards and the flight engineer, Sgt F. J. Watson, stayed to help the pilot. Waugh jettisoned the bombs and dived to 2,500 feet before finally dousing the flames. The engines picked up and he turned for home, desperately trying to gain height.

As he did so the firestorm was beginning. Fifteen blind markers had dropped their TIs by H2S guidance only in the first five minutes of the raid. The marking was concentrated, but instead of falling on the aiming point of the Church of St Nicholas, to the south of the Binnen Alster, it was 2 miles to the east over Hammerbrook.

Flight engineer Sgt Philip Bates was over the target in the third wave in a Stirling of 149 Sqn from Lakenheath. It was at this point in the attack that the flak batteries were given specific orders not to fire above 18,000 feet to give the Wilde Sau their chance without fear of being shot down themselves, but it meant the low-flying Stirlings, which struggled to reach 14,000 feet, caught both the flak and the fighters. Sgt Bates recorded in notes made immediately afterwards: 'A Stirling on our left was coned by searchlights and brought down in flames.* Hamburg was a terrific sea of fire. No city can stand this for long.'[22]

Wave after wave now thundered in over the next thirty minutes to stoke the fires and the inevitable creepback took the bomb pattern slowly north-eastwards into Wandsbek and Horn. S/Ldr Bowes, who had stayed several minutes over the target to see the effects of the attack, reported at Langar: 'Bombing was creeping back from the TIs and seemed to cover most of the town'.

* This was the 15 Sqn aircraft of F/Sgt J. R. Childs, flying his fourteenth operation out of Mildenhall. It was hit by flak over the target, then finished off by a night fighter, crashing at Hamburg-Ochsenwerder. Only the wireless operator, Sgt E. Hurley, managed to bale out.

Re-centerers among later Pathfinders on target took the concentration into the Sankt Georg district towards the city centre and south of the Elbe into the dock area, and aircraft captains reported many fierce fires just north of the docks.

The air the firestorm needed to feed on was now being rapidly sucked in from the outskirts of the city where by an atmospheric freak much cooler air than had been present in the city itself in the earlier part of the day eddied and circled. It created a terrible typhoon of winds sweeping through the streets then rocketing upwards in the natural flue effect over the firestorm area which had been created by the different air temperatures.

As it soared, the firestorm wind, topped by billowing black smoke, carried paper, burning debris and sparks with it to a great height until gravity took over and the debris descended again in a circular motion. A 106 Sqn flying officer who bombed in the closing stages of the attack reported seeing smoke rising above his aircraft more than 4 miles over the city.[23] The torment in Hamburg was not yet at its zenith, however. As further bombs fell, the firestorm area was extended until it measured 1½ miles from north to south and 3 miles from west to east.

Above Hamburg the head of the USAAF VIII Bomber Command, Brigadier General Fred Anderson, watched the burning of the city in the 83 Sqn aircraft Q-Queenie* flown by Canadian F/Lt Richard Garvey. Another unusual passenger was over Hamburg that night. Major T. Southgate, an anti-aircraft expert, was in a Wellington sent to investigate the strange flak a few crews had reported on the previous Sunday's raid. The conclusion was that if it had not been an exploding aircraft, it might have been a signal to Wilde Sau fighters.

One hour and ten minutes after the last of the bombers had departed, the hurricane of heat reached its apogee. From the cellar shelters in Hammerbrook, Hamm and Borgfelde the howling of the unnatural wind could be heard outside as it carried showers of sparks and burning material to be

---

*This aircraft, which went on to complete 144 operations as PO-S of 467 Sqn, is now in the RAF Museum at Hendon.

dropped on buildings so far untouched. Some described it as a weird, organ-like sound in which all the notes were played together.

Those who survived in this area were those who took to the streets. They described seeing trees uprooted in an instant by the hot shrieking wind; walls of fire suddenly shooting out from burning buildings, cutting off means of escape; and the fleeing falling to their knees in doomed exhaustion as the roaring, twisting hurricane of heat greedily gobbled up the oxygen and swept on, its remorseless energy refreshed. The lucky few made it to canals, open spaces such as parks, or water-filled bomb craters. The seeds of fire the Nazis had sown throughout Europe, Russia and Britain had grown into a harvest of horror for the people of Hamburg.

There were countless stories of survivors to be told after that night. Representative of many was that in an official report prepared after the raid for the fire service as Albert Speer, the Reich armaments minister close to Hitler's ear, reeled at the destructive power of Bomber Command.

Water engineer Herr Dehler went to the south-east corner of Hamm as the firestorm was approaching its height to check the condition of pipes. He drove into a bomb crater at the junction of Ausschlager Weg and Suderstrasse as the winds roared towards him from the south. Sparks billowed in through the open windows of his vehicle, setting his clothes alight, so he closed them, but then the heat became so unbearable that he had to break a window to crawl out. In a burst water pipe of the crater he rescued a youth in danger of drowning. By now others fleeing before the raging, searing winds were finding sanctuary in the water-filled hole in the street.[24]

Some, maddened by the temperatures, 'threw themselves in head first and broke their skulls on the broken pipe sections; others drowned in the water,' Dehler wrote.

From time to time I peeped over the rim and saw the street covered with bodies; there were people running, and their clothes suddenly burst into flames. The air was terribly hot. I felt about to suffocate; my lips, mouth and throat were completely dry. I became dizzy and breathing became difficult. I must have been in the crater for at least an hour.[25]

The firestorm to the east of the Alster lakes would rage for two and a half hours, long after the last of Bomber Command's aircraft had reached the middle of the North Sea and was almost within sight of home. The Germans had realised how clearly the Alster lakes would show up on H2S screens and the Binnen Alster, just to the north of the aiming point, had been covered by a complex arrangement of metal, wood and straw bales that gave the appearance of city streets from the air and distorted the picture on radar. Before the night was over the Binnen Alster would be disguised no longer as the flames ignited the whole contraption in a gigantic fireball and it sank into the lake.

The Wilde Sau fighters would now have their moment in history for the Battle of Hamburg. P/O Wilf Elder had lost an engine over the target and had turned on track for 76 Sqn's base at Holme on Spalding Moor when he was bounced from astern by two single-engined fighters. The mid-upper gunner was not in his turret. As Window was introduced, squadrons had been left to make up their own minds about who was best to distribute it. On 76 Sqn the strange decision had been made to give the hour-long task to the mid-upper gunner.

Elder's rear gunner, F/Sgt J. Heggarty, was blinded by searchlights and the raging fires below, so did not see the attackers until the first of them opened fire, wounding him. He ordered a corkscrew, but then the second fighter came in unobserved on the starboard beam and its cannon shells killed the mid-upper gunner, Sgt Arthur Smith, who was standing by the flare chute, and wounded the flight engineer, Sgt W. Berry, in the leg. Berry scrambled with difficulty into the rear turret as Elder desperately corkscrewed to lose his pursuers.

76 Sqn's adjutant later recorded:

Many instruments in the Halifax were by this time u/s and it was impossible for the pilot to be warned by Monica of any approaching enemy. Once again they were attacked and both the rear gunner and engineer, although suffering gunshot wounds, attempted to retaliate. Eventually the fighters were shaken off and the Halifax made for the nearest point of the English coast.[26]

In the same part of the sky a Wilde Sau Me109 also turned in to attack Elder's comrade on 76 Sqn, Sgt Stephen Troake. But Troake's rear gunner, Sgt T. S. Orr, opened fire first, calling for a corkscrew, and the fighter headed away for easier prey.[27]

Flak also could prove deadly for those who got out of the protection of the stream's Window screen. F/Lt Pritchard of 77 Sqn reported back at base: 'An aircraft was seen to be hit by flak over Kiel and fall in flames, followed down by searchlights.'*[28]

F/O Waugh in his 15 Sqn Stirling was still trying to make it home. He had struggled to regain height after his engine fire. Then when he reached the comparative safety of the sea it looked as if he might have to ditch when revs dropped on the port inner. Sgt Boards and Sgt Watson began throwing overboard everything detachable to maintain height. Boards got on the radio set to obtain a fix.

At that time Sgt Bates's Stirling, in the same wave, was also over the North Sea and he went into the astrodome. He says:

> We were about halfway across and I looked back to see there was only one fire in Hamburg. It seemed to be about 3 miles wide and it went up white, then red, then ended in black smoke. It was thousands of feet high. I said over the intercom: 'Those poor bastards down there'. It really was a shocker. I had never seen anything like it. It was just a column of fire miles wide and the actual flame went up thousands of feet. It was dreadful.[29]

F/O Waugh crossed the coast at 3,000 feet and touched down at Mildenhall at 0345. The firestorm had ended as a phenomenon fifteen minutes before, having consumed everything combustible.

P/O ELDER appeared over the USAAF base at Shipdham a quarter of an hour later and ordered the fit members of his crew to bale out. Then he made a successful crash-landing with the two wounded crew members. Within a few days Waugh was told he had been given an immediate DFC

---

*This was the 78 Sqn Halifax of Sgt Leslie Maidment, who was killed with two of his crew.

and Boards and Watson DFMs. Boards had become a medal winner on his first operation.

At High Wycombe the next day, as squadron reports came in of the enormous fires and photoflash photographs indicated the extent of the damage, there was professional satisfaction that Bomber Command had hit the enemy so hard. The raid's immediate interpretation report said: 'In St Georg, particularly, scarcely a building escaped unscathed, and in both that district and Billwerder damage to commercial and industrial property was on a phenomenal scale.' Priority targets known to have been hit included gas depots, electricity works, two railway stations and two tram depots.[30]

Crews themselves had been in ebullient mood at debriefing as, nervously puffing on cigarettes amid sips of rum-laced tea, they related how Window was still keeping the defences foxed, allowing an attack to be made that had raised fires the like of which had never been seen before. The adjutant of 427 Sqn, who like the rest of the air force had no experience of what a firestorm meant but certainly knew how heavily French U-boat ports had been hit earlier in the year, recorded: 'Crews said that Hamburg was beginning to look a lot like Lorient.'[31]

IN Hamburg the trek was beginning out of the city that would eventually make it truly a ghost town. A total of 1.2 million people would leave, taking their war production skills away from the factories that needed them. As they settled throughout Germany they would spread fear and knowledge of what other cities might expect. Implicit was the message of what misery adherence to the Nazi creed had brought Germany. The chill suspicion that the people might not be prepared to go on resurrected in the minds of the hierarchy from Berlin to Berchtesgarden the paranoia of what they had seen as a stab in the back in the Home Front unrest of 1918.

Goebbels wrote in his diary that Otto Kaufmann, gauleiter of Hamburg, had given him the first report of the effect of the British air raid, speaking of

a catastrophe the extent of which simply staggers the imagination. A city of a million inhabitants has been destroyed in a manner unparalleled in history. We are faced with problems that are almost impossible of solution. Food must be found for this population of a million. Shelter must be secured. The people must be evacuated as far as possible. They must be given clothing. In short we are facing problems there of which we had no conception even a few weeks ago. Kaufmann believes the entire city must be evacuated except for small patches. He spoke of about 800,000 homeless people who are wandering up and down the streets not knowing what to do. I believe Kaufmann has lost his nerve somewhat ...

AMONG the green fields of eastern England there was a stand-down on the bomber bases. Commonwealth airmen who had puzzled over how an island could take so much rain and still stay afloat (one of the Northern-based Canadian squadrons describing conditions on a typical day as 'Yorkshire weather – drizzle at dawn followed by more drizzle until night-time') rejoiced at being alive as the hot sunshine continued.

The young Canadian aircrew of 427 Sqn, who liked to call themselves the 'Rocky Mountaineers', lost little time in sleep after returning surprisingly safe and sound from Hamburg yet again. 'Glorious weather made swimming and sunbathing popular,' the squadron diary recorded. 'The Rocky Mountaineers operated in Harrogate and a good time was had by all.'[32]

The Yorkshire spa town had grown tolerant of the rumbustious ways of young men far from parental restraint. It was true that shopping for middle-class matrons could still provide its heart-stopping moments as a Canadian-crewed Halifax or Wellington buzzed the high street chimney pots, but the odd court martial and visits to squadrons by RCAF provost marshals armed with telltale aircraft code letters had rather taken the fun out of it. On Wednesday, 28 July, Harrogate was preparing for the approaching August Bank Holiday and visits by northern factory workers taking their annual leave.

As his crews relaxed in style, Harris's planners at High Wycombe worked on. The C-in-C's intention to destroy Hamburg was only half completed. Two nights following the firestorm and as the *Daily Express* was trumpeting the 'biggest raid of all time' in its story headlined 'Even River Glows Red in Hamburg Fires', 777 bombers were winging their way across the North Sea to approach the city from almost due north and bomb the northern and north-eastern districts. Citizens and the city authorities had been certain the RAF would be back despite the enormous damage caused by the firestorm. They believed Bomber Command was wrecking Hamburg district by district, in a planned anticlockwise direction and avoiding the once Jewish and better-off areas. If night operations could have been so accurate there would have been no need for area bombing.

There were twelve fewer bombers for the raid than had been intended. 100 Sqn, which had put up twenty-seven bombers for the operation of the 27th, hoped to have twenty-five over the target on the 29th. Twelve had roared down the Grimsby runway and lifted away over the boundary hedge when a flight sergeant's Lancaster swung as it followed them down the concrete and he couldn't correct it. N-Nuts spun completely and its undercarriage collapsed. It was plumb in the centre of the squadron's two runways and twelve aircraft had to be slowly and carefully turned round and returned to their dispersals. Hamburg would be spared 78 tons of bombs.

This third raid in the Battle of Hamburg was the same plan and bomb mixture as before with the slight wrinkle that red route markers would be used instead of yellows and spoof route-marker yellows would be dropped to confuse the night fighters. Intruders, which had been introduced into Bomber Command's armoury in June, would be active around the night-fighter aerodromes. There was little more unsettling to aircrew on either side of the air war than to discover that as the flaps went down on final approach and bed and breakfast beckoned, the enemy had followed you home. The Luftwaffe had learned many lessons quickly since the advent of Window and were not fooled by the spoof route markers, but they congregated around the real red track markers and several combats took place.

For a very few, chancing the defences of a city like Hamburg for the third time in a row looked like a gamble too far in the impossible lottery of completing a tour. S/Ldr R. L. Bowes of 207 Sqn, making his second attack in two days, told intelligence officers later: 'It was very disappointing to see one or two bomb loads being jettisoned within a mile or so of the enemy coast and indicates a regrettable lack of determination.'[33]

Fires from the devastating raid of two days before were still sending up clouds of smoke and this, combined with a crosswind, may have been why the blind markers of the Pathfinders put their TIs down in a wide-spread pattern on average 2½ miles to the east of the aiming point. It was a mistake which would have beneficial results for Bomber Command.

All but three of the Pathfinders marked a position over Billbrook and Billwarder Ausschlag not far from the area marked at the start of the firestorm raid. The first wave, therefore, bombed the still burning ruins of Hamm and Wandsbeck. But because of the direction of approach creepback spread bombing into the mainly undamaged districts of Eilbek, Uhlenhorst, Winterhude and Barmbek. It was the later waves which hit the residential suburb of Barmbek and a concentrated attack developed with the bomb loads of 500 aircraft thought to have gone down there.

The defences were improving, but still could not cope with the effect of Window. Sgt Ernie Webb, of 49 Sqn, was making his first operation. He recalls: 'It was a relatively quiet raid for us because it had been so heavily bombed. I thought: "This flak isn't too bad", and we saw few searchlights. It bore no comparison to what we went through later on Berlin.'[34]

A total of twenty-eight aircraft would be lost, 3.6 per cent of the attacking force, one of them from 76 Sqn. The squadron was continuing with its policy of ordering mid-upper gunners to push out Window in the target area, even though two of the squadron's Halifaxes had been caught by night fighters on the raid of the 27th.

Canadian mid-upper gunner Sgt Wilkie Wanless had lately returned to the squadron after two months in the RAF hospital at Northallerton. While he was away his original crew had been lost over Mülheim. Now he was flying as a spare bod and on the 29th he found himself in the crew of S/Ldr Vivian Bamber dropping Window over Hamburg. He recalls:

I had to get out of the mid-upper turret to push out a bundle of Window every minute. I don't think it was the smartest thing to get gunners to push out the bundles. It meant I didn't see a great deal because some time before the target we had to start with the Window, so I was down in the fuselage for most of the time.[35]

Many Hamburg officials and eyewitnesses thought the raid was heavier than that of the 27th and more bombers were involved, but there was no firestorm. Instead there was a widespread fire area, 120 blazes in 2.3 square miles around Barmbek. To the bomber crews later on target it was obviously another colossal blow to the city. Sgt Wilfred Hart, wireless operator on a 51 Sqn Halifax, had been over Hamburg on the first raid of the 24th and was now returning. He remembers: 'It was like putting coals into a furnace. We could imagine the heat from the aircraft. There was a lot of smoke and it was just like a sea of fire.'[36]

Thousands of non-essential civilians had already obeyed Gauleiter Kaufmann's plea to leave the city and had walked to four major gathering points, then been taken by army transport to railway stations outside Hamburg where they had been dispersed throughout Germany, so the loss of life in Barmbek was considerably less than it might have been. The worst incident was in one of the shelters of the Karstadt store in Hamburgstrasse. Not long after the bombing of Barmbek began, an HE bomb started the display windows blazing and at 1.45 a.m. the store collapsed. The next morning 370 people were found to have suffocated, trapped in one of the shelters which contained a burning coke supply. Half an hour into the raid heavy bombing in the eastern districts of Hamburg stretched the fire services too far. There was no way they could now contain the numerous fires and they were allowed to rage unchecked.

This was the object of any Bomber Command area attack. The Blitz had taught Britain's leaders the lesson that to saturate a city's fire and ARP defences was the way to wreck acres of homes and factories. In Barmbek itself over half of an engineering works employing 1,500 people was burned out because firemen had not been able to tackle the blaze. A specialist submarine design firm was destroyed, as were power stations and gasworks. Many assessed the material damage of this third raid as higher than that of the second.

F/Sgt Alex Wood, a Stirling pilot who had lately joined 15 Sqn in 3 Group, was, like Sgt Webb, also on his first operation:

> Window was still being very effective that night. The searchlights were just standing up straight without moving and the flak was completely random like a widespread barrage. I knew it wasn't going to be like that all the time because of Window, but I was still scared stiff. We were very fortunate in that we weren't shot up at all. The whole town seemed like a mass of flames with frequent flashes as high explosive was dropped. We were told the next day the German controllers broadcasting to the fighters were heard to say. 'The English propagate themselves.'[37]

Flight engineer Sgt Philip Bates, above the city in a 149 Sqn Stirling, says: 'It was a good attack. My notes from the time say, "Hamburg again, another load of incendiaries. Defences still heavy, but searchlights wandering aimlessly about. Met twin-engine fighter coming out across coast. Both gunners opened fire then the fighter disappeared."'[38]

However, not all the searchlights were ineffective. Sgt Ken Harvey was back over the city and remembers:

> We had seen one or two go down with the flak and as an aircraft was coned our pilot moved in to bomb. Then we were coned ourselves. He went into a dive to escape and as we got out of the Hamburg area the searchlights flicked off. What we didn't know was we had moved into a fighter zone and that's why they left us. I was in the astrodome. The first thing we knew was the rear gunner opening fire and he must have got him because I saw a black parachute going down.[39]

The Halifax of P/O George Vandekerckhove of 427 Sqn was also one of those attacked. A single-engined fighter came in from astern and his rear gunner, Sgt John McLean, called a corkscrew and blasted it with his four Brownings, the enemy disappearing below.

Mosquitos patrolling the night-fighter bases were giving the Luftwaffe a hard time. The adjutant of 605 Sqn recorded: 'An intruder's dream came true tonight. F/O J. D. Woods found Lüneburg all lit up with 10 to 15 enemy aircraft all orbiting with navigation lights on. Unfortunately weather conditions were far from good and this prevented him getting more than one destroyed and one probable.'[40]

It was smoke from the fires of Hamburg only 30 miles away which had denied Woods greater success. He was not to know what he had nearly achieved. Major Hajo Herrmann, the leader of the new Wilde Saus that were to claim so many Allied aircrew in the months to come, had just landed when Woods began his six attacks and was standing in the control tower when a British cannon shell came through, narrowly missing him.

As the all-clear sounded in Hamburg at 0208 reports came in of raging fires south of the Binnen Alster; in Altona to the west and to the east of the Alster there was a barrier of fire stretching 1¾ miles.

Hans Nossak, still in the Heide park to the south of Hamburg, wrote in his diary:

At about 2 a.m. the trial was over. From an unreal distance one could hear the sound of the all-clear. The northern sky was red like directly after sunset. From the highway nearby one could hear the wailing sirens of the fire brigades, coming from neighbouring towns. There was an endless driving on all streets around Hamburg, day and night, a flight away – not knowing where to.[41]

From 460 Sqn, 22-year-old Australian F/Sgt James English, who had seen burning Barmbek, reported back at base: 'Tremendous fires – almost one huge fire covering a large area.' As he bombed, a 4-lb incendiary had come through his fuselage forward of the mid-upper turret and hit the flight engineer, Sgt A. W. Catty, who was standing by the flare chute.[42]

An exhausted P/O Charles Lawrence landed at Wickenby looking forward to a week's leave. P/O Lawrence, now wearing the DFM ribbon after landing his crippled Lancaster with one gunner blinded and the other about to lose a leg after a fighter attack on a mining operation, had taken 12 Sqn's U-Uncle to Hamburg three times in five days with the gruelling Essen raid in between. Now the week off that operational aircrew were entitled to every six weeks, losses permitting, would be due again in two days. When he returned he hoped to rattle off the last five operations of his tour.

Back at Leeming an excited Sgt McLean claimed one enemy aircraft destroyed, but was only granted a probable. The intelligence officer debriefing the crew recorded: 'The navigator, Sgt William Williamson, then declared: "Jeez they never give you anything in this outfit." McLean replied: "OK Willie, I'll get you another one next time."'[43]

THERE was one more raid to come on Hamburg, but its ordeal was largely over. Bomber Command, which had proved it could defeat much, would be unable to overcome the forces of nature. Harris had intended to send his force out to Hamburg again on 31 July and in 6 Group aircraft had already started to taxi out in thunderstorms when the operation was called off. It would be two nights before bombs fell on Hamburg again and they would be few and scattered.

That day many newspapers were still catching up on what a success the Hamburg raid of the 27th had been. Aircrew in 4 and 6 Groups around York had been able to read in the *Yorkshire Evening Press* that:

> The great Allied battering of Hamburg goes on. Last night our bombers went there in very great strength and gave Germany's biggest port and U-boat building centre its seventh battering in about 120 hours.

But there was a sense of disbelief in a story alongside which read:

> The neutralization of Hamburg would be a tremendous blow to Nazi industry and morale, writes an air correspondent, but it is a very difficult proposition from the bombing point of view. With a population of over one and a half million and a built-up area of 50 square miles the port contains no less than 10,000 acres of water and hundreds of industrial targets.

It was indeed incredible that in six months since the tentative beginnings with H2S Bomber Command had become such a powerful force that the enemy's second-largest city, supplying so many U-boats alone, could virtually cease to exist.

However, for most people in English cities, such as York in bomber country, there were other things to think about as Bank Holiday Monday approached and the hot weather continued. In the time-honoured fashion of newspapers there were pictures of pretty girls sunbathing in parks. There were also advertisements for 'holidays at home' to keep crowds away from railway stations and leave the permanent way free for more goods traffic.

In York a big agricultural show, suspended in 1940, was about to be launched again – on Rowntree's sports ground – as was the ancient Goose Fair in Nottingham. On RAF stations in eastern England the folklore was that Nottingham had a far greater population of women than men, that the girls were the prettiest in England, and that as they were in short supply for chaps they were desperate to meet one. Equally keen and inexperienced young aircrew at operational bases such as Syerston, near the city, would make a beeline for the funfair over its eight days, hoping to carry out their own research among the girls in their summer dresses.

The *Nottingham Evening Post* had chirruped in its leader column: 'This is to be the brightest Bank Holiday period of the war. The great news from the war zones has given the impetus.' The news it was talking about was the kind it reported in its issue after the raid of the 29th that: 'well over 2,000 tons of bombs had been dropped on Hamburg in the latest attack'.

The next day, as many factories closed down for their annual holiday, there was a rush to get away. The need for workers to man the lathes had brought a new affluence to working-class families. The average male wage was now £5 13s 9d (£5.70p) a week and fathers were anxious to take their families for a break in more pleasing country towns or even beyond the barbed barriers of the seaside where a pint of beer in the sunshine while the children played could be had for 7d (less than 3p).

The *Evening Post* reported on 31 July: 'Railway traffic throughout the night was enormous. Nottingham bus centre was the scene of considerable animation by would-be passengers despite warnings.' As was the way with British bank holidays the sunshine wouldn't last and the change in the weather would have a dramatic effect on the final Hamburg operation.

THE last of the four major raids on Hamburg had been planned just as long and meticulously as the first and it was perhaps because he had already had to call it off once because of dangerous weather conditions that Harris, after a thorough Met briefing for the night of August Bank Holiday Monday, put his finger on the map for the broken city again. He had been told that cumulus cloud over the North Sea might well develop into the thunderstorm conditions of cumulonimbus, but there was a possibility it would drift north towards Scandinavia.

The temptation was that Harburg, with its acres of important industries, had not been touched in the attacks. Laying waste to it would be the last piece in the jigsaw of destruction. It was a gamble too far.

There would be the usual six waves. The aiming point for the first four would be Hamburg, then Harburg for the final two. Pathfinders would use the Newhaven method of ground marking, but just in case the weather turned foul there would be 'emergency' Wanganui skymarkers cascading in green with red stars. This time the route through the target would be almost due north to allow for creepback over Harburg.

Crews tucking into the operational meal of bacon and egg expected it to be a treat for which they wouldn't have to pay a price. Ops had been called off for a much less worrying forecast than that of 2 August. As they struggled into the heavy Irvin and Taylor suits and tussled with flying-boot zips the word in crewrooms was that a scrub was on the way. Even as the roaring, spluttering, popping engines of the bombers turned airframes onto perimeter tracks and lined up the first vibrating machine with the wide black yonder, the expectation was a call from control to say all efforts had been in vain. Instead signal caravans flashed green in succession at runway threshold to threshold and the first of the bombers bounded forward along the tarmac as keyed-up pilots tapped brakes to release.

Two brothers in different squadrons took to the night sky within half an hour of each other. Canadian F/O Ernest Kirkham was the navigator in the 44 Sqn Lancaster of F/Sgt Alan Moffatt where Sgt Peter Swan was the bomb aimer. Kirkham's 19-year-old flight sergeant brother, Thomas, was rear gunner in the 432 Sqn Wellington crew of Canadian P/O Deveraux McDonald.

On another RCAF squadron, 419, Sgt John Gilvary was back from his battle course and geared up for his baptism of fire. He wrote in his diary: 'On ops tonight. Spent day in preparation. I might get going at last. Had usual briefing, ops meal and back to kite. Met forecast bloody awful. Took off about 10.30 p.m.'[44]

That 'bloody awful' weather fully lived up to expectations and bomber after bomber soared and sank as it flew into icing conditions and thunderstorms of a ferocity crews had not experienced before. At Scampton six aircraft of 57 Sqn didn't even get off the ground after a Lancaster crashed on take-off and burst into flames, blocking the runway.

The appalling conditions for those who did set out for Hamburg were soon causing problems and no fewer than 186 aircraft would make early returns. Air gunner Sgt Harold McLean, of 427 Sqn, was in one of them. He remembers:

> We were senior crew by this time and it was tradition on our squadron that the senior crew took off last. It was a foul night, but everybody got off, then there was a bit of a break in the weather and we took off straight out without having to circle. We hadn't gone above 9,000 feet over the North Sea when the engineer reported the radiators were icing up, so we had to turn back. It was the only time we abandoned an op. We let the bombs go in the sea on safe and there was a convoy coming down the east coast about 50 miles ahead of where they should be and we flew over them. They put their searchlights on and we were passing between two lines of ships.[45]

This Halifax crew was lucky not to be fired on. The Navy were always informed of where they might encounter Allied bomber fleets going out or returning, but many an RAF crew came back with anti-aircraft damage from British shells.

Sgt Bates of 149 Sqn remembers the particular problems of the low-ceiling Stirlings in such conditions. 'We couldn't get above 8,000 feet that night,' he says. 'The ice was coming off the airscrews and being flung into the side of the fuselage. There were blue sparks coming off the guns. A friend of mine on 15 Squadron came down in the North Sea because of icing in the storm.'[46]

No fewer than four of the Stirling crews of 90 Sqn would have to turn back because ice on the propellers reduced their pulling power or the silent killer on mainplane or tail surfaces dramatically altered the flying characteristics of the aircraft. A Halifax of 419 Sqn would crash because of icing, killing four of its crew, and a Stirling of 214 Sqn would be brought down by ice off Wilhelmshaven. A 115 Sqn Lancaster was struck by lightning near the target and crashed, killing all on board. Two other 428 Sqn Halifaxes were lost without trace over the sea.

Sgt Gilvary, whose 419 Sqn crew were making their first operation together, soon found they were in trouble after disappearing into the mist on take-off and discovering the loop aerial for bearings was unserviceable, as was the standard beam approach equipment. His diary records: 'Got lost in cloud in no time. Unable to establish over base. 35 minutes late at Hornsea.' They struggled on in E-Easy at the tail of the bomber stream, but didn't even reach the enemy coast. Sgt Gilvary noted in his diary: 'Jettisoned bombs having been shot up by coastal batteries and flak ships.'[47]

Despite the weather, night fighters were active. Among those attacked was a 10 Sqn Halifax 30 miles off Cuxhaven. Its gunners shot down the Ju88 which had swooped and the Halifax made a successful landing in Britain with both elevators shot away.

Planners of the last of the Hamburg raids had intended that the first four waves would use the northerly point of the Alster lake as their aiming point, which should concentrate bombing in the wealthy Harvesthude and Rotherbaum areas and the city centre. The aiming point for the final two waves would be the middle of Harburg, 8 miles to the south. As it was, the weather conditions resulted in bombs being scattered all over Hamburg and the countryside around.

Bomb aimer Sgt Dennis Slack of 158 Sqn remembers:

We were told at briefing: 'You will meet a bank of cloud on the way over, but don't worry, it will only be up to 14,000 feet.' In fact when we saw it ahead it was like a brick wall. It went right up to 30,000 feet. The Halifax could only climb to 19,000 feet and we flew straight into it. The aircraft was being tossed around inside. We just hoped we had got to the target. There were flares going down all over the place and flashes of bombs.[48]

Hans Nossack, still in the Heide national park and unable to check on his home in Hamburg, which unknown to him had been burned out, heard the bombers approaching. 'Directly before the attack a heavy thundercloud above the Elbe started to unload when the attack began,' he recorded. 'The attackers could not find their targets so dropped their bombs blindly. One could not differentiate between thunder, bombs and barrage.'[49]

Sgt Bates remembers: 'When we got to the target we couldn't open the bomb doors; they had frozen up. We had to go round a second time while I hand-cranked them down.' Sgt Wilf Sutton, flight engineer in a 35 Sqn Pathfinder Halifax, recalls: 'The propellers were rings of St Elmo's fire, the mainplanes were extended by about a foot of lightning and the tailplane was also extended. The wireless operator tried to withdraw his trailing aerial, but it broke away.'[50]

Peter Johnson, wearing Warrant Officer badges on his sleeves, having risen from F/Sgt in two days due to losses, was making his second trip over the city. He had finally flown on the raid of the 29th after so many scrubs. Now he and other 101 Sqn crews were battling with the thunderstorm Hans Nossack had seen. He reported to debriefing officers: 'There was 10/10s cloud with severe icing in the very heavy electrical storm. The target was identified by dead reckoning position and it was a most disappointing trip.'[51]

W/O Johnson returned to Ludford Magna with a faulty supercharger.

His fellow 101 Sqn captain, F/Lt R. McCulloch described the operation in stronger terms. 'It was a complete fiasco due to weather conditions,' he reported. McCulloch was not in the best of tempers. Flak over the target had shot away his rudder control and damaged the rear fuselage, to the alarm of the mid-upper gunner, Sgt F. J. Burton, only a foot or two away as he scanned the sky. As McCulloch touched down, the port undercarriage of U-Uncle collapsed.[52]

Hamburg, devastated by a freak of atmospheric conditions that had led to the firestorm, was now being saved further torment by another caprice of the weather.

Bomb aimer Peter Swan in T-Tommy of 44 Sqn was suffering at the centre of the storm bellowing its thunder at Herr Nossack and others below in competition with the explosions. He remembers:

> There were absolutely massive cu-nim clouds. It felt as if our aircraft was going up vertically then falling on its back. All our compasses went berserk and in my bomb aimer's compartment in the nose, Window was floating about like confetti. My stomach was churning and it was a very frightening experience. I had to jettison the bomb load, then the starboard outer was hit by flak and caught fire. We put the fire out with the extinguisher, then had to feather it. We turned for home and were still going up and down, but not so severely. It was difficult to know where we were because the compasses had gone. We were fairly well lost.[53]

The bad weather had wrecked Harris's ambitions, but the night fighters were already aloft when the storm broke. Now as the scattered stream, with its Window screen dissipated, crossed the coast for the North Sea the radar screens of the Kammhuber Line would prove they could still be effective.

Sgt Swan's aircraft was down to 4,000 feet as it cleared Holland after F/Sgt Moffatt had tried to escape the worst of the weather. The night fighter of Hauptmann Hans Joachim Jabs of IV/NJG1 was vectored onto his tail. Sgt Swan recalls:

There was no warning, just a hell of a 'rat-tat-tat' noise as it fired its cannon and the flashes as we were obviously hit. I heard the skipper say faintly: 'Bale out.' I went to open the front escape hatch and got it partly open, then it stuck, so I jumped on it. I bashed the back of my head as I went out and saw stars. I came round by a miracle just in time to pull my ripcord, because as the chute opened I went in the water. I went straight in and self-preservation took over because I pulled the CO_2 trigger on my Mae West and found myself floating. I saw part of the aircraft go in the sea. My head must have been in a hell of a state because part of it felt numb for months afterwards.

Sgt Swan was the only one to get out of the aircraft. Others were also being caught by night fighters. Another pilot of IV/NJG1 shot down a 166 Sqn Wellington off Terschelling, a third downed a 100 Sqn Lancaster which had just crossed the Frisian Islands. Flak and bolts of lightning were sending bombers plunging into the Elbe and aircraft away from track were being picked off from Wilhelmshaven to Lüneburg.

Others went into the sea without known cause. One of them was a Wellington from 432 Sqn in which there were no survivors. In the tail was F/Sgt Kirkham, younger brother of the navigator in Sgt Swan's Lancaster. They must have died within minutes of each other. The next day their parents would receive two separate telegrams at their home in Vancouver.

The last of the bombers crossed the enemy coast to leave the rains sweeping away the dust and stench of Hamburg. It would be a battle all the way home against the storm-force winds and as exhausted pilots turned one by one to greet welcoming flarepaths below there could still be surprises in store from aircraft that had been bounced and twisted through miles of electrically charged air.

Sgt John Fell, navigator in a 102 Sqn Halifax, remembers: 'As we were on final approach into base the pilot and the bomb aimer saw a spark fly from the aircraft to the ground like a bolt of lightning. We were only about 60 feet up and it was quite alarming for the pilot trying to keep an eye on the runway.'[54]

The cost of the raid was now being counted. Thirty aircraft were missing, 4.1 per cent – approaching the recent average for raids without the protection of Window. Little could be shown for this last operation. One 207 Sqn pilot told intelligence officers: 'There were scattered small fires over at least 50 miles.'[55]

The adjutant's report for 100 Sqn summed up the debacle. 'Out of 24 aircraft which took off only 15 attacked the primary target. Weather conditions were deplorable and two experienced crews were lost.'[56] One of the skippers, F/Lt R. Howgill, shot down in the sea off Heligoland, had only just been appointed A-Flight commander. 100 Sqn was living up to its reputation that senior aircrew appointments were the kiss of death.

As pilots – knuckles still white from trying to control bucking, plunging, soaring machines across the lightning-lit sky – climbed wearily into bed, dawn was breaking on the Dutch coast where Sgt Swan floated miserably in his yellow Mae West. His wife was five months pregnant and he was sure he would never see the baby:

> I had been in the water for about three hours in total blackness. With the dawn I saw the tail of our aircraft sticking out of the water and further away another part of it. I remember vividly thinking: 'Well, I've had it' and more or less gave up, then at that moment my feet went down and I touched the bottom.
>
> As the light increased I could see the shore with houses on it. A little later an E-boat came out and picked me up. I was about 4 or 5 miles from the shore and it must have been very low tide. The Kriegsmarine sailors on board were very kind to me. I was in a very low state and I vomited and brought up blood. When they got me ashore to their unit in Harlingen they wrapped me up by a fire. I got some cigarettes out of my pocket, but with the water the tobacco was all loose. They dried it off for me. I was then taken to a Luftwaffe station and shoved into a room where a lot of women typists were working. I must have looked pretty wretched to them.[57]

IN Germany the cost of the Battle of Hamburg was being calculated by Reich Armaments Minister Albert Speer. He later admitted Bomber Command had achieved at least temporarily a prime objective of Harris's and Eaker's orders spelt out in the Casablanca Directive – 'the undermining of the morale of the German people to a point where their capacity for armed resistance is fatally weakened'.

Debriefed by Americans after the war at the 'Ashcan' interrogation centre, he revealed that the effects of attacks such as those on Hamburg 'not only upon the population of the town attacked but upon the rest of the Reich, was terrifying, even if only temporarily so'.[58]

In fact Speer told Hitler: 'A rapid repetition of this type of attack upon another six German towns will inevitably cripple the will to sustain armaments manufacture and war production.' Speer added to the Americans that he had spelled out to the Führer 'that a continuation of these attacks might bring about a rapid end to the war'.[59]

Hamburg was by far the biggest producer of U-boats in Germany and completed more than 400 during the conflict. On their own projections the Germans estimated Hamburg was up to 150 short because of bombing. One U-boat can sink a lot of ships, vital to an island nation. Hamburg had been devastated sixteen weeks after Atlantic merchant vessel sinkings had peaked at 385,000 tons and Churchill had feared Britain would lose the war.

Hitler refused to visit Hamburg or any devastated German city to see what his policies had brought to his subjects. That denial helped to keep his fantasies alive. Hermann Roechling, a member of the Reichsministry for Armaments and War Production and the Reichscommissioner for Iron and Steel in the Occupied Territories, was also interviewed many times by Ashcan's American interrogators. He said high-explosive bombs and incendiaries had little effect on foundry sidings, rollings mills and steelworks – they could be easily repaired. However, he tellingly added: 'The most serious throttling of production was due to the destruction of the towns' water main, gas and electricity supplies.'[60]

Add the factors of transport services at a halt for days or even weeks, and the need to train replacement key workers for those dead or missing, and it is clear that area bombing did have a constantly eroding effect on German industry, one which would eventually bring the machines grinding to a halt. It was impossible to choose a power station or waterworks to hit at night, but if a city was devastated some bombs would hit the vital structures that kept a city's machines turning. In the Battle of Hamburg three of the five main transformer stations were knocked out for weeks and thirteen others were damaged to a varying degree. Electricity output was not fully restored until February 1944.

The chief water pumping works at Rothensburgsort had been hit and two reservoirs damaged. There were 847 breaks in the water mains. The Bahrenfeld gasworks had been gutted, the Altona, Grasbrook, Tiefstack, Wandsbeck and Barmbek works hit. Gas mains were only repaired after the roads above them had been cleared of rubble. Germany's largest port was at a standstill; 20 per cent of the harbour installations had been destroyed.

That 'rapid end to the war' Speer feared seemed a distinct possibility on both sides of the North Sea in early August 1943. Bomber Command had not chosen saturation bombing as a means to wage war. It had been forced on it by the inefficiencies of aircraft and equipment employed in the early years of the conflict. A desperate War Cabinet had issued its new commander in 1942, Sir Arthur Harris, with clear instructions on how he must conduct the bombing war in future.

It was obvious to Harris that – efficient subordinate as he was – he must pursue that task with a relentless tenacity intended to end the evil of National Socialism as rapidly as possible, so that Britain and her Allies might survive. The outcome of that titanic struggle was by no means certain when the Battle of Hamburg was launched or indeed won. So, those civilians had not been killed carelessly in Hamburg. The attack might indeed have brought the war juddering to a halt if further raids of such magnitude could be mounted quickly. But they couldn't.

It was the weather and Window which had proved Hamburg's downfall. Bomber Command would not wreak such devastation in one night on a city of huge population for another nineteenth months. Then Dresden would burn because its narrow streets were left largely undefended as the teetering Nazi giant plunged needlessly headlong towards self-destructive, crushing defeat in the iron grip of the Allies stretching across the Rhine and Oder.

The upper hand in war can be a brief tenure and within fifteen days of the last high explosive of the battle falling on Hamburg, Bomber Command would be taking part in the Peenemünde operation to defeat the enormous menace of the Germans' own saturation bombing campaign. Under the Nazi plans there would be no dilemma or debate about morality – human mind, hand and heart would leave off at the moment of launch of a rain of terror that would be truly random.

CHAPTER TEN

THE PERIL OF PEENEMÜNDE

THE hot, turbulent weather of early August settled into a period of calm, balmy days and nights which could only mean an intensification of demands on bomber crews now that Window had offered a respite in the cost of raiding the Reich. August would be Bomber Command's busiest month of 1943 with sixteen nights of operations by the heavies. It would see the squadrons reach further out into Germany as the tidal wave of destruction roared on. There would also be a return to the cities of northern Italy in another attempt to persuade that country its fortunes no longer lay in an Axis.

The timing for working such a conversion would never be better. The terrible lesson of Operation Gomorrah overhung the new leaders of Italy with all the hypnotic fascination of a biblically proportioned disaster. It was clear to them in that time before the atmospheric factor became known that a similar fate must await Milan, Turin or even eventually Naples.

Before the month was out Harris's next major campaign, the Battle of Berlin, would open. But the key raid in August and one of the three most important of the year would be against the rocket research establishment at Peenemünde. It came only a fortnight after the Battle of Hamburg had ended in the fight with the forces of nature. What had been found there had horrified Britain's leaders and threatened the build-up to D-Day and the whole course of the war.

The ideal conditions needed for the Peenemünde operation would not occur until the middle of the month. Meanwhile the bomber war would continue over other targets, but after the nerve-stretching night of the Hamburg thunderstorm the crews had five days in which to rest before they would be needed again.

At Leeming the irrepressible Canadians of 427 Sqn celebrated the safe return of all Hamburg aircraft the night before at a party and concert in the NAAFI described by the adjutant as 'the crowning achievement of our squadron social life'. An admin officer had been dispatched to London a few days before to rustle up some costumes for the show and every member of the squadron turned up at 7.30 p.m., parading a spectacle of drinking receptacles, from tin mugs to tooth glasses.[1]

'The bar soon began to look like Stalingrad at the height of the siege,' the Operational Record Book noted. WAAFs, glad to slip into civilian dresses again from the unforgiving fabric of service uniform, provided the cabaret, though there had been a panic earlier when the leading lady failed to show. Fresh from her duties at station headquarters she dashed back stage to change, minutes before curtain-up.

Bellowing out the familiar Air Force ditties after the show such as 'Once There Was a NAAFI Girl' and 'Bring Back My Bomber and Me', aircrew had a chance to reflect as they drew on their free cigarettes that recent good fortune for the squadron, which had not lost an aircraft since 13 July, was not likely to last as the Luftwaffe caught up.

On 12 Sqn P/O Lawrence, who in five days had completed three of the four Hamburg raids and the Essen operation, discovered that from now on the attrition rate would be abstract. He remembers:

> I returned from leave on 7 August to find that due to Bomber Command losses and a new Heavy Conversion Unit at Faldingworth there was a shortage in 1 Group of pilot instructors. Although I still had five operations to do to complete a tour of thirty I was summarily posted the next day to Faldingworth and my navigator, F/O Kettles, was posted to Blyton as a navigation instructor. Needless to say, the rest of the crew were not amused.*[2]

---

* *The other five members of the crew completed their tour at Wickenby to be posted to OTUs for six months' rest.*

As P/O Lawrence departed for HCU, preparations were being made for a three-pronged attack on Genoa, Milan and Turin that night, which would lay the first steps on the road to Peenemünde. G/Cpt John Searby, the CO of 83 Pathfinder Sqn, was called on for Turin to act as master bomber, a role first demonstrated by Gibson on the Dams Raid. What he learned would be employed ten days later when he acted as master bomber on Peenemünde.

The Turin operation was the second time Bomber Command had employed Gibson's technique. The first occasion had been on another experimental raid six weeks before in which AVM Sir Ralph Cochrane, anxious to set up a rival Pathfinder Force in 5 Group, had sent sixty Lancasters in moonlight to Friedrichshafen to attack at low level a radar works on the shores of Lake Constance. Fortuitously, unknown to Bomber Command at this time, the works was also an assembly plant for V2 rockets and its destruction prevented 300 being built.

To avoid a return across France in the face of alerted night fighters the Friedrichshafen force had flown on to North Africa, the first shuttle raid of the war. More importantly for Peenemünde, the operation had employed for the first time a time and distance technique in which part of the force had dropped its bombs on the factory blindly after counting off the time from an identified landmark. It had also been combined with offset marking whereby some TIs had been dropped outside the aiming point – to avoid smoke, which usually obscured a target in later stages – then bomb sights set for an overshoot, so that they actually landed on the target. This T and D technique would be used by an element of the Peenemünde force.

WIRELESS operator Sgt Ken Harvey was on the Friedrichshafen raid and his CO at 467 Sqn, W/Cdr Gomm, had been nominated as the deputy master bomber. Sgt Harvey remembers:

> Just a few crews from 467 Sqn had been selected. We trained for it over
> a couple of weeks, learning to co-operate at low level with a master
> bomber, practising on the bombing range at Wainfleet. My main job

on the operation was just to make sure that all the channels were open and we kept in contact. As it happened, W/Cdr Gomm had to take over as master bomber because the radio of the actual master of ceremonies was u/s.[3]

Friedrichshafen was meant to be bombed from between 5,000 and 10,000 feet and the assigned master bomber, G/Cpt L. C. Slee, headed for the attack at the lower range of the height band. When he was forced to hand over to his deputy, W/Cdr Gomm, the latter – no fan of the low-level technique – ordered the force up another 5,000 feet.

The 97 Pathfinder Sqn had provided four crews for the operation who dropped their green TIs on the factory roofs, quickly followed up by several Cookies from Main Force. Once dense smoke had covered the target selected crews then adopted the alternative marking method 5 Group was experimenting with by making timed runs from a landmark aside Lake Constance. Bombing was remarkably accurate and later photographs showed that the factory had been badly damaged. Not one aircraft had been lost. The results would help considerably towards 5 Group setting up its own Pathfinder Force, to the chagrin of Don Bennett, the PFF commander.

In fact Cochrane wanted the time and distance technique to be the sole means of wrecking Peenemünde and asked that it be a 5 Group operation. Peenemünde was too important a target, however, not to be destroyed first time and Harris could not take the risk. In the end both techniques were used – Bennett's Pathfinders marked the target by visual identification for Main Force and Cochrane's group carried out a time and distance attack.

The strike against the V2 programme was a long time in coming. Rocket research at the remote Baltic army base of Peenemünde began as early as 1937. Two months after the outbreak of war German technical secrets were passed to British naval intelligence in which the name of Peenemünde was revealed for the first time. They were filed and ignored until March 1943 when the notes of a conversation between two German generals in their bugged quarters at the London Cage were examined by Army intelligence.

In them General von Thoma expressed surprise to his fellow captive General Cruewell that he had not heard the sound of any large explosions and wondered why rockets weren't falling on London in large numbers by now.

The report went up the chain of Army command with mounting anxiety and landed on Churchill's desk twenty-three days later. It was realised the Germans were developing a weapons system to saturate Britain against which there was no defence. Furthermore, there was no clue to what the Germans might eventually put in the payload of those rockets, and chemical warfare was a constant threat readily appreciated by both sides. In fact a spy in the Wehrmacht told London on 12 August that bacteriological weapons were one of three areas of research at Peenemünde.

The urgency to react was obvious and Churchill's son-in-law Duncan Sandys was put in charge of all investigations into the German rocket programme. As Sandys poured over the documents the threat to Britain, it was realised, was extreme. One intelligence estimate was that a single rocket falling on a built-up area could cause up to 4,000 casualties.

At the risk of alerting the Germans to British intentions a series of photographic reconnaissance missions were ordered to be made by a detached flight of 540 Sqn at Leuchars. On 12 June a Mosquito brought back clear evidence of a V2 rocket lying horizontally on its test stand.

Only Bomber Command could effectively remove the menace. Harris fully realised the danger of a weapon that could one day make a force such as his obsolete and it is some measure of how seriously he viewed the German scientific advancement that such an unequivocal leader called a conference at High Wycombe on 7 July of his six group commanders to suggest how the threat could be contained or removed.[4]

The technical difficulties of hitting a small target at night were considerable. The only such precision raids so far had been carried out on the Ruhr dams and on the radar plant at Friedrichshafen – both by small forces. Peenemünde would have to be a maximum-effort raid, and maximum-effort raids outside the range of Oboe could often go totally wrong. The rocket establishment would have to be eradicated at the first blow. A return to the target with a by then fully alerted Luftwaffe would decimate his command.

To achieve success, as in the Dams Raid, it would be necessary to operate in full moonlight and at low level. In the run-up to the projected date of 17 August Harris began husbanding his resources.

To boost morale after the lost Battle of Hamburg the Nazi Propaganda Ministry had begun to circulate stories of new secret weapons. Goebbels would later claim them to be vengeance weapons for the bombing of Germany's cities, but both the V2 and the V1 'Doodlebug', of which the Allies had no knowledge then, had been in development long before the bomber offensive began.

On 6 August, for instance, British newspapers had carried stories from the Berlin correspondent of a Spanish publication about a secret weapon of devastating effect which would be 'out by November' to help Germany dislodge the Americans and British from all their positions and 'to roll up Russia'.

IN the countdown to Peenemünde other German centres of production needed to be raided to keep up the momentum in the settled weather. Mannheim had not been attacked since the Pilsen diversion of 16 April and on 9 August the teleprinters chattered from group to squadron to send bomb trains, fuel bowsers and ammunition trailers snaking to the dispersals of 457 aircraft throughout the bomber counties to prepare them for what was now considered by High Wycombe to be a medium-sized effort. W/O Peter Johnson of 101 Sqn thought he'd arrived over Mannheim before the Pathfinders. As Z-hour approached there was no sign of PFF markers ahead and he expected to orbit among the angry red and white flashes of the flak. Then the TIs suddenly bloomed and he and several others released their bombs. 'Many fires were seen in the target area and there was a very large column of black smoke up to 8,000 feet,' he reported back at base.

As one of the first on target he thought the raid was well concentrated, but the five-tenths cloud cover spoilt the marking and Bomber Command's Operational Research Section judged from the bomb plot photographs that it had been a scattered attack. Crews had been briefed to be careful of bombing a dummy target that the Germans were bound to set alight, but

Sgt W. H. 'Indian' Schmitt of 427 Sqn reported: 'Many bombs seemed to fall on the dummy town.'[5]

The squadron, which had had such a run of good luck, would now lose an aircraft. F/Sgt Billy Biggs, a 22-year-old English skipper on the squadron, had a second-dickey pilot, Sgt R. C. Deegan, aboard and had bombed towards the close of the attack when a single-engined fighter came in from astern and raked the aircraft.

Sgt Harold McLean, now 19, was in the mid-upper turret. He remembers:

> There was ten-tenths cloud quite a few thousand feet below. The search-lights were playing on it like shining a light under a bed sheet. I was looking over the side of the aircraft, feeling a bit cocky as we'd dropped our bombs and thinking: 'Well, that's another one in' and looking at a four-engine aircraft way below us. At that moment a stream of bullets came right under my nose and into the starboard wing root via the rudder on that side. There was this horrible sound like tearing metal.
>
> There had been no warning from the rear turret. There was a fire in the wing root and the flaps had come down. Fortunately the wheels were locked in the up position.
>
> The fighter had just raked down the starboard side and gone. He didn't come back for a second go.

The Halifax's elevator had been damaged in the attack and Sgt Deegan and F/Sgt Biggs had to use all their strength to keep the aircraft from diving. 'The second-dickey pilot had his feet across the pilot's lap and the pilot had his feet on the control column to keep it flying because of the damage,' Sgt McLean recalls.

The American rear gunner, F/Sgt Fisher, was told to keep an eye out for further trouble and Sgt McLean was sent to tackle the fire. McLean remembers:

> I got the escape axe and hacked a piece out of the plane and the flight engineer joined me, bringing a fire extinguisher, and poked the extin-

guisher through the hole I'd cut and fired it, but it went nowhere near the damaged area. The bomb aimer turned up with another extinguisher and I went back in the turret and could see the fire going out. It was just an incendiary bullet in the wing, but it had fractured a hydraulic pipe. There was no manoeuvrability and the navigator told us we were 410 miles from Beachy Head. If anyone had attacked us we would have been powerless, but we got back across France and crossed the Channel at about 9,000 feet.

We crossed the coast in low cloud; we knew there was no way we could land because there were no hydraulics and when we got over the Basingstoke area the pilot said: 'It's about time we got out.' I got the pigeons out of the case and threw them out. The wireless operator, Les Moyler, who was our only married crew member, picked his chute up to put it on but grabbed it by the ripcord by mistake and it opened in the aircraft.

The rear gunner, Bobby Fisher, immediately said he'd take Les's chute, but Les refused. Les sat in the doorway with his arms round his chute and I gave him a push and out he went and it opened OK. I did the same for Bobby and then it was my turn. As I fell away from the plane I remember hearing the engines humming along beautifully and I thought what a waste for a broken hydraulic pipe.

I was swinging quite wildly, it was quite hairy and I was in cloud. Then when I came out I could see a small river below. The harness didn't fit properly and I had a strange urge to hit the quick release buckle. Some high tension wires passed in front of my face and I landed in a blackberry bush in a field.

Biggs, Elliott and Moyler were awarded immediate DFMs and the whole crew were invited to apply for commissions. 'Alf Richards, the bomb aimer, and I applied as did the others. We had one more op than everybody else in the crew,' recalls Sgt McLean. 'But they told us to come back in three months because we were too young. That's always stuck in my craw.'[6]

MANNHEIM had been a long trip and the next day the crews had not risen until lunchtime. To the dismay of many as they reported at flight offices they found they were on again that night. Unknown to them the operation would require even longer time over enemy territory.

Sgt Gilvary of 419 Sqn was one of those who felt a long trip only a few hours after Mannheim was a bit too much to ask. He had got to bed at 5 a.m. after his skipper, F/Sgt Pekin, had had to abandon the previous operation, jettisoning the bomb load in the Channel because the rear turret was unserviceable. Sgt Gilvary recorded in his diary: 'On ops again. Got up about 1.30 and after meal went to flights not feeling so bright after last night's effort. Went for briefing 3.30. Nuremberg the target tonight. 1,600-mile trip.' Only two days before he had been recording in his diary a good night at the Wheatsheaf pub in Darlington, 'sipping gentle brews' and riding back on the crossbar of Stan Pekin's bike. Now it was a distant memory as they were called to the war in earnest.[7]

Nuremberg had not been raided since March. The slowly shortening nights meant it now came within the range of darkness as Harris sought new targets in the wake of the Ruhr and Hamburg. As always, the C-in-C was taking a calculated risk. His Lancasters, Halifaxes and particularly the Stirlings could be prime bait for new techniques the Luftwaffe was known to be developing and this time there would be plenty of opportunity for the night fighters circling their beacons to be fed into the bomber stream before it reached the target. At that time the Luftwaffe was experimenting with a suggestion of Oberstleutnant von Lossberg to employ a technique developed from day operations of feeding a lead aircraft into the head of the bomber stream to broadcast a homing signal once the Main Force or Pathfinders had been found.

Window would from this period gradually become a help, not a hindrance, to the defenders. The clouds of gently descending foil showed clearly on radar screens the bomber track to be followed by the *nachtjäger*, now freed from the Himmelbett fighter boxes.

To reduce the time spent over enemy territory Bomber Command had decided to fly one course to Nuremberg. In an attempt to bamboozle the enemy, nine Mosquitos would fly across Holland at the same time as Main Force then divert to targets in the Ruhr. As it happened, the enemy fighter controllers were confused and just five bombers were shot down by *nachtjäger*, most over Belgium on the way back. But some fighters were active on the way in and P/O John Moss, skippering a 49 Sqn Lancaster, was one of those caught.

His bomb aimer Sgt Len Bradfield recalls:

We had flown base to Beachy Head, across to Le Treport, then straight on to Nuremberg with no dog legs. It was a long, straight strip. We had the flight commander's aircraft that night which was fitted with Monica. We were virtually forbidden to weave because of it. It was supposed to be the greatest thing since sliced bread and it was an absolute death trap.

We started Windowing from the German frontier. We didn't hear anything on Monica, but suddenly from four o'clock high an Me110 opened fire on our port outer engine, setting it ablaze. That engine, of course, supplied the power to the rear turret. The mid-upper was able to have a go at the fighter and I stood up and gave it a quick burst from the front turret just to show I was there. The pilot dived to try to put the fire out, but it didn't work. I was ordered to jettison the load and did so, putting my parachute on at the same time and clearing my cushions away from the escape hatch. I checked through the little window into the bomb bay to see the load had gone, then almost immediately heard the pilot's call: 'Abracadabra, jump, jump!' I yanked open the hatch, dropped it diagonally out and dived head first after it as I saw the flight engineer and navigator approaching to follow me out.

The wireless operator, Sammy Small, had gone back to help the mid-upper gunner out of his turret and the rear gunner, Ron Musson, was hand-cranking his turret to go out through the back. At that very moment I heard the explosion of shells against armoured doors beyond the rear turret from what I think was a second aircraft. I think that cannon fire killed the three at the back of the aircraft.

I was only wearing battledress with the white aircrew sweater and an electric waistcoat and slippers and knew it would be about minus 30 outside, so I waited to pull the ripcord until I got through a cloud belt which I thought was at about 7,000 or 8,000 feet. I could see a series of small fires on the ground which I think was debris from our aircraft, which exploded almost immediately after I left. The two gunners and the wireless op went down in the back of the fuselage after the aircraft broke up. I landed in a little meadow alongside a vineyard at Bad Kreutsaa near Hagen. I got rid of my chute and harness, took out my escape kit and started walking.[8]

The rest of Main Force thundered on overhead to Nuremberg. The Pathfinders leading them had planned a ground-marking attack for Nuremberg, but the target was mostly cloud covered. However, a large fire was started and there was severe property damage. In general the Window effect was holding and only sixteen aircraft of the 653 dispatched that night were lost. Five of the losses were in accidents over Britain or on landing. W/Cdr Johnny Fauquier, CO of the Canadian Pathfinder squadron, 405, was particularly unlucky. He landed safely at Gransden Lodge then while taxiing ran into a ditch and the aircraft was damaged beyond repair.

AS dawn broke over the wine-growing country near Hagen in Germany Sgt Bradfield crawled under an A-frame of vines to sleep for the day until he could start evading again. He remembers:

I was woken up by a boy of about 14, leaning on me with a pitchfork, and a couple of adults with shotguns. They were shouting: 'We have a Tommy.' They were amazed I didn't have any sidearms. Once they discovered that they were fine with me. I was taken into Hagen to the burgomeister, who called the police. They took me to a nearby place where there was an SA headquarters with three cells for Jews in the backyard and they put me in one of these for the night. I was told five of my crew were dead.* The Luftwaffe turned up the next day and I was taken by train to Dulag Luft at Frankfurt.[9]

* Two of Sgt Bradfield's crewmates met particularly cruel ends. One was impaled by vine poles on landing in the next vineyard to Sgt Bradfield and the other fell out of his loose parachute harness as the chute snapped open.

Sgt Bradfield had now to come to terms with the fact that it would be a long time before he saw his home again as he began the journey to prisoner-of-war camp.

The previous day Sgt Gilvary had found it had been hours before he got back to Middleton St George. He had recorded in his diary after the Nuremberg raid: 'Good trip. Flak over French coast and well into France. Had one combat after crossing coast then long stooge to target. Not much flak there, very cloudy.' But as his aircraft cleared France it ran into a storm over the Channel and had to divert. His diary continues: 'Landed Church Rawford at 5.30. Spent most of day there. Bloody tired. Took off about 4.10 and map read to base. Landed 5.40. Interrogated, had meal, bath and shave and flopped into bed with no trouble.' He would have 24 hours to recover as Bomber Command was stood down from operations.[10]

AT Ludford Magna a Scottish wireless operator in W/O Stan Slater's crew who had got to know W/O Johnson suggested they take advantage of the break to go shooting. Sgt Jock Mitchell and W/O Johnson decided the rector of Ludford Magna would be the man with his finger on the pulse of the village. It began a friendship with a farmer that would help both airmen cope with the stress of operations through the late summer and autumn.

Mrs Barbara Guthrie, whose father, Bert Brant, farmed at Ludford Grange, remembers:

> Jock Mitchell asked at the rectory if the rector knew where there was any shooting and the rector sent him down to my father. From then on both Peter and Jock used to borrow shotguns from my father to hunt for rabbits. It took their minds off the operations. Jock was from Scone in Perthshire and used to take the mickey out of Peter as a Londoner because he was scared of the geese on the farm. Jock started laying snares for rabbits and my father used to sell the rabbits for them in Louth to give them a bit of pocket money.*

* _Bert Brant, who proved such a friend to aircrew, was still alive at the time of writing, aged 104._

Peter Johnson and Jock Mitchell would be welcomed into the Brant family home from where 11-year-old Barbara often watched the bombers take off on operations:

> I remember the first time Peter came with Jock. The dispersal points of their two aircraft were alongside and that's how they got to know one another. Jock's aircraft, N-Nuts, was the aircraft nearest to our house at a dispersal in the corner of the field. It had insignia on the front of a pair of nutcrackers with Hitler's head as the nut. M-Mother, which Pete flew, had a witch on a broomstick.
>
> The village was in the middle of the air base. It was all around. The buildings of the base were on one side of the road and the airfield on the other side. My grandmother lived near the WAAF site, so we saw a lot of people from the base all the time. I helped my mother at the WVS canteen in the village for the boys. They were always short-staffed and I used to wash up and my mother would cut up the bread for the sandwiches. It was open every night from 6.30 to 9.30 p.m. and the women would serve tea and sandwiches to the RAF boys and girls. It was always busy. I could see Jock and Peter's aircraft taxi out from their dispersals from my bedroom window and when the aircraft took off they were so close overhead.[11]

The schoolgirl would be watching on 12 August as Peter Johnson taxied out for the seventeenth operation of his tour, on Milan. It would be dawn before the Lancasters were back at their dispersals after a trip of nearly nine hours.

AT Middleton St George Sgt Gilvary found himself back on the battle order. At briefing the squadron commander joked that they might find the Italian defences somewhat tough, suggesting 'there was liable to be a riot there and someone might hit us with a stone'. Gilvary found it a 'long, unpleasant, uneventful trip'. He wrote: 'Did not like the Alps one bit. Grim and foreboding, one poor devil hit them with a full bomb load aboard.

Not much left of him. Stooged right across the target – hell of a mess down below.'[12] Sgt Gilvary's E-Easy had to put down at Dalton at 7 a.m. The tired crew took off again at 10.30 a.m. and landed at base half an hour later.

Turin was also being raided that night with mostly Stirlings and Halifaxes of 3 Group. As both forces approached their targets a drama was being played out which would end in a posthumous VC. The 218 Sqn Stirling of F/Sgt Arthur Aaron had been hit by a burst of fire from the nervous gunner in another bomber, who mistook it for a night fighter. Aaron's Canadian navigator, Sgt Cornelius Brennan, was killed and bullets tore away part of the pilot's face and hit him in the chest, immobilising his right arm. The crew knew they would not be able to return over the Alps and the flight engineer, Sgt M. Mitchem, helped the RCAF bomb aimer, Sgt A. W. Larden, to take the controls and turn the Stirling on a rough heading for Africa.

As the aircraft reached the North African coast 21-year-old Aaron, who had been dosed with morphine, insisted on returning to his seat to help with the landing. He twice tried to take the controls but had to be prevented. Instead he wrote instructions with his left hand for the bomb aimer to carry out a successful approach. The aircraft made a wheels-up landing at Bone on its fifth attempt. Yorkshireman Aaron died nine hours later. With the award of his posthumous VC came a CGM for Sgt Larden and DFMs for Sgt Mitchem and for the wireless operator, Sgt T. Guy.

The two raids, which had caused considerable damage for the loss of only five aircraft out of 650 dispatched, had undoubtedly been a successful persuader to the Italians to discontinue their alliance with the Nazis. An emissary would meet the British ambassador in Madrid within three days.

After a few hours' sleep Gilvary went to the pictures in Darlington and saw *The Man in Grey* starring James Mason and Margaret Lockwood. 'Splendid acting and well worth seeing,' he wrote. It is the last item in his diary. He would be killed five days later.

HARRIS wasn't finished with Italy. Another raid, with 140 Lancasters, was launched on Milan on the 14th and by a further force of 199 Lancasters the next night. Peenemünde was only 48 hours away. A few days before, W/Cdr Gomm of 467 Sqn had been called to a conference at 5 Group headquarters in Grantham where senior airmen were asked their opinion of the group's time and distance technique as practised at Friedrichshafen where Gomm had acted as master bomber.

As he boarded his aircraft for the Milan operation of 15 August Gomm, who had completed one tour with 77 Sqn, flown Beaufighters with 604 Sqn in between, then gone back for a glittering second tour on heavies, knew a special operation was in the wind. He would not take part in it. Only one aircraft had been lost on the Milan raid of the 14th, but on the second the Luftwaffe were waiting over France. Seven Lancasters were shot down including two from 467 Sqn.

In the first was the CO, the brave and ebullient W/Cdr Gomm, killed with all his crew except the flight engineer, Sgt James Lee. In the second, piloted by F/Lt Jack Sullivan, was Sgt Ken Harvey. He recalls:

> I don't know if it was the same fighter that got us. We thought it would be a piece of cake, being an Italian target. We were obviously in the wrong area at the right time.
>
> We were on our way to Milan with a full bomb load and the fighter came from nowhere underneath. He hit the magnesium flare and the back of the aircraft was an inferno. The roaring flames were just behind me and I was virtually blinded by the glare. It was impossible to see what was happening behind me. Jack Sullivan ordered a bale-out and I can't understand why only I and the bomb aimer got out. The pilot seemed to be the only one left in the aircraft and he was trying to hold the controls as best as he could. He was magnificent. He saw me and shouted: 'Get out'. I owe my life to him.
>
> I leaned forward over the escape hatch, which had been opened by the bomb aimer, F/O Terry Entracht, going out. The next thing I knew I was pinned to the roof and I thought: 'That's it', but the pilot

must have done something with the controls because I fell and went straight through the hatch. I pulled my ripcord straight away and almost immediately afterwards I saw the aircraft hit the ground. I came down in a tree, but because of the flare going off I still couldn't see anything and I didn't know how high I was. I was swinging backwards and forwards and grabbed the trunk of the tree and got my arms almost around it and hit the quick release buckle. About a foot below me was terra firma.

I could hear the Germans shouting and I was apparently on the edge of a German airfield. I crawled under some brambles and smoked all my cigarettes and the next morning the Germans found me. They took me to the burned-out aircraft and I could see five unrecognisable bodies of my crew. I was taken before the station's CO and he told me how sorry he was and gave me some lemonade. I was put in a cell at the aerodrome and various pilots came to see me. One told me he had been over London the previous night. They had a whip-round for cigarettes for me. I thought: 'The Germans aren't so bad as they're painted', but I soon changed my mind when I was taken to Dulag Luft interrogation centre at Frankfurt.

I was waiting on Frankfurt station for transport to Dulag Luft and there were a load of Americans on the platform. One of them had derogatory words printed on his jacket and he had been badly beaten up. There were a couple of Americans lying on the platform with flak wounds and some railway officials came along shouting 'Raus'. They couldn't get up, so the railwaymen started kicking them. I thought, 'We've arrived.' But I found good and bad.

Walking into the camp at Dulag Luft I was with a Yank and he said, 'I'm not going to tell them, but my grandmother lives on top of that hill over there.'

I met the bomb aimer from my crew at Dulag Luft. He had broken an ankle on landing, but managed to get to a French farm. The farmer put him up in the hayloft and when he awoke the police had arrived. You can't blame the farmer, he probably would have been shot.[13]

Sgt Harvey shortly found himself on the way to permanent prisoner-of-war camp after being told by his interrogator, 'We've got a lot more coming in and we haven't room for you'.

HARRIS had one more throw of the dice against Italian targets now that the country's leadership was negotiating. A total of 154 aircraft were launched against Turin in a concentrated attack for the loss of four aircraft. He had been conserving his bombers and crews for one of the most important operations of the year and in fact the war. The Peenemünde operation would truly be a maximum effort.

It had been clear there would have to be novel techniques for removing Peenemünde from the map, calling for experiments to be jointly employed which had so far only been tentatively tested in the bombing war. In fact, apart from the fact it would be carried out at low level in the moon period when crews could usually count on not being risked against the Grim Reaper's scythe, there were various new aspects, showing how much Bomber Command had learned since 1 January.

For the first time a master bomber would control a full-scale raid. The Pathfinders would also designate special crews as 'shifters' to move the bombing from the first to the second and third aiming points during the attack. And Cochrane would be allowed to demonstrate the independence of 5 Group by employing the group's time and distance technique as a fail-safe in the closing stages of the operation.

But Harris, knowing that on Peenemünde there was no room for error, insisted that if the special 5 Group crews discovered at the end of their time and distance run from Rügen island that the Pathfinder markers coincided with the position they had reached, they were to bomb there.[14] The crews were only allowed to bomb on T and D alone if the TIs were obscured or obviously misplaced and in any case the master bomber's instructions were paramount.

The next problem the planners at High Wycombe had to address was how to feed approximately 600 aircraft over a small target at low level in moonlight without it becoming a rout by the night fighters. By this point in the year Bomber Command had started to launch spoof raids by small forces of Mosquitos as the Luftwaffe regrouped following the advent of Window.

They would provide the diversion on the night of the Peenemünde raid with such success that it would project a whole range of diversionary raids in the coming Battle of Berlin. In the week before Peenemünde Mosquitos attacked Berlin three times following the same route as had been planned for the operation against the rocket research station and passing within 60 miles of the base to set its sirens wailing.

In case of the operation being postponed at the last minute bomber crews would be told at briefing that Peenemünde was a centre for development of night-fighter radar equipment, a subject that tended to concentrate the mind.

AS the hot days of August drifted by in the run-up to the Peenemünde operation there were changes in the familiar routine at Bomber Command stations. Leave was cancelled for aircrew in 5 Group, unwittingly earmarked for the attack, and they were required to practise time and distance runs on the bombing range at Wainfleet near Skegness, which bore a similarity to the sand dunes of the Baltic. The first results were horrifying, with errors of 1,000 yards or more. An alarmed Cochrane took up a Lancaster to show how it should be done and in the second practice the margin of error was down to 300 yards.

In the Canadian 6 Group – which with 5 Group would bear the brunt of the losses as the last of the three waves – 432 Sqn was undergoing a shake-up at Skipton-on-Swale in the non-operational aspects of air force life. The adjutant's office recorded on 10 August: 'The squadron personnel are looking smarter these days as a regular blitz is in progress. Checking the wearing of caps and of haircuts, shaves and general smartness is being carried out by senior officers and NCOs. It is bearing fruit and the objective is "The smartest squadron in the RCAF".'[15]

The previous night the squadron had helped 408 Sqn mark its departure from its base at nearby Leeming with a party. There was further cause for celebration when 408 Sqn arrived at their new billets at Linton-on-Ouse. They were found to be full of bugs and the squadron was given a week's leave for the quarters to be deloused. 408 Sqn would not be on the battle order for Peenemünde.

In 8 Group 97 Sqn was now operating three flights and on 16 August there had been much grousing as all NCO aircrew were paraded and many were ordered to change quarters at short notice so that A, B and C flights were allotted accommodation sites 1, 2 and 3 respectively.

At Cleethorpes a special party was being arranged on the pier by the aircrew of 460 Sqn in 1 Group. They would be footing the bill for ground crew to celebrate the squadron's one-thousandth operational sortie. It was planned for 17 August. 460 Sqn navigator F/O Alex Flett recalls: 'Glasses had been nicked from all the pubs around for our booze-up and a lot of popsies had been arranged.'

In fact Harris would find no better opportunity than that night to launch the attack on the rocket establishment. That very morning 147 B-17s of the US Eighth Air Force had taken off to attack the Messerschmitt factory at Regensburg, flying on to North Africa. It had been intended that at the same time 230 Flying Fortresses would bomb the ball-bearing works at Schweinfurt, returning to England. As it happened, misty conditions split the departure of both elements. Instead of being a united force the Schweinfurt raiders were three hours late on the same route and the Luftwaffe shot down a total of sixty from both forces. The raids – to mark the first anniversary of the Mighty Eighth's operations from England – had the benefit for the RAF of drawing off Luftwaffe day fighters that might be used in a Wilde Sau role over Peenemünde. F/O Flett remembers:

> The raid was laid on out of the blue. We just couldn't believe it because it was the moon period. I remember at briefing being told: 'Gentlemen, this raid is absolutely necessary and if you don't succeed tonight you will be back tomorrow night and if you don't do it a second time you will be back the night after that.' We didn't know what Peenemünde was. We were told it was a manufacturing plant.[16]

Air gunner P/O Wilkie Wanless remembers the same tense atmosphere on 76 Sqn. He says:

> It was the only briefing I was at where the briefing hut was surrounded with service police. You had to identify yourself at the door and sit with the crew you were flying with. The briefing officer said: 'I can't tell you anything about Peenemünde except that if you don't get it tonight you'll have to go back tomorrow night.' He also said if the operation was scrubbed and the target leaked out the person responsible would be summarily shot. That got our attention.'[17]

P/O Alan Bryett, a bomb aimer on 158 Sq at Lissett, recalls: 'At the briefing when we were told we would be going in at between 6,000 and 10,000 feet, depending on the pilot, there was a moan round the room.'[18]

At Wyton Duncan Sandys attended the briefing of 83 Sqn, sitting at the back as G/Cpt Searby, the CO and master bomber, outlined the marking required by his young crews. Searby himself had been shown a model of Peenemünde at 8 Group headquarters the day before and was anxious to see if the actuality measured up.

Squadron commanders revealed that the operation order called for four phases of attack. First, sixteen blind markers would release one red spot fire each on the northern coast of Rügen island as a vital reference point 7 miles from the aiming point for all approaching bomb aimers.

Then the first wave, consisting of 33 Pathfinders and 145 Halifaxes of 4 Group and 54 Stirlings and 12 Lancasters of 3 Group, would bomb from 0015 to 0030 the housing estate where the scientists and their families lived. The second wave, made up of 113 Lancasters of 1 Group plus 6 Pathfinder shifters and 12 Pathfinder backers-up, would bomb the V2 production factory in the eleven minutes to 0042. The third wave, led by 6 Pathfinder shifters and 12 backers-up and comprising 52 Halifaxes and 9 Lancasters of the Canadian 6 Group and 117 time and distance Lancasters of 5 Group, would aim at the experimental works between 0043 and 0055.

The consensus was that crews would attack at around 8,000 feet, with an absolute minimum of 4,000 feet. It would be a relief for airmen on

Stirlings not to have to worry about being hit by bombs from better-equipped squadrons. There would be the steady climb out from Engand to a point 20 miles from the Danish coast so that the Germans would consider it had the earmarks of a raid bound for Berlin, then Windowing would begin.

The bomb load would be different than on a normal night raid, 75 per cent being made of high explosive. It was also the only time crews were specifically told they were out to take life. Operation Order 176 said crews attacking living and sleeping quarters would be doing so 'in order to kill or incapacitate as many of the scientific and technical personnel as possible'.

As the heavily laden bombers climbed out over their airfields in the warm evening air and set course for the North Sea another force was already in position waiting to make contact with the enemy. Fighter Command were now building up their intruder operations to support the bombers wreaking havoc across Germany. As the balance in radar techniques shifted backwards and forwards in the second half of 1943, RAF Fighter Command's 141 Sqn Beaufighters were being sent over Germany with their Serrate homing device to hunt the *nachtjäger*.

W/Cdr Bob Braham staged his fighters as a screen between the bombers and the German fighter fields in Holland and north-west Germany. That night Me110s of IV/NJG1 at Leeuwarden flew out to intercept the machines sending out such tempting radar echoes to the long-range Freya radar sets, and W/Cdr Braham shot down two.

The eight spoofing Mosquitos of 139 Sqn opened the attack over Berlin at 1140. The commander of the German 1st Fighter Division had been fooled by the diversionary tactics and up to 150 Zahme Sau and Wilde Sau fighters circled the city seeking instructions and looking for targets as the light bombers coming in from different directions dropped their red TIs followed up at random by 500-lb bombs. It was the first time so many Zahme Sau had assembled and would set a pattern for raids on Berlin and other German targets to come.

The flak reacted with traditional fury to greet the full-scale raid it was thought to be and the red and white flashes of the thousands of exploding shells added to the confusion across the city. Twice the guns were ordered to lower their range to give the Zahme Sau above their chance. With so many fighters criss-crossing the sky looking down on the bursting flak it would have been a bloodbath for Bomber Command if they had been there in force. As it was, one Mosquito was shot down. Even after the last Mosquitos had long gone the flak was still firing and orders were being given for more fighters to fly to Berlin. Seldom would a spoof work so well.

THE attack on Peenemünde to the north opened with the red spot fires of the Pathfinders blooming over Rügen island. Flight engineer Sgt Wilf Sutton was at the head of them in a 35 Sqn Pathfinder aircraft captained by P/O Laurie Laney tasked with illuminating the target. Sgt Sutton recalls:

> We had been to Turin, had a night off, then did Turin again and Peenemünde the following night. We were a bit tired. We arrived two minutes before it began because we were doing the early marking on the living quarters. For the first time we carried anti-personnel bombs. Only the marker crews had them and they were dropped with the target indicators. We were a visual marker and I think we were the first crew in. The Germans were putting up only a small amount of flak at that stage because of the spoof raid on Berlin. The flak was just a bit of light stuff and the smokescreen hadn't begun when we bombed. We were right on target, so the master bomber had nothing to say to us, but he was advising Main Force not to undershoot, but to bomb the correct marker. We went in at about 10,000 feet to illuminate and as we turned away the fires were just beginning. Some distance away we started to see the flak or night fighters on the target behind us. We were lucky, getting in early.[19]

F/Lt Jock MacLachlan from 156 Sqn was also one of the first over the target. His navigator, F/Lt Walter Kerry, recalls: 'We had been asked to mark Rügen island, then do a timed run to bomb Peenemünde itself. We found a lot of searchlights. After we had dropped our bombs Jock said: "Let's go down and let the gunners have a go at them", which they did.'[20]

The bombs were now pulverising the scientists' quarters, sending the sea rushing back from the shore with the shock waves. Some of the early bombs also dropped on the Trassenheide labour camp, full of foreign slave labourers, 2 miles to the south and not even marked on target maps. It caused great loss of life before G/Cpt Searby, who would make seven runs over the target in his role of master bomber, realised what was happening and ordered arriving crews to ignore the burning camp buildings.

Bomb aimer Sgt Dennis Woolford was on his first operation in a 90 Sqn Stirling. He remembers:

> The Stirling bomb bay had twenty-six sections so on targets like Peene-münde we carried incendiaries. I could hear the master bomber giving instructions. On all German targets they would drop about twenty red TIs, then the backer-up picked the centre of them and put down greens. A bit crude. Peenemünde was very successful. It wasn't burning when we got there, but it was when we left. As we turned for home we could see the fires going well and growing.[21]

Later aircraft in the first wave of Main Force had some trouble with the smokescreen the Germans were laying along the eastern edge of Peene-münde. The pilot of P/O Wanless, F/Lt 'Sandy' Sanderson, decided to go in at minimum height to make sure of hitting the scientists' accommodation. P/O Wanless recalls:

> We had been used to bombing at 16,000 feet, but Peenemünde was 4,000 feet. That night the navigator in our crew, S/Ldr Bennett, had a movie camera in his hands and took pictures as the first flares went down. We had to keep going backwards and forwards over the target as the camera kept malfunctioning.[22]

Moonlight meant, as F/Sgt Aaron had found on the way to Turin five nights before, that bombers were in sight of each other and the inevitable result was that the more edgy or inexperienced gunners were likely to blast away at any apparently approaching shape without thinking about aircraft recognition lectures.

P/O Ken Hewson of 76 Sqn had the nose of his aircraft hosed by the gunner of another and his navigator was so severely wounded he never flew again. F/Lt Victor Surplice was skippering a 77 Sqn Halifax in the first wave coming off the target at Greifswald when he saw another Halifax on the port bow 200 feet above and putting its nose down. It made a diving turn to port and levelled off 300 yards away. He reported later that it then 'did a steep turn to starboard opening fire from dead ahead and disappeared to starboard'. Fortunately the gunner was a poor shot and Surplice's aircraft was undamaged.[23]

Surplice's bomb aimer, Sgt Herbert Hopkins, also saw one of the first aircraft to be lost over the target. 77 Sqn's Operational Record Book reported: 'At 0027 at 9,000 feet he reported seeing what he believed was an aircraft going down in flames, hit the ground and explode.' This was probably the 158 Sqn Halifax of F/Sgt Bill Caldwell, a 19-year-old New Zealander. Though the defences had been slow to react to the first wave, towards the end of this part of the attack deadly and rapid light flak was hosepiping across the target and Caldwell's aircraft, S-Sugar, was hit in the starboard inner engine. The wing rapidly caught fire and only two of the crew escaped.[24]

A few minutes later another aircraft was hit by flak and exploded in the air. It is believed to have been the Halifax of Sgt Frank Shefford, Surplice's squadron mate. No trace of him or his crew was ever found. These aircraft were the only ones lost in the first wave. It had bombed the scientists' quarters very successfully once bombing had been shifted from the labour camp.

Bomb aimer Dennis Slack of 158 Sqn remembers:

We had an easy run-in in the first wave. We chose to go in at 6,000 feet and I could see the living quarters on fire. We went straight in and out without any bother. As we went in over Denmark we could see the odd V for victory sign being flashed from torches. We were obviously cheering the populace by being there and to see their lights flashing cheered us up.[25]

158 Sqn pilot 'Bluey' Mottershead, by now a pilot officer, also remembers:

We realised how important the raid was. We went out at normal height then dropped down to 8,000 feet to bomb and the target was already burning. The master bomber was flying around and issuing instructions to overshoot by one or two seconds because the fire was moving backwards at that stage.[26]

P/O Bryett of 158 Sqn remembers there was a particular reason the raid had been mounted that night:

The raid was on a Tuesday and that night was chosen because it was on Tuesdays that a one-day course was given to German soldiers and air force personnel who would be launching the V2 rockets from different parts of Germany. Peenemünde was full that night not only of the key men designing and making the rockets, but also the craftsmen who would launch them in due time.

We were in the first wave with the housing estate as the target. We went in at about 8,000 feet. It was perfectly clear and although the smokescreen was operating it wasn't properly ignited until we had gone. It was quite a novelty going in so low. We could see the factories below and they were alight as we got there as we weren't the first in our wave. The fourth or fifth wave who were doing time and distance bombing got the worst of the smokescreen. We never saw a fighter and had no trouble at all.

I remember at the debriefing after landing at Lissett almost the first thing the intelligence people said was that the first wave bombed the wrong target after the Pathfinders dropped the markers on the Trassenheide forced labour camp, just 400 or 500 yards further south. It wasn't even on the target maps. They said: 'We'll wait until your photographs are developed' and when they were they said: 'Well, you're all right, you've bombed where you were supposed to be bombing.'[27]

Crews of 76 Sqn in that first wave returned in triumph to Holme on Spalding Moor and the adjutant, waxing lyrically, reported:

From an average height of 8000 feet our aircraft went into the attack. The Pathfinders were very accurate in their judgement and our air bombers were in paradise. As well as identifying the target by markers the outline of the target could be seen. Careful aim was taken and many report having seen their bombs fall on or around the target. Fires which were already burning became much more fierce and as the aircraft were on their return journey the glow could be seen from 150 miles away.[28]

Some Pathfinders met a heavy German reaction. F/Sgt Robert Gill, rear gunner in a 35 Sqn Halifax, recalls:

We were on Peenemünde as backers-up, dropping flares on the flares that were already there. I could see the vague shape of the Baltic shore below and the photograph we got showed the living quarters. There were flak ships in the Baltic and the stuff was pumping up to us, then we were coned with the bomb doors down. I was immediately blinded. I could hear the crump and the rattle of the fragments of flak coming through and we couldn't get the bomb doors up. We managed to get out of the searchlights, but there was tremendous drag from the open bomb doors all the way back using up fuel and we were very glad to get home.[29]

OVER Berlin the circling fighters still looking for bombers saw the attack to the north and called their controllers. But few in the Luftwaffe would know of the secret base at Peenemünde, and Rostock and Stettin – the only large cities in that general direction – were too far to the west and east. The fighters were told to keep patrolling the capital. Soon many ran short of fuel and had to land. The only fighter pilots who would eventually appear in the Peenemünde area were those who had taken off late and obeyed their own senses. They would not show up until the first and second waves had gone.

That second force of bombers, all in 1 Group, tasked with demolishing the two V2 construction works, each less than 300 yards long, were now to endure their eleven minutes dicing with the multi-coloured light flak streaming across the peninsula.

But before they did so, for the first time in the bombing war the Pathfinders would have to shift the aiming point. There were only five PFF aircraft to do so as one had had to turn back with technical trouble. They used accurately placed green TIs as their mark to undershoot on by setting a false height on the bomb sight. One of the loads fell well to the north and three the same distance to the south.

The remaining load of red TIs, however, fell right across the two buildings where it was planned to mass-produce V2s. Production had already started in one using concentration camp inmates kept under SS guard. 'I can hear Searby now calling out: "Don't bomb the greens, you're dropping in the sea, bomb the reds, bomb the reds,"' remembers F/O Flett. His 460 Sqn aircraft was one of 113 Lancasters led by seventeen Pathfinders to make up the second element in the raid. 'It was very concentrated,' he recalls, 'and the first time we had heard a master bomber.'[30]

Another 460 Sqn crew over the target was skippered by F/Sgt John Goulevitch, a squadron character. He had found an undertaker's top hat in a Doncaster pub on a booze-up and insisted on taking it on every operation. By 0039 when he bombed a pattern of three green TIs, the smoke-screen was obscuring much of the target, but he was confident it was 'a good prang'.[31] Direct hits were scored on the second of the buildings used to store completed rockets, but in the cavernous first building the blast of explosions bypassed much of the machinery.

F/Sgt Bernard Downs, a 19-year-old pilot on 78 Sqn, was making his first operational flight in this second wave. 'I was second dickey to a S/Ldr Badcoe from 77 Sqn at Melbourne,' he recalls. 'We were down at about 8,000 feet and were straight in and out without seeing any combats. As a very naive young man I thought: "If it's no worse than this it's going to be a doddle."'[32]

The shifters now had to move the concentration of the attack further north to the experimental works where the third wave of 117 Lancasters of 5 Group employing the time and distance technique and 52 Halifaxes and 9 Lancasters of 6 Group were about to sweep in and bomb. It was this force which would be subjected to the full fury of the night fighters, arriving at Peenemünde after the debacle over Berlin.

One 76 Sqn aircraft, that of F/Lt Sandy Sanderson, was still in the area though the last of his squadron colleagues had departed fifteen minutes before at the end of the first wave's attack. Air gunner P/O Wanless remembered the aircraft criss-crossing Peenemünde as the navigator tried to take the filmed record of the raid. 'We weren't attacked, but we saw combats towards the end,' he says. 'I've no idea if the movie film was developed. We weren't told about that kind of thing.'[33]

Flight engineer Sgt Sandy Rowe, whose 103 Sqn Lancaster was over Peenemünde in the early waves, remembers:

> We were told there were three main buildings and certain crews were allocated certain buildings to hit. We were asked to do our best to hit a particular building, but as in all raids a lot of bombs went astray. We had no reason to be dissatisfied with our results because our pilot and bomb aimer were excellent and they had a lot of aiming point photographs from previous raids. When I saw the newspaper the next day I was shocked at the losses because our crew never saw a fighter. We were on our way home by the time they arrived from Berlin. The Canadians in 6 Group suffered most.[34]

From 6 Group, Cpt C. A. Taylor, a USAAF officer serving in Bomber Command with 427 Sqn, was right behind the Pathfinders bombing at 0043, the start time for the third wave. He went in at 8,500 feet, but he reported back at Leeming: 'Several aircraft went in very low and may have become victims to light flak or our own bomb bursts.'[35]

W/Cdr R. E. Baxter was one of seventeen squadron commanders who had elected to fly on such an important raid. The CO of 106 Sqn bombed on a time and distance run six minutes after Taylor on the centre of three green TIs on Searby's instructions. He saw 'numerous fires in the target area' from 7,000 feet.[36]

The *nachtjäger* had now arrived in the arena. Sgt 'Indian' Schmitt, who was on the last operation of his tour with 427 Sqn, reported: 'After releasing the bomb load I was attacked by an Me109 which did considerable damage, making holes in the wings, the port tyre and port rudder.' The pilot had found himself on the outside of the stream as the Halifaxes and Lancasters jostled for position over the small target and had been picked on by a Wilde Sau lurking on the edge. It made three attacks then on the fourth pass blew up under fire from the Halifax.[37]

What was unknown to the crews was that a deadly new technique was introduced over Peenemünde that night which would spell doom for hundreds of bombers before it was discovered well into the following year. Two Me110s of V/NJG5 at Parchim had been fitted with twin cannon adjusted to fire at an acute angle through the cockpit roof. The weapon, known as Schrage Musik, contained no tracer. The Me110 identified its target by radar then stealthily positioned itself underneath the bomber with the cannon pointing to the fuel tank between two engines on the port or starboard wing. One burst of fire was enough to set the tank on fire and send the bomber hurtling earthwards. Without telltale tracer the crew would have no idea what had hit them and it would be a poor Luftwaffe crew indeed who would miss, once positioned, as there was no need for deflection shooting.

Five bombers were shot down within thirty minutes by the two Parchim-based aircraft. Others were being pounced on from above by Wilde Sau Me109s and FW190s whose pilots saw them silhouetted against the burning buildings of Peenemünde.

Leutnant Musset of II/NJG1 had been sent all the way from St Trond in Belgium to defend Berlin, then flew north to Peenemünde as he saw the explosions and fires. 'Against the glow of the burning target I saw several enemy aircraft flying over it in close formations of seven or eight,' he wrote in his combat report the next day. He dived and his radar operator in the Wilde Sau Me110, Corporal Hafner, picked up the first contact. Musset wrote:

At 0142* I attacked one of the enemy with two bursts of fire from

* *All times given by Musset are European, one hour ahead of GMT.*

direct astern, registering good strikes on the port inboard engine, which at once caught fire. E/a tipped over to its left and went down. Enemy counter-fire from rear gunner was ineffective. Owing to immediate second engagement I could only follow e/a's descent on fire as far as a layer of mist.

Musset could now pick up other bombers easily and he attacked a second three minutes later and saw it crash in flames at 0147. In another three minutes he hit a third RAF aircraft in the starboard wing from 60 yards and the bomber blew up. 'At 0157 I attacked another four-engined e/a at 6,000ft from 100 metres astern,' he wrote in the combat report. 'Burning brightly in both wings and fuselage it went into a vertical dive. After its crash I saw the wreckage burning at 0158. Heavy counter-fire from the rear gunner scored hits in both wings of own aircraft.' Sixty seconds later he positioned on another target, but the bomber corkscrewed out of the way. In a left-hand turn as he followed it down 40 metres behind, Musset got in a burst which set the port wing on fire. 'Enemy counter-fire from the rear gunner was ineffective,' Musset reported and the aircraft plunged to the ground.

The fighter pilot found one last victim 'which took violent evasive action by weaving'. By now the barrels of his cannon were red-hot after so many combats and they burst as he opened fire. He then made three further attacks with his machine guns and saw strikes in the starboard wing, but without setting it ablaze. Musset reported:

> Owing to heavy counter-fire from the enemy rear gunner I suffered hits in my own port engine. At the same time I came under fire from an enemy aircraft on the starboard beam which wounded my radio operator in the left shoulder and set my Me110's port engine on fire. Thereupon I broke off the action, cut my port engine and flew westwards away from the target area.[38]

In all, forty-two bombers were lost on the operation and twenty-eight went down over the target, many crashing in the Greifswalder Bodden, the Baltic bay between Rügen and the Peenemünde peninsula. There were few survivors. It was here that Sgt Gilvary's remains would lie. Only the bodies of the flight engineer and rear gunner from the crew would be washed ashore. Gilvary had been wrong in his supposition that he would live or die in E-Easy of 419 Sqn. E-Easy had electrical problems and his skipper, Stan Pekin, had been assigned C-Charlie for Peenemünde.

Pekin's crew were part of the dreadful toll the Canadian 6 Group would suffer that night. Twenty per cent of those dispatched would not return. Two more 419 Sqn aircraft would go down, not one crew member surviving; 428 Sqn would lose three, as would 434 Sqn. It was the squadron's first raid on a German target since being formed at Tholthorpe on 13 June. It had sent nine Halifaxes and lost 33 per cent. Lancaster IIs had recently been introduced on 426 Sqn. The CO, W/Cdr Leslie Crooks, chose the honour of leading them on their first Lancaster operation. He was shot down and killed, as was one of his flight lieutenant pilots.

Many more aircraft had been supplied by 5 Group than 6 Group, which had left its Wellington squadrons behind. The percentage loss in 5 Group was less, but still savage. Four Lancasters were lost from 61 Sqn from which only two airmen escaped; three went down from 44 Sqn from which only one person baled out and four of the thirteen dispatched by 49 Sqn were lost from which five crewmen became prisoners of war. Three of 619 Sqn's Lancasters were missing from which no one escaped. They included the CO, W/Cdr Irwin McGhie. Among those missing from 49 Sqn was a flight commander. The squadron had been detailed for time and distance runs in the third wave and were making them when the night fighters arrived. Skipper W/O J. O. McCabe reported at Fiskerton: 'An enemy fighter was destroyed 11 minutes after leaving the target.'[39]

The talk for days to come in the Saracen's Head in Lincoln, the Wheatsheaf in Darlington and the Station Hotel in Harrogate would be of the plunging bombers of Peenemünde, their wing tanks streaming an orange trail across the moonlit sky to be extinguished in an instant in the waters of the Baltic.

FOR the RAF it hadn't all been one-sided, however. Ten Fighter Command Mosquitos had been dispatched to carry out intruder patrols over Luftwaffe airfields along the bomber route. Most found the night fighters had already taken off, but F/Lt D. H. Blomeley of 605 Sqn was orbiting Jagel when he found he was being pursued by an Me109 which opened fire as it roared down from the port quarter. Blomeley reported back at base:

> Tracer was seen going over the top and ahead of the starboard wing. Evasive action of skidding turns was taken and the enemy aircraft was seen silhouetted against the moon. A dog fight took place with the enemy aircraft firing four or five times. Eventually he overshot again and I got a 30 degree deflection shot and one second burst in from 150 yards, port below. Strikes were seen and the enemy aircraft went into the lake due east of Schleswig.[40]

THE last of the bombers streamed across the sea south of the island of Lolland towards the Danish mainland, climbing back up to 14,000 feet, and more were caught by Zahme Sau before they were to exit Denmark's western coast near Esbjerg. P/O F. W. Yackman of 106 Sqn, who had two good gunners aboard in Sgt A. E. Evans and F/Sgt R. J. Talbot, was one of them. He reported succinctly back at Syerston: 'I encountered an unidentified twin-engined fighter on the return journey. There was a short combat and the fighter was shot down.'[41]

Leutnant Musset also lost the battle with his crippled aircraft at this time. He ordered Hafner to bale out as the aircraft passed through 6,000 feet and went out himself immediately afterwards. Me110s weren't easy to exit and Musset hit the tailplane, breaking his right thigh and left shin. He landed near Gustrow, where he and Corporal Hafner were hospitalised.

A second wave of Mosquito intruders had also set out to catch the night fighters as they landed at their bases. F/O A. G. Woods was patrolling Parchim at 0205 when he saw a fighter on its approach halfway down the Lorenz beacon system. 'We attacked from dead astern from 500 feet down to 100 feet with cannon and machine guns,' he told intelligence officers. 'The enemy aircraft is presumed to have crashed off the runway.' Another 141 Sqn Serrate crew shot down two Me110s off the Dutch coast, bringing the total to twelve German fighters downed that night.[42]

Many of the returning crews in 6 Group, anxious for the comfort of familiar surroundings after their mauling over Peenemünde, found they were diverted because of mist over their bases. Sgt Schmitt landed his battered Halifax at Mildenhall. The Me109 had damaged it so badly it was deemed beyond repair two days later. Schmitt and his crew went back by train to Leeming where they were celebrated as the first 427 Sqn crew to finish a tour. Schmitt's progress had been in tandem with Bomber Command itself. He had begun operations at Lorient on 9 January.[43]

His fellow 427 skipper Cpt Taylor was diverted to Newmarket. As his Halifax rolled to a stop a 2,000-lb bomb which had hung up dropped to the tarmac and rolled away. Cpt Taylor had bombed the experimental works from 8,500 feet, but he saw many going in at half that height. 'Several aircraft went in very low and may have become victims to light flak or own bomb bursts,' he reported.[44]

There was considerable enthusiasm in the debriefing reports of the bomber crews back from Peenemünde, only too aware they would be returning if it had not been a success. At Binbrook 460 Sqn pilot F/Sgt Charles C. Smith, an Australian teacher on his twelfth operation, summed it up with: 'Overall a great result'. But for the hard-pressed young crews, most importantly it was another trip among many that one day might lead to a reprieve. Navigator Sgt John Fell remembers: 'It was the last op of his second tour for my pilot, F/O Arthur Middleton. He and the rest of the crew were posted to Transport Command afterwards. But the squadron had suffered several individual navigator casualties and I was kept to stagger on to complete the regulation thirty ops.'[45]

For the planners there was the satisfaction of knowing the raid had indeed been a success, one of the greatest in the year. The three target areas had been hit many times at great risk to the crews, who showed enormous courage in pressing home their attacks at low level, particularly in the last wave, often paying with their lives for their temerity, as Cpt Taylor, who believed some aircraft had crashed because they were too close to exploding bombs, pointed out at debriefing.

Some scientists and many technicians were among the dead, including Dr Walther Thiel, the engineer heading the V2 liquid oxygen propulsion department and second in importance only to Wernher von Braun, the chief scientist, who escaped unharmed to send a rocket to the Moon for the Americans in the post-war world.

The two most northerly aiming points, the production plant and the experimental works, had not been destroyed as hoped and the vital wind tunnel in the latter had survived. But the two plants had been damaged and the V2 programme badly upset.

Much had been learned from the Peenemünde op about the techniques of successful raiding, in particular spoof operations, fitting another piece in the growing jigsaw of aerial bombardment in 1943.

In the government corridors of the Wilhelmstrasse in Berlin there was a new sense of vulnerability. Hitler gave Reichsmarschall Goering a severe reprimand for the Luftwaffe's inability to protect areas important to the Reich. Goering passed it on to Luftwaffe Chief of Staff, Hans Jeschonnek. That morning Jeschonnek had been given a detailed report about the devastation at Peenemünde. Jeschonnek shot himself, leaving a note reading: 'I can no longer work with the Reichsmarschall'.

The Wehrmacht was told control of the rocket programme would in future be in the hands of the SS. Production, now that the secret of Peenemünde was blown, would move to a new underground location near Nordhausen beneath the Harz mountains. The workforce was provided by Buchenwald concentration camp and eventually 13,000 prisoners would work in the tunnels, where a frequently used gallows was erected to ensure efficiency.

It is estimated that the V2 rocket programme was delayed by two months at the minimum by the RAF raid and perhaps by up to six. The first rocket arrived outside a house in Chiswick, London on 8 September 1944, four minutes after being launched from its mobile site in Holland. It killed three people, not the 4,000 once feared. There was no defence apart from overrunning the rocket sites and the missiles continued to arrive until March 1945. More than half of the 2,500 launched fell on Antwerp, the port supplying much of the Allied thrust. It is incalculable what damage a deluge of such rockets would have caused to the jammed roads, camps and jetties of the pre-invasion south of England ports.

The secrecy surrounding the Peenemünde operation remained after the raid. The usually newspaper-conscious Air Ministry, often known as the Royal Advertising Force by the jealous officers of the other two services, put out no bulletin and nothing appeared in British newspapers. When the first rocket arrived in Chiswick the government was still so concerned about public panic that a cover story was released that it was a gas blast. There were several more such 'gas blasts' before Whitehall came clean.

A report of the Peenemünde raid did, however, appear in an Australian newspaper not long after the operation. It read:

> High over the Baltic coastline, in a sky glittering with a moonlight so bright it was like day, the raiders fought out the greatest night air battle the war has seen. No bomber–fighter engagement has been so concentrated, has so congested the sky with aircraft. As the Peenemunde factories shook under the bombs the planes above were milling and wheeling like cars in Piccadilly.

The air and ground crews of the Australian 460 Sqn had their one-thousandth sortie party – with a few more added – a few days later. The squadron's operational record book noted that there had been a lot of disappointment when the party was postponed, 'but as the raid was such a success everyone was more or less satisfied'.[46]

The squadron indeed had much to celebrate. It had sent twenty-four Lancasters to Peenemünde and all had returned. F/O Flett remembers: 'The party was held in a big dance hall on the pier at Cleethorpes. It was just too good to miss.'[47]

The pragmatic Australians considered that standing by the sea at Cleethorpes with a popsie on the arm and a pint in the hand was how moonlight *should* be used, not for finding targets in the Baltic at maximum range and minimum height.

CHAPTER ELEVEN

BACK TO BERLIN

THE ashes of Hamburg were not yet cold before the newspapers were calling for a new air battle to be waged, the Battle of Berlin. It was the target much of the public could identify with, those living in London having suffered so much in the Blitz and others outside realising the degree of loss to the nation's heritage.

On Tuesday, 3 August, as crews were still sleeping off the effects of battling with the thunderstorm on the last of the four Hamburg raids, the national press was revealing under headlines such as 'Hamburg Last Night – Another RAF Hammering' that 'a greater tonnage has now been dropped in little over a week on Hamburg than during 11 months of intensive air raids on London in 1940–41'.

But only 24 hours later under the heading 'Berlin Next?' the *Nottingham Evening Post* reported: 'A forecast that Berlin will be the next German city to be subjected to raids on the Hamburg pattern by the RAF and Allied Air Forces based in Britain was made by usually well-informed sources in Washington yesterday.'

The *Yorkshire Evening Press* said that a fresh appeal had been made for all those not compelled to remain in Berlin, such as workless women or male pensioners, to leave. 'Thousands of Berliners in shirt sleeves and others naked to the waist were working all day yesterday, digging zig-zag trenches and building bunkers,' it claimed. The unequivocal message was that Berlin, with its vast industrial complexes and communication networks, awaited its doom.

Apart from its role as the administrative centre of the new German empire the city was vastly productive as a war machine. Its leading industries were the Alkett factory, which produced half the Wehrmacht's field artillery and many of its tanks; the Borsigwerke, also manufacturers of artillery as well as locomotives; the DWM and DIW conglomerates, pouring out small arms and ammunition; the Siemens complex, which was so vast that, as well as factories all over Berlin, it had its own mini-town, Siemensstadt. Among countless other war factories Berlin also contained three aircraft plants, which alone brought it within the requirements of the Pointblank directive.

The weary crews read the newspaper stories and made their own conclusions. After the Ruhr, Hamburg and Peenemünde they would soon be waging a new war over Berlin in which the chances of completing a tour would be reduced still further.

Three raids to the capital were launched between 23 August and 4 September, with another important raid to Nuremberg in between. The aircrews' gloomy prediction proved right: the losses on Berlin were savage. From 1,669 sorties 125 aircraft went missing, a stunning 7.5 per cent. But if times were tough for Lancaster and Halifax crews they were frightful for their comrades in the low-ceiling Stirlings. Those crews suffered so much that the first steps were taken towards deleting the Stirling squadrons from battle orders for Germany.

On 23 August in the first of the three Berlin raids 16 of the 124 Stirlings dispatched were lost. It was a terrible night of attrition for Bomber Command as a whole: 56 of the 727 aircraft on the raid were shot down, the highest total of the bombing war so far, 7.7 per cent.

One airman was killed before his Lancaster had even left the ground. Flight engineer Sgt Sandy Rowe, who had been so shocked to read of the losses on Peenemünde, was at the heart of a bomb blast as the crew of F/Lt Douglas Finlay prepared for the Berlin raid. Minutes earlier they had been lounging on the grass at Elsham Wolds smoking in the early evening sunshine as they waited for the engine start-up signal.

Sgt Rowe remembers:

We had checked our machine and had to wait to move off, then there was a thump from a nearby aircraft and people started running away from it. We discovered the bombs had dropped out. The CO was nearby and advised our pilot to move our aircraft. As we passed the other machine the bombs went off. They said later the sound was heard in Grimsby about 20 miles away, but I didn't hear a thing because I was in the centre of it. I just saw an enormous flash as the aircraft, the bombs and the petrol all went up at once. I thought I was going to be engulfed. I can see it as clear as anything today. Our aircraft had slewed to a stop and the pilot ordered us out, but I discovered the wireless operator, Sgt Harry Wheeler, had been killed.[1]

Apart from the wrecked aircraft at Elsham Wolds there were others that would never reach Berlin. A total of nine were later estimated by the Operational Research Section to have been shot down on the route in. The 35 Sqn Halifax of flight engineer Sgt Wilf Sutton was among the first, attacked near Hanover.

Sgt Sutton remembers:

The Monica warning device had been pipping all the way across Germany. Of course it just told you an aircraft was near you, not whether it was friend or foe. My skipper asked: 'Shall we turn it off?' and everybody agreed 'yes'.

We had just broken cloud and discovered it was a Ju88. He attacked immediately from the port quarter with his cannons. I was at the back putting Window into the flare chute. The first cannon shell missed me by inches and went right up the aircraft, without touching anybody apart from giving the mid-upper gunner a slight shrapnel wound in the thigh. The skipper corkscrewed, but the two starboard engines and starboard fuel tanks were now alight. I was being tossed around, but I went to try to put the fire out in the wing by poking a fire extinguisher through a shell hole. There was a 250 mph slipstream and it didn't work.

The mid-upper gunner got hold of me and told me we had been told to bale out and I went back with him to the rear escape hatch and went out with the ripcord handle in my hand. I would be about 16,000 feet up, so I was a long time coming down. The rear gunner went out from his turret and the rest of the crew apart from the mid-upper all went through the front hatch. I landed in a field. I went into a wood and cut the top of the flying boots off and all the RAF insignia from my uniform and filled my water bottle. I intended to make for Stettin, but I rested against a tree and promptly went to sleep. I woke up about 6 a.m. to hear German voices and was picked up by a couple of farmers with a shotgun. They took me into the little village of Gintin, not very far from Potsdam.

I was taken to the burgomeister's house. I was joined there by the wireless operator and the rear gunner. One of our crew had wet socks and decided to wring them out in the hall. They didn't like this, so they contained us in a little hand-pulled fire engine until the Luftwaffe came.[2]

The Berlin air raid authorities considered it the heaviest the city had suffered, though it fell far short of RAF expectations. The technique, honed at Peenemünde six days before, of employing a master bomber had been used, but he had been unable to achieve a sufficient concentration of bombs to justify so many missing aircraft. W/Cdr Johnny Fauquier, a later commander of 617 Sqn whose CO had promulgated the method on the Dams Raid, had been called in from the Canadian Pathfinder squadron, 405. Master bombing on a huge target such as Berlin was by no means the same as on a precise moonlit objective such as Peenemünde, and after H2S let the Pathfinders down and they marked south-west of the aiming point Fauquier found he was unable to develop the attack because of the smoke and sheer strength of the defences. The use of a master bomber would be tried twice more, then shelved for six months.

Many of Main Force arrived late after the long journey from England and cut a corner, compounding the marking problems of the Pathfinders. The subsequent report by Bomber Command's Operational Research Section read:

They approached the target from the south-west instead of following the planned route which would have brought them in from south-south-east. Bombing was centred six miles south-south-west of the aiming point. Consequently the Charlottenburg/Wilmersdorf area suffered severely, but the centre of Berlin escaped serious damage.[3]

German wireless traffic intercepted by the Y Service of WAAFs, Wrens and ATS girls in Britain, working in thirty-six-minute stretches taking down streams of Morse coming over the airwaves, showed that the German controllers guessed the target an hour and seven minutes before the Pathfinders' red spot fires bloomed over the city. The running commentary on the progress of the bomber stream, which was now a feature of Luftwaffe defence, ordered all fighters to Berlin at 2304. Cheated by the spoof for Peenemünde, the fighters were now to have their revenge. Bomber crews reported seventy-nine interceptions and thirty-one actual attacks. It was later calculated that at least thirty-three of the losses were due to fighters.

One of the fighters was piloted by Leutnant Wilhelm Johnen of III/NJG1. He had flown from Parchim in his Me110 equipped with SN2 radar and followed the path of burning bombers to the Reich capital where he found a scene he described as 'defying all human description'. In a post-war account he said: 'Hell was let loose. A sea of searchlights lit up the night, thousands of flak guns poured their lead into the air.'

Johnen, who could see the bombers clearly outlined against the flaring sky, shot down a Halifax and a Stirling within five minutes of each other. To do so he had to fly through the same flak as his quarries. He related:

I flew right into a salvo and was flung about the sky by the blast. Right and left, above and below me, burning machines rocketed earthwards. Countless fires had sprung up below. Damaged night fighters fired their distress signals, enemy bombers exploded in the air, spraying the city with a bright-coloured rain of gleaming confetti. A grandiose fireworks display. The constant bursting of the flak shells tortured my nerves. The acrid smell of gunpowder entered the cockpit.[4]

By the caprice of fate some squadrons would make more sacrifices over Berlin that night than others. The unlucky 100 Sqn lost four aircraft, as did 35 Pathfinder Sqn. 78 Sqn lost five, one by collision, and five aircraft of 158 Sqn failed to return to Lissett.

Bomb aimer Dennis Slack was in one of them, skippered by Sgt Thomas Edwards. Sgt Slack remembers:

At the briefing the curtains were drawn back and it brought the usual moans when Berlin was the target. The CO told us: 'As the west of Berlin is heavily defended we will bypass it to the south, make a 135 degree turn to port, bomb the target, make a 90 degree turn to starboard, followed by another 90 degree turn to port when clear of the target then make for home.'

Approaching the first turn we saw five planes go down in quick succession and then we were hit. The rear gunner didn't see the fighter which got us. I saw two lines of tracer going past the port side of the fuselage and yelled to the pilot, 'Starboard, go!', but before he could act the fighter had corrected his aim with a touch of right rudder and hit us in the port wing. I could hear the rapid banging as his cannon shells came up the fuselage from the rear and exploded against the bulkhead behind me. They had come through the rear turret, killing the rear gunner and the wireless operator, who was in the rear of the aircraft pushing out Window. The tanks in the port wing were now blazing and Sgt Edwards dived to try to put the fire out, but it made it worse. The blazing fuel was racing out under pressure acting like an acetylene torch cutting through the wing. The pilot called: 'Sorry lads, you'll have to get out.'

The navigator opened the escape hatch under his feet and pulled it up, making sure it didn't go through the hole and jam in the slipstream. That happened to a lot of aircrew. He went, the engineer followed and I had a last look round through the Perspex to see if I could see the fighter to give him a burst with my gun, but there was nothing to be seen. I got a signal from the pilot and went through the hatch. As I fell away I saw the port wing fold over and the aircraft spun round. I went out at about 10,000 feet and came down in a field at Doberitz. I hadn't got a scratch, so I buried my chute and started walking west hoping to get into France.[5]

Later Sgt Slack would have an opportunity to see at close quarters what damage the RAF had caused to Berlin, as would Sgt Sutton. Sgt Slack's fellow 158 Sqn bomb aimer, P/O Alan Bryett, was also shot down over the city in the Halifax piloted by his friend Australian F/Lt Kevin Hornibrook. P/O Bryett remembers:

We had just bombed on the markers and as we turned away we were caught by one searchlight and in a matter of four, five or six seconds about ten searchlights had come on us. We were in this 400 or 500 feet band of light. All of us were immediately blinded; it was quite terrifying. The German fighters above us at 23,000 feet or so were just waiting for planes to be coned. There were a handful of us lit up and they swept down. You couldn't see them coming until they were right on top of you. They fired incendiary bullets into the plane which set our aircraft on fire in six or eight different places in the fuselage and on the wings. The rear gunner and mid-upper yelled 'Corkscrew!'

As we became a flaming beacon more fighters came round and made a beeline for the rear gunner and mid-upper gunner and killed them both. The pilot said: 'Don't bale out' as he was corkscrewing, but the navigator, engineer and wireless op only heard the 'bale out' as the plane was obviously doomed and went out. I went up and sat with the pilot. It was quite obvious we weren't going to make it, but then the terrifying thing was that as the plane twisted and turned we couldn't get to the escape hatch. We were being tossed around in the nose of the plane. Eventually Kevin did manage to get to the escape hatch, pulled it open, got hold of me and pushed me out with his feet, shouting: 'I'm coming.' We knew we were very low. I pulled my ripcord and was only coming down for seconds before I felt what I thought were bushes. In fact I was in a forest of fir trees about 80 feet up. The pilot was all ready to follow me, but as I was up in the trees I saw the aircraft crash in a bit of open ground. It was burning furiously. He didn't get out.

For the first half-hour or so I was still blinded from the searchlights. Eventually as my sight returned I realised I was up pretty high and I dropped some coins to gauge it. I used a penknife to cut some of the parachute cords and tied six or eight strands round one arm and then put the cords round the trunk and held the other end, letting myself down inch by inch. It took me about two hours to get down. I was quite badly cut and I thought I was going to pass out halfway down and drop. I eventually made it but couldn't get the parachute down so when daylight came the Germans came and found it. I'd got two or three miles away, but about twenty local troops found me. As it got light I had dug a hole in the forest and covered myself with leaves to lay up until dark. Their Alsatian dogs sniffed me. The Germans immediately took me to where the plane had crashed and then to a civilian prison in a village nearby. The rear of the plane had broken off and the rear gunner was dead in his turret, but the rest of the plane had burned out. There was nothing left of the pilot.

Like Sgt Slack and Sgt Sutton, P/O Bryett would also be taken by the Luftwaffe through smoking Berlin.[6]

Flight engineer Sgt Lew Parsons was over Berlin on his first operation. He had arrived on 75 Sqn at Mepal only two days before. Within eight days as the pressure on squadrons mounted he would carry out another four raids and be shot down on the fifth. He recalls:

I was asked by the adjutant to go with another crew skippered by a New Zealander called McGregor because their engineer, a Sgt Bond, was sick. The adjutant said: 'Berlin will be the first target in your log book, that's quite something for somebody to chalk up.' It seemed like a good idea at the time.

It was the first time a master of ceremonies had been used for a normal raid and we were under orders for everybody to maintain radio silence, but we were told afterwards that apparently some crews were ribbing him with remarks such as 'Get some in' and 'Why don't you join up?' Operations were all very new to me. I was in the astrodome over the target looking for fighters and I saw a shadow and said to the gunners; 'There's one on the right.' I got a swift reply from the rear gunner: 'Which is the bloody right?' as of course I should have said starboard, and he didn't know which way I was looking. As it turned out the shadow went anyway. I apologised to the gunner when I got back to Mepal, and he said: 'That's OK, but I was whirling round in my turret like a top, looking for a fighter.' The defences of Berlin were horrific. Flying into the target the shell bursts looked as if they were in one continuous burst in a straight line and I thought: 'I'll never get through this', but once among them you found they were spread out.[7]

Later waves experienced a new procedure by the Luftwaffe, one that would have a devastating effect in the Berlin raid of eight days later: flares dropped by some fighters to light the way for their comrades. Air gunner Sgt Wilkie Wanless of 76 Sqn says:

There were fighters dropping these bright flares way above us and it was like flying down Main Street. The fighters would fly right by you and take a shot at you as they went. One bang and they were gone. I couldn't see anything through the Perspex because the light was reflected on it.[8]

Leutnant Peter Spoden, then a novice Me110 pilot of II/NJG5, later described the raid as the most intensive night battle he ever witnessed, giving him bad dreams for years to come. He attacked two bombers, but was shot down by the tail gunner of the second, a Stirling. Spoden was pinned to the tailplane of his plunging fighter for minutes after baling out and his dramatic escape was described and illustrated in the Luftwaffe *Signal* magazine. He lost consciousness after breaking free and woke up in a Berlin garden, where, significantly, he found himself being walloped by civilians and an SS man until he identified himself.

The 23 August operation may not have worked out as planned – much of the attack falling on villages to the south of Berlin – but more than 2,500 buildings in the capital were destroyed or seriously ravaged and by chance bombs fell on the Wilhelmstrasse, the government quarter, where every building received some damage.

The order for all non-essential personnel to leave the city after the Hamburg raids had not had the required effect on the stoical Berliners and many had refused to go to air raid shelters on this raid. Eight hundred paid with their lives. Now the myth of the capital's invulnerability was being exposed and there were also growing signs of unrest among the population as they increasingly felt that they were being led to disaster.

The next day the *Daily Express* trumpeted: 'Berlin blazes: Himmler rules all Germany'. Gordon Young in Stockholm, who had been given a somewhat inaccurate assessment of damage, told readers:

> Berliners still fighting the fury of an air raid more shattering than even Hamburg has experienced, had tonight not yet been told that all Germany has been placed in the iron grip of 'Butcher' Himmler, Chief of the Gestapo and the Nazi Black Guard. Sweeping changes had been made by Hitler to ensure still tighter control over all the Home Front.

Minister of the Interior Wilhelm Grick had been supplanted by Himmler, a sign of the growing effect on the morale of the German people by Bomber Command's raids as the Russians, advancing on the Kharkov front, exerted psychological pressure from the East.

THE RAF would be back over Berlin on 31 August, but to divert the defences a long-range attack was made to Nuremberg by 674 aircraft on the 27th. Due to the problems demonstrated by H2S on the Berlin raid of four days before, crews of forty-seven PFF aircraft were ordered to check their equipment by dropping a 1,000-lb bomb on Heilbronn along the way. Only twenty-eight were able to identify the town to do so. It did not bode well, but in fact the first Pathfinders did accurately mark the AP on Nuremberg. However, after such a long trip, and perhaps with the losses of Berlin fresh in the mind of some crews, creepback rapidly developed, which the master bomber was unable to halt, and most of the bombing fell in open country to the south-west. A total of thirty-three aircraft were lost, 4.9 per cent. Eleven of them were Stirlings, nearly 11 per cent of those that had taken off. A posting to a Stirling squadron was rapidly becoming a one-way ticket.

Flight engineer Sgt Philip Bates was in one of the Stirlings supplied by 149 Sqn at Lakenheath. He remembers:

> There were hundreds of fighters milling round the target. I saw whitish-red tracer fire from an FW190 to a Lancaster above. The Lanc was weaving like mad and I could see the deeper red of his rear gunner's tracer then the German went down on fire. I saw many combats and many flamers.
>
> A 30-lb incendiary bomb went through our port wing, just missing the dinghy. We weren't conscious of it. But after landing on every trip the bomb aimer and I used to go round the outside of the aircraft with our torches looking for damage and if we didn't find any we were disappointed. On this occasion we could see this big hole in the port flap obviously caused by something going down. It could only have been a 30-lb bomb, because a 4-lb incendiary would have stuck in and an HE would have taken the wing off.[9]

Lew Parsons was on his fourth Stirling operation in five days with 75 Sqn, having gone on two mining ops after the first Berlin raid. 'Nuremberg was a very long trip, about seven and a half hours,' he remembers. 'But we actually got the best bomb plot photograph in 3 Group. My New Zealander skipper, Doug Henley, got commended. When we went to Berlin the next time he wanted to get another good photograph.'[10] It would have fatal results.

The attrition rate on squadrons was now proving too much for a few. Rear gunner F/Sgt Robert Gill, whose 35 Sqn Halifax had flown back from Peenemünde with bomb doors hanging down, remembers of the long-distance Nuremberg raid:

Our pilot nodded off on the way back, I think. Instead of turning at the French coast he flew straight on and we ended up over Cherbourg. We could see the docks and everything and the bomb aimer said it was Portsmouth. There were searchlights and the flak started coming up and the pilot said: 'Fire the colours of the day.' That really did it; they knew who we were then and a lot of flak hit us. We got out of there with thirty-odd holes in the aircraft. We got very short of fuel and had to make a Mayday landing at Tangmere. When I went down the fuselage the wireless op was sitting on the Elsan toilet and I said: 'Come on, open the door.' He said: 'I'm not doing that; a German might come in.' He refused to fly again, was reported as LMF and was sent off to the discipline centre.[11]

AS the bombers had been prepared for Nuremberg Sgt Dennis Slack, shot down just short of Berlin, was being taken under guard into the city after being on the run for three days. He had been spotted when he broke cover to get water to cope with a raging thirst caused by his issue condensed milk. 'I was taken by truck to Luftwaffe headquarters in Berlin where there were a lot of other captured aircrew,' he recalls. 'The guards were pointing out the bomb damage; there were gaps and some of the buildings were still smoking. There was no anger about it. Berlin hadn't been raided heavily until then and they hadn't seen many aircrew.'[12] Eventually he would be taken to Stalag IVB.

Alan Bryett, whose pilot, Kevin Hornibrook, had given his life to save his, was taken to the same building on the same day. He says:

I was in a cellar with about forty others who had been shot down. Many of them were terribly badly injured, with shrapnel wounds and so on. Gradually the injured chaps were taken away and others would come in. We were in that hellhole being fed on bread and water and soup for some days and were then taken to the Dulag Luft interrogation centre at Frankfurt on Main.

When I was taken to the Luftwaffe building there were certain

signs of damage from the raid, but I couldn't see much from the closed
police van. On our way to Dulag Luft we were marched part of the
way to one of the Berlin railway stations. I could see some damage.
I've never forgotten that when we got to the station we saw a group of
about twenty or so young men and women all wearing the Jewish star
on their back. They were all being herded into a cattle truck and that's
when I first realised what persecution of the Jews meant. It was a horrifying sight. Until then I'd thought what we had been told was just
propaganda. All of us were incredulous to see it really was happening.[13]

Wilf Sutton, shot down on the way to Berlin, was also able to inspect the
city. He says:

Twice they took us in a bus to the Potsdammerbanhof to catch a train
for Frankfurt and the interrogation centre at Oberursel, but there were
no trains available and they took us back again. Berlin was virtually
untouched then. It was a very lovely city. I was in the Unter den Linden
and there were beautiful lime trees along it and the Brandenburg Gate
was undamaged.[14]

ANOTHER milestone would be passed on the road to ruin for Berlin with
the raid of 31 August. The public, who had listened to the bombers droning
eastwards night after night in the past week, were eager to read of their
results, but the *Daily Express* had struck a cautious note the day before with
the news: 'More than 1,000 front-line fighters are believed to have been
thrown into the night battle of Germany in the past week to stop Bomber
Command's inexorable and systematic obliteration of German cities. This
is more than treble the force the enemy was using a few months ago.'

There had been a change in the weather between the two Berlin raids, a
chill in the days bringing the first hint of autumn. Fitters and riggers had
had to cope with heavy dews as they prepared the aircraft in their isolated
hard-standings for another maximum effort. There had been talk on the
squadrons that Bomber Harris had wanted to launch 1,000 aircraft on the
capital, but heavy losses meant only 613 could be made available.

Lew Parsons had at last managed to get off his base at Mepal for a night out. He recollects:

There were four New Zealanders in our crew and three Brits. 75 was a New Zealand squadron but was about fifty-fifty New Zealanders to other nationalities on the squadron. The three Englishmen in the crew had one night out between the Nuremberg op of the 27th and Mönchengladbach of the 30th. We stayed overnight in the Lamb in Ely, sharing a room for a guinea, and that was the extent of our getting to know the area.[15]

Sgt Parsons' gruelling eight days as an operational airman was about to come to an end. The fighter flares that some had seen on the raid of the 23rd would now be demonstrated with awesome efficiency by the Luftwaffe. The Stirlings would suffer 16 per cent casualties and 75 Sqn would lose four of its Stirling crews from sixteen that took off. Another of its aircraft would crash in England. From Lissett 158 Sqn, which had lost five Halifaxes on the first Berlin raid, would lose another four.

Thick banks of cloud, grim defences and problems with their H2S sets again prevented the Pathfinders finding the aiming point and the TIs spilled out their red flame in the blackness south-south-west of the city centre. Bomber Command's Operational Research Section later reported:

The backers-up and Main Force attacked still further south owing to cloud obscuring all but the nearest TIs. Thus the bombs fell mainly 8 to 30 miles from the aiming point in suburban districts and outlying villages. Enemy aircraft were very active, especially in the target area, and the majority of the 47 bombers lost probably fell to fighters.[16]

The thick cloud brought its own problems to Stirling crews on their way to the target. F/Sgt Alex Wood, a 15 Sqn pilot, recalls:

There was complete cover below as we were approaching a turning point towards Berlin, so the navigator took a number of astro shots and announced that the turning point was closer than we expected. We altered course to the east almost immediately. After about thirty minutes ice began to form on the front turret and the wings. I tried to climb above the cloud but, although I could see stars through the gaps,

I could not coax any more height from the Stirling, so dropped through the cloud to 5,000 feet below it.

Some time later the navigator said I should be able to see the target ahead, but there was no sign of it although I could see searchlights and what looked like fires 20 miles to the south. I turned towards it and as we got closer I could see we had been way off track so I joined the bombing run westward. We had clearly avoided the defences before joining the bombing run by approaching from the opposite direction to the Main Force.

The Germans were dropping flares from high altitude to illuminate the bombers. We were in the flares over the target and a fighter did come in to attack over the target, but the rear gunner opened up and he sheared off. We weren't hit and we flew home with the rest of the main stream.

I was fortunate in having a very good crew. The reason we were lost was due to an error in the Astro Almanac for the time the navigator took his sights and we later learned a number of Main Force had made the same mistake.[17]

Flight engineer Sgt Philip Bates, who had had a 30-lb incendiary bomb go through the port wing of his Stirling four days before, found the type's lack of ability to climb was cutting a swathe through squadrons: He says:

The Stirling casualties for the raid are listed as 16 per cent, but I would say that with the damaged Stirlings that crashed in England the write-off was 20 per cent.

Most of the aircraft lost were shot down by fighters on or near the target because of the flares they sowed once they knew the track in. We were in the third wave so they knew the track by then. Ju88s flying very high put down these brilliant white flares either side of the track. It was like flying down the Mall in daylight. I was in the astrodome looking for fighters behind and I could see our aircraft on either side. It was pretty horrifying, there was nowhere to hide. We were between 11,000 and 13,000 feet.

It was a curious route we were on that night. The night before we had been to Mönchengladbach, so we followed the same route and went straight on. We went south of Berlin, way past Berlin and then made an acute angle and went in a north-west direction into Berlin. It was at that turning that the flares were sown, but a lot of people seeing the fires and realising that they had to go another 20 miles or so just cut across and avoided the flares. We were too conscientious and got caught in them. I didn't see any combats, but there was a huge explosion which threw a tremendous light round the starboard inner. It was probably a Cookie going off, but I thought we had been hit at first.[18]

Sgt Roy Child was an 18-year-old mid-upper gunner in another of the East Anglia-based Stirlings, a 90 Sqn aircraft captained by F/Lt Robert Roger. He remembers:

As we climbed over England at about 2000 hours we saw some Fortresses returning to their bases nearby from a daylight raid. About 20 miles from the target the German fighters put down a line of flares on either side of the stream. It made you feel naked. I could see other bombers and fighters in the light and saw a couple of planes blow up after they had been hit by Schrage Musik.

As there were a lot of fighters around, the navigator was asked to go into the astrodome as lookout. He had never seen a raid before because he had stayed at his curtained-off desk. It was so light I could see his head in the dome from my turret. He came out after half a minute and said he couldn't do it; he hadn't realised what a target was like and he couldn't watch. He was no coward; he just didn't want to see.

As we came in to bomb we were attacked by a Ju88 from underneath. They made a habit of just firing off one burst from below, hoping it would bring you down, then moving on to another target. It missed us, fortunately, because we were corkscrewing at the time. I returned his fire and the main fire came from me because the rear gunner was having trouble with his turret. That particular raid the Germans seemed to have us dead on. They seemed to know where we were coming in and it was just like daylight. It was the most vivid of my operations.[19]

The RNZAF 75 Sqn were now to find themselves in the right place for the Luftwaffe at the right time, just as P/O Doug Henley tried to repeat the success he had had on Nuremberg four days before. His flight engineer, Sgt Lew Parsons, remembers:

We were flying straight and level after the bombs had gone, trying to get a good photoflash photograph. We were surrounded by a line of fighter flares and that's when we got hit by two Ju88s. They came in one behind the other. The port inner engine was knocked out and the tailplane was badly damaged and the rear gunner, Jimmy Grant, injured in the face, foot and hands. The pilot went into a corkscrew and the mid-upper gunner, Doug Box, was concussed being thrown around the turret, so both our gunners were out of action. Fortunately by then the fighters had gone. We lost a lot of height in the corkscrew and had lost one engine, so had a hell of a job keeping it in the air. The damage to the tailplane was making it fly nose-heavy. We balanced out and I jettisoned the fuel to No. 2 engine.

The aircraft flew on as the crew tried to make it home.[20]

Other 75 Sqn aircraft were beating off attacks. A Ju88 approached F/Sgt G. Wilkinson's Stirling from 500 yards astern and his rear gunner fired a long burst. The adjutant's report later stated:

The enemy aircraft replied and stalled. The mid-upper gunner then fired three long bursts and the rear gunner fired a short burst. The enemy aircraft was seen to fall away and is claimed as probably destroyed.

The aircraft captained by F/O A. Alexander sighted two Me109s, the first opened fire from the starboard quarter and the rear gunner replied with a short burst as did the mid-upper gunner. The enemy then dived to the ground and exploded. The second Me109 opened fire with a short burst from the port bow. The rear gunner fired a short burst and tracer was seen to enter the enemy which dived. The aircraft of W/O P. Moseley sighted an Me110 on the port quarter, the gunners fired a long burst and the enemy aircraft turned over and dived with smoke pouring from it.[21]

The Stirling of Sgt Parsons had now been heading eastwards for an hour. He remembers:

We were throwing stuff out as we went, all the armoured plate, the oxygen bottles and belts of ammo. I could imagine it all wrapping itself round chimneys down below. We had got just across the Rhine and I think we were not much above 1,000 feet when the skipper said: 'Bale out, bale out.' I was the only one on the intercom at the rear, throwing stuff out of the hatch, and I told the wireless operator and he baled out and I followed him. My parachute got caught in a tree which I think saved my life. The bomb aimer and navigator went out through the front and both were killed because there wasn't time for their parachutes to open properly. The gunners and the pilot were still in the aircraft when it crashed. The pilot was killed, but the rear of the aircraft broke away and both gunners survived uninjured.

There was a range of hills where the aircraft crashed at the side of the Ahr valley and I think the pilot saw them and knew we would hit them. I could see the kite burning on top of the hill. I had lost a flying boot coming down, but I started walking west along a gravel footpath. I heard a burst of machine-gun fire in the distance and thought, 'The Germans are shooting my mates.' I carried on walking, crunching on the gravel and as I turned a bend there were three Jerries with guns waiting to greet me.

In fact the machine gun fire had been meant to rally other troops after a German soldier had come across the wireless operator, Bob Quelch, who was unhurt.

The Lissett-based 158 Sqn had been hit hard again. P/O 'Bluey' Mottershead, who had been over Berlin, recalls:

The searchlights playing on the under side of the cloud made it like daylight above and I could see other aircraft. After bombing I saw a Halifax bomber below being chased by four fighters. Its rear turret wasn't working and all the return fire was coming from the mid-upper.[22]

As the returning bombers flew back over the enemy coastline the Stirling of Roy Child was involved in a strange incident. He remembers:

We spotted a plane above us to the left. As it came closer we decided to open fire, but our guns had frozen up. The bandit followed us all the way across the North Sea. Then I swear he waggled his wings at us before peeling off and flying home. At that time German aircraft were coming back with the bomber force and shooting them down as they landed.[23]

P/O Mottershead brought his Halifax over the familiar friendly bulk of Flamborough Head and into the Lissett circuit. He says:

When I got back to base I discovered the wing commander, Jock Calder, was missing, and I found out the next day it had been him I had seen attacked over Berlin. He had made it into Manston and I was detailed to fly down to pick him up with his crew because his aircraft was so badly shot up.

The loss rate overall had been 7.6 per cent, slightly better than for the previous Berlin raid, but the damage had been negligible for such a heavy operation, only seven industrial buildings being hit in the whole Berlin area. The Stirling casualties had indeed been horrendous again and it was obvious they could not continue to be risked against the Nazi capital. Another attempt to wreak havoc in Berlin would be made in three days' time, but the Stirlings would be left at home. The Command was now changing into a force of truly efficient heavy bombers. Within weeks the doughty Wellington would be withdrawn from Main Force operations and the Stirling would vanish from German skies in November.

Bomber Command's strength on 2 September was 840 heavies, spread across fifty-two squadrons. The airfield expansion programme was nearing completion, as teams of Irish labourers, who had helped to change many rural retreats for ever, prepared to depart. They had laid miles of runway in the year, working in lines behind rows of six big concrete mixers, ten men to each mixer in a constant machine-like action of cutting bags and tipping in concrete, an army in solid grey, only the streaks of sweat down their faces breaking the colourless conformity.

Many villages of eastern England were now excitedly poised to welcome air force blue as squadrons were switched to the new bases to make way for others. From Scampton 57 Sqn departed in its Lancasters to the new base of East Kirkby 29 miles away. Villagers today remember the summer Sunday lunchtime the Lancasters arrived, roaring over cottage roofs into the circuit of the new airfield and performing an impromptu display as they were called down one by one to the unsullied concrete. Two nights later, 31 August, the same Lancasters had lined up for Berlin.

The Lancasters of 57 Sqn would in fact fly the most sorties to Berlin of any 5 Group Sqn and share with 44 Sqn the highest losses, losing sixteen aircraft in twenty raids. One of them would be lost on 3 September in the last of the three late summer Berlin operations.

The Main Force which flew out over the North Sea that night was entirely composed of Lancasters after the heavy losses among Stirling and Halifax squadrons. It did reduce the attrition, 22 failing to return from 316, and showed the lowest loss rate of the three operations. However, it was still 7 per cent – a rate no military commander could sustain.

There had been various new elements in the planning which it was hoped would make this op a success where the previous two had largely failed at great cost. The bombers would sweep in for 350 miles from the Dutch coast on an almost straight line, a risk the planners considered worth taking now that the Germans seemed to be concentrating most of their night fighters over the actual target.

After the bombs had started to fall it was hoped to fool the alerted Luftwaffe by departing almost due north to Sweden and in fact invade Swedish air space before turning beyond the tip of Denmark for the North

Sea. Four Mosquitos would drop spoof fighter flares on a false route out of the target, demonstrating how quickly Bomber Command's experts had responded to the Luftwaffe's full-scale introduction of such flares only three nights before. The extended route to save casualties would mean extra fuel, reducing the bomb load in each aircraft by approximately a ton.

For once the weather worked in the bombers' favour. Thick cloud over the route in prevented the night fighters assembling, yet it cleared near the target to allow the Pathfinders to use ground markers. One load went down almost on the aiming point, the others a couple of miles to the west. The raid had been planned to take sixteen minutes only instead of the forty-five of the previous two, so only slight creepback occurred and the industrial area of Siemenstadt was badly hit.

The city's defenders had laid dummy fires on the route in, but few crews were fooled. Flight engineer Sgt Barry Wright was on his second operation with 103 Sqn in a tour that would end with a CGM. He remembers:

> The defences were very heavy, lots of searchlights and lots of flak. I remember it particularly for the dummy fires. You could tell they weren't from bombs because they were such a pale colour, like sodium and in little spots, obviously separate pieces. We could see them from 50 or 60 miles away the same time as we saw the searchlights weaving and the flak bursting ahead. We thought: 'How on earth are we going to get through that?'[24]

Flak and fighters over the target accounted for most of the bombers lost. The thick cloud had saved all but five on the way in and the unusual routeing and spoof flares prevented interception on the way out. However, the percentage loss rate on Lancaster squadrons was much higher than it had been on the previous two Berlin raids when Halifaxes and more particularly Stirlings had been present to take the fury of the defences.

THE comparative statistics had proved the beginning of the end for Stirlings. They would not be seen over the Nazi capital again until the second raid of the winter campaign against Berlin on 22 November. A total of fifty would take off; twelve would turn back and five would be shot down. It was the last raid of Stirlings over Germany. The sacrifices of their brave crews, seen as flak bait by the Lancaster squadrons above, had been great. In the three Berlin raids in which Stirlings participated (23 August, 31 August, 18 November) 280 Stirlings took off, 46 made early returns and 37 were shot down, 15.8 per cent of those that had reached enemy territory.

Ever since taking over the Command in February 1942 Harris had realised the Stirling was a grave liability, unable to climb above 14,000 feet operationally, and the Halifax, with a ceiling of 18,000 feet, was at that time only slightly better. He began a campaign to have Stirling production facilities switched over to the making of Lancasters and Halifax production cut back in favour of Lancasters.

August had indeed been cruel for the Stirling squadrons, but it had been truly dreadful for a Halifax squadron, 158. Two-thirds of the squadron present on 31 July had gone, fourteen aircraft and crews. One crew had been lost on the last of the Hamburg raids of 2 August, three on the Nuremberg raid of 10 August, one on Peenemünde, five over Berlin on 23 August and another four on the raid of the 31st.

The losses on Berlin had been savage for the Command as a whole. The returns in terms of industrial damage had been insufficient for such a high cost, but Berlin knew it was doomed. A million and a quarter women and children were at last being evacuated from the city, creating a massive logistical problem of where to find them accommodation in country areas – where they were often resented. Morale was heading inexorably downwards in the Reich. In August the rations for bread, general food-stuffs, meat and potatoes had all declined and Berliners left behind in the city awaited the inevitable cataclysm in a Wagnerian fever, best summed up by the Berlin reporter Ursula von Kardorff, who wrote at the time: 'The thing is to have as many parties as possible and to make the most of one's house while it is still there.'

In the meantime Bomber Command licked its wounds. Berlin, with its geographical and architectural advantages, had proved it would not be quickly defeated in the manner of Hamburg. It was too distant a target at present and as autumn approached Harris withdrew, hoping to persuade the US Eighth Air Force to join a later, greater assault. The new 3-cm H2S would then be available to assist the Pathfinders' marking and the high losses that were being seen as inevitable on such a distant and well-defended target could at least be offset by considerable damage. The hope had been to make the Nazis reel again as they had over Hamburg and there was still confidence this could be achieved, but first the Command would have to be strengthened with more Lancasters.

Harris decided to turn to other important centres of industry deep into Germany, cities that would not be as fiercely defended as Berlin, communities such as Mannheim and Munich The first would be devastated, but the Pathfinders would be defeated by the second.

CHAPTER TWELVE

STRETCHING TO SUCCEED

THE weight of war, which now fell on cities in central and southern Germany as Bomber Command withdrew wounded from Berlin, showed an immediate improvement in loss statistics and in some cases results as summer shortened towards the chill of autumn.

Mannheim was devastated in September by two attacks of more than 600 aircraft each, and in this period the technique of diversionary raids by heavy bombers to draw away the night fighters was developed. But two medium-sized raids on Munich proved disappointing after lacklustre marking by the Pathfinders, and they and other anticlimatic operations would sow seeds of doubt in the effectiveness of PFF, still struggling with H2S. As if to highlight how remarkably effective Oboe was compared to its sister bombing aid, a return to the Ruhr to confuse the Luftwaffe about Bomber Command's intentions with two raids yielded important results at little cost. But to the British public, eager to read of the RAF taking the war to the enemy, every night the bomber boys went out was a success. The losses revealed by the BBC's post-raid reports were a constant reminder to those listening in living rooms and at factory bench of what sacrifices were being made by teenagers on their behalf. Aircrew found that girls sometimes now made the first move, striking up conversations on Tubes and in shops, to win the prize of a winged airman on the arm.

F/Sgt Harold McLean, a veteran air gunner at 19 on 427 Sqn, re-members how grateful the public was. He says:

You couldn't go in a pub in London, or in Yorkshire where I was based, and buy yourself a drink because before you sat down the waitress would be over with a couple of pints. For instance, I went in a pub in Leeds with another aircrew chap and a couple of girls we'd picked up, and as we sat down there were a couple of pints in front of us. I thought: 'That's quick service', but the waitress pointed to a table with a big crowd round it. They had bought them.[1]

There were other perks for those risking their lives over Germany. 'Aircrew got petrol coupons,' 101 Sqn pilot Peter Johnson remembers, 'and for a very small sum, tax and insurance to go on leave in your car. I had an Austin 7 myself, which had cost me £25. If anyone went missing the authorities came along and took his car off the camp.'[2]

Most aircrew found their wages would just stretch from week to week – there was no point in saving, after all. New RAF pay rates had come in from 1 January, giving sergeant pilots, navigators and bomb aimers 13s 6d (about 68p) a day and equivalent-rank wireless operators and flight engineers 12s daily. Sergeant air gunners felt badly done to, earning 8s a day for the same risk. If the putative air gunner had decided to stay on the ground and not risk his life for his country, and perhaps risen to the same rank as an engine fitter or even a carpenter, he would have been paid 10s 6d a day.

Perks or otherwise, the price the bomber boys were paying would be demonstrated clearly in the raid of 5 September on Mannheim in which 34 aircraft of 605 sent out would be lost and 174 airmen would lose their lives as the Wilde Sau gathered beneath fighter flares. As usual the Stirlings and Halifaxes would suffer most, 78 Sqn at Breighton losing no fewer than four of its Halifaxes.

A double blow had been planned on Mannheim/Ludwigshafen in which ground markers were placed on the eastern side of Mannheim, so that the creepback of Main Force approaching from the west would move across Mannheim and the Rhine on to Ludwigshafen on the west bank. The riverside towns were considered to be prime targets. Mannheim was the second biggest inland port in Europe with one-third of its 247,000 population engaged in the electrical and engineering industries. Ludwigshafen was an important centre of the chemical and armaments networks. The plan formulated at High Wycombe to overwhelm the defences of both at one strike worked with cataclysmic effect.

Flight engineer Sgt Philip Bates was in one of the eight Stirlings lost of the 111 dispatched. He says:

Ours was a sad story. Our navigator, who was absolutely spot-on at his job and a big chap with a very big personality, went sick so they gave us this other chap. He was with us five days and I don't think we spoke more than a couple of words. We weren't happy.

We were briefed for Munich with a big petrol load and small bomb load and we were told: 'The weather might not hold for Munich, so we're going to brief you for Mannheim as well. We'll tell you later which one it is.' As we were waiting to take off the CO came round and said: 'OK, forget Munich, it's Mannheim.' It meant we were carrying a lot more petrol and a lot fewer bombs than we should have done for Mannheim.

In order to ensure the attack went from due east to due west so that any creepback would fall on Ludwigshafen the Pathfinders were putting a red flare down at the final turning point. We turned for it and saw a red flare go down to our left and another to our right. The navigator decided the one on our left was the correct one, east of the target, so it meant we were running up to the target five minutes early – not a happy situation. And of course they picked us up as we started to go in.

A master searchlight hit us, a cone rapidly built up and there we were, flying straight and level with the bomb doors open, so the bomb aimer got his sight and we jettisoned the lot at one go and didn't wait for a photograph. I was in the astrodome and could see an Me109 so close in the searchlights I could see the mask on the pilot's face. We weaved hard and nearly got away from the beams; there were only two still on us and I thought I'd better get down and check the engines as they were getting full power and you could only get away with that for about five minutes.

As I got down, a Ju88 came in. Its fire immediately killed the rear gunner and hit the hydraulic lines to the rear turret, starting a huge fire in the fuselage, and wounded the wireless operator, who was Windowing down the rear hatch at the back. He came running up towards me screaming and tripped over my long flight-engineer's intercom lead, pulling it out and cutting me off from everybody.

So while I was wondering what was the priority, him or the fire, I saw the mid-upper gunner get out and put his parachute on and I turned round and saw the navigator was putting his chute on. So I followed. Later I learned from the mid-upper that almost simultaneously as the fighter started firing the flak knocked out an engine and started a fire in the mainplane and when the mid-upper got an order to bale out from the skipper it sounded as if the skipper was badly hurt.

I followed the navigator down to the front hatch. I got my legs through the hatch after he went, then felt a pressure on my back. I looked round and the bomb aimer had his knees pressing on my back. I gave him the thumbs up and went, but the bomb aimer never got out. As I went I thought I felt the aircraft lurch and I think it broke in half and the bomb aimer was thrown back into the cockpit because the rear gunner's body was the only one which was salvaged unburned.

My harness had stretched a lot with moving about the aircraft and when I bent down the shoulder strap used to fall off, so I daren't open the chute until my body was absolutely straight. I looked down and could see the D-ring glinting in the searchlights. I pulled it and felt a tug and thought 'That's it', but it was only the pilot chute pulling out the main chute. The main chute opened with a tremendous jerk and I came down in agony because all the weight was on my leg straps.

As I saw the ground coming up I whipped my knees up to roll

myself into a ball as I'd been taught and the leg buckle on the left side came up and broke three ribs. It was very painful as I lay on the ground and also frightening as I thought any movement would pierce some vital organs. We had flown over the target and I had landed near Hockenheim. Finally I got up and started heading west hoping to get to France and then things turned into farce. I came across a solitary house that I skirted, but a young girl in a windmill spotted me, so I gave her a wave and shouted: 'Guten Morgen' and kept going. After a little while I heard a shout and saw this chap running after me with something long and menacing in his hand.

Until then there were two things I didn't believe. I didn't believe fighting men put their hands up like in the cowboy films and I didn't think ordinary Germans went around saying 'Heil Hitler.' But in fact without any thought on my part my right hand shot up, but I was now so stiff I couldn't get my left hand up. So there I was with my right arm in the air and this chap must have suddenly thought he had made a dreadful mistake and he came to attention and shouted: 'Heil Hitler'. I burst into hysterical laughter.[3]

The German's wife proved more knowledgeable. She pointed out to her husband that he did in fact have an RAF flyer on his hands and Sgt Bates was marched off to the police station and eventual prisoner-of-war camp. He and only two others in the crew had survived.

The damage in Mannheim caused by the bombing was so severe it was rated as a 'catastrophe' by the authorities and in Ludwigshafen more than 2,000 separate fires were recorded in which the centre and southern parts of the town were devastated.

Albert Hitzfeld was working as a journalist in Mannheim and had to get from the Lindenhof in the centre to the eastern part of the city. He described in a report of that night:

It seemed as if I was running through a burning tunnel. On the left and right were rows of houses and burning curtains were fluttering out of the windows and flames bursting metres high into the air. Then a powerful firestorm developed which kindled the fires even more and caused flying sparks like snowstorms.[4]

To the bomber crews the defences were more awe-inspiring than the fires below. Flight engineer Sgt Barry Wright of 103 Sqn, who had found Berlin's defenders so impressive two nights before, was now to find those of Mannheim even more fearsome. He recalls:

We had just dropped our bombs and could see the blue master beam searching the sky. It locked onto us and the other searchlights followed. We were coned. The pilot went into a dive and corkscrewed. The flak stopped then a fighter came in and holed the outer tank in the port wing and left quite a few holes in the aircraft. We managed to give the searchlights and fighter the slip, but we lost 113 gallons before I could pump the fuel to the next tank. We had to feather the port outer and came home on three engines.[5]

Sgt Grenville Jones was the bomb aimer in one of the four 78 Sqn Halifaxes that were lost. He says:

The flight engineer, Harry Mott, reported the oil pressure was low, which would make us late on target. I wanted to turn back. I said: 'Let's find somewhere to drop this lot and get out of it', because an awful lot did turn back. But the navigator, Sgt Sam Muldoon, didn't want to. He had done six ops then his pilot said he wasn't going to fly any more and they did the pilot for LMF. It should have been unfit for further service in that job, not this thing they called lack of moral fibre. Muldoon had this hanging over him, so didn't want to turn back.

We were only on the squadron three weeks, just long enough to go to Betty's Bar. They usually started you with a gardening op, but I had only done one flight over Holland looking for survivors from another raid, then we were on ops. It seemed to be a bit quick. I'd never talked to another crew. The pilot had been on a second-dickey trip, to Hanover, that's all.

I saw the glow of the target coming up when the rear gunner said,

'I can see a fighter sitting off our tail.' I think it was an Me110 cat's eye fighter holding off and radioing to the others. The bomb doors opened then the rear gunner shouted: 'I've got one, I've got him, skip.' I was lying down looking through the bomb sight and had just dropped the bombs when a piece of cannon shell came through the aircraft and took away the tip of the glove covering my little finger and went out through the front blister. I'm sure it was Schrage Musik from a fighter below.

The plane was suddenly on fire. I think the fighter had fired through the open bomb doors and caught the fuel lines. The navigator next to me got up to have a look and came back pretty quick and said: 'We're getting out of here.' The pilot had put the aircraft into a dive to try to blow the fire out and he called up and said: 'There's something the matter with the controls. Abandon aircraft'. The navigator went out through the front hatch and I went out. The wireless operator was just sitting there, smiling at me. Why he didn't go out I don't know. It was a matter of seconds, you couldn't think about it.

I counted to ten and I saw the aircraft pass above me. It was like a burning cross. We had flown past the target as we dived, but we were very low when I went out. After the war the flight engineer, who went out through the rear door, put in a report saying that he had seen the Australian mid-upper gunner with his chute on, so why he didn't get out I don't know.

I think that's why the rest of the crew were killed; they didn't have time to get out. I looked down and I could see the ground already. I thought: 'Blimey, I thought I was higher than that.' I landed in a ploughed potato field, spraining my ankle slightly. I could see a fire in the distance, which I think was our plane. I buried my chute, then a German home-guard chap walked down the field, so I hid behind some potato plants. He walked straight past me, concentrating on the fire. When he got a fair distance away I was up and off. I filled my battledress jacket with potatoes and started walking west using my escape compass. I hoped I might come across some foreign workers who could help me.

It was light then and I skirted round a forest then came to a river with a gantry over it. I walked on and came up against a flak battery. They spotted me and told me to put my hands up. They took me to their officer. He laughed when all the potatoes came spilling out of my jacket. They also found it pretty funny when they found the silk escape map in my shoes. They gave me a bowl of soup and I slept overnight in their billet. Later, because they thought I couldn't walk they gave me a bike to ride while the guard marched along. Of course, I went to the wrong side of the road.

Sgt Jones was taken to the local train station to be sent on to Dulag Luft and saw the navigator and flight engineer, who had also survived. 'Some civilians on the station shook their fists at us, but the guards waved them off,' he remembers. Before the month was out he was in Stalag IVB at Mühlberg.[6]

AT Ludford Magna W/O Peter Johnson, who in August had found shooting expeditions on the land of farmer Bert Brant a welcome relief from operations, had now settled into a routine of visiting the Brant family at Ludford Grange and in the dawn after an operation he would go back to the farmhouse instead of his billet. It was so after the Mannheim raid; he trudged up the lane alongside the airfield, across the main Louth–Market Rasen road where villagers lay sleeping in their mist-enshrouded cottages and up the hedged track to the Grange. Waiting for him as always was a bowl of Weetabix and jug of milk on the kitchen table.

Afterwards he would wearily climb the stairs to the room set aside for him. In the morning young Barbara Brant would see by the empty bowl that he had returned and look forward to hearing of his adventures when she came home from school. 'I used to spend most days shooting and snaring rabbits on the farm,' W/O Johnson remembers. 'Somebody from the crew would come over and tell me if we were on ops.' Usually his friend Jock

Mitchell, wireless operator in another crew, would go out shooting with him. 'Jock could load, aim and drop a rabbit while I was still fumbling with the cartridge,' Peter Johnson remembers.[7]

IT was a demanding period for aircrew and by 7 September W/O Johnson had carried out five operations in ten days. There followed the six days' leave aircrew were given every six weeks, but on 23 September he found himself back on the battle order for the second of the Mannheim raids in the month.

The plan was to wreck the northern part of Mannheim, which had escaped the devastation of the raid on the 5th. The Pathfinder marking was accurate and a concentration of bombs went down on north Mannheim. Creepback hit the northern part of Ludwigshafen, wrecking the I. G. Farben factory, but it also spread to the small outlying town of Frankenthal, where a backer-up target indicator – known to German civilians as a Christmas tree – seems to have gone down, and the centre of the small town was burned out.

Walter Osterpey was a flak helper in an emplacement by a lake used for bathing. He later recorded:

> The searchlights played in the air and the barrage roared its iron greeting. We had to work fast because the enemy flew usually just over our area. But our hearts stopped as we saw the 'Christmas trees' above us. Now we knew it was Frankenthal's turn. We in the barrages got something of it. After the attack we saw big fires in the city. The chief of the barrage let us locals go so that we could help our families. As I arrived home I could see the roof of my whole block in Morscher Street was on fire, but after hours of work the united community managed to halt the fire.[8]

Teenager Anton Stosser had just waved off a friend at the railway station and gone home for dinner at Parseval Square when the air raid warning sounded. The family of four ran into the cellar and his father reported a target indicator over the town. Herr Stosser reported later:

The bathing beach flak position fired not more than 10 times then stopped. More and more people came into our air-raid shelter from the burning houses. Panic broke out as two firebombs were dropped in front of our cellar windows and thick smoke streamed in. My mother wanted to get out with my 18-month-old brother, so we walked to Edigheimer Street where the Fuchsbach emptied into the Isenach. Our eyes were running with tears because of the smoke. The baby buggy stuck at an obstacle. A Polish prisoner of war was lying on the street with a smashed head, my first dead body.[9]

The citizens of Frankenthal were not the only Germans to be shocked that night to find their community was a target. The technique of mounting a diversionary raid by heavy bombers was born in this period, now that the fighters were being directed into the stream by a running commentary, guessing at Main Force's intentions. As the Main Force roared on to the Mannheim area on the 23rd, twenty-one Lancasters and eight Mosquitos broke away from the stream for Darmstadt, dropping quantities of Window to lure the Luftwaffe. For such a small force they caused much damage to Darmstadt.

There was initial confusion, though it failed to fool the Luftwaffe for long because the night fighters could see the fires building in Mannheim only 20 miles away. Seven bombers had been shot down before they reached Mannheim and Bomber Command's Operational Research Section later calculated that nineteen of the thirty-two aircraft lost on the raid fell to fighters.

That night Luftwaffe ace Martin Becker claimed the first of his fifty-eight night victories as both Zahme and Wilde Sau dived and climbed into the bomber stream, their cannons flashing across the blackness of the night. The percentage loss by Bomber Command was 5.1 per cent, the level of attrition crews had suffered in the Battle of the Ruhr.

P/O Ron Heatherington, bomb aimer in Lancaster ZN-C from Syerston, had just dropped his bombs on Mannheim when disaster struck. He remembers:

We were flying straight and level for the photoflash to go off when we were coned and the starboard wing caught fire. We didn't know if it was flak or a fighter. The pilot, P/O Stan Trill, corkscrewed and we were losing height all the time and the skipper gave the order to stand by for baling out. Finally he gave the order to bale out as both starboard engines were now burning.

I put my chute on and jettisoned the escape hatch. I had discarded my helmet and was standing by the open hole and I could see the flight engineer standing on the step-down to my position. He had his chute on and was all ready to follow. I remember standing astride of the hole and pushing myself through. I can't understand to this day why at least the engineer didn't get out. I don't think we were very high, but it was enough for me to feel a bit sick with the swing of the parachute. As I floated down I shouted to the other members of the crew to see if anyone responded in the darkness. Nobody did.

Apparently the aircraft was blown apart. I came down north of Mannheim near the village of Neuleiningen in the middle of the wine-growing area. I landed on a railway line and my parachute hit the telephone wires running along the track. I hid up in a patch of nettles then started walking in the direction of where I thought France was. Three days later I came across a vineyard. As I walked along the vines pinching grapes a soldier was walking down the other side. I tried to dodge him, but he got fed up and pulled out his pistol. He took me to the local police station and from there I was taken to the interrogation centre at Dulag Luft then on to Stalag Luft III North.[10]

The 77 Sqn Halifax of Sgt Bill Grant was one of those which fell to a night fighter. The navigator, Sgt Bob Murty, who had transferred to the RAF after being evacuated from Dunkirk as a soldier, was one of only three who got out. Sgt Grant was not among them. Sgt Murty related afterwards:

I came down in the target area of Mannheim and as dawn was breaking, to avoid meeting angry civilians, I climbed a tree and hid there all day. The following night I came down and started walking. I came to in a forest and because I was so tired I rested by a tree and fell into a deep sleep. I woke to see a forester standing over me holding a big axe and for me the war was over.[11]

The Lancaster of wireless operator Sgt Tom Hall of 103 Sqn also nearly became a victim. He remembers: 'A 109 came into attack immediately astern. Our rear gunner spotted him before he opened fire and started firing himself, calling for the pilot to corkscrew. It was a clear night with no clouds to hide in and fortunately the German didn't pursue us.'[12]

For others from 103 Sqn engagement with a fighter was more conclusive. Oberleutnant Lenz Finsler of IV/NJG1 made one firing attack against the Lancaster of F/Lt Douglas Finlay then flew alongside out of range watching it burn as crew members fell away from the fuselage, their parachutes blossoming.

Flight engineer P/O Sandy Rowe was one of them. He recalls:

We were north-west of Mannheim when the night fighter made one pass, which knocked out the two port engines and set the port wing ablaze. The pilot asked my opinion and I suggested he told the crew to prepare to bale out. He finally gave the order to jump. I lifted the front hatch cover and tried to push it out of the hole, but the wind caught it and it jammed. I gave it a jolly good kick and I followed it, then the bomb aimer and navigator followed me. I pulled the ripcord too quickly because I was doing about 200 mph and my body would have slowed down to about 160 mph if I'd waited. There was quite a jolt. I came down in a clearing in a wooded area. As I was picking up my parachute I saw another chute come down on the top of a tree nearby. It was the navigator, John McFarlane. I went and asked him if he could get down and he replied: 'How do I know? I didn't climb up.' He managed to get down OK with a few scratches.

The two began an evasion attempt which would last a week.[13]

The Lancaster of F/Sgt Ernie Webb of 49 Sqn was also hit by a night fighter as he left the target. He recalls:

The mid-upper gunner called out: 'Fighter corkscrew port' and I went down left, then as we climbed up the other side I saw the tracer going below us to the right and we were hit. I heard the banging and smelled the cordite as the fire went through the rear turret towards the centre of the aircraft. The rear gunner, Sgt Philip Horton, was wounded and immediately the intercom was knocked out so we couldn't communicate. I put the nose down, dropping 4,000 or 5,000 feet, and lost the fighter. Because of the dive when we levelled out we were going very fast and I turned back onto course. We were belting along. The wireless operator went back to check on the rear gunner and found he had got to the rest bed. He had three bullet holes in the left thigh.

F/Sgt Webb's troubles were not over and he would find the condition of his aircraft critical as he brought O-Orange into land at Fiskerton.[14]

Others faced different perils over Mannheim. As on all raids there was a considerable risk of being hit by a missile from another RAF aircraft. Some airmen considered that and collision a bigger risk than the flak as an increasing number of aircraft jockeyed for position to line up a green or red TI. Skipper P/O 'Bluey' Mottershead of 158 Sqn remembers:

There were 600-odd aircraft all heading over the target in the same direction and we had just dropped our own bombs when a 30-lb incendiary hit the port inner engine and cut all the propeller blades off to the stubs. The engine ran away and was shaking up the aircraft severely. We shut down the engine and were down to about 5,000 feet before I could make any forward progress without diving. One of the other engines was a bit dickey, but we struggled back home.

However, as the port inner controlled the hydraulics I couldn't be sure the undercarriage had come down when I came into land, so I had to fly down the runway as the control tower put a searchlight on me. When I landed I dropped rather hard, which caused the rear gunner to complain a bit. We were OK though and I taxied her round to her usual dispersal, but it took seven weeks to put the aircraft right.

I had had NP-T for twelve operations since the Hamburg raid of 2 August, but I had to finish my tour on another aircraft.[15]

F/Sgt Webb also had a tense approach into Fiskerton. He says:

We had lost all our hydraulics. A bullet had gone through the hydraulic system and drained it. We had to use the emergency air bottle to lower the undercarriage. Once you had used it you were committed; you couldn't raise the undercarriage again. I made quite a good landing apart from discovering the rear tyre had been punctured in the attack and there was a banging noise as we went along the runway. I was very relieved to be back.

By the time I got out of the aircraft the ambulance had taken the rear gunner away to the sick bay. The next day we went to look at the aircraft and the rear turret was badly damaged and there were holes from the cannon shells through the rear fuselage slanting to the bomb bay. Luckily the bay had been empty. We had spare gunners for various trips, but Percy Horton came back to us towards the end of our tour.

Despite the losses the raid had been a remarkable success. In northern Mannheim and Ludwigshafen twenty-two industrial premises had been burned out and 2,000 separate fires had been started. The centre of Frankenthal was now a blazing ruin.

P/O Rowe and Sgt McFarlane left the fires of the three communities burning behind them as they tried to evade. P/O Rowe remembers:

McFarlane and I wanted to get away from the parachute in the tree and we came across an autobahn. We got our silk escape maps out and found it led to Saarbrücken, but there seemed to be a crossroads on it and the road from there was more or less north and south so we thought when we reached the junction we would head south for Nancy. We walked at night and hid up during the day for about a week and never found a crossroads because as we now know motorways don't have them. It must have been a bridge and of course we thought bridges were for railway lines. We kept walking and got into Saarbrücken, so we retraced our steps and hid in a hay loft under bundles of straw. We heard footsteps coming up the steps to the loft and the next moment a bundle was whipped off and the woman saw me. She was as white as a sheet. She disappeared down the steps and brought half a dozen people. Then the police came.[16]

The two airmen began the new journey which would end in prisoner-of-war camp.

In England by this time the cost and causes of such losses in the two Mannheim raids had already been calculated, processed and filed, but sometimes it was weeks before the relatives of RAF personnel missing on operations heard if they were dead or alive. The parents of P/O Heatherington would not know he was safe until they received a prisoner-of-war card from him in Sagan on 9 November. In the meantime his closest friend on 106 Sqn, RCAF bomb aimer Al Porter, wrote to P/O Heatherington's girlfriend, Margaret Hutchinson, telling her of that last flight:

As we were going to our aircraft we shouted our cheerios: 'Good luck, see you in the morning.' Over the target we saw one aircraft shot down and, although I did not see it myself, the crew told me that all of the other crew were able to bale out. That may have been them, but of course we did not know.

Our crew first knew that something was wrong when we arrived over the 'drome and did not hear 'C-Charlie' calling for permission to land. As I came away from the flight office, their bikes were still there. After interrogation I waited till about 5 a.m. when a call came through to Air Ministry stating that they were three hours overdue and had not landed in this country.[17]

F/O Porter, who promised to write with any further news, was dead within less than a month, shot down on a Leipzig operation which claimed his whole crew.

THE success Bomber Command had found with its raids on Mannheim would not be repeated further south in two raids on Munich, though the losses in percentage terms would be lower. Shortly after the bomber stream took off on the first of the raids, on 6 September, a 12 Sqn aircraft came down in the sea. Five of the crew were rescued from their dinghy, but the bomb aimer and rear gunner had gone down with the aircraft.

The bombers, a force of Lancasters and Halifaxes, were routed over London to demonstrate how strongly Bomber Command was now taking the war to the enemy. Crews of the 404 planes, which creaked and reverberated as the remorseless wedge of aircraft split the darkness on the long flight from the Channel, found cloud covering Munich as they approached. The Pathfinders, marking on H2S, dropped both sky and ground TIs, but most of Main Force resorted to a timed run from the Ammersee lake, 21 miles to the south-west. The bombing was inevitably short, and scattered over the south and south-west of the city, though most fell in countryside.

It was a bad night for 156 Sqn of the Pathfinders. Two of the three Lancasters lost were theirs and a third returned so badly damaged after a fighter attack that it never flew again. The squadron had also lost one on Mannheim the night previously and one on Berlin two nights before that.

Navigator F/O Walter Kerry was in the 156 Sqn aircraft of F/Lt A. Maclachlan:

We did a lot of raids in a row and Munich was our fourth operation in a week. We released our markers and bombs and minutes later fighter flares were dropped and we were silhouetted against them. A fighter came up underneath with Schrage Musik and hit us in the wing, setting the petrol tanks on fire. We hadn't seen anything and the sound of the attack was hardly noticeable. There was a sort of rattling sound, but I thought that was our gunners.

The pilot ordered a bale-out straight away as soon as the wing caught fire, but only four of us got out in time. The Canadian rear gunner, Sgt 'Duke' Ducat, went out through the back of his turret, but believes the aircraft exploded as he went out. The pilot, the mid-upper gunner, 'Red' Chambers, and the wireless operator, Colin Dalton, were still in the aircraft when it exploded. I was the third to go out. The aircraft wasn't spinning, it seemed quite steady. The flight engineer, Dave Evans, and bomb aimer, Nick Carter, had already gone and I went forward to the open hatch and went straight through it. I don't know what happened to the bomb aimer; he was never seen again. I was tumbling around in the pitch-black and went to feel for the D-ring, but it had slipped out and was dangling around my waist. I thought I had lost it, but when I dropped my hand I felt it. I then followed the drill and counted to ten before I pulled the ripcord.

I came down in a tree just outside Munich. I was dangling in the darkness and after I hit the quick release box I held onto the trunk, but I slipped and wondered how far I was going to fall. Fortunately it was only a foot or two and I went flat on my back. I couldn't get the chute out of the tree and I could hear the voices of people walking along a road near me, so I thought the best thing to do was to get out of the area. I headed towards Switzerland throughout the night and the next day and at about six that evening I walked out of a thicket right in front of a German policeman marching some slave workers home. I was only about 5 feet in front of him and out came his gun and he actually used the words, 'For you the war is over.'[18]

The Luftwaffe defence of the whole of southern Germany was now centred in Munich and a total of sixteen aircraft were brought down, a rate of 4 per cent, nowhere near the recent losses on Berlin raids, but the Munich operation was particularly hard on the Halifaxes: thirteen of them were lost, two of them from 427 Sqn.

Mid-upper gunner F/Sgt Harold McLean was in a 427 Sqn Halifax hit by a fighter. He says:

That last flight was a very long, tedious one in which we were passing in and out of the tops of clouds and as we got to the target area the searchlights were causing a strobe effect. We got on the bombing run and some very heavy tracer shells went past some way behind us from starboard to port, about the same height, but nowhere near. I thought it had been aimed at someone else. I reported it as a bad miss. I asked the pilot, Billy Biggs, to do something even though we were on the bombing run as I couldn't see the fighter. Of course, it meant we would have had to go round again. Just as the pilot said 'OK', this fighter fired again and got us in the overload tank in the back of the bomb bay under my seat. Flames started coming up. I called up the pilot and told him: 'We won't put this one out, Billy', so he said: 'All right, good luck, lads, bale out.'

My chute was actually in the flames in its storage box, but I got it out, clipped it on and went to the back of the plane to open the rear door and it seemed to be jammed, then I passed out, I think from petrol fumes. When I came to, the front of the plane was gone.

I was lying in the back with the wireless operator, Les Moyler, across my legs and the ammunition over the pair of us. I kept fading in and out of consciousness. I remember thinking: 'This is bloody silly', and at one time tried to brace myself against the ammunition racks for the crash. Then I prayed for a quick death; I didn't think I would survive. I asked Les to get off me. But he replied: 'I can't.' Those were his last words.

I thought I would try to get out, but whether I managed to climb up to where the front had been or was thrown out I don't know because the next thing I knew I was in the air in my parachute. I actually saw the front of the plane go past with flames streaming from it. I went unconscious again and landed in a tree. The flight engineer, Jack Elliott, was in the front of the plane and when it got near the ground it must have flattened out because after it crashed he just walked out of the back of it with a couple of bruises. Alf Richards, our bomb aimer, survived by being thrown through the front Perspex when the petrol tank exploded, blowing the aircraft apart. He wandered around for a few days before he was caught.

There I was, stuck in the tree, and after a bit I got hungry and thought I'd better try to get out so I started swinging and I heard a cracking sound. I came to across the roots and I had hurt my back, fracturing my fourth lumbar vertebra as I discovered later. I'd lost one flying boot and thought I'd lay up for the day. But I heard dogs barking, so I walked on and strolled by mistake into the end of a farmhouse. A door opened, I was challenged and I replied: 'Ich bin englischer Flieger.' The farmer went for the police and while he was gone his daughter rubbed my back, which I thought was a very Christian thing to do.

The Germans came with an ambulance and about a quarter of a mile down the road picked up Jack Elliott. They took us to the local jail in Tutzing, on the edge of the Starnberger See in Bavaria. I could hear kids jabbering, going to school. I looked out and one of them, aged about 7, shouted: 'Good morning, Mr Englishman, how are you?' He told me his name was Richard and he brought me some apples. I could have cried. I'd only been in Germany about seven hours and I'd met nothing but kindness.[19]

The day after the Munich raid, as his comrades put out their best blue for a run-in to the delights of Betty's Bar in York, Harold McLean was being taken with flight engineer Jack Elliott to see his wrecked aircraft and discovered what had happened to the wireless operator, Les Moyler. He remembers:

Three army officers took us round to the wreckage in a *kubelwagen*. I could hardly walk so Jack had to identify the bodies and he said Les was lying near the rear portion of the aircraft with one arm up, so whether he crawled out of the back when it landed and died or was flung out at the same time as me I don't know.

They took us to Fürstenfeldbruck aerodrome where we stayed overnight and on the way we passed a signpost to Dachau. I was aware that there was something sinister about that place. I was asked if I wanted to go to hospital but I didn't fancy being in hospital with a lot of bomb victims. So they gave me some anti-neuralgia pills and the next morning took them off me again. We went by ordinary train to

Dulag Luft and a woman with a heavy American accent asked me: 'Who do you think is going to win the war?' I said: 'Mr Churchill tells us we're going to win' and she said: 'Our leader tells us we are.'

I was treated quite well at Dulag Luft. They didn't put too much pressure on. My interrogator could see I was in pain. He said he had worked for Whitbread's brewery in London before the war and said: 'We've got a wing commander in the RAF working for us and I suppose you've got one of our people working for you.'

F/Sgt McLean found himself bound for Stalag IVB at Muhlberg.

BOMBER Command was now a vastly different organisation than it had been at the start of the year and the war had developed a harder edge. The call was for maximum efforts as Harris planned the Battle of Berlin, which he saw as the final blow to the Nazi hierarchy. Sometimes the desperate need to win led to seemingly impossible demands on aircrew, demands that allowed for no excuses, valid or not.

It was against this background that the second Munich raid was launched on 2 October. Only 1 and 5 Group were employed, with marking by 8 Group's Lancasters equipped with H2S. Among the 5 Group Lancasters were those of 50 Sqn at Skellingthorpe, near Lincoln. Bomb aimer Sgt Joseph Porter had reported with his crew to the squadron in September and had rapidly been drafted in as a spare on another crew because their bomb aimer had been injured. He recalls:

It was the third op I had been called in to do with this pilot and I still hadn't operated with my own crew. We were on the runway to take off when the mid-upper gunner reported his turret wouldn't turn. They'd already tested it before moving on to the runway and it was OK, but as the skipper revved up his engines the mid-upper tried his turret again and it was faulty. The pilot called up the CO and he told them: 'That won't hurt, off you go.' The pilot and crew had done several trips and had been shot up once before and the skipper asked them what they should do and they all said no. They excluded me.

The pilot pulled off the runway and we were made to walk all the way across the airfield to the CO's office. He told them they would go on every operation until he'd got rid of them, but didn't include me in his ticking off because I wasn't part of their crew. I don't know what happened to them because I was shot down shortly afterwards.[20]

The Munich raid was important because 5 Group's chief, Sir Ralph Cochrane, saw the virtually undamaged target as an ideal opportunity to demonstrate his time and distance technique, which had failed on Friedrichshafen in June and had struck problems on the Peenemünde operation. In fact the 5 Group bomb aimers were unable to pick up the Würmsee lake from which to start their timed run and bombs were scattered up to 15 miles along the approach route to Munich. On the positive side only eight Lancasters were lost of the 294 dispatched, 2.7 per cent – a low figure indeed for such a distant target.

It had been flight engineer Sgt Charles Marshall's first operation. He would be shot down within a week, two months to the day since he made his first training flight. He remembers:

We last flew at 1662 HCU at Blyton on 20 September and were posted to 460 Sqn at Binbrook. We were on the squadron barely two weeks. We never got the chance to go out anywhere. We arrived and had to see the CO and he said: 'We're not quite ready to send you tonight but you'll be on tomorrow', and we were.

We were briefed every night, but the op was put off because the weather was too bad or the aircraft wasn't right. On 4 October we went to Wickenby to pick up an aircraft to fly back to base and the port inner engine ran away and caught fire. We couldn't feather it because all the oil had run out. We got the fire out, but the propeller was windmilling and we had to land at base with a fully fine prop.

On the Munich operation I had to stand up all the time because we took a squadron leader from the base to guide us through our first op and he sat in my position. It was a seven hour fifty-five minute trip. Our aircraft was in the first wave. I found it astounding looking down.

It looked like embers glowing in a bonfire, but as we got nearer it was obvious this was the city. We were lucky with our position in the stream and didn't have any trouble with flak or fighters. Coming back we did three overshoots before we managed to get in because there was a crosswind on the runway. We had 1,900 gallons of fuel when we set out; 2,154 was the maximum, but we were getting very low when we came in to land. It took 40 gallons to go round again and according to my calculations we had about 10 gallons left at the end. The squadron leader said: 'Oh, you've got bags of fuel', but when they tested the tanks there was only 10 gallons left.

We actually landed at East Kirkby. We were talking to our own base at Binbrook a few miles away, but somehow or other we were in the circuit for East Kirkby. We taxied off the runway and then found we were on the wrong aerodrome. Their crews had all come back except one,* so they put us in that crew's accommodation. We were woken up when the padre, the orderly officer and the military police came in to empty the missing crew's lockers. It wasn't very nice.[21]

In this period, as Pathfinders were beset by problems with H2S, two medium-sized raids were launched against the Ruhr, which showed how splendidly Oboe worked by comparison. They also achieved their object of confusing the Luftwaffe about Bomber Command's intentions, 2.6 per cent being lost from the raid on Bochum on 29 September and a remarkably low 0.8 per cent from another operation on Bochum.

Nine Oboe-equipped Mosquitos marked Bochum for the 343 Lancasters and Halifaxes of Main Force and in concentrated bombing nearly 1,300 buildings were destroyed or badly damaged. Five Halifaxes and four Lancasters went down. On the Hagen raid three days later only two Lancasters were lost of the 243 sent out. The Oboe Mosquitos dropped their skymarkers extremely accurately over cloud and half of the town's industrial areas were severely damaged. No fewer than 46 firms were put out of action and more than 150 damaged. Among the latter was the largest

* This was the crew of P/O R.K. Clements RCAF, who had all been killed.

accumulator works in Germany, which held up U-boat production.[22]

It was a prime example of what Oboe could achieve, but Oboe's beams would stretch no further and other cities needed to be raided as the longer hours of darkness crept in, ready for the most crucial air bombardment battle of all, Berlin. The Pathfinders would be tussling with the uncertainties of 10-cm H2S in four heavy raids on Hanover, one of which would lead to a crisis of confidence in their abilities. The four raids would also cost 110 aircraft.

AUTUMN

CHAPTER THIRTEEN

ATTRITION TO ACHIEVEMENT

THE winds of autumn, which swept leaves pattering across dispersals and into orderly piles by the wheels of crouching, shrouded black aircraft, ushered in technical changes in the air war. They would give Bomber Command a temporary edge over the Luftwaffe. The season would also see two important raids on Kassel – the second of which would turn out to be the most devastating punishment of a German city since Hamburg. But it was the four raids on Hanover for which the autumn of 1943 would be remembered, and the first of them would spark a long and detailed letter from Don Bennett to Harris explaining why it had failed.

A total of 711 aircraft set out for Hanover on the night of 22 September, the first time it had been raided in strength. The city had long been on the Air Ministry's target list, however. Hanover had sizeable locomotive and tank works, oil refineries and textile mills. It was also home to Germany's largest producer of synthetic rubber.

The die had been cast to destroy the city, no matter at what cost over how many operations. It was unfortunate, therefore, for the Pathfinders in the first raid of 22 September that although they arrived over the target in good weather, there was a stronger wind than forecast and most of the attack fell miles from the aiming point. According to Bomber Command's Operational Research Section the error was compounded by the backers-up aiming their TI greens at reds instead of yellows.

There had been disappointment of late in some Pathfinder marking, for instance over Berlin on 3 September and Munich on the 6th, and the method of attack had called for PFF to mark the aiming point with red TIs using H2S, checked by a carefully timed run from the Steinhuder Meer. Visual markers were to mark the aiming point with yellow and green TIs.

In fact, the ORS reported:

The blind markers appear to have dropped their TI reds and their flares about three to four miles south-east of the aiming point, the marking being somewhat scattered. The visual markers, with the help of their own flares, marked the aiming point accurately with TI yellow and TI green, but all but two of the backers-up seem to have aimed at the greatest concentration of TI, irrespective of colour, instead of backing up the yellows.[1]

The wind had been unexpectedly strong and many aircraft approached on the wrong track, which meant the Main Force bombing on green TIs was led astray and the main weight of attack fell 2–5 miles south-south-east of the aiming point. Towards the raid's end the bombing was spreading as far as 9 miles from the AP. The ORS report went on: 'As a result some 2,500 tons of bombs were dropped mainly in suburban areas and open country.' The lack of success was balanced somewhat by the low loss figure of twenty-six aircraft, 3.7 per cent.

A diversionary raid by twenty-one Lancasters and eight Mosquitos furiously releasing Window had been made on Oldenburg, and intercepted German wireless traffic showed that the running-commentary controllers then expected the main assault to be on Berlin to the east, at one point directing all fighters there.

Most of the danger in the target area was from barrage flak and searchlight activity which was described as 'intense' by the normally terse post-raid report. Sgt Alec Taylor was a wireless operator in a 102 Sqn Halifax unusually brought down by searchlights alone. He says:

It was our thirteenth operation and it turned out to be unlucky. We were coned over Hanover for what seemed like ten minutes and after the skipper got us out of the beams by strenuous efforts we found the starboard inner engine was over-revving. The propeller came off and scythed through the nose of the Halifax. The fuse panel was blown out with a big bang and everything went black.

A course for home had already been plotted by the navigator and with the aid of a torch held by me the pilot was able to turn onto it. But the damaged engine caught fire and the pilot ordered us to bale out. I seemed to be a long time in the air before I landed in a field. I had lost one flying boot and was on my own. I struggled out of my harness and hid it and my parachute in a ditch. I had no idea where I was and I crawled beneath a hedge and went to sleep. I got out my escape kit and found I had two silk maps of northern Germany and two small compasses. I moved on the next evening and travelled for the next three nights, sleeping during the day. I had nothing to eat in that time except some blackberries. Finally on the fourth day a farmer found me as I slept.

He took me to a house occupied by German soldiers and they took me to the wreckage of our aircraft. There was a body of one of our crew by the plane and I got a flying boot to replace the one I had lost. I wore it for the rest of my time in captivity. I thought it was the body of the pilot, P/O Jack Hanby, but at interrogation I was told it was the rear gunner, Sgt Roland Maund. I was taken to a German airfield where I was held the whole weekend, then I was taken to Dulag Luft where I met up with Frank Windmill, the Australian mid-upper gunner from our crew.[2]

For the first time the Americans had joined in night bombing of a German target, sending five B-17s from the 305th Bomb Group, and Harris – who was hoping to persuade the Eighth Air Force to switch to night bombing for the coming assault on Berlin – was not pleased that the USAAF commanders looking over the post-raid reports would not find much in the way of results for an effort by 711 aircraft.

The Pathfinders chief Don Bennett felt his ire and three days after the attack wrote the C-in-C a long letter defending his force. He said PFF had not been able to achieve the required policy of 'nothing but the best' because 'in short (a) we are not getting the very best of crews and (b) we have to take our crews with no experience whatsoever'. In fact the top crews passing out of OTUs were being asked at that time if they wanted to volunteer for the forty-five-trip double tour required by Pathfinders instead of the thirty-op first tour of Main Force. A surprising number agreed to the extra immediate risk.

In the post-Hanover inquest a senior officer from 5 Group, headed by AVM Cochrane, who wanted to set up his own Pathfinders, had told Bennett that the group could easily produce twelve crews who would be better at the job of backing up than the PFF backers-up. By way of reply the needled Bennett asked Harris: 'I should like to suggest that we should be permitted to select any or all of second-tour crews who are returning to ops.' He also repeated an often-made request that he be allowed to fly the occasional operation to see what improvements could be made. Bennett was forced to admit that 'the results obtained with H2S have been extremely bad', but used the letter as an opportunity to again demand 3-cm H2S as 'our most vital requirement'.[3]

It was in fact 13 November before the first three Mk III H2S sets, operating on the shorter wavelength and giving a clearer picture of terrain, arrived on a Pathfinder squadron. H2S had proved particularly problematical over Hanover when only ten of the twenty PFF aircraft in the target area had serviceable sets. Nine of them dropped their TIs to open the attack on H2S and the tenth bomb aimer released his TI on an existing one.

There was another reason, however, why the Pathfinders had found it so difficult to read the target on their H2S sets. The Maschsee lake immediately south of Hanover's main railway station, which the Pathfinders needed as an H2S fix, had been camouflaged by the civil defences. In error PFF identified the interconnecting lakes of Ricklinger Teiche about 5 miles further south as the Maschsee and consequently marked too early. It was therefore more a fault of planning than of execution.

The truth trickled through to RAF squadrons in weeks to come. F/Sgt Alex Wood, who had been skippering a 15 Sqn Stirling over Hanover, says:

> It looked like a successful raid to us; we were credited with an aiming-point picture as we were on all our raids. I had a very good bomb aimer. Unfortunately the aiming point was wrong because the Pathfinder force had been duped by the lake in the town being covered by barges. The target indicators were dropped some miles south. There was a lot of flak and searchlights and the incendiaries were burning anyway, but of course you couldn't tell whether it was incendiaries or buildings burning.[4]

There was no doubt Hanover would have to be attacked again and it was, five days later, but again the Pathfinders were misled by winds and again the centre of Hanover was spared. Not surprisingly, the missing rate was up, thirty-eight aircraft or 5.6 per cent, and, worryingly for Harris's attempts to woo the Americans, a B-17 was lost.

There was also a disturbing new trend of Luftwaffe fighters following the bombers home. On the previous Hanover raid the fighters, sent off to Berlin, did not catch up with the stream until 20 miles onto the homeward leg, but intruders had attacked eight of the bombers over their bases, destroying two. After the second Hanover raid the *nachtjäger* would be circling the circuits of the bomber bases again, waiting for the steady arc down the sky of a heavy aircraft, navigation lights glowing, its crew on final approach for debriefing, bacon and eggs, and the safe familiarity of bed after a long flight. This time a 101 Sqn Lancaster would be shot down and the threat would continue into October, before Hitler temporarily called a halt to such operations.

It was not until 1 October – four days after the unsuccessful second Hanover operation – that Harris replied to Bennett. He agreed that introduction of 3-cm H2S was a priority, but with the new Hanover bomb plots in front of him the C-in-C still had harsh words for PFF's recent performance.

He told Bennett that the crews must not rely on H2S at the expense of basic navigation. The C-in-C added: 'It seems to me that on a certain number of occasions there is evidence that crews, who ought to know better, have failed to mark the target accurately through over-reliance on H2S and neglect of other methods.' Harris also turned down Bennett's request to fly on ops.[5]

Another week would pass before Bennett's force would be able to take the pressure off their chief with the third Hanover raid and accurate marking of the city centre which led to a highly concentrated attack.

The raid of the 27th had been very concentrated, but fell in an area 5 miles north of the city centre, entirely because PFF navigators were using faulty winds. Only four visual markers reported identifying the aiming point, although some made as many as four runs over the city in an attempt to get it right. Bomber Command Operational Research Section considered the lack of illumination over the AP spoiled what would otherwise have been an excellent raid.

Luftwaffe controllers had guessed the target long before the bombers arrived and the night fighters were waiting. The sky was soon criss-crossed with tracer among the stabbing lances of the searchlights as Zahme Sau and Wilde Sau picked off aircraft on their bomb runs. The ORS post-raid report read:

> Over the target there were so many observations of falling aircraft in a short time that no definite number can be assigned either to flak or to fighter, but the majority are believed to have been shot down by fighters. More than half of the observations in the target area mentioned that aircraft were coned before being shot down and this applied equally to flak and fighter victims.[6]

Sgt Robert Taylor was in one of the aircraft seen coned, then shot down – a Stirling of 199 Sqn, skippered by Sgt Maurice Hodgson. He was the sole survivor of his crew and in a moving letter just after the war to the mother of his friend Sgt Doug Wood, the wireless operator, he recorded those last moments:

There was quite a lot of fighter activity over the target and hundreds of searchlights. We had just started the bombing run and I being the bomb aimer was seeing to the bombing. Unfortunately we were picked up by the searchlights and held by them. The plane was lit up like day. Almost immediately after this the gunners reported two fighters coming in, one from the rear and one from the port side.

In the meantime Maurice was endeavouring to get out of the searchlights, but to no avail. The fighters then attacked and scored hits in their first attack. Maurice told us to get ready and put our parachutes on, as this seemed to be 'it'. Repeated hits from the enemy cannons were coming into the plane. The intercommunication was shot away and all this time Maurice was trying in vain to get out of the search-lights. Suddenly the aircraft went out of control after a terrific explosion. I assumed then that Maurice had been killed and I baled out. Being in the bomb aimer's position I was fortunate enough to be near the front escape hatch. Unfortunately for me I was knocked unconscious on leaving the plane, so I did not see it crash.[7]

Before he was taken to prison camp the Germans showed him the belongings of the rest of his dead crew.

The attrition continued even over England. W/O Peter Johnson was letting down to enter the circuit at Ludford Magna, looking forward to breakfast at the Brant farm, when he heard P/O Desmond Skipper call up that he was funnelling on the glide slope in King Two. He smiled as he remembered Skipper's Australian rear gunner, Rex Liersch, who had been before a commissioning board, larking as they struggled into flying clothing in the crew room hours earlier that he also was a P/O, but in his case it stood for *Potential* Officer. 'Skipper had his nav lights on and I suddenly heard him call "Bandits",' W/O Johnson remembers. 'All the runway lights went out and the intruder got Skipper. I'd known him at Binbrook before we joined the squadron. The rest of us were diverted to Lindholme.' P/O Skipper's blazing aircraft crashed near Wickenby to the south. There were no survivors.[8]

THE Pathfinders heading a stream of 430 Lancasters, Halifaxes and Wellingtons to Hanover on the third raid, of 8 October, were aware how keen Bennett was to see the target at last marked properly and a blitz on H2S servicing staff had paid off. All forty-eight Pathfinders so equipped found their sets working perfectly as they approached the city in clear visibility.

This time there was no 20-mile timed run from the Steinhuder Meer to confuse as there had been on the first and second operations and the initial blind markers placed their yellow TIs very accurately around the aiming point in the city centre, which was brilliantly illuminated. Unfortunately the first four visual markers overshot by 2–3½ miles, but the next two dropped their salvos of red and green TIs within half a mile of the AP. The academics of the Operational Research Section, who of course didn't know what it was to face the mind-numbing terror of a well-defended German target, noted: 'The Main Force, following their usual procedure, bombed the first red TI that they saw, which in this instance were those nearest to the AP.'

Their report continued: 'About 70 per cent of the Main Force bombed before these TIs were extinguished with the result that an exceptionally concentrated attack developed in the centre of the city.'[9]

On the ground the air-raid precautions services, mindful of those who had died in their thousands in the cellars of Hamburg, persuaded people to leave their shelters and collect in open areas between the fires, saving many lives. Reconnaissance the next day showed that the central area and south of the main railway station had been very seriously damaged, as had the industrial district of Linden, south-west of the city centre. Fires still burning as the photographing Mosquito flew over covered an elliptical area 2 miles long by 1 mile wide. It was estimated that 54 per cent of the town's built-up area had been destroyed by fire. At last the Pathfinders had triumphed and the night raid report crowed: 'This was undoubtedly one of the most successful attacks hitherto made using the Newhaven* technique.'[10]

---

* *Visual marking after H2S-guided blind illuminators had lit up the target.*

The cost had again been high. The Luftwaffe controllers had correctly guessed Hanover was the aim as the stream thundered in over the German border from Holland – although the planners had hoped their route would make the Luftwaffe think it was Berlin – and the night fighters were on time to meet the bombers over the target. A total of twenty-seven aircraft were lost, 6.3 per cent. The operation was the last time Wellingtons were used over Germany, 300 Sqn and 432 Sqn supplying thirty-six between them. They all returned safely, although on the first Hanover raid of the four 432 Sqn had lost a Wellington off Flamborough Head, only three of the crew being rescued after twelve hours in a dinghy.

The Hanover raid of 8 October was the first operation of 19-year-old rear gunner Sgt Norman Page of 78 Sqn. It was also his last. His short RAF career from call-up on 12 January spanned the build-up of Bomber Command in 1943, from tentative beginnings with raids of fewer than 100 bombers to the 504 including Pathfinders that were now raiding Hanover as a matter of course.

In a diary kept at the time he wrote that his pilot, F/Lt Bill Williams, had been warned by the navigator, P/O Les Heaney, fifteen minutes before the target came up to look out for the TIs going down. He wrote:

Bill called out: 'There are our target flares to starboard', and we started to see the flashes of the Cookies going off. When it was our turn the skipper turned towards Hanover from a point north-east of the city. Suddenly I saw the outline of a Ju88. It appeared from underneath our plane, to starboard. I shouted: 'Dive to starboard, go, go' and started to fire my guns.

The fighter attacked twice, but they managed to corkscrew into the darkness. However, within five minutes sparks were streaming past Sgt Page's turret as the port inner engine caught fire. Sgt Page continued:

The skipper tried to feather the engine, but had no success. By now the port inner was a blazing mass, which was quickly spreading to the wing and fuselage. It was all happening so quickly. There was nothing

Bill could do to bring the fire under control and he gave his last order: 'I'm sorry, chaps, this is it, emergency, abandon aircraft, jump, jump.' The next thing I knew I was falling over and over through space. We must have been at about 16,000 to 17,000 feet when I baled out at around 1.30 a.m. I hadn't even time to get out of my parachute before I was surrounded by three men and a woman who were saying excitedly, 'Engländerflieger'.

Sgt Page had come down near the village of Harsewinkel near Detmold and was taken to the Luftwaffe base at Gütersloh where he was told he was the only one to get out of his aircraft. 'To my horror I was then taken to the local hospital to identify,' he wrote. 'As the mortuary door was opened I came to a sudden stop. In front of me lined up on the cold floor were the six members of my crew.'[11]

The raid was also the last operational trip of Lancaster flight engineer Sgt Charles Marshall of 460 Sqn, who had flown for the first time in training only two months before. He remembers:

As a new crew we didn't get top-line aircraft and on the pre-flight checks the mid-upper turret failed to rotate. This was corrected, but after take-off the mid-upper's intercom wouldn't work. I had to supply the turret with an intercom extension lead from the rest position, which was too short for the gunner to sit upright in his turret, reducing his area of vision.

We were in the last phase of the attack and by the time we were approaching the target the defences were well aware of our route. They were illuminating it with flares from above. It was more like going down a well-lit main road. This made us obvious targets for night fighters operating from below us. We were on our bombing run when I saw a plane to the right of us going down on fire and I thought, 'Poor devils'. You never think it's going to happen to you, but the next thing we were attacked by two night fighters. I think they came up from below and behind. The first thing any of us knew was a sudden shud-dering of the aircraft as the cannon shells came through. I could see tracer coming through the plywood doors at the back of our compartment and they went straight past me and the bomb aimer without hitting us.

I looked out to starboard and saw the 500-gallon starboard wing tank catch fire. The wireless operator was looking out the other side and saw the same thing happen on the port wing. We had just switched over to those tanks and they were full. The jettison toggles for the bomb load were just in front of my position so I didn't wait for the bomb aimer; I jettisoned the bombs myself and closed the bomb doors. The pilot put the nose down to try to put out the fires but it just seemed to make them worse. The skin was magnesium alloy and the fire just turned whiter. The fighters came in from behind again and I could see tracer going over the top of the canopy. I looked down the fuselage and there were fires down there as well. The wing root rivets were now showing red inside the fuselage.

The pilot told us to bale out and I got my chute from behind the pilot's seat and fitted his. I was the last out except the pilot. The only instruction we had about baling out was to count to ten before pulling the ripcord, so I did. We must have been doing about 140 mph and it felt as if I was going up, not down. The aircraft passed above me well on fire in both wings. I wore my harness slack because as a flight engineer I was always moving round the aircraft and the chute opened with quite a jerk. I had pins and needles in my pelvis for several days afterwards. My helmet came off, but my new escape boots stayed on. It was so quiet after the noise inside the aircraft, then the fighters dropped flares either side of me and I thought I was going to be shot at, but I now think they were counting us out. All seven of us had baled out. The pilot told me later his chute hadn't opened when he pulled the ripcord and he had to reach inside his chest pack and pull the chute out.

I could see the target burning at one point. We had turned north away from Hanover after being hit and as I came down I could see a big lake – I thought I was going to fall into it, but I landed not far from the shore. On the ground I cut the tops off my escape boots with the knife supplied to turn them into shoes, but later discovered most of the Germans wore boots. I stuck out a bit. It was dark, but I could see I was out in the country.

I hid my chute and started walking north as I thought Denmark would be a good place to aim for. After about half an hour at about 2 a.m. the all-clear sounded. I remember thinking it sounded just like ours. I saw people walking towards me apparently as they returned from air raid shelters and they greeted me with 'Good morning' in German and I replied and walked on. This happened several times and eventually I came to a crossroads and saw masses of people coming back from the shelters. I decided it would be better to avoid them, so took a lane towards some trees and hid in some undergrowth and fell asleep.

I woke about 8 a.m. and made for a road where a man in navy-blue uniform came towards me, smiled and said, 'Heil Hitler'. My response gave the game away and I was taken to the local pub where I found my Australian bomb aimer, F/Sgt Norman Wulff. He was sitting in a bar in complete flying clothing with his parachute on a table.[12]

Sgt Marshall met up with the rest of his crew at Dulag Luft, including his pilot, F/O Murray Caffyn, who had a big bruise to his head, caused by a train door in transit. Within three weeks Caffyn died in Stalag Luft III from a blood clot.

For some unlucky aircrew their lives could be snuffed out even before they left the ground. P/O 'Bluey' Mottershead of 158 Sqn, whose original rear gunner had gone LMF after the Krefeld operation in June, lost his mid-upper gunner, Bill Martin, who had been briefed for Hanover. P/O Mottershead says:

Bill had last flown with me on the Kassel operation of 3 October. Because I'd done an extra op as second dickey the crew were detailed to fly an extra op to catch up. The aircraft Bill Martin was in was taxiing on the perimeter track when the pilot got a red from the control caravan and one or two got out to have a cigarette. The pilot got a green and opened up, not knowing one of his gunners wasn't aboard and Bill was blown under the tail wheel of a fully laden Halifax behind and it killed him. I wasn't on the squadron that night and didn't find out until the next morning.[13]

Crews of the heavy bomber squadrons who had suffered so much in the past six weeks over Mannheim, Munich and Hanover were now rested in the moon period. For Halifax squadrons there was a stand-down which lasted two weeks. It was an opportunity to put the memories of flaming bombers, walls of bursting flak and seemingly impenetrable forests of search-lights behind them with a dash for the liberty bus into the nearest town and whichever pub had been marked as the squadron's own.

The Canadian 432 Sqn were about to begin conversion to Lancasters from their Wellingtons, which would take them off the battle order for a few weeks. They had moved to East Moor from Skipton-on-Swale on 18 September and some atonement was due to the town council of Harrogate. The Air Ministry's Provost Marshal's branch had felt bound to visit the station just before the move about another complaint of a Wellington buzzing the town. Over the next few nights Betty's Bar at York would make a better target. To the east Bridlington was the attraction for Halifax crews from 466 RAAF Sqn at Leconfield and of 158, less than 5 miles away at Lissett.

Val Clarkson was a young secretary in Bridlington Town Hall who had moved to the resort after being bombed out of her Hull home with her widowed mother on her nineteenth birthday. Her friends, as Bomber Command hit back in the autumn and winter of 1943, were the boys from the bomber stations. She remembers:

158 Sqn's pub was the Brunswick in Bridlington town centre; the flyers and their girlfriends had a special room downstairs we called the 'Ops Room' where we used to meet and have sing-songs. If anyone had just been commissioned his friends would pour beer into his new hat and

then drink from it. It was a way of screwing up the new hat, making it look operational.

We used to meet up with the boys from the bomber stations at the Spa Ballroom and the Pavilion Ballroom at Bridlington. There was a dance practically every night. They would come in from Lissett and from Driffield and Leconfield. They were very young, some of them only teenagers, and they loved to be in the company of girls and of their parents as well. No doubt they were missing their own mums and dads. My own mother was frequently in our company, joining in the jollity at the dances and pubs we frequented. She was a young widow and the boys liked to have older people around. If when we were dancing we saw any of our crowd we would link arms and bellow, 'Are we downhearted, noooo!' The spirit was fantastic.

In the moon period stand-down between 8 October and 18 October the young RAF, Canadian and Australian aircrew from Lissett were in Bridlington on most nights. Val Clarkson recalls:

To find out if the boys would be coming in that night for the evening dance, beer, sing-song and fish and chips one of the girls would ring the aerodrome and ask to speak to her particular friend in the sergeants' or officers' mess. If the telephone operator said: 'I'm sorry, I can't connect you' we knew they were on ops. It was a real giveaway. We would later hear the bombers going out over Flamborough Head. There was quite a noise in the sky and we would hope for their return.

In a long stand-down there would be a chance on most bases to organise a weekend squadron dance. From Lissett buses would be sent into Bridlington to pick up the girls who had planned to go and would bring them home again. Sometimes, amid the gaiety the war would intrude, death peeking with dreadful certainty over a girl's shoulder as she waltzed in her best frock with an airman in best blue.

Val Clarkson remembers one such night at another air force station, Leeming:

I went to a dance in the sergeants' mess and was dancing with a young man in aircrew. He asked me if I would like to see inside a Halifax bomber. I'm sure it was against the rules but he walked me across to his dispersal in the dark. The aircraft looked huge, looming out of the darkness. When we went into it it seemed so bleak, there was a smell to it and I found it frightening to be in it, even on the ground. I told him I found it very scary even without being fired at. He told me he was frightened when he was in it too.

Then he broke down and cried. He was embarrassed and after a while he recovered himself and we went back to the dance. I was so sad for him. Significantly, I never saw him again.

It happened such a lot that people you knew went missing. I remember meeting one particular nice aircrew boy at a dance and arranged to meet him there in two days' time. He did not arrive. When I asked his friends where he was I was told: 'He went for a Burton over Germany last night.' We developed a hardness to such news, but it was exciting when someone you thought you would never see again 'walked it' back. There were two occasions when this caused considerable trouble because the girl left behind had taken up with someone else. Friendships were so fleeting.

The aircrew wouldn't tell you of their experiences over Germany; they just laughed it off. If someone started to talk about a trip and they thought he was shooting a line as they called it, they would interrupt and say: 'There I was at 2,000 feet, nothing on the clock', and everybody would laugh.[14]

THE last of the four Hanover operations, on 18 October, would not require the Halifax boys to dice with death. Their time would come four days later in a Kassel raid, which would claim three aircraft from the much-battered 158 Sqn.

The Luftwaffe controller directed his fighters into the stream of 360 Lancasters heading for Hanover fifty-one minutes before the Pathfinders arrived over the city and Bomber Command's post-raid report considered that possibly a record number of fighters were in the area as the first target indicators went down. But the poor weather conditions over Hanover spared the crews from a bloodbath and the inhabitants from another colossal attack. Wireless operator Sgt Tom Hall, now with 166 Sqn, recalls the confusion: 'The Pathfinders weren't successful in marking the target. It was covered by cloud and we were just able to unload on fires. In fact we couldn't be sure if it was a raid or not.'[15]

It was also only the second time Bomber Command had employed a new technique in ruining the Reich, the use of a German-speaking special radio operator in 101 Sqn Lancasters to jam the broadcasts of the *nachtjäger* controllers. The equipment, coded Airborne Cigar (ABC), had first been used in a Stuttgart raid on 7 October. The operators looked for signals as blips on a cathode ray tube then flicked a switch to listen in. If the blip was a broadcast to fighters the special operator could tune one of his three transmitters to the frequency and broadcast a warbling tone.

Four nights later the RAF would add to its bank of jammers with Corona, a team based at West Kingsdown in Kent monitoring the German running commentary to night fighters on a captured German receiver. The German-speaking operators, many of them Jews who had fled from Hitler, would then broadcast false instructions to the fighters, ordering them off on spurious courses or even to land. It proved a continuing irritation to the German controllers and *nachtjäger* crews in months to come. When not engaged in giving false instructions to the anxious night-fighter pilots desperately seeking news of the bomber stream, the Corona operators broadcast recordings of the Führer's speeches to them.

The advent of ABC caused a stepping up in security at 101 Sqn and the ban on the use of cameras on operational stations was even more strictly enforced at Ludford Magna, where the Lancasters now sprouted extra radio aerials. W/O Peter Johnson, now coming to the end of his tour, remembers: 'The special operator on our crew was a Czech called Otto Fischel. We called him "Official". The special operators had their own briefings and were sort of implanted into the aircraft. You didn't even pass the time of day with them. It was very hush-hush.'[16]

ABC had given Bomber Command an enormous advantage on the Stuttgart raid, only 1.4 per cent of the 343 Lancasters being lost, but it seldom took the Luftwaffe long to catch up and on the Hanover raid of 18 October, despite poor weather hampering the night fighters, eighteen Lancasters were lost, 5 per cent of those that had set out. Eleven bombers returned with damage from fighter attacks and two reported destroying enemy aircraft. One of those lost was the five-thousandth RAF bomber to be shot down since the war began. PFF's marking problems resulted in most bombs falling in open country north of the city.

Bomber Command would not return again that autumn. Instead, the build-up would continue for the Battle of Berlin as more new squadrons were formed in Bomber Command. It meant that experienced aircrew were recalled at short notice for a second tour and F/Lt Alex Flett suddenly found himself planning routes for the first operation of 625 Sqn on Hanover on the 18th, as the new squadron's navigation leader. He had finished his first tour on 460 Sqn with the Berlin raid of 31 August, his twenty-sixth op. He says:

> Every crew wanted to have at least one Berlin raid in their log book and when we got home we thought: 'One more done, one more less to do', but after we got off the aircraft we were told: 'You've finished.' At that time on 460 Sqn the chances of getting through a tour were between five and ten to one.
>
> I was sent to Faldingworth as a navigator instructor and was only there a month when I got a call to go up to 1 Group headquarters at Bawtry Hall where I was asked if I would like to go as navigation leader at 625 Sqn, just forming. We started from scratch, we didn't even have any tables, we were doing the charts on the floor. They were calling maximum efforts all the time. If a navigator got a cold or something they wouldn't let him fly, so that was another aircraft they couldn't put up, so I stepped in as spare nav. I flew with eight or nine different crews. One navigator went completely off and was sent to the discipline centre at Sheffield and I finished my tour with his crew.*[17]

The new 625 Sqn found itself pitched into battle at a time when the second of two very heavy raids was made against Kassel, which would have shades of Hamburg in intensity. The first big operation on Kassel, important for its aircraft and locomotive works, had been launched on 3 October. It was an example of how in area bombing an attack could go completely wrong and yet still succeed. H2S misled the PFF blind markers and they considerably overshot the aiming point. As a result, bombing by the following Main Force of more than 500 aircraft was scattered, most bombs falling on the western suburbs of Kassel and outlying villages instead of the town centre. But creepback resulted in devastation of the eastern suburb of Wolfshanger and a nearby ammunition dump went up, destroying eighty-four military buildings.

RCAF Sgt Lance Buttler had come over to England in February 1943 as an airframe mechanic with 405 Sqn at Leeming. After a while there was a recruiting drive for air gunners and flight engineers to replace those lost in the Battle of the Ruhr and Buttler volunteered. He didn't tell his parents. In the chilly, damp evening of Sunday, 3 October he found himself a fully fledged flight engineer waiting by the 428 Sqn aircraft of Sgt Ken McArthur at two-squadron Middleton St George to board for his first operation. It was the third time in three days he had been briefed. Bad weather over Germany had scrubbed the op until now.

In his later private memoirs he wrote:

> Planes were lined up on either side of the runway, 419 Moose Sqn and our Sqn, Ghost. I remember the padres with their bicycles – the Protestant, the Roman Catholic and the Salvation Army with their baskets full of gum, chocolate bars and other goodies. I remember their words of encouragement even though they knew full well that some of us would not be returning.

A flare arcing into the blackness signalled the crews to board their aircraft and one by one the Halifaxes from each squadron trundled noisily,

---

* Alex Flett, by then a squadron leader, finished his second tour in 1944 on exactly the same day and month he had finished his first and was awarded a bar to his DFC.

barking and coughing, down parallel lines on the perimeter track divided by the airfield itself and lined up to take off. At Sgt McArthur's signal Sgt Buttler put his gloved hand behind the pilot's and applied full power, to send the Halifax bounding along the runway for the North Sea and Germany.

The novice crew were coned over Hanover, but corkscrewed out of it with minor flak damage. They had lost several thousand feet but went on to Kassel to bomb and had turned for home when they were hit by flak. Sgt Buttler wrote:

> The pilot had just started evasive action when the second shot hit us full on and I think we knew we were finished for the night. The plane was on fire, the engines had cut out, the intercom was gone and hydraulic oil was everywhere. I emptied two fire extinguishers, which did little good.

The aircraft was now down to 3,500 feet and Sgt McArthur ordered a bale-out, with the wounded wireless operator being helped out first. The bomb aimer, F/O Tom Elliott, should have been next, but instead he waved Sgt Buttler to go in front. 'The pilot and bombardier were right behind me but didn't make it,' Sgt Buttler wrote. 'My chute had no sooner opened than I was in pine trees and the trees saved me from serious injury.'[18] The first thought of Sgt Buttler, who would be captured two days later, was what a shock it would be to his parents to find out their son had volunteered for aircrew.

F/Sgt Alex Wood, skippering a 15 Sqn Stirling, didn't get as far as Kassel before he was shot down. He recalls:

> We were due a turning point and the navigator couldn't get an astro fix because of cloud cover, there were no landmarks on the ground and radio fixes weren't reliable, so we dropped an incendiary bomb for the rear gunner to take a drift reading with his gun sight. It wasn't the first time we had done it and you couldn't just press on regardless, but we were attacked by a fighter from starboard below. The rear gunner

shot him down. But we had been hit in the flare chute, which exploded the photoflash there. It blew the flare chute out of the aeroplane and left a big hole in the bottom of the fuselage. The wireless operator had been there because he put the incendiary through the flare chute and was wounded in the knee.

The cannon shells coming up the fuselage killed the engineer and several shells exploded in the aircraft, but didn't do any damage apart from leaving the bomb aimer suffering from shell shock. The incendiary bombs in the bomb bay were set on fire and the electrics were shot up and the starboard inner engine was burning. I tried to put out the fires by diving but it didn't work.

We couldn't open the bomb doors to jettison, so didn't have any alternative but to get out. We had no intercom, of course, so I used the battery-operated signalling device to signal to everybody else to bale out. I flew the aircraft while the bomb aimer, wireless operator and navigator went out from the front. I kept flying long after I thought was necessary for the crew to get out, then set the autopilot on a gentle climb because I didn't want the aircraft exploding when there were other Stirlings about and went down the stairs between the seats to the front escape hatch. I found I couldn't open the hatch.

So I went round to the front of it and it still wouldn't come and I thought it must be because the aircraft's climbing. But I thought: 'It'll stall in a minute', and when it stalled the hatch shot up and I dived straight out. We had lost a lot of height and I got out at about 3,000 feet. The parachute opening had temporarily knocked me out and broke a tooth and I came to just before I landed – in a ploughed field at Haste, near Osnabrück. Apparently the aircraft hit a block of flats at Osnabrück and killed about ten people. I had sprained my left ankle and left knee and my back had been injured getting out of the aeroplane. I got up and found myself facing a farmer with a shotgun.

He took me to his farmhouse and his teenaged daughter dressed a wound in my head where I think a bullet or shrapnel had shot across the scalp. He called the Luftwaffe, who took me to an aerodrome. I was put in a hut with two guards and was given food and the next morning I was taken by ambulance to a military hospital in Lingen and there I met up with the bomb aimer and wireless operator. The bomb aimer was suffering from shell shock and was mentally wandering. We were in hospital about a week. We were taken by train to Frankfurt, changing at Cologne, and at Dulag Luft I met up with Jack Curtis, the navigator. The two gunners were apparently dead. I don't know if they were killed in the aircraft.

At Dulag Luft I was in a cell on my own and the heating was turned up high and then cold and high again. I was interviewed by a hauptmann who said he came from Hamburg and told me: 'I'm going to have you shot because you killed my family in Hamburg.' They seemed to know all about our squadron; they knew the CO had been killed in a flying accident and the new CO had been shot up on the aerodrome by an intruder. Eventually I was taken to Stalag IVB at Mühlberg.[19]

P/O Wilkie Wanless, the 76 Sqn air gunner who found himself flying eleven operations with six different crews after his own crew were shot down during his prolonged stay in hospital, was about to meet up with his old skipper at Stalag Luft III. He remembers:

It was my twenty-fourth op. We had flown towards Magdeburg then were supposed to turn to head towards Kassel partly back on ourselves. After the turn a night fighter came underneath and hit us in the fuselage and the starboard wing. Straight away it was blazing like a torch. I think the mid-upper gunner had been killed and the pilot told us to get out. I told him I was baling out from the rear turret and everybody else had gone. I made quite a delayed drop because I was afraid of being hit by another aircraft in the stream. After pulling my ripcord I saw the aircraft fly on a long way, then it made a sudden turn to the right and went straight in. I don't think the pilot, Arthur Thorpe, got out.* I didn't know him very well; I'd talked to him a bit in the

---

* P/O Thorpe was in fact killed, as was the mid-upper gunner.

mess. I came down at Detmold. It was about 9 p.m. and I got rid of the parachute and started walking. I thought I'd get to Switzerland, but I was picked up a few days later.[20]

THE raid on Kassel had been effective, damaging both the Henschel and the Fieseler aircraft factories, but bore no comparison to what happened on the second operation nineteen days later. Again H2S led the blind markers to overshoot the aiming point, but the visual markers following on correctly found the centre of the town in the light of their flares. 'They concentrated their TIs most accurately and were admirably supported by the backers-up,' said the post-raid report. 'Reconnaisance photographs revealed extraordinary destruction.'[21]

The devastation was indeed awe-inspiring. The bombing had been so concentrated that it produced 3,600 blazes the services were unable to cope with and for a while created a firestorm. That meant more buildings would be completely destroyed than lightly damaged, unlike in a normal raid. More than 5,500 people died, many trapped in their shelters as in Hamburg. More than 60 per cent of the town's living accommodation was lost.

The uncontrollable conflagrations destroyed more than 150 industrial buildings and the local Gestapo headquarters. Crucially, the Fieseler aircraft factory, making V1 flying bombs, was so badly damaged that the raid further delayed the doodlebug assault on Britain. Another piece of the Peenemünde puzzle begun at Friedrichshafen in June had fallen into place. The RAF's raid report read:

Seven days after the attack fires were still burning in Kassel. The central city area presented a scene of utter devastation and the damage extended to the industrial districts on both sides of the river Fulda as well as to suburbs. In the oldest part of town in the main business shopping centre between the river and Konigsplatz no building was left intact.[22]

WHAT happened in Kassel was what Bomber Command was always trying to achieve: to finish the war quickly without the need for invasion and before the Nazis could develop a doomsday weapon such as a nuclear bomb. The cost to the Command itself had been dreadful, forty-three aircraft going down, mostly to fighters. It was an attrition rate of 7.6 per cent and would undoubtedly have been higher if 125 of the 569 bombers that set out had not had to turn back because of problems caused by the severe freezing weather en route.

Sgt Wilfred Hart was a wireless operator in one of the Pathfinder aircraft, from 35 Sqn, one of the first to go down, but as a result of flak:

We were hit by a shell burst over the target. There was a sound like hail on a tin roof. The pilot got a piece of shrapnel in his chest and the two starboard engines caught fire. The pilot didn't say anything, but my position was underneath him and I saw blood dripping in front of me and realised he was hurt. The bomb aimer went to take over, but he couldn't hold it on course. It wasn't spinning, but it lurched round in a circle to the left and was going down. We decided we had to bale out.

We could hear nothing from the gunners, so I went back and couldn't get any reply from the turrets and realised the gunners were dead. We were then pretty low, about 5,000 feet. I gave the pilot a morphine injection then threw him out. I put his hand on the D ring knowing the slipstream would jerk his arm, pulling the chute open. I was next out and glimpsed the burning aircraft above me.

I don't remember pulling the ripcord. It was quite a relief when I heard it crack open. I didn't see the ground, but landed in a field on my back on an outcrop of rock. Two of the boys, Sgt Wally Kingham, the engineer, and Sgt Arthur Jordan, the navigator, came down near the pilot and heard him cry out on the ground and found him.* We had gone out some way away from the target and I couldn't see any of the other crew. I got up and started walking and I was picked up at a road block a few hours later.[23]

---

* The pilot, P/O S. A. Durrant, survived.

Navigator John Fell of 102 Sqn, now a pilot officer, was on his twenty-seventh operation. He says:

> I remember the intense fires. I stood over the bomb aimer's shoulder as he dropped the bombs. I went back to my table to check the course for base when within two or three minutes one of the gunners called up to tell the pilot to turn. Shortly afterwards there was a sort of panic on the intercom and the starboard wing was on fire. The pilot, F/Lt Ned Kelly, said he was trying to put the fire out. We were diving and there was a lot of confusion on the intercom then F/Lt Kelly suddenly came through with 'Parachute, parachute, bale out'.
>
> My station was right over the escape hatch and it was my job to be first out, so that the others could get out. I moved my seat back, opened the escape hatch and dropped it through the hole then followed it. I guess we were then at about 12,000 feet. It was about minus 30 degrees outside and I immediately froze. I tried to count to twelve then pulled the ripcord. I was frozen all the way down. I didn't see the ground, so was very relaxed when I landed in a field.
>
> It was pitch-black and I could see the fires of Kassel burning in the distance. I must have landed a few miles outside. The most sensible thought I had at the time was I must keep Kassel at my back and keep walking. I tried to bury my parachute, but the ground was frozen hard, so I eventually tucked it under the roots of a tree. I walked all night. The following morning I was walking through a forest and saw someone coming as I turned a corner. He was in a grey uniform. I couldn't hide. As I passed him he said: 'Guten Tag' and I replied, 'Guten Tag' then as I walked on I heard a bellow and when I turned round he was pointing a gun at me.

P/O Fell's air war was at an end. He discovered later that all but one of his crew had survived.[24]

Flight engineer Sgt Robert Williams was in the first wave of the attack on Kassel in a 78 Sqn Halifax. He remembers:

We were headed for Frankfurt on Main as it appeared to be. A short distance from Frankfurt all the aircraft with the exception of about twenty-four Lancasters turned north and headed towards Kassel. This was to fool the Germans who would assume the target was Frankfurt and send up the fighters in large numbers to deal with us, which was evident.

But on the new course the navigator calculated they were three minutes early, making them highly vulnerable to radar-predicted flak in the first wave. They made three circuits to delay their arrival, then bombed the target. Sgt Williams remembers:

Shortly after this there was an uncomfortable explosion near the aircraft followed by another which must have been an anti-aircraft shell resulting in a fire in the port inner engine and damage to the wing. The pilot instructed us to bale out.

The navigator, bomb aimer and radio operator, all being located in the front, left through the nose hatch followed by the second pilot who was with us for experience, which I don't suppose he expected to be this. As the aircraft was flying straight and level I looked at the pilot and he said to me in a somewhat urgent manner: 'Bale out.'

I realised that the aircraft must have been severely damaged and probably the pilot intended to leave himself. I decided to establish if the gunners had managed to free themselves from their turrets so I started to go to the rear of the aircraft and noted that the rear hatch was open.

As I approached the rear door the aircraft lurched to the left, no doubt out of control. The G-force made it almost impossible to move. With extra effort I rolled to the hatch and in a final burst of energy rolled out of the aircraft. I then saw it some way ahead with the port wing well alight.

Sgt Williams's troubles were just beginning. He landed on a main road in Kassel and as he got rid of his chute and harness.

I noticed a mob of unfriendly yobs armed with sticks approaching me. I took to my heels and ran ahead turning left and almost collided with a Luftwaffe officer. He took me into a large building nearby which appeared to be a Luftwaffe administration centre. I was treated gently except for a massive middle-aged woman who shouted to me that Churchill was a mad old man. I was very imprudent and answered 'So is Hitler.' She attempted to strike me on the face, but two officers forcibly removed her.

Before I was taken to a night-fighter station and locked up for the night one of the officers enquired if the aircraft I was in performed orbits some way from Kassel and said his radar had located an aircraft orbiting and fired at it. I pretended I didn't understand, but felt sure it was us.

There was a further ordeal for Sgt Williams the next day. He was taken in an open-topped car around smoking Kassel. He says:

It was alarming as the car stopped frequently and the driver would talk to people. At one stage the car stopped near a large grassed area and there was our aircraft. I was told the pilot had been killed in the crash. I was also told that the second pilot was dead.[25]

Dead too was the rear gunner.

THE 50 Sqn aircraft of bomb aimer Sgt Joseph Porter, whose Munich operation of 2 October was cut short by a faulty turret, paid the price of facing a fully alerted enemy. He recalls:

Going in, there didn't seem to be so many searchlights and flak, but there seemed a lot coming out. I could see a big blaze spreading and fires joining up. We were in the last wave on the target and the Germans knew where we were coming out.

About half an hour after we left the target the Germans dropped a line of flares. It lit up the sky like daylight. We flew right into the middle. The next thing we knew was a fighter came underneath in our blind spot and there was a 'bang, bang' as the cannon shells hit and a fire broke out in the back, setting off the ammunition, then the engines and wings were on fire. The pilot just had time to call out 'Jump' before the intercom went out.

The bomb aimer is supposed to be the first one out. I opened up the hatch and dropped it through, but I heard cases of the bomb aimer going out first, then the crew managing to get the fires out and bring the aircraft home, so I waited. The engineer, Sgt Tudball, went out; the navigator came down and went out, then the wireless operator came down. He only had one side of his chute clipped on, so I clipped it on then he went out. The mid-upper gunner, Sgt Nicklin, couldn't go out through the rear door because it was all on fire back there, so he came up to the front. He got stuck in the hole with his bulky electric suit, so I had to stand on his head to push him out. The Australian rear gunner, Bob Easdown, had gone out through his doors at the back of his turret.

I looked up to where the pilot was sitting in his seat and gave him the thumbs up to say I was going and he gave me the same sign back, so I thought he would follow, but that was the last I saw of him. What happened to him I don't know, but he died.

I think we were at about 5,000 feet when I went out. The plane was a ball of flames as it went over the top of me. I saw the top of a tree, then the next thing I had hit the side of a bank in the middle of a field, apparently near a place called Hexum, hitting my knee and shoulder. I now have a replacement knee and the nerve has gone in my shoulder. The wireless operator came down in a tree. He survived but his face was cut to pieces.

After I landed I hid my chute and flying gear under a tree and headed down to a lane. A car came round with an armed soldier in plus the navigator, Jock. I didn't let on that I knew him. We were taken to a German barracks and we were stripped to our underwear and left in the cold. The navigator, whose boots had come off when he baled out, spoke a bit of German. I was laying the law down because it was so cold and the navigator said: 'I'd be quiet if I were you; they're talking about shooting us.'

We were taken to an aerodrome and were treated fairly well and were then taken by train to Frankfurt. About half a dozen aircrew were on the station while we waited for the train to Frankfurt and these civilians were shaking their fists and shouting at us. Our guards kept them off. I'm sure we would have been beaten up and I think a lot of aircrew were killed after baling out.[26]

Kassel joined the list of targets Bomber Command would not need to return to until the closing stages of the war. The industrial output of Hanover and Mannheim had also been savagely curtailed, though there would be a return to Mannheim the following month. In the period another rung in the ladder of technical development had been climbed by Bomber Command with the advent of ABC and Corona.

But the Luftwaffe too had grown in size and ability. Losses on the last Kassel raid had been a crippling 7.6 per cent of British aircraft. The *nachtjäger* were about to climb to their zenith of achievement. A sweeping reorganisation of the command structure of the night-fighter arm had taken place in mid-October. The fighters were also rapidly being equipped with SN-2 air interception radar, unaffected by the Window then in use. Its use with Schrage Musik upward-firing cannon made for a deadly combination.

Harris, aware of what was ahead in the Battle of Berlin, had visited various stations in mid-September to gauge morale. He had visited 76 Sqn, which had lost eight aircraft in two weeks and was showing a high rate of early returns. Earlier in the year he had visited 57 Sqn and told them only one in three of them would be still alive in six months. They cheered him. This time he reminded 76 Sqn aircrew of their duty in forceful terms, then he travelled to 460 Sqn at Binbrook – where Hughie Edwards VC was the station commander – and 101 Sqn at Ludford Magna.

W/O Peter Johnson remembers:

When Harris came to Ludford all the aircrew were called into the briefing room to meet him. Everybody was pretty apprehensive – this was the commander-in-chief, after all – but he said: 'I'll answer any questions you like, except about air gunners' pay.' That got a laugh because gunners had pretty strong feelings about what they got. It was all pretty good-humoured after that.[27]

Any light relief was welcome in the briefing rooms, billets and messes of Bomber Command that autumn. The euphoria which had gripped Bomber Command headquarters after Hamburg and Peenemünde was slipping away into the possibility that there would be no knock-out blows, simply slow erosion of German industrial ability, which would cost crews and aircraft in great numbers.

CHAPTER FOURTEEN

'THE GREATEST OF AIR BATTLES'

The campaign which was to become known as Bomber Command's Passchendaele opened deceptively. The weather in the first two weeks of November was unusually mild and as the Battle of Berlin began, losses on the first two raids were comfortingly low. There was further hope at Bomber Command headquarters in new equipment coming on stream. The technical war would step up another gear with the formation of 100 (Bomber support) Group on 23 November, a mix of heavy bombers and night fighters with a range of the new electronic and radio countermeasures equipment to jam and deceive. And the growing technology would further advance with the Pathfinders' acceptance of the first three Mk III H2S sets on 13 November for trials. Another three would soon arrive as Main Force began to be equipped with the less precise 10-cm sets.

As the nights rapidly lengthened, ahead lay the prize target. On 3 November Harris wrote his oft-quoted letter to Churchill giving a brief survey of Bomber Command's great achievements in the year and listing what targets still had to be destroyed. At the head of the list was the Reich capital. 'I await promised USAAF help in this, the greatest of air battles. But I would not propose to wait for ever, or for long if opportunity serves,' he wrote. Then he added: 'We can wreck Berlin from end to end if the USA will come in on it. It will cost us between 400 and 500 aircraft. It will cost Germany the war.'[1]

In fact there was no hope of the USAAF coming in on it, by night or by day. The Americans were not trained for night bombing and there were not the long-range fighters available then to support a daylight offensive on distant targets. Ira Eaker's force was still regrouping after the Schweinfurt raid of 14 October which had had a temporarily dramatic effect on German ball-bearing production, but at a cost of 20 per cent of the crews dispatched. Schweinfurt had proved for the second time in weeks it was a target too far and the doctrine of the self-defensive bomber formation was dead. It was in 1944 that the Eighth Air Force would come into its own – 1943 had proved to be the year of the RAF's great bomber offensive.*

As the British and Commonwealth crews waited, poised for the on-slaught on Berlin, they were ordered not to a distant target, but to make a return to other dangerous territory, the Ruhr, which had been spared the weekly rain of fire and high explosive since the devastating raids of the spring and summer.

The night he dispatched his letter to Churchill Harris staged a new demonstration of Bomber Command's might with an operation by 589 aircraft to Düsseldorf at the same time as 52 Lancasters and 10 Mosquitos carried out a diversionary raid on Cologne.

It had been five months since Düsseldorf had been raided and, as its industry recovered, much had changed in the air war. The static defence system of the Kammhuber Line had made way for free-ranging attacks by fighters guided into the stream by a running commentary. On this night ABC, Corona and the diversionary raid to Cologne confused the night-fighter force, which was first ordered to Bonn, then to Dortmund and Cologne. A minimum of 80 fighters, however, turned up over Düsseldorf, most of them twin-engined.

One of these ended the operational career of a young RAF flight engineer on the night it began as he replaced an injured man on another crew at short notice. Sgt Malcolm White had arrived on 12 Sqn at Wickenby

---

* The Americans would not bomb Berlin until 6 March 1944 although they would eventually cause the greatest loss of life in a single raid on the capital, at least 8,000 dying in the daylight raid of 3 February, 1945. Some estimates put it as high as 25,000.

in the middle of October. He and his crew carried out cross-countries, night flying and bombing exercises, waiting to be put on the battle order. He remembers:

> We were in A Flight and the flight commander told me in the middle of the afternoon of the 3rd that I was on that night as a relief flight engineer because the engineer from another crew, Sgt Fouhse's, had broken his leg in a motor accident. It would be the second operation for Sgt Fouhse's crew. On the first they had shot down a night fighter. Our crew asked if we could all do the operation together – my skipper even said he would pilot the other crew or come as a spare – but they were turned down.
>
> It was overcast, cold and drizzling as we taxied out. I wasn't worried, I remember; the first trip is exciting until you realise what it's all about. Soon after take-off the aircraft developed a fault in the oxygen supply and then engines overheating caused us to throttle back, losing speed and rate of climb so falling behind the main stream. We had managed to climb up to 18,000 feet just before we reached the target, but we were struggling to get to the 20,000 feet required. It was bright moonlight by that time and we got picked up by a searchlight or two. The pilot went into a corkscrew then a Ju88 came into attack, but the gunners saw him, firing back and we seemed to lose him.
>
> We climbed back and made our bombing run, but as we turned away, still with the bomb doors open, in came the Ju88 again and we were riddled. The pilot was corkscrewing as best he could, but the fighter raked us from end to end and the whole of the back of the aircraft was on fire as well as the port wing. I could hear the thump of the explosions. The gunners were shouting instructions to the pilot, but then ended up screaming. Their turrets were alight and they were trapped.
>
> It all went quiet and there were flames everywhere and holes in the canopy. The pilot said: 'Bale out.' He couldn't raise anyone but me on the intercom. I handed him his chute and he clipped it on, then the aircraft plunged out of control in a steep spinning dive. I was floating

around the canopy when I blacked out. I came to in my chute about 30 feet off the ground. The aircraft had exploded.

I think the rest of the crew except the pilot were already dead when that happened. I came down in a field near Düsseldorf. I could see the target burning in the distance. I had lost one flying boot, but I took off my flying gear and harness and hid it all in a ditch with my chute.[2]

The pilot, Canadian Sgt Ray Fouhse, has no idea how he got out of the aircraft. Back in Canada he wrote that after the Ju88 had raked his aircraft front to rear three or four times with cannon fire he realised there was no hope. He recorded:

The fuel tanks and front and rear turrets were on fire, flames were coming through the windscreen and the plane was in a spinning dive. Not knowing whether the crew was still alive I shouted, 'Bale out, bale out.' Somehow I retrieved my chute and snapped it on and managed to release the escape hatch in the canopy. But because of the flames and the wind pressure I couldn't get more than my head out, so I dropped back into my seat and struggled to pull the plane out of the dive. Watching petrol and flames streaming out of holes in the wings I blacked out.[3]

On the ground Sgt White checked his assets for evasion:

I had the escape pack consisting of a compass, some silk maps and paper French and German money. I also had some chocolate and a packet of wine gums. I started walking west, using the compass. I reached a little village and hid in some woods. It rained throughout the night. The next morning I woke to find I was in a little triangle of a wood with farm workers, mostly women, digging potatoes nearby. So I crawled back into the bushes and ate my chocolate bar for breakfast.

A little later I heard voices, looked out and saw a line of farm workers with pitchforks and a policeman with a revolver working their way through the woods. It seemed one of the women in the fields had seen me and raised the alarm. There didn't seem much point in running, particularly with only one boot, so I stood up and waited.

I was escorted to the local jail and kept there overnight where they took my insignia off me and my remaining flying boot. The next day an SS officer with a man in civilian clothes arrived in a big open tourer. I was put in the rear seat between them, and the civilian, who I imagine was Gestapo, made it clear that if I attempted to escape, the SS man would shoot me. I was driven through the outskirts of Düsseldorf, the car stopping several times and I was shown off as a *terrorflieger*. Civilians would gather round and would shout and gesticulate until it got too hectic, then my guards would drive off again to stop somewhere else. I was quite worried. I think I was lucky to survive. A lot of aircrew were killed by civilians.

Eventually I was taken to a nearby Luftwaffe field where I met lots of other aircrew who had been shot down. The Luftwaffe treated us well, allowing us a wash and giving us some food, but I got no shoes. The next day with one Luftwaffe officer to each RAF man a bunch of us were taken by train to Dulag Luft. At Frankfurt station they cleared a waiting room for us for the night and shared their rations with us; they were as good as that.

Sgt White was eventually sent to Stalag IVB at Mühlberg, where he met up with the pilot of his stricken aircraft, Sgt Fouhse. Months later he learned from a 12 Sqn airman, newly arrived in the camp, that his original crew had gone on to complete a full tour with a replacement flight engineer.

Another airman on his first operational flight made a remarkable escape from his exploding Lancaster on the Düsseldorf operation. P/O John Teager was acting as second dickey to F/Lt C. G. Thomas of 49 Sqn when they were attacked by an Me110 on the way in to the target near Cologne before they had split away from the diversionary force. P/O Teager recalls:

There was a lot of flak coming up at the time and he just came straight in, and in the first pass his cannon hit the 4,000-lb bomb and it exploded. I remember lots of light and the sensation of being lifted up then I went through the roof of the Lancaster. Fortunately I had my chute on and as I fell outside the aircraft I pulled the ripcord. We were very high, but I drifted down and landed in a bush in a field. I picked myself up and was on the run for three days. Eventually I made my way into a barn where I fell asleep. Unfortunately someone must have seen me because I woke up to find myself in the hands of the authorities.[4]

The most remarkable story of survival came from a young pilot on 61 Sqn, Bill Reid. The Luftwaffe running commentary for its fighters was already operating as the bomber stream crossed the Dutch coast and an Me110 picked up F/Lt Reid's aircraft, O-Oboe, just after he crossed into enemy territory. It made a head-on attack, smashing the windscreen and wounding Reid in the head and shoulder. He told a journalist afterwards:

I just saw a blinding flash and lost about 2,000 feet before I could pull out again. I felt as if my head had been blown off. Other members of the crew shouted: 'Are you all right?' It was no good telling them that I felt half dead and I said: 'Yes, I feel all right.' I regained course and managed to get my goggles on. My shoulder was a bit stiff and it felt as if someone had hit me with a hammer.

F/Lt Reid said he had never thought of turning back. 'Well, you see, there were lots of other bombers behind us and if we had turned back we might have been a danger to the rest,' he explained. Soon afterwards the Lancaster was attacked again and raked by cannon fire. The navigator was killed and the wireless operator fatally injured. Reid was again wounded and the oxygen system was knocked out. The flight engineer, Sgt James Norris, gave Reid oxygen from a spare bottle. 'I looked for the Pole Star and navigated by that for a bit, then I could see Cologne and turned for Düsseldorf,' Reid said. He unloaded on the target, his bomb aimer getting an aiming point picture. Reid then collapsed and Sgt Norris, who would be awarded the Conspicuous Gallantry Medal, took over. The wounded pilot rallied in time to bring the aircraft in to the USAAF base at Shipdham, where the undercarriage collapsed.

To Reid's astonishment he was visited in hospital by his 5 Group commander Cochrane, told he had won the VC and asked what posting he would like. Reid asked to go to the Dambusters, where he again survived, being blasted through the roof of his exploding Lancaster on 31 July 1944 in an attack on a flying-bomb site. Fortunately he was wearing a seat-type parachute.

THE Düsseldorf operation had been a successful attack; 525 of the aircraft dispatched had got there, unloading Cookies and incendiaries over the centre and south of the city. Despite the heavy Luftwaffe presence at the target only eighteen aircraft had been lost, a manageable 3.4 per cent in the dreadful calculations Bomber Command's statisticians had to make. Of the fifty-two Lancasters and ten Mosquitos sent to Cologne not one was missing.

Another important test had been carried out that night – thirty-eight radial-engined Mk II Lancasters, slowly replacing the Stirlings of 3 Group and Wellingtons of 6 Group, had carried the G-H bombing apparatus on operations for the first time. The device, which operated like Oboe with a transmitter and receiver but in the aircraft, not on the ground, had been used against the Mannesmann-Rohrenweke, manufacturing tubular steel on the northern outskirts of Düsseldorf. The equipment had failed in half of the force, but the remainder had bombed accurately, several of the steelworks,' buildings being burned out. G-H would achieve much in the final year of the war.[5]

Bomber Command now turned away from Germany as squadrons prepared for the Battle of Berlin. There would only be two more operations, on French targets, before the campaign against the Reich capital was opened in two weeks' time. Aircrew found time for nights out at the Saracen's Head in Lincoln, the Eagle in Cambridge or even at the pictures in Nottingham, where *Flying Tigers* starring John Wayne was climbing the cinema circuit and trailers promised that the new Walt Disney masterpiece *Victory Through Air Power* would be coming shortly.

There were lectures on dinghy drill, evasion, landing in fog, and fighter techniques. To keep sharp with the latter even experienced crews sometimes found themselves on fighter affiliation exercises with local Fighter Command training bases.

The crew of the 18-year-old air gunner Sgt Roy Child, who had been followed home by the Luftwaffe from the Berlin raid of 31 August, found themselves detailed for such an exercise in their 90 Sqn Stirling on 9 November. Sgt Child was having hospital treatment that day so wasn't with his crew when they took off from Tudenham to rendezvous with a Newmarket-based Hurricane. Within an hour the Hurricane had collided with the Stirling and the bomber's crew were all dead, one of the approximately 1,500 aircrew lost in training accidents in 1943. 'After the accident I did not want to stay on the squadron and requested a transfer,' Child says. 'The request was granted and in December I was posted to 7 Sqn Pathfinders, flying in Lancasters from Oakington.'[6]

There were other crashes as aircraft were delivered from factories and hurriedly prepared for operations. F/Sgt Ernie Webb, the 49 Sqn pilot attacked by a fighter over Mannheim on 23 September, found himself on the battle order at Fiskerton on 11 November for a raid by 313 Lancasters of 5 and 8 groups on railway yards at Modane in southern France. As his regular aircraft, O-Orange, had been shot up over Mannheim, he had been assigned a different aircraft on each of the eight operations since. He remembers:

For Modane we were given P-Peter, a new aircraft on the squadron. We hadn't even given it an air test and as we sped down the runway I suddenly felt the aircraft turning to port because the tyre pressure on that side had gone down. We careered off the runway through the FIDO fog dispersal pipe system, did a 180-degree turn and came to a halt as the undercarriage collapsed. All four engines burst into flames and I went out quickly through my side window onto the wing and jumped off backwards. I ran round the back of the aircraft and saw the rear turret had broken off and the rear gunner was trapped in it.

He couldn't move his leg and called out to me. I straightened his leg and got him out. It was just bruised.

Everybody else was out but we couldn't account for the wireless operator and the navigator. The fire crew arrived and there were five of us there pretty confused when the MO came up with the ambulance and asked about the others. I said we didn't know where they were, so the MO said: 'Let's go and look for them in the aircraft.' It wasn't very pleasant to go back into the burning aircraft, but he and I went in where the rear turret had been. We couldn't find them so we went off in the ambulance to sick quarters. The nav and wop walked in about twenty minutes later. They had taken off in a different direction.

We were fortunate because we didn't have a Cookie on board. We were carrying eight 1,000-lb bombs which weren't armed until we were on our way, so they were safe. A Cookie would have gone off. I have thought many times how lucky we were.[7]

The brand new P-Peter was a write-off, lost through faulty tyre pressure. F/Sgt Webb and his crew recovered from their ordeal in time for the first operation in the Battle of Berlin seven days later. They would make seven raids to the capital, including the last of the year.

JUST before 9 a.m. on 18 November the staff of the underground ops room at High Wycombe snapped to attention as the C-in-C arrived for his daily conference, which he liked to call 'Morning Prayers'. Harris sat down and was surrounded by his immediate staff and liaison officers from the Navy and USAAF as he listened to the weather forecast and target possibilities. He paused for a moment, then with customary brevity ground out the one word: 'Berlin'. He stood up and walked to the door where he was handed his cap, then as it closed behind him the feverish activity began of route planning, selecting bomb loads and PFF TIs, and alerting groups to put up 440 Lancasters.

This was the moment Harris had waited for, the battle that would prove his theory that war could be won by bombing alone. The head would be removed from the dragon.

That night as F/Sgt Webb lined up on Fiskerton's main runway in U-Uncle, eyes peering through the damp blackness for the control caravan's green flare, he and the hundreds of other Lancaster skippers now holding their bucking charges against brakes at airfields throughout Lincolnshire prepared to cast the first die in a campaign that Harris was sure would bring Germany's leaders to the negotiating table. The year that had begun with tests by a few on how to destroy the Ruhr promised to end with a trial by many of the Nazis' ability to continue.

No fewer than 835 heavy bombers would be in German skies that night, a huge diversionary raid of 395 Halifaxes, Stirlings and a few Lancasters heading south for Mannheim/Ludwigshafen to draw the fighters as the other force flew to Berlin. It was the highest total so far that year of bombers in the air on one night and they would cross the enemy coast simultaneously 250 miles apart.

There were also two important technical changes: aircraft would be fed over the target at a new, increased rate of twenty-seven per minute to swamp the Wilde Sau, and the all-up weight of Lancasters was increased to 65,000 lbs, allowing another half-ton of bombs. They would help to make up for the ones that would not be arriving by the USAAF's Flying Fortresses.

As it was, Harris, who had waited so long, could not have picked a worse time to begin the Battle of Berlin. The weather, which had been so unseasonably kind in the weeks of November, now closed in. Over the next two weeks there would be snow flurries over Lincolnshire and Nottinghamshire with frost on seven nights. And it would be cloudy over Germany. The cloud would continue for four weeks, covering five Berlin raids, and it would not be until the middle of December that photo reconnaissance would give an inkling of what had been achieved. The cloud over Berlin on the night of the 18th was so thick that the post-raid report could only conclude:

The TIs could be seen cascading to the ground and much of the effort undoubtedly fell on the city. The comparative failure of this operation resulted from unserviceable Y (H2S) sets; an unexpectedly light wind en route delaying the backers-up so that for five or six minutes only one green TI could be seen burning; and a smokescreen hampering visibility.[8]

The only working Mk III set had developed a fault on the way across the North Sea and its host aircraft had to return as eighteen of the twenty-six 10-cm H2S sets in the other Pathfinder aircraft also failed. A total of thirty-two industrial premises were hit in scattered bombing. However, the bad weather and the diversionary raid had kept the fighters away. Only nine Lancasters were lost, 2 per cent, and there was no evidence any had gone down to fighters. In terms of losses the Mannheim/Ludwigshafen raid with its Halifaxes and Stirlings had fared far worse – twenty-three aircraft were missing, 5.8 per cent. There too the cloud blanket led to a haphazard attack, destroying more than 300 buildings across the two towns.

If the raid of 18 November was disappointing, the one mounted four nights later was a resounding success, the greatest achievement of the campaign against the capital.

The forecast had been for clear conditions over the bases, broken medium-level cloud over the target and low cloud or fog over much of the rest of Germany, which would hinder the night fighters. The planners took the risk of a straight route in and out with no diversions and the rate of aircraft over the target was increased to thirty-four per minute despite the considerable collision risk.

F/Sgt Bernard Downs, who had begun his tour with his own crew over Hanover on 22 September, was detailed for Berlin with 78 Sqn. He recalls:

> It was my first raid on the capital and I can recall a great friend of mine who wasn't flying that night, Tommy Smith, coming up towards the cockpit at dispersal to wish me luck and I was shaking almost. I suppose it was because it was the No. 1 target. It passed off very quickly once we got going, but the defences lived up to my expectations – lots of flak and many searchlights.[9]

Every squadron in Bomber Command, apart from the Dambusters and the two Oboe Mosquito squadrons, was on the battle order – 764 aircraft, a new record for one target. Harris was taking a massive risk, as he had had to do many times. If the forecast had been wrong and the night fighters had been able to get airborne and into the stream early, as they would on a Nuremberg raid in four months' time, the carnage would have been extreme and the Battle of Berlin would have been over almost before it had begun.

The first Pathfinders arrived over the city just before 8 p.m. to find the forecast for the target itself had been incorrect. Berlin was again covered by ten-tenths cloud. And three of the five Lancasters carrying the new 3-cm radar had had to turn back with faulty equipment, but two Mk III sets were showing a clear outline and the special blind markers accurately dropped four red TIs over the aiming point slightly to the east of the city centre.

The ordinary blind markers quickly followed with both sky and ground markers – a new technique of mixing the two whatever the conditions, which would become known as the Berlin Method – and the first of five mixed waves of Main Force droned remorselessly on in swelling resonance, their bomb doors gaping to begin releasing their Cookies and incendiaries.

Those bombs tumbled through thousands of feet of cloud to flash, crack, blast and roar across the administrative area near the Brandenburger Tor. Each type of bomb had its own familiar sound: the 'pressure–suction–pressure–suction' thump of the Cookies, the rustle like a flock of birds of the showering 4-lb incendiaries, the short, sharp explosion of the 30-lb incendiary bomb.

At last the true nature of war was brought home to the Nazi hierarchy, who, apart from Josef Goebbels, did not visit the bombed cities. These bombs were falling in their own back yards, destroying their offices and apartments. One by one the sources of Nazi evil, which had spread from the Baltic to the Urals and west to the English Channel, were being ground to dust along the Wilhelmstrasse. The Gestapo headquarters, where victims suffered in the cellars, was hit that night, as were the official residence of Himmler, the Ministry of Justice, the Foreign Office, the Propaganda

Ministry, the Treasury and the Ministry of Transport, which facilitated the final journeys of the Jews. All were damaged by fire and high explosive.

And, amazingly, it was all happening through such thick cloud that the night fighters were largely grounded. Goebbels recorded the Nazi shock in his diary:

> The attack began shortly after the alert had been sounded. It was a major, grade-A attack. I was in the bunker in the Wilhelmplatz. It wasn't long before fires started all around. Bombs and land mines of notable size were dropped over the whole government quarter. They destroyed everything around the Potsdamer Platz. The pressure was so strong that even our bunker, though constructed deep underground, began to shake.

He went on that the State Playhouse and the Reichstag were aflame and:

> people keep coming and going in our bunker just as at a command point. Well after all we are living in a war and many a sector at the front would certainly not want to trade with us, so enormous is the strain. Hell itself seems to have broken loose over us. Mines and explosive bombs keep hurtling down upon the government quarter. One after another of the most important buildings begins to burn.

Marie Vassiltchikov, a Russian-born aristocrat who worked in the district at the German Foreign Ministry's Information Department, described in her own diary how she and her family had rushed to shelter in the basement of their home not far from her office:

> We had hardly got there when we heard the first approaching planes. The barking of the flak was suddenly drowned by a very different sound – that of exploding bombs, first far away and then closer and closer, until it seemed as if they were literally falling on top of us.
>
> At every crash the house shook. The air pressure was dreadful and the noise deafening. For the first time I understood what the expression *bombenteppich* (bomb carpet) means. At one point there was a

shower of broken glass and all three floors of the basement flew into the room. We pressed them back into place and leant against them.[10]

Within twenty-two minutes the raid was over and the huge air fleet flew on to the east of the target, turned south then thundered home across Belgium and Holland along the same route they had taken in. Crews over the target reported seeing a huge explosion, possibly the Neukölln gasworks being destroyed. More than one hundred people had died in a shelter nearby. Twenty-six aircraft had been lost, 3.4 per cent. The enormous gamble decided upon at High Wycombe twelve hours before had worked.

The newspapers, which had so promoted 'Berlin Next' after the Battle of Hamburg, had been slow to realise that the Battle of Berlin had finally arrived, but on 23 November the *Daily Express* trumpeted: 'Berlin again: Twice in Five Nights'. Even the German radio was admitting at 1.30 a.m. 'reports of destruction of irreplaceable historic and cultural buildings and damage to buildings housing diplomatic missions of neutral States'. It was useful information. Many embassies had been hit, including the former British embassy, and they were all based around the Wilhelmstrasse. The bombers' photoflash pictures would reveal nothing but cloud. They had taken off into cloud, bombed through cloud and returned through cloud, without seeing a scrap of land. The destruction would not be revealed to reconnaissance until the overcast cleared in mid-December.

The comforting murmur of the bombers returning was heard along the east coast of Britain from the Wash to the Tees as weary pilots let down in the blackness, steering from Occult to Pundit lights and peering out for the arrangement of searchlights that meant the welcoming Sandra lights of the home airfield. Ten per cent of the fifty Stirlings that had set out eight hours before would not be back and the high rate of attrition of Stirling crews meant the type would now be withdrawn from German targets. At Pocklington there was a sudden flash in the circuit, a Halifax of 10 Sqn and another of 77 Sqn colliding and plunging to earth. None of either crew survived.

F/Sgt Downs felt the slight bump as the wheels of R-Robert touched then held the tarmac of the main runway at Breighton. There was the slight hiss of the brakes as he turned off at the end of the strip and onto the perimeter track to dispersal, his first Berlin raid behind him. He remembers:

> When I got back and climbed out of the aircraft at dispersal all these flashbulbs were going off. There were a lot of photographers and reporters. Why 78 Sqn had been picked and my crew in particular I don't know. It may have been because I had a mixed Commonwealth crew. The flight engineer was Canadian, the navigator was from New Zealand and the two gunners were Australian. Our photograph appeared on the front page of the *Daily Telegraph* the next day and in various other national newspapers. I don't think we were the youngest crew on Berlin that night but I was the youngest in my crew. I had had my twentieth birthday less than a month before. I'm amazed when I look back now at how young we were. I did five Berlin raids in all.[11]

There was also a surprise for 21-year-old P/O 'Bluey' Mottershead, whose 158 Sqn Halifax had been hit by a 30-lb incendiary over Mannheim on 23 September. He remembers:

> My wireless operator was complaining about the Berlin raid because he said it wasn't our turn to operate and another crew should have been on. I never gave it a thought. When we got back the CO, W/Cdr Jock Calder, realised what stress we were going through as very young men and after debriefing he said: 'That's it, Bluey, no more.' We had done twenty-seven instead of thirty. It was jubilation. We were so relieved not to have to go again. This had been our third Berlin operation and the Battle of Berlin was a terrible strain. I was posted to an Oboe course and went to a transmitter station in Norfolk.[12]

For those with a tour still to complete there would be no rest, as there would not be for the people of Berlin. Within hours the city would be selected as the target again. It would be the same route as before with the same zero hour of 1958 and this time the Wilde Sau would be waiting.

Berliners, aided by more than 50,000 soldiers drafted in from up to 60 miles away, had laboured all day in a pea-soup-like fog of smoke and ashes to clear the devastated streets while firemen still tackled the blazes. The 337 bombers arriving over the city were guided from 50 miles away by eleven huge fires, the glow pulsating through the blanket of cloud, and many unloaded on those. Staging another major raid within twelve hours of aircraft returning from the first had proved beyond the capability of most squadrons and only 443 aircraft, nearly all Lancasters, could be got ready in time. There had also been a high proportion of early returns, the highest percentage from 1 Group, which was loading maximum bomb tonnage in its Lancasters, 10,050 lbs compared to the 9,600 lbs of others.

Goebbels had had another bad night, recording in his diary:

> It was 4 a.m. when I got to bed. This was one of the worst nights of my entire life. Although the flames are still soaring skywards we hope to overcome the worst difficulties by noon and get ready for the next night. It would be wonderful if we had one night's rest.

Marie Vassiltchikov wrote in her own diary of trying to reach her office the next day. She recorded that only one block away from her home all the houses were burnt out.

> As I continued down Lützowstrasse the devastation grew worse; many buildings were still burning and I had to keep to the middle of the street, which was difficult on account of numerous wrecked trams. There were many people on the streets, most of them muffled in scarves and coughing, as they threaded their way gingerly through the piles of fallen masonry. At the end of Lützowstrasse, about four blocks from the office, the houses on both sides of the street had collapsed and I had to climb over mounds of smoking rubble.[13]

When she arrived at her office on the Kurfürstenstrasse she found it burning and made arrangements to leave Berlin.

It was on this raid of 23 November that female operators were brought in to handle the Corona service to jam the German running commentary to night fighters. The male German reportage controller was heard giving accurate instructions to the circling *nachtjäger*, so Corona broadcast a false version. The Germans then switched to a female controller, believing the interruptions were coming from British aircraft. Kingsdown had a female standing by and she went on the air telling the night fighters to fly south. There then followed an argument over the airwaves, both women accusing the other of lying and the British operator telling the night fighters to land because of fog.

Some did and eight Mosquitos dropping spoof TIs to the north also caused a diversion, but enough night fighters were present over Berlin to shoot down twenty aircraft, a loss rate of 5.2 per cent. There were also six crashes in England by returning bombers, a sign that the anxiety and exhaustion of two Berlin raids in two nights was more than a test of aircrew skills, a 49 Sqn pilot landing on the beach at Chapel St Leonards by mistake when approaching Fiskerton.

Lancaster pilot P/O John Josling was one of those who had been over Berlin two nights running. As the tired 20-year-old sipped his rum-strengthened tea after debriefing he told waiting reporters: 'You could see the city itself through an occasional gap. Soon there was a big area of new fires. Just after we bombed there was a large explosion, not as large as the one I had seen the night before, but still big enough to light up the sky.'[14]

There would now be little rest until the Battle of Berlin was over, and the spectre of increasing attrition was appearing from the shadows. The Lancaster squadrons were alerted for Berlin again two nights later with a large diversion to Frankfurt by the Halifax units, which had largely escaped the demand to return to Berlin on 23 November. A forecast of worsening weather caused cancellation of the Berlin raid in the late evening, stretching the nerves of crews, but the Halifax raid went ahead and twelve were lost out of 262.

The next day the Lancaster crews trudged through the puddles of a darkening, damp afternoon into the briefing rooms at their Lincolnshire bases once more to see the red line stretching south across the Channel, due east across Belgium and then north-east – back to the flak and searchlight belts of Berlin. A groan went up, airfield after airfield anticipating the agony of another ordeal by flak and cannon fire.

F/Sgt Ernie Webb, on the 49 Sqn battle order for his fourth Berlin raid in a week, remembers the mood:

> We half expected it, but when we saw the target revealed we thought, 'Oh no, here we go once again.' There had been a hush as the screen was pulled away.
>
> We were fortunate to go and come back without any trouble. The searchlights seemed so close together as we approached, but it was a matter of heading straight for them and hoping to find a way through. From far away the flak seemed very intense and there was an angry red glow of the fires and the occasional flash of a bursting bomb.[15]

To the north of Ernie Webb's Fiskerton base the Halifax squadrons saw the same route as far as Frankfurt, then a turn to the south to raid Stuttgart. It was another maximum effort, 443 Lancasters bound for Berlin and 157 Halifaxes headed for Stuttgart.

Crews had read in the national press that day that Butch Harris had sent a reply to Sir Archibald Sinclair congratulating him on the Berlin raids, reading: 'The Battle of Berlin progresses. It will continue as opportunity serves and circumstances dictate until the heart of Nazi Germany ceases to beat.' It was clear many young English hearts would cease to beat before it was over.

The sound of 2,400 aircraft engines straining above the clouds brought many citizens of southern England to their doors and windows. The armada took forty-five minutes to cross the coast. It was music to the ears of the British public, one regional newspaper commenting the next day: 'I am sure we have all been greatly heartened by the knowledge that Berlin, which gave the orders to level Warsaw, Rotterdam and Belgrade, is now receiving due and proper payment.'

For the people of Berlin trapped in a weird world of aerial siege the apocalyptic chaos reached new heights that night as the Berlin Zoo was hit and crocodiles and other wild beasts, lit by the flash of exploding

Cookies, headed for the streets near the once-elegant Kurfürstendamm.

New techniques were now rapidly following each other and for the first time Mosquitos flew in advance over Berlin dropping clouds of Window to attract the predicted flak that had downed seven Pathfinders on the previous raid. The Windowing Mosquitos would become a regular feature of bomber operations. This time more factories were hit, particularly in the industrial suburb of Reinickendorf and Siemenstadt, the Bournville-like complex in western Berlin. The carefully planned route fooled the German controllers, who identified Frankfurt as the target. The cloud had cleared briefly over Berlin, however, and the flak took its toll. A total of twenty-one bombers went down over the capital. Another five had been lost to fighters near Frankfurt.

Among the industrial plants accurately hit was the important Alkett armament works. Goebbels recorded in his diary on 29 November: 'The Berlin munition industry is still in bad shape. Alkett is almost completely destroyed, and, worst of all, valuable and virtually irreplaceable tools and machines have been put out of commission. The English aimed so accurately that one might think spies had pointed their way.'

The cost to the RAF was high, the attrition rate rising to 6.2 per cent. Mid-upper gunner Sgt Jack Patterson was in a 207 Sqn Lancaster spotted by a night fighter near Frankfurt. 'We were attacked from low astern with a burst that blew our starboard rudder away and struck the starboard engine, puncturing the fuel tank,' he remembers.[16]

The attack also started a fire in the bomb bay. This crew had already decided to press on even though the rear gunner had reported his turret unserviceable as they crossed the English coastline. Now the pilot dived to port, jettisoning the bomb load and dousing the fire. He headed for cloud cover and the Lancaster limped back across the North Sea, making landfall at the emergency airfield at Woodbridge, Suffolk.[17]

Apart from the increasing chop rate there was another worrying aspect to the raid. There was fog over many airfields as bombers returned that night and six aircraft were lost in crashes, bringing the attrition rate up to 9.3 per cent. Flight engineer Sgt Barry Wright found his 166 Sqn Lancaster couldn't land at his home base of Kirmington because of the poor visibility. He recalls:

> We were diverted to Skipton-on-Swale. They thought they had bandits in the area, so as we approached they just switched the runway lights on for us, let us land and immediately switched them off, so there we were, left taxiing round the perimeter track of a strange airfield without lights. Suddenly we ran into the back of a Lanc that had been parked sideways along the track. The rear gunner of that aircraft was just getting out of his turret when our starboard engine started chopping up the tailplane and rear fuselage just behind his head. Luckily everybody got out.[18]

The foggy weather was a startling omen. It would return the following month after another Berlin raid when twenty-five Lancasters had been lost and would cause the crashes of another twenty-nine. The attrition rate would shoot up to an appalling 12 per cent.

There would be other raids on the Reich capital as the year drew to a close, which would also cost more lives than Bomber Command could afford. The dream of ending the war by bombing alone was ending in the ashes of burnt-out aircraft.

WINTER

CHAPTER FIFTEEN

A MISERABLE END

THE Battle of Berlin was truly a shot in the dark. It was fought in frightful weather and during the whole three months of the battle hardly a single crew saw anything of the city below. On many nights aircraft took off into overcast skies, flew in cloud all the way across western Europe, bombed in nil visibility and returned in zero visibility conditions, only catching sight of the earth again as they let down to join the circuits of their home airfields. Mist followed rain, fog trailed mist, and at the end of the sodden weather blanket came snow. At one time in the winter of 1943–4 the front-line station of Binbrook, its runways sliding away to an escarpment, was cut off by drifts for three weeks, supplies being dropped by parachute. Operations never wavered.

It was a miserable time of conflict. The oscillating chop rate was showing an inexorable overall rapid rise as Schrage Musik took its toll. It would be well into the following year before Bomber Command recognised that the stealthy, unseen killer existed, the blooming of bombers in the blackness into brilliant orange balls dripping red rain still being explained away as 'Scarecrow' shells.

Night after night, trucks splashed across shimmering tarmac to drop new crews beside waiting bombers to join the bomb train to Berlin. Day after day, other trucks would arrive at airfield guard rooms to deposit hopeful, fresh-faced replacements for those lost the night before. The lifeblood was being drained from the Command.

The first shocking intimation of this debt that an Empire would owe its airmen came in the newsrooms of the newspapers, which had so vigorously captured the public mood of satisfaction that the Nazi leaders were themselves now experiencing the horrors of war. Newspapers were desperate for their own first-hand accounts of what a bombing raid on Berlin was like and had been badgering the Air Ministry for weeks for operational permits. No fewer than four reporters were allowed to go on the raid of 2 December. Only one returned, the American radio journalist Ed Murrow, whose report under the headline 'Berlin – Orchestrated Hell of Light and Flame' appeared in the next day's *Daily Express* in the absence of one from the newspaper's own reporter, 24-year-old Lowell Bennett, now a prisoner of war with most of a 50 Sqn crew.

An Australian war correspondent, Norman Stockton, had been assigned to 460 (RAAF) Sqn at Binbrook, as had Cpt Grieg, working for the *Daily Mail*. 460 Sqn lost five aircraft that night including the two with the reporters on board, who were both killed. Murrow had flown with the CO of 619 Sqn, which that lost two Lancasters.

There were only two routes to Berlin, straight across Europe or up to Denmark, then down. High Wycombe chose the former for the raid of 2 December. Another maximum effort had been planned, but late in the afternoon all but fifteen of the 225 Halifax crews detailed for the operation were taken off because of fog forming at the Yorkshire airfields.

The 458 aircraft bound for Berlin climbed through cloud to meet the last rays of the setting sun, but found a towering front over the North Sea and many aircraft had to turn back because of icing. The forecast had also failed to predict the wind direction correctly and the stream started to straggle as navigators worked on different winds from their groups. As a result, the Pathfinders were unable to unite to mark the target correctly and the bombing was scattered over southern Berlin and the countryside beyond.

The Luftwaffe guessed the target at 0745, nineteen minutes before the first bombs were due to fall, and Ju88s laid lines of fighter flares to the capital from as far as 50 miles away. Over Berlin itself the Wilde Sau were waiting. Forty aircraft were shot down, a horrifying 8.7 per cent.

Sgt Gordon Penfold, a wireless operator on 9 Sqn, who would make nine trips to Berlin, remembers how daring the Wilde Sau were on that operation. 'An FW190 attacked us from the front, extremely unusual at night,' he says. 'He was firing as he came towards us, but the Canadian mid-upper gunner, Sgt Nicky Sorge, had seen him and was shooting back. The fighter missed, but the gunner hit him and he didn't come back.'[1]

F/O Ronald McIntyre, who had heard five of his fellow captains on 460 Sqn were missing, told waiting reporters at Binbrook:

> There were blocks of searchlights, hundreds of them. They were trying to probe the clouds and the rear gunner saw two aircraft coned. The flak was pretty solid. The enemy seemed to be using the type that looks like hose-piping when it comes up. It gives you the impression that it is impossible to get through it, but you do somehow, though we had one or two holes in the bomb doors.[2]

The 20-year-old Australian would be called to Berlin again and again, dying on the last raid of the year.

To complete the publicity blitz the Air Ministry had allowed a British Movietone News team into Skellingthorpe to interview a 61 Sqn crew when they returned. They were introduced to P/O Tony Bird, back from his sixth trip to the Big City. The newsreel featuring him was shown throughout the country and was seen by his mother at a Croydon cinema. In her amazement she jumped up and cried out: 'That's my Tony!'

The photographs of British aircrew lost over Berlin were now beginning to litter the pages of regional journals, and towns and villages throughout Britain were starting to wonder if it was worth the cost. In an article in the *Daily Express* at this time Basil Cardew asked: 'Why Do We Bomb Berlin?' He said many people had asked him that question in the past few days and he had assured them it was not mere retaliation for the 1940–41 Blitz on London. In fact it was because Greater Berlin employed about 10 per cent of Germany's industrial workers, it had a rail centre in which twelve main lines converged and it was Europe's focal point for air transport. An RAF commentator had told him: 'The north-west is largely occupied by scientific and military institutions; the west and south-west is residential intermingled with factories; the north is machinery works; the south houses vast railway workshops.'[3]

On 7 December Harris wrote to the Air Ministry saying he expected in the next three months to have forty Lancaster squadrons that would be able to drop 13,850 tons a month, sufficient to destroy between 40 and 50 per cent of the principal German towns. He concluded: 'From this it appears that the Lancaster force alone should be sufficient but only just sufficient to produce in Germany by 1 April 1944 a state of devastation in which surrender is inevitable.'[4]

In fact, by 23 December there were thirty-nine Lancaster squadrons and sixteen Halifax squadrons, giving Bomber Command a front-line strength of 1,072 bombers.[5]

To encourage the High Wycombe hierarchy there were reports from neutral countries of what destruction the air raids of 1943 had caused to Germany's cities. The Berlin correspondent of the Swiss *Neue Zürcher Zeitung* said that month that repairs were likely to take the strength of a whole generation. Damage in Berlin was very great, but things looked even worse in northern and north-west Germany. Hamburg, Hanover and Kassel were 'really dreadful sights'. Practically all industrial workers in Mannheim and Ludwigshafen were engaged in clearing-up operations.[6]

It was satisfying to read that the road to ruin was also the path to victory, but the eye was more likely to be drawn to the picture of a little English girl with USAAF personnel under the headline 'Her Uncle Sams'. It carried the explanation that she had been taken under the wing of American flyers since her own RAF aircrew father had gone down over Germany.[7]

As Christmas approached it tugged at the heartstrings, and pictures of Santa Claus in department stores and tips on what days markets might have mistletoe didn't help those who tried to keep the reality of war at bay. The cruelty of combat was an image crews were ever trying to forget as they rested in the moon period of early December, but as they checked in at flight offices in the grey, misty morning of 16 December the long, red yarn was being stretched once more across those eye-riveting maps in operation rooms to mark the fear-filled route to Berlin.

In fact the moon period was not quite over. Harris was so anxious to continue the battle after a stand-down of almost two weeks that he was prepared to risk a three-quarter moon later in the night with an early take-off of 4 p.m. He was also taking a great gamble with the weather. The ORS report for the raid gave the forecast as 'widespread fog for the return as far as the West Coast of Denmark with 10/10s cloud over the North Sea'.[8]

As it turned out, the fog would follow the bombers all the way home and would cause the most savage attrition of all the Berlin raids. The loss rate over the target would be twenty-five bombers, 5.2 per cent of the 483 all-Lancaster force, but a further twenty-nine aircraft would crash in Britain, rocketing the loss rate to 11.2 per cent. In North Lincolnshire 1 Group would suffer the greatest blow with thirteen wrecked aircraft, but the highest individual toll was on 97 Sqn in 8 Group, with seven aircraft plunging in the vicinity of the Bourn, Cambridgeshire, base.

Bomb aimer F/Lt Maurice Colvin was in 5 Group, on 467 Sqn, less affected by fog. He was making his first trip to the capital. F/Lt Colvin had begun his tour in August, but the crew had carried out only five operations so far because they had had to divert to North Africa after a fighter attack over Milan and hadn't been able to return to Britain for six weeks. F/Lt Colvin kept a diary of his operations. He recorded:

This was the trip I had been waiting for; raiding the Nazis' capital is something to be proud of. I admit when I walked into the briefing room I felt a queer feeling in my stomach when I saw the target. There was to be 10/10s cloud on Berlin and once again that fact made me feel a bit better. The route they gave us was very good indeed.[9]

That route was the direct approach, straight across Holland to the target. Many crews weren't as lucky as F/Lt Colvin's and despite very low cloud and icing, German fighters took off and picked up the bombers at the Dutch coast. One of them was the 7 Sqn Pathfinder Lancaster of bomb aimer Sgt Dennis Woolford, who had begun his tour on Peenemünde in a

90 Sqn Stirling. His Lancaster was unfortunate enough to be located by the SN2 nose-mounted radar of a Luftwaffe ace, Prince Heinrich zu Sayn-Wittgenstein, kommandeur of II/NJG2 at Parchim.* There would be little chance of escape from the Schrage Musik of Sayn-Wittgenstein's Ju88.

Sgt Woolford remembers:

The port wing suddenly caught fire between the two engines. We didn't see or hear anything. We'd never been warned about fighters with upward-firing cannon, but that's what it was. The flames were shooting back about 30 or 40 feet.

I was sitting next to the navigator, Sgt Alex Smillie, working the H2S set, and the pilot, P/O Geoff Tyler, ordered an immediate bale-out. But the fighter must have gone past and come round in a circle, because the aircraft was suddenly hit by cannon in the centre of the fuselage. It felt like we had run into a brick wall as the cannon shells exploded. It was surprising, you felt the sensation. I got a bullet through the wrist, so I decided it was time to get my parachute. I went into the nose and opened the hatch, but the aircraft was spinning and there was a lot of G force. I had to wait till it eased off. I tried to drop the hatch through the hole, but it stuck, so I kicked it and it fell out.

I didn't see the aircraft again. As we were at about 17,000 feet when I jumped I counted to thirty before pulling the ripcord. We were fairly well trained about what to do. The chute snapped open. I didn't see the ground coming up. I landed in a field and the parachute went over a wire fence.

I saw a barn and tried to get the doors open, but I didn't realise it was attached to a house. The next thing was the old German farmer came round with a gun and I was taken into the farmhouse. All the neighbours came in to have a look and everybody was quite good to me. In the morning the Luftwaffe came in a truck to pick me up. There were five coffins in the truck and I knew it was members of my crew

---

* The anti-Nazi Sayn-Wittgenstein, brought up in Switzerland, was a friend of the Berlin diarist Marie Vassiltchikov. She wrote in her journal on 25 January of her shock at discovering at a dinner party that he had been killed.

who had been killed. There was a smell like pork and I knew they had been burned. They took them to a mortuary in the town of Wilsum and took me to the local aerodrome where the night-fighter pilot that got us was based. It was about 30 miles from where the aircraft crashed. I was kept there for a couple of days.

Our navigator was at the Luftwaffe base. He got out of the aircraft unscathed. He told me he hadn't got a chute and the pilot handed him his, saying: 'Take mine.' I think everybody except the pilot had been killed in the fighter attack. They told me at the Luftwaffe aerodrome that it was a fighter from their base which had shot us down. They interrogated me for their own benefit and for cussedness I said it was flak that got us. The officer got a bit shirty because he could see it was a bullet wound I had. The Prince had to put a proper claim in whereas normally they just credited him anyway.

I was sent under guard to the sergeant's mess where my wounded wrist was seen to. I also had some superficial cuts and bruises from getting out. I had a meal with them. They were young sergeants like me and they sang me a song. It was 'We're going to hang out our washing on the Siegfried Line'.

We had only done a couple of ops with 7 Sqn when we were shot down. The pilot had volunteered us for Pathfinders because they were talking of turning over the Stirlings for odd jobs like glider towing or even anti-submarine work. The pilot said: 'I haven't come over from Australia to do odd-jobbing.' I couldn't see anything wrong in it myself.[10]

In all, 7 Sqn lost four of its aircraft to night fighters over Holland. One of them was picked up by another *nachtjäger experten* equipped with Schrage Musik, Oberleutnant Heinz-Wolfgang Schnaufer of IV/NJG1, based at Leeuwarden. He took off into cloud only 100 feet above the runway and ice built up on the wings of his Me110 as he climbed through 15,000 feet of overcast conditions to break out into a brilliant starlit sky.

The fighter box Polar Bear directed him onto the Lancaster of Sgt

Woolford's squadron mate, W/O Wallace Watson. Schnaufer's SN2 radar picked up Watson half a mile away and the ace quickly positioned himself unseen under the 21-year-old Australian's wing tank to dispatch him with the upward-firing cannon. Watson's wrecked aircraft, its target indicators burning furiously, left a multi-coloured pyre on the ground. There were no survivors. Schnaufer went on to shoot down three more bombers, but weather conditions were so bad that when he returned to Leeuwarden he overshot four times before the low cloud dispersed sufficiently for him to land.

A total of eighteen combats were reported by crews. *Nachtjäger* had also been sent to assemble at Brandenburg near Berlin, though they shot down no bombers over the target.

The badly mauled Pathfinders arrived over Berlin to find almost total overcast there as well, but the marking – led by four aircraft equipped with 3-cm H2S – was accurate for the conditions and most of the bombs rained down through the clouds onto built-up areas of Berlin, the attack spreading from the centre to the west and to the east of the city, which had not been hit before. The railway system was particularly badly affected, holding up important supplies for the Russian front.

Many of the airmen on the Berlin raid were new, replacements for those lost in November. Among them was RAF flight engineer Sgt Alan Morgan, who had joined 49 Sqn at Fiskerton. Unknown to him as he approached the target, a 49 Sqn crew had already died, one of Oblt Schnaufer's victims over Holland. Before December was out Sgt Morgan would raid Berlin three times in total. He remembers:

We had done a lot of training on the squadron over three weeks and we were proud and excited to be doing something for the war effort and I was with my pals.

The searchlights and flak on my first raid impressed me. I could see the lines of white tracer from the Berlin light flak screaming through the air and the explosions of the heavy flak. We didn't think the light flak was real. We were in the second wave and went in at 19,500 feet.

The heavy flak was at the front and the side of us and we could smell the cordite. There was one big orange glow under the cloud.[11]

F/Lt Colvin's easy run to Berlin also twisted to tension. He recorded in his diary:

At the last turning point before the target things really began to pop. The first thing we noticed was tracer flashing across the sky and an aircraft going down. Fighters were really doing their best to get the route into the city marked with flares, but for some reason they didn't quite succeed. The target area was quite easy to pick up as the search-lights were just visible on the cloud. Gee! There must have been hundreds of lights down below us and I really thanked God there was plenty of cloud. There was a lot of heavy flak, but most of it was in barrage form; their light flak was very, very thick indeed. Round the target area it looked as if there was a solid wall of 47 mm guns spurting tracer all over the sky.

F/Lt Colvin wrote that below him he saw an aircraft

burning from the starboard wing tip right along to the fuselage. It flew along straight and level for a minute or two, so the crew most likely got out OK, then it started a long shallow dive and disappeared in the clouds. A few seconds later there was a large explosion reflected in the overcast. Gee! It takes a long time to fly over Berlin.[12]

F/Lt Colvin's crew made a safe return to base at Waddington from what he coolly described as 'a quite enjoyable trip'.

Sgt Morgan in the same 5 Group also got in to his home airfield, helped by fog-dispersing equipment burning oil along the sides of the runway. 'We landed back at Fiskerton because we had FIDO,' he recalls. 'You could see the flarepath from 500 to 1,000 feet up to 3 miles away. As you came in over the threshold you would go up in the air again because of the updraft from the heat.'[13]

Few airfields in Bomber Command were so equipped and now the fog was echoing with the sound of bombers, their engines straining as they made approaches only to climb away again at the last moment as unforeseen obstacles loomed. Soon the mist would flash and glow with exploding aircraft as their crews ran out of fuel and baled out or simply failed to find a place to land in time. Aircraft were diverted to fields miles away and badly damaged bombers were often stacked up on circuits thirty-six deep as controllers at training aerodromes struggled to cope with the sudden influx.

The reaper swung his scythe from freshmen crews to the most experienced. Among those killed on 16 December was W/Cdr David Holford, CO of 100 Sqn, which had proved so unlucky for senior officers. He crashed on the approach to Grimsby. A total of 127 aircrew would be killed by the fog and for ever afterwards this night was known throughout the Command as Black Thursday. It had been particularly heavy among the Pathfinders, eight crews being lost in the crashes in Britain adding to six aircraft lost on the raid itself.

On the plus side the technical department of the Allied air war had taken another step forward. The recently formed 100 Group had its first success with Serrate, the radar device that picked up the transmissions of the *nachtjäger's* SN2 searching radar, when a 141 Sqn crew recently transferred with the squadron from Fighter Command damaged a hunting Me110 with cannon fire. The Serrate-equipped Mosquitos would now demonstrate growing success and Sayn-Wittgenstein himself would be shot down by one after a Schrage Musik attack on a Lancaster, his eighty-third kill, on 21 January 1944.

Schrage Musik itself was by now cutting a swathe through the ranks of Bomber Command. The advantage had always been to the nimble night fighter as it sought the wide bomber stream, the laden aircraft's glowing exhausts sending a 10-mile signal across the black sky. Schrage Musik – whereby the fighter, having spotted the bomber by the new SN2 radar immune to Window, was able to take a position out of sight below the rear gunner's field of vision – made it an unequal contest indeed.

If by some great good chance the bomber's gunners did see the night fighter, their .303 machine guns were no match in range or firepower against the *nachtjäger* 20 mm or 30 mm cannon, pumping out explosive shells. For this reason Bomber Command's gunners were under strict orders throughout 1943 not to fire unless they were attacked, in case they gave their aircraft's position away.

The 5 Group C-in-C, AVM Sir Ralph Cochrane, was not in favour of this policy. He wrote to Harris's deputy, Air Vice Marshal Sir Robert Saundby, in July, contending that a greater willingness on the part of Bomber Command bombers to open fire might 'convert the German night fighter trade from one of the safest in the German Air Force to one of some peril' and coldly concluded: 'In the process we shall no doubt put a number of .303 bullets into our aircraft, but I doubt whether that will matter very much.'

The views of other group commanders were sought as the longer nights approached, but the policy remained unchanged after a minute from 8 Group's Don Bennett, dated 3 September, warned that 'the great readiness on the trigger which this theory encouraged would merely help the German fighters to find their quarries'.

In captivity Oblt Schnaufer, who ended the war as the Luftwaffe's highest-scoring ace with 121 victories, told RAF interrogators that on a light night he opened fire at 660 feet. On a dark night it was half that. Browning .303s were thought by Bomber Command to be seriously effective at up to 300 feet. Only on a dark night, therefore, could the bomber's .303s come anywhere near matching the range. He also said 90 per cent of the bombers he attacked did not see him positioning. Even after attack 40 per cent of the bombers did not fire back or attempt evasive manoeuvres.[14]

Harris was well aware how poorly defended his heavy bombers were and fought hard for two years for a turret equipped with .5 machine guns. Eventually, despairing of official channels, he approached a small Gainsborough firm to design one and it was introduced in 1 Group Lancasters in the closing stages of the war.[15]

Of even more use would have been a .5 ventral gun to defeat Schrage Musik attacks. Early Halifax IIIs were equipped with this weapon. It was removed in favour of the radar blister to improve target finding as H2S spread throughout Main Force squadrons. Target finding was judged more important than crews. Tellingly, Schnaufer informed his interrogators that when he heard some RAF bombers were being fitted with .5s he was very worried until he found very few were carrying them.[16]

The front turret fitted in nearly all Lancasters until the war's end was hardly ever used. Some consider it would have been better to remove all turrets from bombers, giving an extra 50 or 60 mph in speed and for Fighter Command to have made a greater contribution by training on Serrate-equipped Mosquitos.

An Air Ministry analysis of the views of captured Luftwaffe reported: 'Pilots among PoWs said they became very homing conscious after the discovery of the first Serrate aircraft, although in their own homing endeavours they did not have much success.'[17]

It may have been true that the majority of night-fighter crews, who only shot down one or two bombers or more likely didn't score at all, didn't have much success picking up the signals of the bomber fleet, but the aces – twenty-one of whom had been credited with fifty or more kills by the war's end – did and there was a plethora of signals to home in on.

They ranged from H2S pulses, to ABC transmissions in 101 Sqn, to Monica, a tail device to warn of the approach of night fighters, which sadly proved more effective in directing the hunting night fighter onto the bomber. It was withdrawn in 1944 after it was realised countless inexperienced bomber crews had been shot down because they had been told to rely on it.

The complex deception now being mounted by Bomber Command as the Luftwaffe night-fighter arm reached its peak of efficiency in the closing weeks of 1943 included fooling the enemy about the air fleet's nightly intentions, despite the fact it had become obvious a major campaign was being launched against Berlin to try to finish the war by bombing.

To this end a huge raid was mounted on Frankfurt only four days after the 12.2 per cent loss on Berlin and despite the difficulties of bringing widely dispersed aircraft back to their squadrons. The Luftwaffe controllers were not duped. They plotted the 650 aircraft as they left the coast of Britain and kept up with them all the way to Frankfurt, despite a diversion by forty-four Lancasters and ten Mosquitos to Mannheim. There were combats all along the route and forty-one aircraft were lost, 6.3 per cent – no better than on a Berlin raid. The Pathfinders had been told the target would be clear and prepared accordingly, but found eight-tenths cloud. A large decoy fire was also lit by the Germans 5 miles south of the city and attracted several bombs, but many Cookies and incendiaries did fall on Frankfurt, causing considerable damage.

Among the Pathfinders 35 Sqn had recently been re-equipped with the efficient Halifax III and lost two of them on the Frankfurt operation of 20 December. Rear gunner F/Sgt Robert Gill, in another of the squadron's aircraft, remembers how tough Frankfurt proved:

> We were coned and there were a lot of flak holes in the aircraft as a result. At the time we were being told the explosions we could see in the air were Scarecrow shells, but it was absolute rubbish, they were exploding bombers. On Berlin, particularly at that time, you would see strings of fighter flares across the sky then an exploding aircraft. There would be a bright glow, then if it was a Pathfinder greens and reds spilling out of it. Bomber crew suffered very much because there was virtually no defence underneath and you wouldn't see a fighter with Schrage Musik. On a dark night a gunner's view downward wouldn't be more than 100 to 200 feet, but we could be seen, silhouetted against the sky, plus the Me110s simply bristled with antennae to pick up your H2S radar emissions and we were simply sitting ducks.[18]

It was 78 Sqn in Main Force that would suffer the most, however, losing five of its captains. F/Sgt Bernard Downs, the young pilot whose picture appeared in the papers after the Berlin raid of 22 November, nearly became a sixth. He says:

> We had turned into the target and had about ten minutes to run when three things happened almost simultaneously. Both gunners called 'corkscrew', some tracer came up between the rear of the starboard

mainplane and the fuselage and I immediately started to evade. I think
it was a night fighter with Schrage Musik. The tracer was inches away.
We managed to lose him. I think he must have had a very poor aim
and he only made the one pass.[19]

Arguably the most continually nerve-stretching time of all was had by
F/Lt Colvin, the 467 Sqn bomb aimer. He recorded in his diary the next
day:

This target is rated as one of the toughest in the Reich and to us it kept
up its reputation. Everything was going just dandy until we ran up on
the target. If the rear gunner's mic had been working the following
may never have happened. The fighter was seen by the rear gunner
and identified as an Me210 at 800 yards, closing fast. He gave corkscrew
but as his mic was frozen no one heard him, the first thing we knew
was a rattle in the rear of the aircraft and showers of sparks and the
smell of powder.

The pilot corkscrewed at once and the gunners opened up at the
enemy aircraft. As we changed direction in the corkscrew we received
another burst which put all turrets out of action and ripped the bomb
doors all along their length. A terrific punch in the back knocked me
over the bomb sight and made me think I had had it. We continued
on the bombing run as the fighter had by now broken off.

Just as we finished bombing we collected some incendiaries from
an aircraft above us. One put our starboard outer out of action, but we
found it wouldn't feather and stuck at 1,700 revs. The dead-reckoning
compass was also u/s, so we had to rely on the P4 [a compass in the
pilot's position] for our courses being correct. When we got back to
base we informed them we had been badly knocked about and they
told us to circle until all aircraft had landed.

After landing we looked over the aircraft and found six bullets in
the mid-upper turret, one sticking in the gunner's boot; cannon shells
and machine-gun bullets all over the fuselage between the rear and
mid-upper turrets; cannon shells through dead reckoning compass;

bomb doors badly ripped by bullets and cannon shells; cannon shell through port aileron; a 30-lb incendiary bomb in starboard engine and another in port wing. The punch I felt in the back was a bullet that had hit the Window packets I had stowed behind me. If they hadn't been there I wouldn't have been writing this now.[20]

He and his crew were given much-welcomed leave and would not operate again in 1943, missing the next two Berlin raids.

While F/Lt Colvin and the other members of his crew had been fighting for their lives over Frankfurt the RAF's Photographic Interpretation Unit at Medmenham, near Aylesbury, had been poring over the first reconnaissance photographs of Berlin obtained since the battle began. That day and the next Mosquitos crossed the city in clear skies from west to east and north to south, their cameras clicking, building up a montage of destruction. The weather would not be kind enough for reconnaissance again until the middle of February.

It was impossible to determine what damage had occurred in which of the six major raids since the Battle of Berlin started apart from in the Reinickendorf/Tegel districts where on the operation of 26 November the clouds had parted sufficiently for some crews to show on their bomb-load photoflash pictures that the raid had been concentrated there. But the havoc of the six raids had been impressive and encouraging for the future. Bomber Command's Operational Research Section reported to their chiefs:

> The largest area of devastation, covering eight square miles and resulting almost entirely from fire, stretched from the east side of the central district of Berlin to Charlottenburg in the north-west and to Wilmersdorf in the south-west. Severe damage was also caused in the important industrial districts of Reinickendorf and Spandau. In the Tiergarten district whole island blocks were gutted including various legations. The great War Office building was partly demolished.[21]

The greatest satisfaction was to be found in the destruction in the central area of Mitte and especially along the Wilhelmstrasse, which the ORS described as Berlin's Whitehall in case anyone should miss the point. It listed the buildings hit from Hitler's Chancellery to Gestapo headquarters. Applied to the geography of London it was as if Whitehall, the Houses of Parliament, Westminster Abbey and the Mall had been left as smoking ruins.

In fact Bomber Command had reduced the housing capacity of the vast metropolis of Berlin, the world's third largest city, with an area of 900 square miles, to 75 per cent of pre-war figures. The temptation must have been great to assume that the Nazi State was on the brink of collapse. There were some signs of panic. Even the resolute Marie Vassiltchikov admitted to her diary on 24 November, after the heavy raid on central Berlin of 22 November, that as she walked in the Lützowplatz area near her home and office:

> The sight of those endless rows of burnt-out or still burning buildings had got the better of me and I was beginning to feel panicky. The whole district, many of its houses so familiar to me, had been wiped out in just one night!
>
> I started to run and kept on running until I was back in Lützow-strasse [her home street], where a building collapsed as I passed. A fireman shouted something unintelligible to me and some people close by; we all flung ourselves to the ground. There was the rumble and clatter of yet another collapsing wall.

A few days later she had ignored Goebbels' diktat that all young people should stay in Berlin by leaving for Konigswart, near Leipzig. Within days the centre of Leipzig with its important Junkers aircraft works was blitzed in a very accurate H2S-guided attack. She described how she missed the express out of Berlin and had to take a more circuitous route. When she finally picked up the train 24 hours later, 'it was jammed and we had to literally pull ourselves aboard. A woman was pushed on the track just in front of me and pulled back by the hair in the nick of time.'[22]

Regional newspapers in Britain used a Reuters report at the time from a Stockholm businessman who had travelled with great difficulty by train from east Germany to Berlin. 'When I arrived I had the impression that all gaiety had gone from the city,' he said. 'The children had been sent away, only those on work of national importance are left.'[23]

A phenomenon was occurring in Berlin that was being called cellar influenza, he said. It was caused not only by long vigils in shelters, but by smoke and grime in the atmosphere after air raids. A Berlin film actress, Ingeborg Wells, described in an account published just after the war a new sense of desperation among those trapped in the city at that time which was like dancing on a volcano.

And there were rumours of capitulation. Goebbels recorded in his diary after the shattering raids of late November:

London expects a new German peace offensive. It is believed that envoy Bismarck, who is at present visiting relatives in Sweden, and the former Secretary of State Kuehlmann have been selected to conduct these peace negotiations. In reality there isn't a word of truth to either.

The Allies had already decided they could not negotiate with those who led children into gas chambers – as had already been revealed to them by concentration camp escapees in 1943 – and nothing less than unconditional surrender would suffice. Hitler was determined his people would fight to the last for him, his SS summarily executing 10,000 troops and other Germans in the closing stages of the war who could follow him along the path of insanity no longer.

The aircrew who had returned from the Frankfurt operation, which had followed so closely on the almost crippling losses of the last Berlin raid, hoped not to operate again before Christmas. The heartfelt desire for Christmas at home had already been dashed with the news that no leave or passes for any distance over 20 miles would be issued to RAF personnel between 23 and 28 December. There would be few exceptions.[24]

The only solace was to be found with a quick run into the nearest town. In York there was a chance to meet a winsome WAAF in the crisp night air outside the newly opened Services Hostel. In Nottingham *Striptease Lady*, starring Barbara Stanwyck, was a big attraction at the Astoria. Many local airmen looked forward to admiring the long legs of the principal boy as Dick Whittington opened the pantomime season at the Theatre Royal on Christmas Eve. It was not to be. Some who had held tickets were missing from another gruelling Berlin raid in the early hours and most of those who had returned were too tired to go.

The 390 crews of the mainly Lancaster force that climbed out of the Nottinghamshire and Lincolnshire bases just after midnight on 24 December carried higher hopes than those who had set forth on the 16th. The lesson of what penalties bad weather could cause had been learned and take-off had already been postponed from early afternoon because of poor conditions. It had finally been decided to stage it to allow for a return in daylight in case of fog or low cloud.

A small diversionary raid was organised for nine Mosquitos on Leipzig, just off the route of the last north-eastern leg to Berlin. For once the weather favoured the attackers. Cloud and icing conditions over their bases prevented most of the night fighters intercepting on the track to the capital, reducing the losses.

Berlin was cloud covered as usual and there were the ubiquitous serviceability problems for Pathfinders still using the old 10-cm H2S sets. The attrition rate among Pathfinders had been extreme on the raid of the 16th and some crews were new to their task. The marking was scattered and bombs that fell within the city went down on the south-eastern suburbs. However, only sixteen Lancasters were lost, 0.8 per cent below the 5 per cent figure that made Berlin operations almost supportable. One other Allied aircraft went down, however, a Serrate-equipped Beaufighter, the first 100 Group fighter to be lost on a raid and one of three operating that night.

Many of the *kellergemeindschaften* crouching in their shelters beneath the whump, crack and thud of exploding bombs thought it mean of the RAF to operate on Christmas Eve. The aircrew, anxious to forget about the war and celebrate the birthday of the Prince of Peace, thought so too. As they munched their ration chocolate on the way back to base they could reflect on the recent Cadbury's advertisement in the newspapers showing a keen, searchlight-lit pilot explaining that there would be a shortage of chocolate for children or girlfriends this Christmas because four out of every five tons produced was going to the armed forces to fight fatigue. Free chocolate was a precious perk for airmen among much pain.

The heavy-legged crews who stumbled from debriefing tables to billets in the dawn, rubbing stinging eyes, could easily calculate how few of them were alive that Christmas of those they had known the Christmas before. The persistent, nagging thought inevitably followed before sleep mercifully blotted out all consciousness of how few of those who were left would meet the dawn of Christmas Day, 1944.

At home the relatives of those airmen, who worried ceaselessly about sons, husbands and boyfriends among the bomber boys, tucked into American pork that Christmas Day of 1943, made available by the new Food Minister, Colonel Llewellin. As an extra festive treat he had also allowed a real egg in the ration instead of the powdered version.

As the sons of servicemen played with second-hand Frog aeroplanes or Meccano bought at the last minute from the 'For Sale' columns of local newspapers, mothers and older sisters relaxed, stretched out before the heavy, oak-cased radio listening on the Home Service after the post-lunch King's Speech to the satirical pantomime 'Is Your Journey Really Necessary?'

On the air bases officers among the aircrew carried out the traditional task of serving the airmen. The sound of engines was stilled, there was a stand-down throughout Bomber Command. After lunch the war-weary nearing the end of their tours were glad to slump in the shapeless leather of mess armchairs leafing through *Tee Emm* for the current mishaps of P/O Prune. In the Christmas issue there was a picture of him putting his bomb aimer, Sgt Straddle, off his aim in an article entitled: 'Are you a good bomber pilot?' The advice was that skippers should share a noggin or two with their air bombers in the mess, to find out where they were going wrong.

On at least one station those new to life on an operational squadron and innocent of what lay ahead yielded to the temptation of waking up the slumberers in front of the mess fire by shinning up the roof and dropping a clip of blank .303 cartridges down the chimney. There were mess games where sprog pilots were held upside down on a pyramid of furniture to leave the mark of their soot-covered feet on the mess ceiling or roped in for Flarepath where they had to run through a tunnel of hand-held burning newspapers. It was too much fun to last and four days later the battle orders were posted from Dishforth to Skellingthorpe for the final operation of 1943. It was inevitably Berlin.

The newspapers were in reflective mood as the year drew to a close and, traditionally, it was a time for statistics. They revealed that 6,500 awards had been received by those in air force blue in 1943 – including 7 VCs, 3,247 DFCs, 1,832 DFMs and 61 CGMs.[25]

It had been a year of profit for some, but loss for many more. Because of those losses many aircrew who had finished their tours in the first half of 1943 were now being recalled after their statutory six months' rest. One of them was air gunner Albert Bracegirdle, whose first tour had been completed on Guy Gibson and John Searby's 106 Sqn. He would join the crew of a flight commander, S/Ldr Steve Cockbain, a replacement for an officer who had just got the chop. He remembers:

I reported for my second tour on 27 December 1943 at 44 Sqn, Dunholme Lodge. I had been instructing at 1661 HCU at Winthorpe. I had got there in June and left in December, so it was only a few days over six months. Gunners were particularly likely to be recalled because pilots on second tours wanted them for their crews. They thought it gave them a better chance. At Winthorpe I'd got to know a flight engineer, Walter Faraday, who was then flying a lot with Steve Cockbain in training. He was going back for a second tour with Cockbain and he came to me and said: 'If you join us you'll go home for Christmas, how about it?' So I said: 'OK'.

I got back to my mum and dad's house near Manchester Airport at 10 p.m. on Christmas Eve. Walter and I reported back to Winthorpe on the 27th. I found they had had a Christmas raffle in the sergeants' mess and I had won a box of cigars. They took us in a truck that day down to Newark station and we got the train to Lincoln, before being taken on to Dunholme Lodge. Walter and I made ourselves sick on that train journey, smoking those blessed cigars.[26]

As F/Sgt Bracegirdle settled in at his new station High Wycombe ordered a maximum effort for the last operation of the year. A total of 712 Berlin-bound Lancasters and Halifaxes took off in the dark of 29 December, the largest air fleet since the crushing raid on the capital of 22 November. The planners had had time to design new arts in deception and Mosquito crews were ordered to carry out a double-bluff. Some raided Magdeburg on the final leg to Berlin, intending it to look like a diversion, while other Mosquitos turned south to bomb Leipzig, hoping to convince the Luftwaffe controllers that was the real target. It worked. The spoof raids and bad weather kept all but the most experienced night fighters away and only eighteen aircraft were lost, 2.8 per cent, the second lowest rate of all the operations in the Battle of Berlin.

The damage, however, was limited after the Pathfinders arrived three minutes late, though the *Daily Express* the next day trumpeted: 'Very big evening raid on Berlin' and quoted a Swedish reporter who had been able to telephone to Stockholm: 'There are heaps of ruins around my office and a big smoke pall is hanging over the city.'[27]

The raid was the twenty-ninth of Ernie Webb's tour with 49 Sqn, which had begun on the third of the four Hamburg raids in July. It was his fifth Berlin raid in a row and he was now a warrant officer. The squadron was in the first wave and met heavy flak in barrage form.

He remembers of the approach to the target:

There was a reddish glow to the cloud below and green skymarkers drifting down. We were fortunate in our bomb aimer and he dropped the bombs first time on a marker. It was always a worry whether you'd be asked to go round again, but he never asked me to and the photographic results were usually good.[28]

Back at base he reported: 'Ran up on six flares. Bomber concentration good. Glow of fires visible from Hanover.'[29]

As W/O Webb left the target, nearby was another 49 Sqn aircraft in which Sgt Alan Morgan was the flight engineer. He was carrying out his fourth raid in two weeks and the third of six he would make on Berlin. He recalls:

> We seemed to go to no other targets. We were coned twice on Berlin raids at 22,000 feet and had to corkscrew out of the lights. The skipper dived like mad to get in a cloud, then we trusted to luck.
>
> On the night of 29 December a Ju88 and two FW190s attacked us as we left the target. We could see the FW190s flying alongside just keeping their distance. Then the Ju88 came underneath us as we were distracted. I think a lot got shot down in that way, but we corkscrewed down into cloud.[30]

The last of the 15,832 operational Bomber Command airmen to die in 1943 were those in a Lancaster of 50 Sqn, returning from Berlin in the early hours of 30 December. Damaged by flak, the aircraft was forced to ditch in the North Sea. The Lancaster rapidly sank, taking the 29-year-old pilot, F/Lt Donald McAlpine, and his British crew members with it, but the Australian rear gunner, F/Sgt H. E. Groves, clambered out of the floating tail turret and drifted away in his buoyant yellow Taylor suit as the last evidence of his comrades vanished from the sea.

At the beginning of the year the first to die had been F/Lt Douglas Lonsdale and Canadians F/Sgt Robert Dickie and his hometown friend W/O Robert Moore, who had been shot down on an Essen raid near Arnhem on 3 January. Then only three aircraft had been missing in a operation that involved only nineteen. Now Bomber Command was a mighty force indeed, hitting the enemy with 700-odd aircraft a night and losing aircraft in proportion – often twice the number of the total force that had set out on that Essen raid.

Those losses would mount into 1944 as the Battle of Berlin continued to snatch airmen in an instant from the sky, the rate on consecutive Berlin raids in the first two days of the New Year rising to 6.7 then 7.0 per cent, a total of fifty-five aircraft. Sometimes there were remarkable escapes and

F/Sgt Groves's was one of those. A British destroyer came across him in the dark in the vastness of the black North Sea in the middle of the night. He was plucked from the water and carried ashore for treatment to shrapnel wounds in his arms.

For the rest of 50 Sqn and the other squadrons of Bomber Command the Battle of Berlin went on, night after freezing night combating a night-fighter force now at the peak of efficiency. On the night of 15 February, seen as the true end of the Battle of Berlin, the losses were 43 aircraft from 891 dispatched. The much-battered Nazi capital still functioned, but Bomber Command was short of 427 aircraft and crews.

There was a new cynicism among the bomber boys, similar to that suffered by the infantry at Passchendaele a generation before, as the odds against survival shortened night by night. It is summed up by this verse found scribbled on a bomber base at the time:

Down the flights each ruddy morning,
Sitting waiting for a clue,
Same old notice on the Flight board
Maximum effort – guess where to!

Butch Harris had been 50 per cent right in his prediction of 3 November to Churchill: the Battle of Berlin had indeed cost approaching 500 aircraft – half of the Command's front-line strength. Another quarter had been lost in the other major raids in the period. It had not ended as he had predicted, costing Germany the war. We will never know if it would have done if Harris had been able to obtain the 4,000 aircraft he wanted.

On the day of that last operation of 1943 as the teleprinters were chattering out another maximum effort against Berlin the newspapers were reporting an event that would signal the end of Harris's vision. The Allied military chiefs had been meeting in Cairo. There the Supreme Commander, General Dwight D. Eisenhower, and his deputy, AVM Sir Arthur Tedder, had presented what was described as 'the final mammoth plan for the invasion of Europe from the West'.[31]

Within weeks Harris would be ordered by Portal to end the Battle of

Berlin and prepare to begin support for D-Day. His command would be suborned to the will of Eisenhower. It would be mid-September before Harris got it back and Bomber Command would never operate again with the same freedom it had enjoyed in 1943.

The year – which had seen such developments in the jigsaw of ruining the Reich from tentative raids with Oboe and H2S in the weeks of winter to the remarkable performance by the Dambusters in the spring; the awesome destruction of Hamburg and technical prowess over Peenemünde in the summer; and the devastating demonstration of aerial might over Kassel, Mannheim and Hanover in the autumn – was closing in a draw over Berlin. The brave young crews of Bomber Command had achieved much against tremendous odds. Because they had taken the war to the enemy homeland night after night it was now becoming shockingly clear to all but the most diehard Nazis that eventual defeat was inevitable.

In January 1943 the total tonnage dropped by Bomber Command had been 103,119. In December it had been 264,506 tons. The average bomb lift per aircraft had also increased in proportion, from 1,146 among all types in January to 2,966 in December as the twin-engined Wellingtons and inefficient Stirlings and Halifax IIs and Vs were phased out.[32]

Bomber Command's aircraft were now flying from 128 operational airfields compared to 105 at the beginning of the year and the airfield expansion plan was complete; the aerodromes in operational use would show a steady decline to 111 by May 1945 as methods of dispersal and dispatch were honed to greater efficiency.[33]

Ranged against the bomber boys during the year had been 642,700 anti-aircraft personnel, compared to 439,500 the year before, and eventually two million soldiers and civilians would be engaged in ground anti-aircraft defence.[34] There had also been a 16 per cent boost in production of twin-engined fighters to 4,100 and a 37.7 per cent increase in single-engined machines, before 1943 used seldom at night but now being fed into Wilde Sau units.[35] As the year ended, 9,626 had been manufactured and 68 per cent of the German fighter force would eventually be facing the attacks of Bomber Command and the US Eighth Air Force, to the detriment of the battle against Russia. Germany's resources would continue to be bled to feed the air battle in the West, 81 per cent of all German fighters being thrown into the fight ten months later.[36]

Apart from this draining away of Germany's industrial might in the bombers' direction – great achievement though that was for Harris's command – questions were beginning to be asked by some in Whitehall as to how effective the application of 7 per cent of British industry to bombing had been in 1943. Intelligence assessments indicated that some areas of the German economy were not so much declining under bombing as expanding.

In fact those plans to grow had been laid in the middle of 1941 when it was realised the comparatively low level of economic mobilisation in the early war years would prove woefully inadequate. The bombing of 1943 kept a crippling rein on that expansion, which if it had been allowed to flourish in Germany and its conquered territories might even have been measured against that of an unbombed economy such as the United States. The bombing of Germany's cities in 1943, which throttled gas and elec-tricity supplies, halted transport and prevented the homeless worker attending to his lathe, as well as destroying the factories themselves, paved the way for enforced dispersal with its attendant inefficiency and allowed the RAF and the US Eighth and Fifteenth Air Forces to cut off those lines of supply in the following eighteen months.

The bomber offensive of 1943 had forced the Nazis from an offensive to a defensive strategy. Wars are not won by defence. Had not the high explo-sives and incendiaries blasted and burned out Germany's city-based indus-tries and infrastructure in 1943 she probably would have continued until either the Allies felt forced into using nuclear bombs in Europe or Germany's scientists unleashed equally deadly destruction. It was an offensive largely conducted that year by the RAF and Commonwealth airmen. These crews, who made up only 7 per cent of Britain and her empire in uniform yet took 25 per cent of the total fatalities, dropped nearly four times the tonnage of bombs compared to that dropped by the Eighth Air Force. The tonnage from the USAAF, who suffered so much in Europe's fight, would leap the following year.

In the post-war report by the 1,150-strong United States Strategic

Bombing Survey team, which also investigated the damage done by Bomber Command to Germany's economy, the conclusion was drawn that night bombing had done little to curtail war production. The British Bombing Survey Unit assembled hurriedly to conduct its own investigations consisted of no more than a dozen RAF officers, now faced with a hopeless task of comparison. Its reports constantly complain of too great a task for so small a team.[37]

It left a false legacy the bomber boys have suffered from ever since: the belief that their sacrifices and therefore the sufferings of those on the ground were to naught. Yet the gaunt testimony of the ruined Ruhr, Hamburg, Hanover, Kassel and the other industry-saturated German cities told a different story where normal life and, therefore, work had ceased to function.

Little account has been given of the decrease in a German worker's ability brought about by the destruction of his standard of living and constant nervous tension over sleepless nights. The German spirit was not broken by bombing any more than that of Britons in the Blitz, but logic must serve that his abilities were much reduced.

There were other effects of the 1943 RAF bomber offensive which can only be guessed at. The RAF raid on the Peenemünde rocket research establishment had checked development work severely and driven it underground. The payload of a rocket is designed for massive effect because its weight compared to that carried by conventional bombers is small. It seems likely, therefore, that a nuclear or biological warhead had been the original intention for the investment programme in the V2.

The Nazi leaders themselves could now only pin their hopes on such miracle weapons. The bombs that tumbled through cloud to destroy their offices and apartments around the Brandenburger Tor on the night of 22 November had starkly revealed that their days were numbered. The destruction of Hamburg had happened to other, lesser Germans. Suddenly the massive, accurate power of Bomber Command was being unleashed on the head of the dragon itself. In six months the invasion would begin and the Nazi empire of evil would be squeezed from east and west until the hierarchy turned on its own people.

The Allied armies would quickly be able to consolidate as Germany collapsed under the transport plans and oil campaigns of 1944 and 1945, the accuracy of which had been made possible by the techniques learned in the city night-bombing offensive of 1943. Before 1944 such damage would not have been achievable and if it had, it would have been too readily rectified.

As 1943 closed, the bomber boys' C-in-C could look back on a year of remarkable achievements, sending a clear message to Stalin and the conquered countries of Europe that Britain had opened a Second Front of the air. But the main prize was to elude him. Harris, an enlightened yet single-minded commander, had proved the saviour of Bomber Command, conducting a campaign in the only way possible after the Butt Report. Mindful of his experiences in the First World War as a pilot on the Western Front, he had then stuck with his theory that the war could be won without the need for a land campaign that might see the carnage of the Somme visited on a second generation of soldiers.

In fact, the Battle of Berlin was becoming Bomber Command's Passchendaele, a war of attrition in which the weaker nation was meant eventually to yield, as operation after operation headed towards further losses that would decimate the RAF squadrons. It was now clear that the prospect of a victory achieved by bombing alone had vanished. Harris's bomber dream was at an end.

CHAPTER SIXTEEN

CLOSURE

Other aspects of the bomber boys' story were just beginning as 1943 ended. For many of them there would be further ordeals as they returned for second tours, and for a few, accolades – for instance air gunner Eric Hadingham, who survived six days in a dinghy on his first tour, winning a bar to his DFC on his second, as did navigator Alex Flett. Others went on to fight a different kind of war as prisoners of war, several helping in the 'Great Escape' from Stalag Luft III for which fifty flyers were shot.

For some there was the sadness of discovering that close friends they had left behind on squadrons had not survived. Pilot Peter Johnson returned from HCU to the Brant home at Ludford Magna to discover the bike of his shooting pal Jock Mitchell still leaning against the farmhouse wall, yet Mitchell had died the night before on his twenty-ninth operation.

Within two years the men in these pages – the youngest of whom was 18 when they took part in the events which shaped their lives and the oldest 27 – would find themselves out of air force blue and back in a life of normality they had never expected to see, where subsistence now took the place of survival. It was an austere world in a rush to forget the past and make something of the peace. Along the way the old sacrifices of the men of Bomber Command were quickly forgotten by a new government and a war-weary population. It would be ten years before the achievements of the Command were looked at again in film and book. In the meantime as realpolitik beckoned, a decision was taken not to award a separate Bomber

Command campaign medal, a churlish gesture which still rankles among those whose generosity with their very lives knew no such cynicism. Bomb aimer William Garfield, a prisoner of war for two years, says: 'When I came back all my friends in the Army and Navy had campaign medals. I asked: "Where's the Air Force medal?" and I was told: "You don't get one; the British people as a whole don't like you."'

Instead the bomber boys of 1943 shared with Fighter Command the Aircrew Europe medal, but the rules for awarding it could be inflexible in the extreme. Bomb aimer Joseph Porter who was shot down on his fourth raid only three weeks after joining 50 Sqn was told he didn't qualify. 'I wrote to the Air Ministry about it and was told you had to be on a squadron for one month and do at least one operation in that month or be on longer than a month and do at least five in that period,' he says. 'If I'd lasted another week without doing any more ops I would have qualified. I was very annoyed.'

For the free spirits of the RAF it was tempting in such a rigid world to turn away from blitzed Britain as wartime rationing made way for a decade of austerity in which the tired mother country struggled to pay her debts to the New World. Several made new lives in those countries their aircrew comrades had told them so much about, in Canada, Australia and New Zealand, even in America. A few were able to visit the relatives of those who had not returned from a war so far away.

They and their former comrades at home pushed aside their ordeals as they married, had children and built careers. Eventually the nightly battle with flak and fighter seemed but a dream, though a sad section were sufficiently tormented by the experience of baling out from blazing bombers into the unknown that they were driven to early deaths. A few have found their wartime experiences so harrowing, particularly those who fell into the hands of the Gestapo, that they are still reluctant to talk about them. A number are still suffering the physical effects of wounds or privations suffered during the war.

Yet another group are daily aware that they owe their continued existence to the sacrifices of young skippers and have dedicated their own lives to ensuring their saviours are remembered. Bomb aimer Alan Bryett named his son after the Australian pilot who pushed him out of a blazing Halifax over Berlin. 'Kevin Hornibrook knew we were desperately low and he got to the escape hatch first and all he had to do was jump out and he would have had sixty years of life,' he says. 'In fact he got me out and gave me those years which I never for a moment thought I was going to have as we were coming down.'

In the past few years, in an attempt to find closure, ex-airmen have returned to the sites in Germany where their aircraft crashed and discovered how lucky indeed they were to survive, learning from local inhabitants, now able to talk with freedom because of their efforts, how close they came to being summarily executed by police or, in some cases, civilians. Others forged new friendships among those very civilians the RAF was bombing – bomb aimer Ron Heatherington, the sole survivor of his Lancaster shot down on a Mannheim raid in September, returned fifty years later to the nearby village of Neuleiningen where he came down and was taken on a flight over his crash site by a former mayor of the village and given an official dinner.

The men of Bomber Command are not the kind to bleat, but if pressed most will admit they have not had the recognition they deserved. Air gunner Cliff Hill, who speaks for many, says: 'On Remembrance Sunday I watch the whole ceremony from the Cenotaph on television and tears spring to my eyes when I think of so many aircrew friends who didn't return. Apart from their role on that one day in the year the country appears to have forgotten Bomber Command.'

If at home the courage of the bomber boys has been too easily laid aside as the years pass, it has been remembered by individual acts in those former occupied countries the bomber offensive of 1943 helped to liberate. Wireless operator Norman Leonard, shot down on the way to Cologne, bears witness to the gratitude of one small Belgian town to his skipper, F/Lt Bill Kirk. He says:

> My abiding memory of my skipper was of his courage and calmness in
> an emergency. He did all he could to save our aircraft and his crew,

staying with the doomed plane and losing his life to avoid crashing in the inhabited area of the town of Meerhout.

Part of the tail assembly was salvaged and erected in the mid-seventies as a memorial to him and his co-pilot and navigator who did not survive. Local residents pay their tributes every year with Belgian veterans on the date of their liberation by the British Army, on Armistice Day and also on the day of the crash. The memorial is a reminder that the war's unsung heroes like F/Lt Kirk and two of his crew did not die in vain, when sixty years later they are still remembered not only by their contemporaries, but by the countryfolk among whom they died.

AS the decades pass, a dwindling band of ex-Bomber Command aircrew come back to the airfields they once knew, bases from where so many of them flew off into history one night not to return. It is often those from the Commonwealth countries who are most keen, holding locked in their memories the vision of pretty English farmland humming with the sounds of war. They travel back by jet to a country and time so different it seems to allow no handle on the past.

But as they return to the villages that once were home, familiar pubs, churches and occasionally abandoned billets tug at fronds in the pool of memory. Then they stand, old boys with sticks, at the end of broken, grass-tufted runways now stretching to pasture and plough. With closed eyes and furrowed brow they hear again the growing sounds of laden, trundling machines, lining up for take-off in the night, long-forgotten aircraft crewed by those they once were – the bomber boys of 1943.

NOTES TO THE TEXT

ONE **TO THE HEART OF DARKNESS**

1 AIR 27–833, Public Record Office
2 Interview with author
3 *Daily Express*, 18 Jan. 1943
4 AIR 27–127
5 AIR 27–833
6 Interview with author
7 AIR 27–127
8 Interview with author
9 *Daily Express*, 18 Jan. 1943
10 John Mitchell (a Dimbleby pseudonym), *The Waiting Year*
11 Interview with author
12 *Daily Express*, 18 Jan. 1943
13 Interview with author
14 *Daily Express*, 18 Jan. 1943

TWO **A SIGNAL SUCCESS**

1 Sir Arthur Harris, *Bomber Offensive*, p. 137
2 Volume II of the Air Ministry-sponsored history *Royal Air Force 1939–1945*, p. 282
3 Interview with author

4 *Royal Air Force 1939–1945*, Vol. II, p. 282
5 Interview with author
6 Michael Cumming, *Pathfinder Cranswick*
7 Sir Arthur Harris, *Bomber Offensive*, p. 137
8 Gerrit Zijlstra research
9 Letter to author
10 Interview with author
11 Ibid
12 Ibid
13 AIR 27–487, Public Record Office
14 Ibid
15 Ibid
16 AIR 27–833
17 Ibid
18 AIR 27–538

THREE **PIERCING THE GLOOM**

1 AIR 14–2697, Public Record Office
2 Interview with author
3 Ibid
4 AIR 27–890

5 Interview with author
6 AIR 27–646
7 AIR 27–1849
8 Interview with author
9 AIR 27–538
10 Interview with author
11 AIR 27–487
12 AIR 14–1310, Night Raid Report 257
13 AIR 27–767
14 AIR 27–890
15 Interview with author
16 Ibid
17 AIR 27–127
18 Interview with author
19 Ibid
20 AIR 14–3410, Night Raid Report 264
21 Interview with author
22 AIR 27–833
23 AIR 27–127
24 AIR 27–492
25 Clifford Hill's diary
26 AIR 27–1908
27 Interview with author
28 Ibid

FOUR **RUINING THE RUHR**

1 Interview with author
2 Clifford Hill's diary
3 AIR 27–890, Public Record Office
4 Walter Hedges, diary
5 Interview with author
6 Hedges diary
7 Interview with author
8 AIR 27–450
9 Interview with author
10 Ibid

11 Ibid
12 Hill's diary
13 Interview with author
14 Letter to author
15 Interview with author
16 Ibid
17 Ibid
18 AIR 27–796
19 Interview with author
20 Ibid
21 Ibid
22 Ibid
23 Hill's diary
24 Interview with author
25 AIR 27–450
26 AIR 27–1849
27 AIR 27–1908
28 Clifford Hill's letters
29 Ibid
30 Ibid
31 Ibid
32 AIR 27–1930
33 Hill's diary
34 AIR 27–1048
35 Interview with author
36 Letter to author
37 Ibid
38 AIR 27–1930
39 Interview with author
40 Sgt Stewart's recollections
41 Interview with author
42 Sgt Stewart's recollections
43 AIR 27–1930
44 Speer Papers, FD 3063/49, Dept of Documents, Imperial War Museum
45 Ibid
46 Ibid
47 Ibid

FIVE **THE BITTER TASTE OF PILSEN**

1 Interview with author
2 Eric Hadingham's personal notes
3 Interview with author
4 AIR 14–3410, Public Record Office, Night Raid Report 312
5 Ibid
6 Interview with author
7 Ibid
8 Historie IX of Böhmische Museum, Pilsen
9 AIR 27–450, Public Record Office
10 AIR 27–1930
11 Skoda Museum archives
12 AIR 27–656
13 Ibid
14 Ibid
15 AIR 27–127
16 AIR 27–1908
17 Interview with author
18 AIR 27–1908
19 Interview with author
20 Skoda Museum archives
21 Ibid
22 AIR 14–3410, Night Raid Report 312
23 Interview with author
24 Eric Hadingham's personal notes
25 Alan Lord's reminiscences
26 Clifford Hill's diary

SIX **THE TOSS OF A COIN**

1 Interview with author
2 Ibid
3 AIR 27–1908, Public Record Office
4 AIR 27–1930
5 AIR 27–1322
6 Interview with author
7 Letter to author
8 AIR 27–796
9 AIR 27–1908
10 Interview with author
11 Ibid
12 Ibid
13 'Camp History of Stalag Luft III' compiled for Air Ministry, RAF Museum Dept of Records
14 Ibid
15 SS Report, 'Herren Engländer', RAF Museum Dept of Records
16 AIR 14–3410, Night Raid Report 315
17 Ibid

SEVEN **THE POWER OF WATER**

1 AIR 14–840, Public Record Office
2 AIR 14–383
3 Interview with author
4 Ibid
5 Ibid
6 AIR 14–2087
7 AIR 4–37
8 Interview with author
9 AIR 27–2128
10 AIR 14–840
11 AIR 14–1195
12 AIR 14–1195
13 AIR 14–840
14 AIR 27–2128
15 AIR14–2087
16 AIR 14–2087
17 AIR 14–2087
18 RAF Museum Dept of Aviation Records B7086

19 AIR 14–2087

20 AIR 14–2087

21 AIR 14–2087

22 AIR 27–2128

23 RAF Museum Dept of Aviation
Records B7086

24 AIR 14–2087

25 AIR 14–2087

26 *Royal Air Force 1939–45*, Vol. II

27 Speer papers, FD 3063/49, Dept of
Documents, Imperial War Museum

28 Goebbels diaries

29 AIR 27–2128

30 RAF Museum Dept of Aviation
Records B7086

EIGHT POINTBLANK AND RETURN TO THE RUHR

1 Interview with author

2 AIR 27–1930, Public Record Office

3 Interview with author

4 AIR 27–796

5 Interview with author

6 Ibid

7 Ibid

8 Clifford Hill's diary

9 Interview with author

10 Ibid

11 Ibid

12 Ibid

13 AIR 27–1322

14 Interview with author

15 AIR 14–2697

16 F/O Harris's account *A Blinding
Duty*

17 Sgt Walsh's private recollections

18 Account to author

19 AIR 27–656

20 AIR 27–167

21 Interview with author

22 Ibid

23 Ibid

24 Ibid

25 Ibid

26 Account to author

27 Interview with author

28 Ibid

29 Ibid

30 Ibid

31 Ibid

32 Sgt Walsh's recollections

NINE THE POWER OF FIRE

1 AIR 24–257, Public Record Office

2 Sgt Gilvary's diary, RAF Museum
Dept of Aviation Records

3 Interview with author

4 Ibid

5 Ibid

6 Ibid

7 AIR 27–1858

8 AIR 27–380

9 *The Setting* (Suhrkamp Verlag:
Frankfurt am Main, republished
1976). Written November, 1943

10 AIR 27–380

11 Interview with author

12 Ibid

13 AIR 27–1041

14 Ibid

15 AIR 27–1858

16 AIR 27–1849

17 AIR 27–802

18 AIR 27–833

19 Interview with author

20 AIR 27–1908
21 Interview with author
22 Ibid
23 AIR 27–833
24 Hans Brunswig, *Feuersturm über Hamburg*
25 Ibid
26 AIR 27–651
27 Ibid
28 AIR 27–656
29 Interview with author
30 AIR 14–3411
31 AIR 27–1849
32 AIR 27–796
33 AIR 27–1234
34 Interview with author
35 Ibid
36 Ibid
37 Ibid
38 Ibid
39 Ibid
40 AIR 27–2090
41 *The Setting*
42 AIR 27–1908
43 AIR 27–1849
44 Sgt Gilvary's diary, RAF Museum Dept of Aviation Records
45 Interview with author
46 Ibid
47 Gilvary's diary
48 Interview with author
49 *The Setting*
50 Interview with author
51 AIR 27 802
52 Ibid
53 Interview with author
54 Ibid
55 AIR 27–1234

56 AIR 27–796
57 Interview with author
58 Speer Papers, FD 3063/49, Dept of Documents, Imperial War Museum
59 Ibid
60 Ibid

TEN **THE PERIL OF PEENEMÜNDE**

1 AIR 27–1849, Public Record Office
2 Interview with author
3 Ibid
4 Sir Arthur Harris, Bomber Offensive, p. 182
5 AIR 27–1849
6 Interview with author
7 Sgt Gilvary's diary, RAF Museum Dept of Aviation Records
8 Interview with author
9 Ibid
10 Gilvary's diary
11 Interview with author
12 Gilvary's diary
13 Interview with author
14 *Bomber Offensive*, p. 183
15 AIR 27–1858
16 Interview with author
17 Ibid
18 Ibid
19 Ibid
20 Ibid
21 Ibid
22 Ibid
23 AIR 27–656
24 Ibid
25 Interview with author
26 Ibid

27 Ibid

28 AIR 27–651

29 Interview with author

30 Ibid

31 AIR 27–1908

32 Interview with author

33 Ibid

34 Ibid

35 AIR 27–1849

36 AIR 27–833

37 AIR 27–1849

38 Bundesarchiv, Freiburg, ref R/L 10/540

39 AIR 27–481

40 AIR 27–2090

41 AIR 27–833

42 AIR 27–2090

43 AIR 27–1849

44 Ibid

45 Interview with author

46 AIR 27–1908

47 Interview with author

ELEVEN **BACK TO BERLIN**

1 Interview with author

2 Ibid

3 AIR 14–3410, Public Record Office, Night Raid Report 408

4 Wilhelm Johnen, *Duel Under the Stars*

5 Interview with author

6 Ibid

7 Ibid

8 Ibid

9 Ibid

10 Ibid

11 Ibid

12 Ibid

13 Ibid

14 Ibid

15 Ibid

16 AIR 14–3410, Night Raid Report 415

17 Interview with author

18 Ibid

19 Ibid

20 Ibid

21 AIR 27–646

22 Interview with author

23 Ibid

24 Ibid

TWELVE **STRETCHING TO SUCCEED**

1 Interview with author

2 Ibid

3 Ibid

4 *Mannheim im zweiten Weltkrieg*

5 Interview with author

6 Ibid

7 Ibid

8 'Die Bombennacht der 23 September 1943' in Frankenthal, Erkenbert-Museum

9 Ibid

10 Interview with author

11 Account to author

12 Interview with author

13 Ibid

14 Ibid

15 Ibid

16 Ibid

17 Ron Heatherington's personal papers

18 Interview with author

19 Ibid

20 Ibid

21 Ibid

22 AIR 14–3411, Night Raid Report 437

THIRTEEN **ATTRITION TO ACHIEVEMENT**

1 AIR 14–3411, Public Record Office, Night Raid Report 430

2 Account to author

3 AIR 14–2701, File 20A

4 Interview with author

5 AIR 14–2701, File 20A

6 AIR 14–3411, Night Raid Report 447

7 W/O Taylor's personal papers

8 Interview with author

9 AIR 14–3411, Night Raid Report 443

10 Ibid

11 Sgt Page's diary

12 Interview with author

13 Ibid

14 Ibid

15 Ibid

16 Ibid

17 Ibid

18 P/O Buttler's private memoirs

19 Interview with author

20 Ibid

21 AIR 14–3411, NR 451

22 Ibid

23 Interview with author

24 Ibid

25 Account to author

26 Interview with author

27 Ibid

FOURTEEN **'THE GREATEST OF AIR BATTLES'**

1 Dudley Saward, *'Bomber' Harris*, p. 218

2 Interview with author

3 Recollections of Ray Fouhse

4 Account to author

5 AIR 14–3410, Public Record Office, Night Raid Report 456

6 Interview with author

7 Ibid

8 AIR 14–3411, Night Raid Report 470

9 Interview with author

10 Marie Vassiltchikov, *Berlin Diaries 1940–45*

11 Interview with author

12 Ibid

13 Marie Vassiltchikov, *Berlin Diaries 1940–45*

14 *Yorkshire Evening Press*, 24 Nov. 1943

15 Interview with author

16 Account to author

17 AIR 27–1254

18 Interview with author

FIFTEEN **A MISERABLE END**

1 Interview with author

2 *Nottingham Evening Post*, 3 Dec. 1943.

3 *Daily Express*, 25 Nov. 1943

4 Webster and Frankland, *The Strategic Air Offensive Against Germany*, pp. 54–57

5 AIR 14–2697, Public Record Office

6 *Nottingham Evening Post*, 6 Dec. 1943

7 *Yorkshire Evening Press*, 19 Nov. 1943

8 AIR 14–3411, Bomber Command ORS Night Raid Report 489

9 F/Lt Colvin's diary, RAF Museum Dept of Records, B2142

10 Interview with author

11 Ibid

12 Colvin's diary

13 Interview with author

14 AIR 40–2397, Night Fighter Interrogations Report 337/1945

15 Sir Arthur Harris, *Bomber Offensive*, p. 163

16 AIR 40–2397, Night Fighter Interrogations Report 337/1945

17 AIR 40–1397, Night Fighter PoWs, interrogations

18 Interview with author

19 Ibid

20 Colvin's diary

21 AIR 14–3411, Night Raid Report 489

22 Marie Vassiltchikov, *Berlin Diaries 1940–45*

23 *Yorkshire Evening Press*, 30 Dec. 1943

24 *Nottingham Evening Post*, 2 Dec. 1943

25 *Nottingham Evening Post*, 31 Dec. 1943

26 Interview with author

27 *Daily Express*, 31 Dec. 1943

28 Interview with author

29 AIR 27–481

30 Interview with author

31 *Nottingham Evening Post*, 29 Dec. 1943

32 Richard Overy, 'Bomber Command Statistics', *Bomber Command, 1939–1945*

33 Ibid

34 Volume III of the official history *Royal Air Force* 1939–45, p. 386; and Richard Overy 'Bomber Command Statistics', *Bomber Command, 1939–1945*.

35 Richard Overy, 'Bomber Command Statistics', *Bomber Command, 1939–1945* and *Royal Air Force, 1939–45*, Vol. III, p. 387

36 Richard Overy, 'Bomber Command Statistics', *Bomber Command, 1939–1945*

37 AIR 14–843

ACKNOWLEDGEMENTS

I AM particularly grateful to the following British, Commonwealth and Allied aircrew who participated in various ways in the preparation of this book. It is their unstinting help that made it all possible. Ranks and awards are those when they left the services:

7 Sqn: W/O Richard Ormcrod DFM; W/O Dennis Woolford. 11 OTU: F/Lt George Hunt. 9 Sqn: F/Lt Gordon Penfold. 12 Sqn: F/Lt Charles Lawrence DFM; Sgt Arthur Madelaine; W/O Malcolm White; W/O Ray Fouhse (deceased). 15 Sqn: F/Sgt Alexander Wood. 35 Sqn: F/Lt Alan Mundy; F/O Allan Vial DFC; W/O William Higgs; W/O Wilf Sutton; W/O Roy Macdonald; W/O Frank Tudor DFM; F/Sgt Terry O'Shaugnessy. 44 (Rhodesia) Sqn: F/Lt Raymond Worrall; P/O Colin Watt DFM; W/O Peter Swan; Sgt Jim Taylor. 49 Sqn: G/Cpt John Teager OBE, AFC; F/Lt Ernest Webb DFC; F/Sgt Alan Morgan; W/O James Arnold; W/O John Bryan; W/O Leonard Bradfield; F/O Steve Putnam (deceased). 50 Sqn: W/O Joseph Porter; W/O Jim Wilkie; W/O George Stewart. 51 Sqn: W/O Wilfred Hart, W/O Eddie Hilton. 57 Sqn: S/Ldr Alfred Fripp; W/O Kenneth Hulton. 61 Sqn: F/Sgt Donald Clement. 75 Sqn: W/O Lew Parsons; W/O Ron Brown. 76 Sqn: W/O Clifford Hill DFM; F/Lt Wilkie Wanless. 77 Sqn: F/Lt Dennis Bateman DFC; F/Lt Alec Pawliuk; W/O Geoffrey Haworth; W/O Bob Murty (deceased); Sgt John Walsh (deceased). 78 Sqn: S/Ldr V. A. Robins DFC; F/Lt Bernard Downs DFC; Sgt Grenville

Jones; W/O Howard Marshall; W/O Robert Williams; F/Sgt Norman Page (deceased). 83 Sqn: F/Lt Kenneth East DFM; F/Lt Gerry Mitchell. 90 Sqn: F/Sgt Roy Child. 97 (Straits Settlements) Sqn: F/O Jack Hannah DFC. 100 Sqn: F/Lt Eric Hadingham DFC and bar. 101 Sqn: F/Lt Peter Johnson DFC; F/O Dennis Goodliffe; F/Sgt Gordon Wallace (deceased). 102 (Ceylon) Sqn: F/Lt John Fell; W/O Walter Hedges; W/O Alec Taylor; F/O Reid Thomson; Sgt R. Day (deceased). 103 Sqn: F/Lt Don Charlwood; F/Lt Sandy Rowe DFM; W/O Graham Briggs DFM. 106 Sqn: F/Lt Ron Heatherington (deceased); W/O Albert Bracegirdle DFM; F/O Graham Allen DFM. 115 Sqn: W/O Arthur Smith. 138 Sqn: F/O W. R. Peake DFM: W/O Alfred Dove. 149 (East India) Sqn: W/O Philip Bates; W/O Derek Jackson; W/O R. Bell; F/Sgt Albert Miller. 153 Sqn: W/O Frank Etherington. 156 Sqn: F/Lt Walter Kerry. 158 Sqn: F/Lt Alan Bryett; F/Lt W. Clark; F/Lt Herbert Mottershead DFC; F/Lt Joe Hitchman DFC; Sgt W. Maxwell (deceased); F/Sgt Trevor Marlow; W/O Robert Gill DFM. 166 Sqn: F/Lt George Barclay; F/Lt Leonard Isaacson; F/Lt Sam Small DFC; F/O Fred Sim DFC; W/O Barry Wright CGM; W/O Tom Hall DFM; W/O James Wright; Sgt L. W. Diggines; W/O Norman Smith; F/Sgt Jack Dunlop. 199 Sqn: Sgt Robert Taylor (deceased). 207 Sqn: Sgt Kenneth Freeman. 218 Sqn: P/O Rowland Mason. 408 Sqn: W/O John Taplin. 419 (Moose) Sqn, RCAF: F/Lt Tom Jackson; F/Lt Albert Wallace; W/O Edwin Jury; F/O Russell Lowry; F/O James Eddy. 428 (Ghost) Sqn, RCAF: P/O Lance Buttler (deceased); W/O Harold McLean. 429 (Bison) Sqn, RCAF: F/Lt Otto Sulek; W/O Oswald Davis. 433 (Porcupine) Sqn, RCAF: S/Ldr Wilbur Pierce DFC; F/O Robert Madill. 460 Sqn, RAAF: S/Ldr Alex Flett DFC and bar; F/Lt William Bateman DFC; F/Lt Jack Murray DFM; F/O Claremont Taylor DFC (deceased); F/Lt David Francis DFC; F/O Edney Eyres; W/O Donald Gray DFM; F/O Don Roberts DFC; W/O Charles Marshall; Sgt John Cornish. 466 Sqn, RAAF: W/O William Garfield; W/O Norman Leonard. 467 Sqn, RAAF: W/O Ken Harvey. 515 Sqn: F/Lt Alan Shufflebottom. 617 Sqn: S/Ldr Les Munro DSO, DFC; S/Ldr George Johnson DFM; F/Lt Jack Patterson; F/Lt Dave Rodger DFC; F/O Grant McDonald. 619 Sqn: F/Lt Stewart Harris. 622

Sqn: P/O Bruce Sutherland. 625 Sqn: F/Lt Harold Sutton DFC; F/Sgt
Robert Pyett (deceased); W/O Tom Howie; W/O Norman Jones. 630 Sqn:
W/O Edwin Watson.

I have also received much help from civilian sources and organisations
including Mrs Val Charlton; Mrs Barbara Guthrie; Lars Biester, of Hanover,
who helped particularly with translations of German documents; Dr
Stephan Pieroth, of Bad Dürkheim, who provided much information about
the Mannheim raids of 1943; staff of the Skoda Museum, Pilsen; Stephen
Walton, Archivist at the Imperial War Museum Department of Documents;
Peter Elliott, Senior Keeper, Department of Research and Information
Services at the RAF Museum, Hendon; Keith Lowe, a wise editor at
Weidenfeld & Nicolson; and David Hepworth, a good companion on many
an airfield visit and an unerring source of contacts.

There are four people, particularly, without whom this book could not have
been written, namely Ken Hulton and the late Cliff Hill of the Manchester
Branch of the Aircrew Association; Albert Bracegirdle of the North West
and North Wales Branch of the RAF Ex-PoW Association; and ex-101
Sqn pilot Peter Johnson, with whom the journey began.

Sadly, the following have passed away since being interviewed: F/Lt Gordon
Penfold; Sgt Arthur Madelaine; W/O Frank Tudor DFM; W/O Clifford
Hill DFM; W/O Bob Murty; F/Lt Eric Hadingham DFC and bar; F/Sgt
Gordon Wallace; F/O Claremont Taylor DFC; F/Lt Dave Rodger DFC.

GLOSSARY

ABC   Airborne equipment for jamming Luftwaffe night-fighter
              transmissions

AP   Aiming point

ASR   Air Sea Rescue

Erk   Aircraftsman 2nd Class, the lowest RAF rank

Cookie   4000-lb bomb

Corona   Ground-based listening and broadcasting system for sending
              false instructions to German night-fighter crews

Cpt   Captain

DFC   Distinguished Flying Cross

DFM   Distinguished Flying Medal

DSO   Distinguished Service Order

Experten   A recognised Luftwaffe ace with five or more confirmed
              victories

F/Lt   Flight Lieutenant

F/O   Flying Officer

F/Sgt   Flight Sergeant

FW190   Focke-Wulf single-engined fighter, a favourite of Wilde Sau
              pilots

G/Cpt   Group Captain

Gee   Airborne device receiving signals from one master and two slave radio stations by which a navigator was able to plot his exact course on a grid

HCU	Heavy Conversion Unit
Himmelbett	Box fighter control system introduced by General Kammhuber
H2S	Radar scanner carried underneath bombers supplying features of terrain below to operator inside
Ju88	Twin-engined multi-purpose Junkers aircraft, often used in the Zahme Sau night-fighter role. Armed with Schrage Musik in the autumn of 1943
Kammhuber Line	String of Luftwaffe fighter boxes made defunct by Window
LMF	Lack of moral fibre, the harsh judgement made by the RAF on those who felt unable to continue operational flying. The words were stamped on their files
Me109	Single-engined Messerschmitt day fighter adapted for Wilde Sau role
Me110	Twin-engined Messerschmitt night fighter, lethal with Schrage Musik
Monica	Device warning bomber crews of a night fighter's rearward approach
Nachtjäger	Night-fighter aircraft or aircrew. The command structure was in staffels of nine aircraft, three staffels making a group, three groups making a *geschwader*. In abbreviated form the Third Group of the First Night Fighter Geschwader would be III/NJG1
Newhaven	Pathfinder marking by visual identification of the target
Oboe	Highly accurate radar tracking and transmission system, signalling to a PFF aircraft the exact point at which to drop its TIs
Offset marking	Technique of dropping TIs outside an aiming point to avoid obscuring by smoke and setting bomb sights for an overshoot, so bombs actually hit the target
ORS	Operational Research Section at Bomber Command headquarters
OTU	Operational Training Unit

Parramatta	Pathfinder ground marking by the use of H2S
PFF	Pathfinder Flare Force
P/O	Pilot Officer
Schrage Musik	Upward-firing guns in the fuselage of German night fighters
Serrate	Night fighter airborne radar hunting *nachtjäger* transmissions
Sqn	Squadron
S/Ldr	Squadron Leader
T and D	A bombing technique developed by 5 Group where a force bombed blind after counting off the time from an identifiable distant landmark
TI	Target indicator
U/S	Unserviceable
VC	Victoria Cross
WAAF	Women's Auxiliary Air Force. Members known by the same name
Wanganui	Skymarking in very poor visibility. The prefix 'musical' meant the use of Oboe
Wilde Sau	Freelance night fighters, usually over targets and single-engined
Window	Metallised paper producing spurious responses on Luftwaffe radar
W/Cdr	Wing Commander
W/O	Warrant Officer
W/T	Wireless telegraphy
Zahme Sau	'Tame boar' fighters controlled by means of a running commentary

BIBLIOGRAPHY

BENNETT, D. C. T., *Pathfinder* (Frederick Muller, 1958)

BECK, Earl R., *Under the Bombs: German Home Front, 1942–1945* (University Press of Kentucky, 1986)

BEKKER, Cajus, *The Luftwaffe War Diaries* (Macdonald & Co, 1967)

BRICKHILL, Paul, *Dam Busters* (Evans, 1951)

BRUNSWIG, Hans, *Feuersturm über Hamburg* (Motorbuch Verlach Stuttgart, 1979)

CHESHIRE, Leonard, *Bomber Pilot* (Hutchinson & Co, 1943)

CHORLEY, W. R., *Bomber Command Losses, 1943* (Midland Counties Publications, 1996)

COOPER, Alan W., *The Air Battle of the Ruhr* (Airlife Publishing, 1992)

CUMMING, Michael, *Pathfinder Cranswick* (William Kimber & Co, 1962)

FISCHER, Josef, *Köln 1939–45* (J. P. Bachem, 1970)

FREEMAN, Roger A., *The Mighty Eighth* (Macdonald & Jane's, 1970)

GIBSON, Guy, *Enemy Coast Ahead* (Goodall, 1986)

HARRIS, Sir Arthur, *Bomber Offensive* (Collins, 1947)

HARRIS, Stewart, *A Blinding Duty* (Pentland Books, 2001)

HASTINGS, Sir Max, *Bomber Command* (Michael Joseph, 1979)

HINCHLIFFE, Peter, *The Other Battle* (Airlife Publishing, 1996)

JACKSON, Robert, *Storm from the Skies* (Arthur Barker Ltd, 1974)

JOHNEN, Wilhelm, *Duel Under the Stars* (William Kimber, 1957)

JONES, R. V., *Most Secret War* (Hamish Hamilton 1978)

MAYNARD, John, *Bennett and the Pathfinders* (Arms and Armour Press, 1996)

MIDDLEBROOK, Martin, *The Battle of Hamburg* (Allen Lane, 1980)

   The Berlin Raids (Viking, 1988)

   The Peenemunde Raid (Allen Lane, 1982)

MIDDLEBROOK, Martin and EVERITT, Chris, *The Bomber Command War Diaries* (Viking, 1985)

MORPURGO, J. E., *Barnes Wallis* (Longmans, 1972)

MUSGROVE, Gordon, *Operation Gomorrah* (Jane's, 1981)

OTTAWAY, Susan, *Dambuster* (Leo Cooper, 1994)

OVERY, Richard, *The Air War 1939–45* (Europa Publications, 1980)

   Bomber Command, 1939–45 (HarperCollins, 1997)

RICHARDS, Denis, *Royal Air Force 1939–45*, Volume I: *The Fight At Odds* (Her Majesty's Stationery Office, 1953)

   The Hardest Victory (Hodder & Stoughton, 1994)

RICHARDS, Denis and ST G. SAUNDERS, Hilary, *Royal Air Force 1939–45*, Volume II: *The Fight Avails* (Her Majesty's Stationery Office, 1954)

RUMPF, Hans, *The Bombing of Germany* (Frederick Muller, 1961)

ST G. SAUNDERS, Hilary, *Royal Air Force 1939–45*, Volume III: *The Fight Is Won* (Her Majesty's Stationery Office, 1954)

SAWARD, Dudley, '*Bomber' Harris* (Cassell, 1984)

SPEER, Albert, *Inside the Third Reich* (Weidenfeld & Nicolson, 1970)

SWEETMAN, John, *Operation Chastise* (Jane's, 1982)

TAVENDER, Ian, *The DFM Register for the Second World War* (Savannah Publications, 2000)

TERRAINE, John, *The Right of the Line* (Hodder & Stoughton, 1985)

VASSILTCHIKOV, Marie, *Berlin Diaries* (Alfred A. Knopf: New York, 1987)

WALKER, Nigel, *Strike to Defend* (Neville Spearman, 1963)

WARD-JACKSON, C. H. and LUCAS, Leighton, *Airman's Song Book* (William Blackwood & Sons, 1967)

INDEX

All Orion/Phoenix titles are available at your local bookshop or from the following address:

Mail Order Department
Littlehampton Book Services
FREEPOST BR535
Worthing, West Sussex, BN13 3BR
telephone 01903 828503, *facsimile* 01903 828802
e-mail MailOrders@lbsltd.co.uk
(Please ensure that you include full postal address details)

Payment can be made either by credit/debit card (Visa, Mastercard, Access and Switch accepted) or by sending a £ Sterling cheque or postal order made payable to *Littlehampton Book Services*.
DO NOT SEND CASH OR CURRENCY

Please add the following to cover postage and packing

UK and BFPO:
£1.50 for the first book, and 50p for each additional book to a maximum of £3.50

Overseas and Eire:
£2.50 for the first book plus £1.00 for the second book and 50p for each additional book ordered

---

BLOCK CAPITALS PLEASE

name of cardholder ....

address of cardholder ....

....

....

postcode ....

delivery address
(if different from cardholder)

....

....

....

postcode ....

☐ I enclose my remittance for £...................................

☐ please debit my Mastercard/Visa/Access/Switch (delete as appropriate)

card number ☐☐☐☐☐☐☐☐☐☐☐☐☐☐☐☐

expiry date ☐☐☐☐   Switch issue no. ☐☐

signature ....

prices and availability are subject to change without notice